Outrage and Insight

Berg French Studies

General Editor: John E. Flower

ISSN: 1354-3636

John E. Flower and Bernard C. Swift (eds), *François Mauriac: Visions and Reappraisals*

Michael Tilby (ed.), *Beyond the Nouveau Roman: Essays on the Contemporary French Novel*

Richard Griffiths, *The Use of Abuse: The Polemics of the Dreyfus Affair and its Aftermath*

Alec G. Hargreaves, *Voices from the North African Immigrant Community in France: Immigration and Identity in Beur Fiction*

Colin Nettlebeck, *Forever French: The French Exiles in the United States of America during the Second World War*

Bill Marshall, *Victor Serge: The Uses of Dissent*

Allan Morris, *Collaboration and Resistance Reviewed: Writers and the Mode Rétro in Post-Gaullist France*

Malcolm Cook, *Fictional France: Social Reality in the French Novel 1775–1800*

W. D. Halls, *Politics, Society and Christianity in Vichy France*

Outrage and Insight

Modern French Writers and the 'Fait Divers'

David H. Walker

BERG PUBLISHERS
Oxford / Washington, D.C.

HUMCA

First published in 1995 by
Berg Publishers Limited
Editorial offices:
150 Cowley Road, Oxford, OX4 1JJ, UK
13590 Park Center Road, Herndon, VA 22071, USA

INDEXED IN *E G L I*

Cover Photograph: © AFP Documentation Photo, France.

Library of Congress Cataloging-in-Publication Data

A catalogue record for this book is available from the Library of Congress.

British Library Cataloguing-in-Publication Data

A catalogue record for this book is available from the British Library.

ISBN 0 85496 780 X

Printed in the United Kingdom by WBC Book Manufacturers, Mid-Glamorgan.

for Cathy

fée d'hiver

Contents

Acknowledgements

A section of part I and a section of part IV appeared in slightly different forms in *Nottingham French Studies* and *French Cultural Studies* respectively. I am grateful for permission to reproduce the material here.

Abbreviations

A	Louis Aragon	*Anicet ou le panorama, roman*, Paris, Gallimard, 1921
AA	Marguerite Duras	*L'Amante anglaise*, Paris, Gallimard, 1967
BI	Simone de Beauvoir	*Les Belles Images*, Paris, Gallimard-Folio
CII	Albert Camus	*Carnets II, Janvier 1942–Mars 1951*, Paris, Gallimard, 1964
CIII	Albert Camus	*Carnets III, Mars 1951–Décembre 1959*, Paris, Gallimard, 1989
E	Albert Camus	*Essais*, Paris, Pléiade, 1975
F	J.M.G. Le Clézio	*La Fièvre*, Paris, Gallimard, 1965
FD	Jean-Jacques Gautier	*Histoire d'un fait divers*, Paris, Julliard, 1946
JOC	Alfred Jarry	*Œuvres complètes*, vol.2, Paris, Pléiade, 1987
JV	Jean Genet	*Journal du Voleur*, Paris, Gallimard, 1949
LM	Alain Robbe-Grillet	*Le Miroir qui revient*, Paris, Minuit, 1984
M	Roger Grenier	*Les Monstres*, Paris, Gallimard, 1953
MR	Jean Genet	*Miracle de la Rose*, in *Œuvres complètes de Jean Genet*, vol.2, Paris, Gallimard, 1951
MC	Marguerite Duras	*Moderato cantabile*, Paris, Minuit, collection Double
NF	Jean Genet	*Notre-Dame-des-fleurs*, in *Œuvres complètes de Jean Genet*, vol.2, Paris, Gallimard, 1951
N	Jean-Paul Sartre	*La Nausée*, in *Œuvres romanesques*, ed. M. Contat and M. Rybalka, Paris, Pléiade, 1981

NJP	André Gide	*Ne Jugez Pas*, Paris, Gallimard, 1969
O	Marguerite Duras	*Outside*, Paris, POL, 1984
PP	Louis Aragon	*Le Paysan de Paris*, Paris, Livre de Poche
PV	J.M.G. Le Clézio	*Le Procès-verbal*, Paris, Gallimard-Folio
PI	Nathalie Sarraute	*Portrait d'un inconnu*, Paris, Union Générale d'Editions, collection 10/18
POC	Charles-Louis Philippe	*Œuvres complètes*, vol.5, Moulins, Editions Ipomée, 1986
RRS	André Gide	*Romans, récits et soties, œuvres lyriques*, Paris, Pléiade, 1958
R	J.M.G. Le Clézio	*La Ronde et autres faits divers*, Paris, Gallimard, 1982
RA	Michel Tournier	*Le Roi des Aulnes*, Paris, Gallimard-Folio
T	François Mauriac	*Thérèse Desqueyroux*, Paris, Livre de Poche
TA	Marguerite Duras	*Le Théâtre de l'Amante anglaise*, Paris, Gallimard, collection L'Imaginaire, 1991
TCF	Simone de Beauvoir	*Tout compte fait*, Paris, Gallimard, 1972
TRN	Albert Camus	*Théâtre, récits, nouvelles*, Paris, Pléiade, 1962
V	Alain Robbe-Grillet	*Le Voyeur*, Paris, Minuit, 1955

1

Introduction: The *Fait Divers*

The label *fait divers* is used in the world of French journalism to denote a certain type of newspaper story. The *Petit Robert* dictionary defines such phenomena as 'nouvelles peu importantes d'un journal', while the *Petit Larousse* resorts to the phrase 'événement sans portée générale qui appartient à la vie quotidienne'. There is a measure of agreement, then, on the notion of triviality which attaches to the *fait divers*. But this can be taken as a defensive reaction, a measure of its potential to unsettle those categories which define what is significant.

The *Trésor de la langue française* indicates that the term was in use by 1859. The creation and dissemination of the label may be connected with the transformation, which occurred during the latter part of the nineteenth century, of the political broadsheet, the staple of the press until then, into the modern newspaper.[1] News values as such were introduced only with difficulty into what had hitherto been organs purveying opinion, propaganda and entertainment.[2] The creation of a modern newspaper providing information was, and remains to this day, constantly under threat from functions inimical to objective documentation; as one analyst puts it: 'Qui dira avec assez d'éloquence le rôle pernicieux du divertissement ou de la psychothérapie sur l'effort de documentation sociale?'[3] The news function defines itself by excluding what challenges it: hence the term *fait divers*, which separates out that which cannot be classified systematically, that which has no social consequence and therefore no news value.

As the above quotation indicates, newspapers serve a number of needs, some of which are psychosocial. These latter are met by the *fait divers*, which speaks of scandal, sensation, disruptions of the norm. As society increasingly represses individual idiosyncrasies in favour of consensual values, frustrated impulses seek displaced gratification: 'Les faits divers satisfont surtout [. . .] le besoin psycho-social de libération des contraintes et de compensation aux frustrations qui rongent les civilisations de masse. Comment expliquer autrement la lecture quotidienne par de nombreuses personnes de ces colonnes interminables et monotones d'incidents (vols, viols, accidents, etc.) en trois lignes, qui, chaque jour, répètent leur litanie?'[4]

However, incidents which occur in the byways of everyday life and do not find their way into the mainstream of public affairs may owe their marginal status not to any intrinsic triviality but to the fact that the dominant ideology cannot accommodate them properly. The *faits divers* fall outside the central concerns of a society; but precisely because they are located on the margins of the social consensus they may point to, or illustrate, realities that the conventional wisdom leaves out of account. In this respect the rubric of the *fait divers* has a dual function: on the one hand, by reporting odd or bizarre items, it seeks to translate them into the language of common concerns; but, because of its secondary status, it marginalizes such items, keeps them at a safe remove from the centre of society. The *fait-diversier* thus lays claim to the off-beat or grotesque on behalf of bourgeois humanism or conventional society. 'Nil humanum me alienum puto' translates into modern journalistic parlance as 'All human life is here.' But at the same time, the reporter holds these items at arm's length, labels them marginal or odd in order to fend off any disturbing implications they may have for conventional wisdom. Thus, in a very real sense, the *fait divers* might be said to map the sensitive outer edges of public opinion.

This accounts for other features that *faits divers* frequently embody. A story may be horrific, challenging our sense of what is the norm; or it may hinge on an enigma, highlighting phenomena for which we have no ready explanation; or – as is frequently the case – it may arise from judicial proceedings, and involve accounts of incidents which pose a threat to customary behaviour or conventional patterns of thinking as codified in the law. In this guise, the *fait divers* is traditionally, and still today, presented in highly-coloured language that resorts to sensationalism, eliciting and articulating standard reactions of horror, indignation or mystification. Here again, it can be considered a therapeutic exercise. By means of the rubric reporters exorcise that pernicious taste for the novelistic and the emotional that jeopardizes properly-informed, impartial news reporting,[5] while society – individually and collectively – lets off steam at the excesses within it. Thus these excesses are contained within manageable bounds.[6]

However, the boundary between *fait divers* and news story proper cannot be fixed. Different reporting styles compete in the presentation of a suicide, for example, when the victim happens to be a government minister such as Roger Salengro in 1936 or Pierre Bérégovoy in 1993; conversely, an apparently momentous event may ultimately entail no serious consequences. The *fait divers* and the news item constantly interpenetrate, which accounts for the sensitivity of purists who try to keep them apart, and for the diligence of *faits diversiers* who see their function as unjustly demeaned. In an interview recorded for the communicative French course *Lyon à la une*, two journalists explain that if a reporter works on an up-market national daily the relevant rubric is referred to as 'faits et société'. In a middle-ranking respectable paper like *Lyon Matin* the term is 'faits divers'; at the bottom end of the scale one is dealing with 'chiens écrasés'.[7] Thus social class, cultural interests – and, as we shall see, the sociopolitical climate at given points in history – also determine shifting levels of interest in the facts, and shifting approaches to their presentation.

Most regular readers of French newspapers will know what a *fait divers* is when they see one, and this intuition is usually reliable. But the question of defining the *fait divers*, even in its own terms, is not straightforward. A symptomatic response to the problem can be found in the 1872 edition of Larousse's *Grand Dictionnaire Universel du XIXe siècle*:

> Sous cette rubrique, les journaux groupent avec art et publient régulièrement les nouvelles de toutes sortes qui courent le monde: petits scandales, accidents de voitures, crimes épouvantables, suicide d'amour, couvreur tombant d'un cinquième étage, vol à main armée, pluie de sauterelles ou de crapauds, naufrages, incendies, inondations, aventures cocasses, enlèvements mystérieux, exécutions à mort, cas d'hydrophobie, d'anthropophagie, de somnambulisme et de léthargie; les sauvetages y entrent pour une part et les phénomènes de la nature tels que veaux à deux têtes, crapauds âgés de quatre mille ans, jumeaux soudés par la peau du ventre, enfant à trois yeux, nains extraordinaires . . . etc.[8]

This compendium-definition is the first of many we will come across as we map the place of the rubric in the culture. We are confronted by a phenomenon which seems to elude classification, which appears to stand for fragmentation and heterogeneity as well as cultural slumming. Indeed Roland Barthes, in his essay on the *fait divers*, makes the point that in a sense the form is characterized by the fact that it cannot be integrated into a system of meaning. A political assassination is not a *fait divers*, because it draws meaning from the political context within which it can be located. The significance of the *fait divers* is immanent: by its nature it actually challenges pre-existing meaning systems.[9]

Be this as it may, it is an indisputable fact that millions of readers attend to the *faits divers* daily. They are not therefore to be lightly dismissed. It is also worth stressing the peculiar status of the *fait divers* in French. There is no readily available translation of the term into English or other European languages, which seems to suggest that the *fait divers* has a specific function within French culture. Such, indeed, is the conclusion of those numerous specialists – historians, sociologists, philosophers – who have considered the phenomenon.

Romi offers a history of 'cinq siècles de faits divers' which owes much to the compendium tradition, but which suffices to show that the modern *fait divers* derives from the age-old taste for sensational tales, as made manifest from ancient chronicles through to the *occasionels* and *extraordinaires*, so-called 'feuilles de colportage' illustrated with engravings, that circulated from the sixteenth century onwards.[10] This colourful and entertaining compilation is complemented by Jean-Pierre Séguin's scholarly study of the great flowering of a subgenre, *Canards du XIXe siècle*.[11] These pamphlets, which came to characterize the romantic era, existed alongside the mainstream press they sometimes plundered for material (though the clientele of the more respectable organs, being mainly bourgeois, was less overtly given to sensation-seeking than the newly-emerging working class), flourishing as their up-market rivals intermittently fell foul of the authorities and censorship. However, they rapidly became redundant after 1863 with the commercial triumph of Polydore Millaud's *Petit Journal*, which put both news and *faits divers* within the reach of bourgeois and worker alike.

Such histories of the press take their place within broader social and cultural history. Louis Chevalier, in his study of crime during the first part of the nineteenth century,[12] pays telling tribute to the impact of the *fait divers de presse* by repeatedly invoking it as an indicator of the way criminality was perceived and the way this perception evolved. Hence, in the novels of Balzac and Hugo, Chevalier discerns traces of an outmoded conception of criminality deriving from the abiding impact of *canards* from another age: their criminals tend to be superhuman figures, embodying a 'criminalité limitée, pittoresque, aventureuse, sans rapport avec la criminalité confuse qui monte de la foule et qui naît de la misère'.[13] The extravagances that mar the plots of *La Femme de trente ans* and *La Cousine Bette* stem from the same source and could have been avoided if Balzac had drawn more closely on his awareness of the *faits divers* of his own time.[14] Even Hugo, clearly detaching himself from the lurid criminality of *Le Dernier jour d'un condamné* and pursuing a more modern notion in *Les Misérables*, is intermittently betrayed by the same vestigial attachment to an anachronistic vision of 'brigands légendaires' flatly contradicted by contemporary press reports – which Chevalier adduces in order to correct or ratify the picture as appropriate.[15] 'La psychose du crime', says Chevalier, had infected an entire generation largely under the influence of publications such as *La Gazette des Tribunaux*, launched in 1825.[16] We know too that Stendhal found in the same source the story of Antoine Berthet which was to become *Le Rouge et le Noir*.[17]

If the early nineteenth century was thus characterized by *faits divers* – and concomitant literary works – which glorified the spectacular exploits of illustrious bandits, Michel Foucault, developing Chevalier's thesis, confirms that the new society evolving under the influence of the Industrial Revolution progressively produced mechanisms for controlling the 'gloire douteuse' of the criminal and subjecting the delinquent to detailed definition, monitoring and discipline.[18] Foucault simultaneously shows how the *fait divers*, reflecting social evolution, constructs one dimension of a criminality ambivalently conceptualized 'à la fois comme très proche et tout à fait étrangère'.[19] Specifically, it propagates the anonymity that characterizes the modern world: 'les journaux [. . .] reprendront dans leurs faits divers quotidiens la grisaille sans épopée des délits.'[20] It is as a result of this evolution, perhaps, that while the *fait-divers*-inspired heroes of Balzac, Hugo and Stendhal achieve notoriety in their struggle to conquer society, a later novel such as Flaubert's *Madame Bovary* brings to our attention an adulterous wife the story of whose life and death would otherwise have remained unnoticed in the *fait divers* rubric of a provincial newspaper.[21] Similarly, in *Thérèse Raquin* the *crime passionnel* is undiscovered by the outside world, while *L'Assommoir* hinges on the private consequences of a fall from a rooftop of a *couvreur*, a typical anonymous *fait divers* among those we have seen listed in the *Dictionnaire Universel* at the time Zola was writing his novel. At the start of the century the *faits divers* were plundered for 'des exemples de l'énergie humaine';[22] after 1870, the influence of Taine's preface to *L'Intelligence*, with its insistence on the importance of 'de touts petits faits bien choisis' in scientific investigation, was further to determine an approach to the *fait divers* that saw it above all as a 'document humain', validating the fictions of day-to-day realism and naturalism: 'de là l'usage du fait divers, judiciaire ou médical, et ce *reportage* acharné qui est la forme vulgaire de la chasse aux *petits faits*', as Gustave Lanson disparagingly puts it.[23]

However, notwithstanding the repudiation of the heroic in the *fait divers*, its peculiar sensationalism continued to tempt literary artists. Bernard Shaw was driven to find fault with Zola for basing *La Bête humaine* on the story of Jack the Ripper:

> The majority of Frenchmen [. . .] like to read [. . .] the police intelligence, especially the murder cases and divorce cases. The invented murders and divorces of the novelists and playwrights do not satisfy them, because they cannot believe in them; and belief that the horror or scandal actually occurred, that real people are shedding real blood and real tears, is indispensable to their enjoyment. [. . .] As an example of how to cater for such readers, we may take Zola's *La Bête humaine*. [. . .] [I]nto it Zola has violently thrust the greatest police sensation of the XIX century: the episode of Jack the Ripper [. . .]. One is tempted to accuse Zola of having borrowed it from the newspapers to please his customers just as Shakespear used to borrow stories of murder and jealousy from the tales and chronicles of his time [. . .][24]

Such direct literary exploitation of the peculiar *frisson* procured by the *fait divers* is usually the preserve of the *feuilleton* and sensation novels[25] – or surrealists. From a literary point of view the *fait divers* is an ambiguous entity. Its substance may be brutal raw reality: and in this sense it offers a challenge to the writer, moralist or psychologist to go beyond prevailing representations and provide an account of what society has chosen to dismiss either by explaining it away or by labelling it inexplicable and circumscribing it within the stereotyped responses we have discussed. On the other hand, the fact that the newspapers present it in such a way as to limit reflection and substitute emotional orgies for rational analysis means that its form is also likely to provoke a critical reaction from the serious artist.

Specialists from a variety of disciplines have been drawn to these and other features of the *fait divers*. Georges Auclair adopts the approach of a social anthropologist in his *Le 'Mana' quotidien: structures et fonctions de la chronique des faits divers*.[26] His analysis and documentation are indispensable to any study of the phenomenon, and this work will be a point of reference throughout what follows. Auclair shows how the *fait divers* engages with the symbolic systems of a culture, calling on 'la pensée naturelle' to make sense of the 'scandale logique' which defies rational categories. Its themes include mystery, chance and destiny, and unconscious fears and impulses which activate the collective imagination and bring into play various forms of projection and identification. The spectacle of catastrophe triggers fantasms which haunt both the public at large and writers as divergent in other respects as Dostoyevsky and Proust. The form also connects with semiological issues, raising questions about the relation between the imaginary and the real, about the conventions of verisimilitude based on norms determining representations of the real – norms which the *fait divers* flamboyantly subverts, the better to confirm them.

At the same time, the *fait divers is* real, as Shaw's comment on Jack the Ripper and *La Bête humaine* indicates: it exists independently of the news report, and as such generates concomitant phenomena such as a concern for the actual scene of the event, for relics of the disaster, which offer 'des court-circuits possibles entre le référent et le réel'[27] and the chance of a more direct participation in the drama. A discussion that complements Auclair's consideration of these aspects, as well as his elucidation of the 'portée sociologique des faits divers',[28] is provided by Jean Baudrillard, in the context of the general commodification of experience he discerns in *La Société de consommation*.[29] For Baudrillard, the *fait divers* is *the* cardinal category of thought in the consumer society: it is the form, at once anodyne and miraculous, that articulates political, historical and cultural information in terms which accord with our fantasms of involvement in the dramas of reality. Baudrillard's argument helps explain why in a society of affluence and security (at least for some) the *fait divers* should continue to have compulsive attractions. The media offer fantasms of violence and disruption – 'le plus vrai que le vrai [. . .] le fait d'y être sans y être' – for consumption by a public whose comfort cannot be appreciated unless it seems to be precarious, constantly under threat: 'Il faut la violence et l'inhumanité du monde extérieur pour que non seulement la sécurité s'éprouve plus profondément comme telle (cela dans l'économie de la jouissance), mais aussi pour qu'elle se sente à chaque instant *justifiée* de se choisir comme telle (cela dans l'économie morale du salut).'[30]

The universality of the *fait divers*, graphically illustrated by Baudrillard, owes something to its particular mode of propagation. It is not exclusively dependent on the press or other media: as Edgar Morin has shown, it is also transmitted by hearsay and *la rumeur*. This provides perhaps the most dramatic illustration of its insidious attraction and its pervasive influence. Morin's study of epidemics of what are also sometimes called 'urban myths' once more links a phenomenon of the modern world to practices redolent of primitive cultures and which can, on occasion, prove independent of and resistant to the official media.[31] However, the methodological discussion which Morin provides helps justify and orientate our consideration of the phenomenon. For his 'Sociologie du présent' the *événement* is a crucial factor, since it vindicates an approach whose object of study is not a system in a state of equilibrium, but one which is seeking to reconstruct its regular functions by incorporating or otherwise neutralizing what has disrupted them: a 'sociologie événementielle' elects to examine the 'processus de modification et résorption provoqués par l'événement'. Moreover, 'l'étude de la virulence événementielle ne peut être séparée des processus de communication des événements et des caractères symboliques, voire mythologiques, qu'ils acquièrent dès qu'ils entrent dans la communication sociale.'[32]

The writers and texts we shall be examining might be seen as sophisticated contributors to both the manifestation of these cultural reactions and the study of them that Morin calls for. A philosopher such as Merleau-Ponty, for example, while less explicitly concerned with the contagion of gossip the *fait divers* gives rise to, nonetheless sees in the phenomenon itself a series of challenges that need to be met and are too often neglected. Initially a bloody incident he witnesses 'troublait l'ordre, il fallait bien vite l'effacer, et que le monde reprît son aspect rassurant'. The spectacle reminds him what it is to see such violence: 'se rendre présent en gardant ses distances, et sans participer', which in turn highlights 'notre parti pris de regarder sans comprendre'.[33] The criticism of this perception shows there is little significant distinction between reactions to the actual event and those elicited by the mediatized event which claims to make present 'la chose vue' without our needing to be there, as Baudrillard puts it.[34] However, for Merleau-Ponty the *fait divers* does offer the prospect of a revelation since it both dramatizes 'ces rencontres avec le préhumain' and constitutes 'l'invasion d'une vie dans celles qui l'ignoraient': it reminds us of what we see without taking it in. 'Le fait divers appelle les choses par leur nom,' Merleau-Ponty asserts: and for him it is the only point of comparison for the novel. Both are concerned with notions of truth, though they converge only too rarely:

> Le roman est plus vrai, parce qu'il donne une totalité et qu'avec des détails tous vrais on peut faire un mensonge. Le fait divers est plus vrai parce qui'il blesse et qu'il n'est pas beau. Ils ne se rejoignent que chez les plus grands, qui trouvent, comme on l'a dit, la 'poésie du vrai'.

The ideal novel achieves a synthesis between the event and the totality, between the *fait divers* and the context, between two complementary truths.

Merleau-Ponty has in mind the novels of Stendhal, who as we have seen offers a possible example of his ideal in *Le Rouge et le Noir*. In the same connection we might recall André Gide's commendation of Dostoyevsky's *The Brothers Karamazov*: 'On sait qu'un vulgaire *fait divers*, une "cause" ténébreuse, que prétendit éclairer la subtile sagacité du psychologue, servit de premier prétexte à ce livre.'[35] Many other authors (not least Gide himself) have had their texts explicated through reference to sources in newspaper items.[36] This book does not seek to add to the number of such authors or such studies. The writers discussed are presented as a sample of those in the twentieth century who have deliberately addressed themselves to the *fait divers*, making it the overt subject of their writing – fiction or journalism – and commenting thereby on its place within the culture and within modern literature. We shall examine texts which may feature violent or unusual events, but which also concern themselves explicitly with the 'processus de communication des événements et des caractères symboliques, voire mythologiques, qu'ils acquièrent dès qu'ils entrent dans la communication sociale', as Morin puts it.[37]

Equally, the intention is not to duplicate the work of specialists on the *fait divers* whose studies have been rapidly surveyed here nor to provide systematic illustration of their theses through literary examples. The purpose of the foregoing discussion has been to sketch in the context – thematic, methodological, historical – within which our subject can be located. At various points in what follows we shall inevitably refer to elements from this body of material, though the approach will be predominantly literary. The corpus assembled hereunder, while inevitably far from comprehensive for the period covered, does raise questions about the appropriate framework within which to place it. No single pattern seemed to meet all the requirements of the subject, so that, borrowing justification from the miscellaneous nature of the *fait divers* rubric itself, I have adopted several different angles of approach in an attempt to show what each can produce and to suggest how each could be applied separately across a fuller range.

The book begins with a group of studies in which the literary project is viewed in a wider perspective; it then focuses progressively on individual writers and readings of individual texts. The writer as journalist, or journalistic endeavour in relation to literary preoccupations, is the subject of part one, which considers two periodicals from different eras. Part two presents examples of the approach to the *fait divers* of a literary movement on the one hand and of two writers with significant literary affinities on the other. Part three seeks to illustrate the contribution that historical developments can make to the treatment of *faits divers* in the press and in literature. Part four presents a pair of case-studies, with the aim of circumscribing the individual profile of two writers whose careers as a whole are substantially marked by a familiarity with the rubric. Parts five and six offer contrasting viewpoints on violence in the news, the former based on writing by female authors, while the latter considers texts by male authors. Finally, part seven elects to analyse certain significant works of fiction by an author who manifests in them a comprehensive preoccupation with the *fait divers* and offers therefore a kind of overview on my subject.

It may be some consolation to the reader to learn that the first draft of this book was twice as long as the present volume. For the author its present relative brevity is barely adequate testimony to the considerable support and encouragement from which it has benefited. The British Academy generously provided a grant to enable me to pursue research in Paris. In addition to allocations of study leave, Keele University conferred a research award which freed me from teaching and administration and made it possible to bring the project to fruition. My colleagues in the Department of Modern Languages at Keele, and the French section in particular, shouldered the extra burden of work this entailed. I wish to express my sincere thanks for all these material and moral contributions.

Many colleagues supplied material and helped with information, criticism, and displays of interest or enthusiasm, and without them I may not have found the sustained impertinence required to develop my quirky topic into a book. They include David Bancroft and the staff at CPEDERF in Paris, David Bellos, Rick Caldicott, Rosemary Chapman, Ceri Crossley, John Flower, Johnnie Gratton, Trevor Harris, Michael Holland, Diana Holmes, Christopher Johnson, Andy Leak, Silvano Levy, Roger McLure, David Meakin, Walter Redfern, Paul Reed, Michael Sheringham, Edmund Smyth, David Steel, Jeremy Stubbs, Tony Williams and Geoff Woollen. I am very grateful to them and trust they will not feel let down by the outcome.

Notes

1. See Roger Clausse, *Le Journal et l'actualité*, Paris, Marabout Université, 1967, pp.95–7.

2. See Claude Bellanger *et al.*, *Histoire générale de la presse française*, Tome III, *De 1871 à 1940*, Paris, Presses Universitaires de France, 1972, p.278.

3. Clausse, *Le Journal et l'actualité*, p.96.

4. Ibid., pp.26–7. See also pp.14–15, 17, 35.

5. Ibid., pp.18, 23–4.

6. See Roland Barthes, 'Structure du fait divers', in *Essais Critiques*, Paris, Seuil, 1964, pp.188–97.

7. Andrew L. Walker *et al.*, *Lyon à la une*, Communicative Competence in French, Module 7, 'Chiens écrasés', Edinburgh, Scottish Universities' French Language Research Association, 1986, p.7.21 of the transcript.

8. Quoted by Alain Monestier *et al.* in *Le fait divers*, catalogue of an exhibition organized at the Musée national des arts et traditions populaires (Paris, Editions de la Réunion des musées nationaux, 1982, pp.50–1). Quoted also as epigraph in Romi, *Histoire des faits divers*, Paris, Editions du Pont-Royal, 1962.

9. Barthes, 'Structure du fait divers.'

10. Romi, *Histoire des faits divers.*

11. Jean-Pierre Séguin, *Nouvelles à sensation. Canards du XIXᵉ siècle*, Paris, Armand Colin, 1959.

12. Louis Chevalier, *Classes laborieuses et classes dangereuses à Paris pendant la première moitié du XIXᵉ siècle*, Paris, Plon, 1958.

13. Ibid., p.66.

14. Ibid., p.68.

15. Ibid., pp.73–134.

16. Ibid., pp.ix–x.

17. See *Le Rouge et le Noir*, ed. H. Martineau, Paris, Garnier, 1960, pp.x–xii, and extracts from the report in the *Gazette des Tribunaux*, December 1927, reproduced in Paul Lidsky, Christine Klein-Lataud, *'Le Rouge et le Noir'*, Paris, Hatier, 1992, pp.7–8.

18. Michel Foucault, *Surveiller et Punir*, Paris, Gallimard, 1975, p.114.

19. Ibid., pp.292–4. The evolution Foucault traces takes in *en passant* various other types of 'réécriture esthétique du crime' aimed at keeping its potential exoticism well beyond the reach of 'les gagne-petit de l'illégalisme' (p.72).

20. Ibid., p.72.

21. See Romi, *Histoire des faits divers*, p.197; Enid Starkie, *Flaubert, the making of the master*, Harmondsworth, Penguin Books, 1971, pp.331–3; *Madame Bovary*, ed. E. Maynial, Paris, Garnier, 1961, pp.403–8.

22. Albert Thibaudet, *Histoire de la Littérature Française de 1789 à nos jours*, Paris, Stock, 1936, p.206.

23. *Histoire de la littérature française*, Paris, Hachette, 1910, p.1043.

24. *Three plays by Brieux. With a preface by Bernard Shaw*, London, Fifield, 1917, pp.xi–xii.

25. Classic instances include Eugène Sue, *Les Mystères de Paris* (1842–3); Ponson du Terrail, *Les Exploits de Rocambole* (1859). For a penetrating study of the sensibilities involved, see Christopher Prendergast, *Balzac: Fiction and Melodrama*, London, Arnold, 1978. A typical English equivalent would be Mary Braddon, *Lady Audley's Secret* (1862).

26. Georges Auclair, *Le 'Mana' quotidien: structures et fonctions de la chronique des faits divers*, Paris, Editions Anthropos, 1970; a second edition, with a preface and an extra chapter, 'Le double imaginaire de la modernité dans la vie quotidienne', is dated 1981. Page references are to the 1970 edition.

27. Ibid., chapter 10.

28. Ibid., chapter 7.

29. Jean Baudrillard, *La Société de consommation*, Paris, Gallimard Folio-Essais; first published in 1970.

30. Ibid., pp.30–5.

31. Edgar Morin *et al.*, *La Rumeur d'Orléans*, édition complétée avec *La Rumeur d'Amiens*, Paris, Editions du Seuil, 1969; see in particular p.119.

32. Ibid., pp. 247–8.

33. M. Merleau-Ponty, 'Sur les faits divers', *Signes*, Paris, Gallimard, 1960, pp.388–91.

34. Baudrillard, *La Société de consommation*, p.31.

35. 'Les Frères Karamazov', in *Dostoïevski*, Paris, Gallimard, Collection Idées, 1970, p. 63. Dostoyevsky is of course a classic case of the novelist finding inspiration in *faits divers*: see the illuminating chapter on the subject, informed by an appropriately French perspective, entitled 'Le grand dialogue: le fait divers', in Jacques Catteau, *La Création littéraire chez Dostoïevski*, Part 2, Paris, Institut d'Etudes Slaves, 1978, chapter 8, pp.237–51.

36. See for example Louis Mandin, 'Les origines de *Thérèse Raquin*', *Mercure de France*, vol.297, 1 May 1940, pp.282–98. More recent instances include: Charlotte Schapira, 'Maupassant et le fait divers', *Hebrew University Studies in Literature and the Arts*, Spring 1987, pp.23–32; Ida-Marie Frandon, 'Fait divers et littérature. En marge d'une exposition' [on Barrès, *Les Déracinés*], *Revue d'Histoire Littéraire de France*, vol.84, 1984, pp.561–9.

37. Morin, *La Rumeur d'Orléans*, pp.247–8.

PART I

Writers and Journalism

2

From *Fin de Siècle* to *Fait Divers*: Alfred Jarry, Charles-Louis Philippe and *Le Canard sauvage*

Although frequently characterized as an other-worldly age of aesthetes, the decades spanning the turn of the century mark the high-point of the down-to-earth news industry.[1] The era saw the Panama Canal scandal (1892–3), the Dreyfus affair (1894–1906), a campaign of anarchist outrages culminating in the assassination of the President in 1894, Jack the Ripper on one side of the Channel (1887–91) and Vacher l'Eventreur on the other (1895–7), not to mention a volcanic eruption in Martinique (1902) and regular road, railway and metro disasters as new forms of transport, especially motor cars, became a feature of everyday life. Not even artists could remain aloof from this heady broth.

Newspapers trafficking in such matters became more than ever a staple of cultural life. A shift in their role[2] and a surge in their prominence was reflected in feverish editorial and managerial changes during the era. *Le Petit Journal*, which by 1880 had been the first to sell over a million copies through its sensational reporting style, launched an illustrated supplement for *faits divers* in 1889. Its upstart rival *Le Petit Parisien* which, under new ownership, had done the same a year earlier, was soon to reach 1,500,000 copies and feature on its masthead the claim 'Le plus fort tirage des journaux du monde entier.'[3] *Le Matin* came under new and ruthless ownership in 1897, and aimed at similar heights – only to be surpassed by *Le Journal*, founded in 1892 but the object of takeovers and a relaunch in the years following 1895.[4]

The fundamental fare through which all these organs pursued success was *fait divers* and *roman feuilleton*, sensational fact and fiction. Zola's 'J'accuse' sold 300,000 copies of *L'Aurore* in a matter of hours on 13 January 1898. We should not underestimate, then, the importance of *fait divers* as a feature and a form of cultural life at the turn of the century.[5] The responses of intellectuals and artists range from a wary or reluctant submission to enthusiastic engagement with it. 'Nul n'échappe, décidément au journalisme,' wrote Mallarmé in the *avant-propos* to his *Divagations* in 1897. In fact it has been argued that in professional as well as material terms, journalism and literature were more closely interrelated during this period than at any other.[6] Félix Fénéon, the distinguished art critic, prominent as the director of *La Revue Blanche* and thus publisher of the most renowned aesthetes, was to produce some of his finest writing in the *Nouvelles en trois lignes*, witty, elegant, subtly subversive renderings of agency reports he contributed to the *fait divers* rubric in *Le Matin* during 1906.[7] Gide was to use *faits divers* from the turn of the century in *Les Caves du Vatican* and *La Séquestrée de Poitiers*, to say nothing of the news reports of 1906 and 1909 which form the basis of *Les Faux-Monnayeurs*. The narrative of Proust's 'Sentiments filiaux d'un parricide', written in 1907 for *Le Figaro*, lingers over the experience of 'cet acte abominable et voluptueux qui s'appelle *lire le journal*', explicitly savouring the miscellany that typifies the *faits divers*: 'tous les malheurs et les cataclysmes de l'univers pendant les dernières vingt-quatre heures, les batailles qui ont coûté la vie à cinquante mille hommes, les crimes, les grèves, les banqueroutes, les incendies, les empoisonnements, les suicides, les divorces, les cruelles émotions de l'homme d'Etat et de l'acteur, transmués pour notre usage personnel à nous qui n'y sommes pas intéressés.' Proust's narrator points out that reading the news is a method of communicating with society and being integrated with the world: 'dès les premières nouvelles sensationnelles [. . .], ces nouvelles sensationnelles que nous aurons tant de plaisir à communiquer tout à l'heure à ceux qui n'ont pas encore lu le journal, on se sent soudain allègrement rattaché à l'existence qui, au premier instant de réveil, nous paraissait bien inutile à ressaisir.'[8] During 1908 Proust was to use the contemporary *affaire Lemoine* as the pretext for a famous series of pastiches, news reports after the manner of Balzac, Flaubert, Sainte-Beuve, Henri de Régnier, the Goncourt brothers, Michelet, Emile Faguet, Renan and Saint-Simon.[9] A host of his contemporaries chose to express themselves by writing about actuality in its rawest form.[10] Even Mallarmé the master, the patron saint of cloistered aesthetic refinement, had devoted a section of his *Divagations* to what he called 'Grands faits divers'.

Alfred Jarry and Charles-Louis Philippe are typical of their generation, having much in common with each other as well as presenting significant contrasts. Their lives spanned the same thirty-five-year period between the mid 1870s and the first decade of the twentieth century (Jarry died in 1907 aged thirty-four; Philippe in 1909 aged thirty-five). They were not *faits-diversiers* as such but they commented on *faits divers* and on the way the newspapers dealt with them, from the point of view of the literary artist and the nonconformist. To adopt a formula coined by Foucault, they were 'contre-fait-diversiers'.[11] Their aim was to get at the facts behind the news or to demystify its authority by subjecting to critical scrutiny the process whereby the news was produced. The form of the *fait divers* doubtless attracted them for differing reasons. In the 'pataphysical perspective of Jarry, the *fait divers* provides documentary evidence that every phenomenon is an exception, while the oddities which characterize the items in the rubric present a challenge to his 'science of imaginary solutions' which duly comes up with weird and wonderful explanations. Jarry contributed a regular series of what he called 'Spéculations' or on occasion 'gestes' to *La Revue Blanche* from January 1901 to December 1902 when the review closed down, and to *La Plume* and others for a year or so thereafter. (These articles he later collected for a volume entitled *La Chandelle verte, Lumières sur les choses de ce temps*, published after his death). Philippe, for his part, given his provincial artisan background, retained a fellow-feeling for the *petites gens* who people the *chronique*; moreover his anarchist sympathies drew him to the criminals and delinquents whose exploits also feature there. Philippe published a series of articles under the heading 'Faits divers' in *La Revue Blanche* from late 1901 to early 1902, with some related items in *L'Ermitage* during the same period. The two authors' writings on current affairs thus appeared side by side in some numbers of *La Revue Blanche*; but more significantly, perhaps, on the demise of this review, they became the principal (indeed the only regular) contributors to *Le Canard sauvage*, a weekly illustrated review devoted to *faits divers* which was launched in March 1903 and ran until October of the same year.[12]

With its sixth issue, *Le Canard sauvage* inaugurated a format whereby each number adopted a theme inspired by current affairs.[13] The contributors tailored their articles to these themes with varying degrees of scrupulousness, as can be seen if we consider the number for 27 September–3 October, devoted to 'Faits-divers'. Philippe's article, entitled 'Un fait divers', turns out to be a sequence from part one of *Marie Donadieu*, the novel he was then working on, relating Marie's first brief infidelity to Raphaël (here called Ferdinand), which takes place in Lyon (here transposed to Paris through the removal of 'Place Bellecour' and 'Allée des Veuves' and the insertion of 'au Luxembourg'). It is a feature of so-called 'populist' or 'proletarian' fiction that it is happy to pass itself off as, or acknowledge its debt to, the *fait divers*.[14] It is characteristic of Philippe that he should adopt this strategy; but it is significant too that he should change the location of his story, an apparent acknowledgement that Paris is established as the appropriate setting for both the anonymity and the urban poetry of the *fait divers*. From a technical or formal point of view the tale does stand up well on its own, both psychologically and aesthetically; but insofar as the episode represents, in the novel viewed as a whole, an isolated incident, a narrative parenthesis which nonetheless sows the seeds of later calamities – 'la suite eut lieu un jour' as a key phrase later in the text has it[15] – we can see in this respect too how Philippe might have justified its inclusion here as a *fait divers*: an 'anecdote futile qui renvoie à l'essentiel', as an analyst of the *fait divers* puts it.[16]

Something of what makes it possible to adduce this line of reasoning emerges from other articles in this number. One Thomas Griffon, who we can assume was Franc-Nohain, vouchsafes a tongue-in-cheek 'Philosophie du fait-divers'. Firstly, the *fait divers* is a departure from the norm: 'S'il en était autrement, il serait terrible de penser que nous ne vivons qu'au milieu de gens écrasés, noyés ou chiourmés, et que l'histoire du temps présent a comme grands premiers rôles les Apaches de Belleville et les Administrateurs du Métro.' Secondly, the *fait divers* is constructed – nay, created, lived – by the journalist. 'Cela est si vrai que le même événement, immersion en Seine, chute d'une cheminée, ou chute de voiture, accident de chasse ou de bicyclette – le même événement devient un fait divers, suivant que le reporter était absent ou présent.' This, it is asserted, is what makes a real *fait divers* of 'chien écrasé, incendie, suicide, vol à la tire, ou mort subite'. While these remarks help enlighten us on the form, the sheer drollery of Franc-Nohain's lists emphasizes the intractably miscellaneous character of what we are dealing with.

Jarry, in his article on the subject, adds the necessary rider that we must 'abandonner l'idée que le mot "divers" implique quelque variété dans ces incidents' since 'l'on ne trouve jamais autre chose, sous la rubrique "faits divers", que les "crimes et accidents"'; in other words, Jarry highlights the recurring patterns followed by incidents in the rubric even though its content is invariably that which 'n'est pas conforme à l'ordre social'. But the term itself gives rise to difficulty: 'un fait' cannot be 'divers' since it is singular; and what does 'divers' mean? We have here a phenomenon which is singular and heterogeneous, in which language has trouble circumscribing its referent, whose very name simultaneously implies and evades patterns of classification. At the heart of the rubric lies a double enigma, linguistic and ideological, which is inscribed in the very words used to denote an instance which in fact is poised at an angle to everything. It is in this respect above all, as we shall see, that Jarry will engage with it.

Jarry insists that the *fait divers* is 'la menue monnaie de l'information', 'tout ce qui n'est pas important'. Hence he claims to exclude from the category a number of items: 'un voyage de Président de République, un décès de Pape', which are 'trop considérables et trop rares'. But he has specifically dealt with these items in the pages of *Le Canard sauvage* (nos. 17 and 18), with deadly punning irony that confirms they are being brought down to the level of the 'menue monnaie de l'information' (the articles on President Loubet's journeys are entitled respectively 'Loubing the Loub' and 'Le Président migrateur'). The *fait divers* does not just record the minor incidents of everyday life: it challenges the hierarchy of information, and can make minor incidents out of ostensibly grandiose exploits, subjecting them to scrutiny of a kind which deflates the unquestioned respectability supposedly conferred by grand political or historical designs. A year or so earlier, in *La Revue Blanche*, Jarry had provided a catalogue of his intended topics every bit as heterogeneous as the lists furnished by Franc-Nohain (or Proust, for that matter) and had asserted: 'Tous ces gestes et même tous les gestes, sont à un degré égal esthétiques, et nous y attacherons une même importance. [. . .] Tel mariage mondain ne mérite pas de nous distraire de la cérémonie des justes noces de tel étalon dans un haras' (JOC, 332).

Such news items are as good as a *feuilleton* for *connaisseurs* such as *concierges*: 'le fait-divers est-il autre chose, sinon qu'un roman, du moins qu'une nouvelle due à la brillante imagination des reporters?' asks Jarry. But he will demonstrate his superiority over reporters by bringing a greater linguistic inventiveness and an even more fertile aesthetic vision to bear on the material of the *fait divers*. Why should he feel impelled to do so? Because, as he says in conclusion, 'le fait divers . . . C'est un fait'. Like reality, it cannot be ignored. Just as Jarry sought to transfigure the rest of the world around him, so he will tackle this particularly factitious feature of it.

Ultimately though, the *fait divers* is a fact of the *cultural world* more than of any putative actual universe. Jarry agrees with Franc-Nohain that the phenomenon is constructed by journalists – sometimes in collusion with those they serve – for a specific set of purposes, because 'ça fait vendre les journaux, et, de même que la justice, il n'est pas mauvais que la presse vive' (JOC, 498). In 'L'Affaire' of *Le Canard sauvage* for 9–15 August 1903 he discusses the recipes and strategies used by the press and the judiciary for the successful exploitation of a '"bonne" affaire': 'Pour inventer une affaire, il faut du flair [. . .] Une affaire, cela se découvre, se médite et se construit comme une pièce de théâtre' (JOC, 498). Ingredients to seize upon are treachery – hence the Dreyfus affair – or large amounts of money – hence the Humbert-Crawford affair, that hinged on fraudulent claims of a vast inheritance from a mythical 'oncle d'Amérique'. And it's a good thing too that 'il n'y a jamais qu'une seule affaire "pendante": autrement, l'attention publique se disperserait' (JOC, 499). In a later article he will pick up this idea and discuss how the news of different cases is managed in order to keep the public occupied: 'Avec deux affaires ingénieusement alternées, un gouvernement sagace sait ne jamais laisser manquer le bon Public de distractions aussi saines que variées' (JOC, 531).[17] Jarry too will be happy to alternate, but with anarchic abandon, blending and confusing different 'affaires' for his own purposes.[18] Hence at a point when the powers that be are striving to keep in focus the key issues of the Dreyfus affair in an effort to contain its subversive ramifications,[19] Jarry inserts into his report on allegations of forgery in the corridors of power a reference to another contemporary affair, that of the so-called tiara of Saïtapharnès, an archaeological fake that had been bought by the Museum of the Louvre.[20] 'Un vrai faux, mais il est plus vrai que nature,' he declares, impugning the reliability of officials in both cases but at the same time raising a philosophical issue of some importance and considerable subversive potential. In earlier remarks on the affair of the tiara, he had highlighted the question of verisimilitude that is so often at issue in such matters: 'Le faux peut quelquefois n'être pas vraisemblable' (JOC, 417),[21] he writes, spoofing Boileau: 'Le vrai peut quelquefois n'être pas vraisemblable.'[22]

The *fait divers* often arises, indeed, along that curious spectrum where truth, plausibility, belief, rumour and falsehood mingle and are confused. In the miscellany of current affairs that the media rain down on the public the distinctions are frequently blurred: one of the functions of the *fait divers* is actually to test such distinctions. And it is precisely because it is located in a zone where the facts challenge verisimilitude, and thus do not necessarily command credence, that the elements in play generate doubt as to their stable placing in the signifying circuit. Jarry, who in any case loves to push at the limits of credibility, sends up this very point when he marries and cross-fertilizes different but equally unlikely components. He does so most readily where important points of conventional ideology or morality are at stake. A particularly juicy instance arises in the *Canard sauvage* series as he writes about a diplomatic incident that occurred at Figuig in North Africa when the Algerian Governor-General, Charles Jonnart, came under fire in an ambush on the frontier between Algeria and Morocco, resulting in the dispatching of an expeditionary force to the region. 'Il est remarquable que tout, dans ce mythe, repose sur des mots,' declares Jarry – who sets about undermining the reliability of the words in question. Glossing the initial ambush of the governor-general, he reports this as an encounter with a mythical beast, the 'Guet-Apens', of which, he alleges, several species are wont to maraud in the desert: the 'Guet-à-Pinces', the 'Guet-à-Panse', and the 'Guet-à-Pans'. Jarry deliberately confuses the diplomat with the leader of the punitive military force, called O'Connor; he refers variously to a composite 'M. le général O'Jonnart' or 'O'Jonnor' (JOC, 461). In any case, reliable information was in short supply, since the press was excluded from the zone of operations, whence dispatches were communicated by field telegraph. 'Commencez-vous à comprendre?' enquires Jarry. 'Le bombardement [. . .] s'effectue par dépêches, savamment pointées, coup sur coup, sur . . . le public parisien.' In the final analysis, the General 'n'aurait pas eu besoin de se déranger de Paris pour ça. [. . .] La télégraphie est le bombardement moderne' (JOC, 462). Jarry highlights the dubious epistemological status of information in a media-saturated culture.

Further examples of notoriety exploited to similar effect emphasize the point. Saturation coverage of the Pope's death in July 1903 occasions a dialogue in *Le Canard sauvage* in which it emerges that 'on l'a élu parce qu'il devait mourir prochainement', the better to perpetuate the papal image: 'Sa Sainteté ne serait qu'une invention, canard en quelque sorte, de journalistes' (JOC, 487–8). In terms which could well have inspired Gide's *Les Caves du Vatican* and Genet's *Le Balcon*, Jarry indicates how the press de-realizes the person *per se*, and creates in its place a fiction that inhabits the collective imagination only. This collective imagination, whose basic currency is the *fait divers*, becomes a kind of common ersatz knowledge that supersedes reality. Jarry's exercises in spoof verisimilitude contribute to the devaluation of the common currency masquerading as truth.

Strategies such as these are essential, in any case, if the raw material is to achieve any value at all. Mallarmé, for example, in his 'Grands faits divers', refers to the anarchist bombing of the Chamber of Deputies as being interesting only 'en raison de la lueur'.[23] The Panama Canal scandal, with its financial figures amounting to an inert heap of zeros, cries out for the writer to 'amonceler la clarté radieuse avec des mots qu'il profère'.[24] 'A part des vérités que le poète peut extraire [. . .] rien, dans cet effondrement de Panama, ne m'intéresse,' he declares.[25] Writers who fail to refine the gold from the dross 'offensent le fait divers'.[26]

It is generally agreed that the 'rêve mallarméen' is what underpins Jarry's writing project, in *La Chandelle verte* and elsewhere.[27] By undermining the conventional signifying elements – linguistic, ideological and moral – which habitually frame the *fait divers*, Jarry is making it available for just such a transfiguration as Mallarmé is asking for. The particular teleologies of literature and the autonomy of language take precedence over other considerations. Jarry's attachment to the sensational is motivated by overriding aesthetic considerations. 'Tous les gestes [. . .] sont à un degré égal esthétiques, et nous y attacherons une même importance' (JOC, 332), we have seen him write.

The aesthetic features of the enterprise are reinforced, and can be clarified, through reference to a work whose impact on Jarry's generation seems to have been telling. Thomas de Quincey's *On Murder as a Fine Art* was published in France in 1901 in a translation by André Fontainas and was reviewed enthusiastically by Jarry in *La Revue Blanche* for June of that year (JOC, 616–7).[28] Justifying his approach to his shocking subject, the English writer says: 'Everything in the world has two handles. Murder, for instance, may be laid hold of by its moral handle (as it generally is in the pulpit, and at the Old Bailey); and *that*, I confess, is its weak side; or it may also be treated *aesthetically*, as the Germans call it – that is, in relation to good taste.'[29] The point about approaching such matters aesthetically is not that this rules out moral considerations, but that it denies a monopoly to moral reactions. As Gide put it: 'Le point de vue esthétique [. . .] reste le seul point de vue qui ne soit exclusif d'aucun des autres.'[30] Such a point of view thus opens up perspectives, it enables us to view things in the round. It also facilitates a proper critical appraisal of, for example, to quote Jarry in his review of De Quincey's book, 'ce que nous entendons de façon confuse et embryonnaire quand nous disons un "beau" crime.'

De Quincey affords a connecting link between Jarry and Philippe, since both French writers refer to him in articles each wrote on the criminal Gilmour. Jarry's piece, published in the *Revue Blanche* of 1 May 1901, dates from shortly after the arrest in mid April, following Gilmour's nocturnal attack on the female owner of a luxurious apartment in the rue Henri-Martin. Jarry greets the case as fit for de Quincey's 'société des connaisseurs en assassinat', on the grounds of the elaborate planning and weaponry that went into it, including a piece of cloth containing sand, to serve as a silent cosh. 'Un euphuiste dans son art', says Jarry, who advances the deadpan argument that he was actually the Sandman, understandably startled into violence when the light was switched on. While Philippe too views the murderer as an 'artiste' worthy of de Quincey, he evokes the need for pity in the face of the ill-luck and discomfiture of a man who was raised as an orphan and was merely a pawn in the manipulative hands of organized criminals.[31] However, under the influence of Nietzsche, Philippe is ready to see incarnated in Gilmour 'the strong man in unfavourable surroundings, the strong man made sick', to quote *The Twilight of the Idols*. In contrast to Jarry's sardonic detachment, he identifies with Gilmour as he reconstructs the crime, assimilating it to an aesthetic experience, the accomplishment of an intellectual project. He offers, in effect, the complex articulation of a number of positions, mediating matters through a number of moral, political and artistic discourses. John Flower expresses very well how Philippe's writing 'hovers indeterminately between an imaginative account of a real social problem, a vehicle for a number of Philippe's reflections on life in general and a projection of his own inner contradictions and ambitions'.[32] We certainly witness this hovering here. Philippe has unpicked the one-dimensional figure who was judged guilty in the law court and the press. Philippe's aesthetic dictates subtle modulations in point of view to construct a multidimensional close-up perspective, making the facts available to a diversity of discourses. The oscillation John Flower finds fault with in the fiction is here strikingly vindicated. Such is Philippe's aesthetic of the *fait divers*; the contrast with Jarry's virtual absence of engagement, achieved by standing well back from the spectacle, could hardly be more marked.[33]

By virtue of the intervening time-lag and the fuller documentation it draws on, Philippe's article on Gilmour might be seen to contain a plea for a more considered view than the cursory assessment Jarry's earlier text arguably set out. We can assume they did read each other's work: Jarry pronounced Philippe's *Bubu de Montparnasse* 'ce petit chef-d'œuvre' and more than enough justification for the presence of syphilis in France (JOC, 304).[34] They probably talked also on those not infrequent occasions when they met. However, the regularity of their parallel work for *Le Canard sauvage*, the likelihood that they collaborated editorially and may have had a hand in deciding the themes they would be required as contributors to write on, all this offers the possibility of some overlap and interaction in their writing during this period.

A number of issues provoke reactions which are fairly straightforward and produce texts which, setting aside technical or stylistic differences, are broadly similar in import. The collision and sinking of the passenger ship the *Liban*, from which most of the crew escaped while most passengers perished, drew a brace of sarcastic essays on the moral and professional competence of those in charge and on the state of repair of the equipment. The government's dissolution and expropriation of religious congregations brought from both writers protests about the distortion of the values of freedom and truth under the Republic, as well as warnings that this policy would actually enhance the dissemination of religious influence. Similarly, they were not alone in lambasting the mediocre qualities of President Loubet, though both came separately to the same conclusion that while on one of his numerous diplomatic trips to other countries some public-spirited individual might arrange for Loubet to take up permanent residence abroad (JOC, 484; POC, 55).

There are, however, some instances when what each writes arises from or integrates so closely with habitual personal preoccupations that it is hardly susceptible to the impact of outside influences. In Philippe's case this occurs most obviously when he fudges the thematic imperative in order to win time for work on his current novel *Marie Donadieu* and simply reuses material written for another purpose. More significantly, topics such as crime and politics consistently activate his anarchist or Nietzschean proclivities. In fact, several of Philippe's articles seem to carry as a systematic subtext a memorial to and a meditation on the 'propagande par le fait' practised by the anarchist terrorists a decade earlier.[35] Thus 'Le Visiteur', in a number of July headed 'A Rome' and devoted to the death of the Pope which caused the postponement of a planned visit to Paris by King Victor Emmanuel, recalls the exploit of Caserio, another notorious Italian, described as 'un saint' by Philippe, who visited Lyon in 1894 and assassinated Sadi Carnot, then President of the Republic. 'Voici plus de neuf ans que tu es mort et il y a toujours des rois,' Philippe writes (POC, 58). Similarly, he uses the number devoted to the opening of 'La Chasse' to highlight the class differences which put the poor on the side of the hunted animals, evoking 'L'humanisation de la bête . . . Jusqu'à ce qu'un jour lâchant tout, un Emile Henry,[36] un Vaillant,[37] en arrivent à déshumaniser les hommes et, par un retour qui n'est pas sans logique, à les frapper, comme on chasse, au hasard de la rencontre' (POC, 83). When King Victor Emmanuel did eventually arrive in France in October, Philippe responded with 'Un autre Italien', an article about an unnamed Calabrian brigand apparently on the run from the military, who had also come to France, who 'n'a recherché ni les fêtes ni les fanfares', but who 'n'[a] pas besoin de lire Nietzsche pour posséder les grandes vertus', and who through his exploits was 'une des grandes victoires de l'esprit humain' (POC, 97–9). Italy could be proud of his like, says Philippe: 'Depuis Caserio qui fut un saint, depuis Luccheni qui sans se rendre compte, frappa comme un enfant,[38] depuis Angelo Bresci,[39] ton sang noble, ton cœur fort ont trouvé d'autres hommes [. . .]' (POC, 97). His defence of these rebellious spirits extends to the repudiation of supposed scientific discoveries for dealing with social deviants, reported from America by *Le Journal*, 'toujours à la tête des initiatives généreuses'. No more Dostoyevsky, Poe, or Rousseau, complains Philippe; 'Caserio, Ravachol,[40] [. . .] le peuple en gésine, tout ce qui dépasse, sera trépané sciemment, car nous voulons socialiser les hommes' (POC, 34). These masses in labour he elsewhere offers as a bitter response to the political campaign to increase the birth rate, which merited its own number of *Le Canard sauvage* in July. 'Quand les fils des pauvres seront le nombre [. . .], nous les rassemblerons sur la place et nous leur dirons: "Mes fils! [. . .] Allez, et taillez-vous chez les riches, taillez-vous à coups de couteau de quoi manger plus que vous-mêmes et plus que vos pères n'ont mangé. Allez! Et s'ils vous parlent de leur droit, de leur justice et des principes, frappez-les au visage [. . .]"' (POC, 52). It is fair to say, then, that part of Philippe's purpose in what he wrote for *Le Canard sauvage* was to continue the anarchists' *propagande par le fait* by means of *propagande par le fait divers . . .*[41] Philippe made no secret of the fact that he used the form of the *fait divers* as a vehicle for the articulation of his most deeply-held convictions. This had been his explicit aim in the series of articles written between December 1901 and February 1902 under the heading *faits divers*, a title also used on their subsequent publication in book form. He looks back to them in a letter of December 1902, saying 'J'y donnais raison aux assassins parce qu'ils sont actifs et qu'ils "introduisent le hasard dans leur vie" (ce sont les mots dont je me servais).'[42] We have considered Gilmour, who falls into this category; when the opportunity arises in *Le Canard sauvage* to defend criminals against convention and society, Philippe's line is remarkably unchanged.[43]

A similar unswerving attachment to certain key themes can be seen in Jarry when social comment awakens the sleeping Ubu within: hence 'Cambronne et Edouard au Jockey-Club' in early May has His Majesty discussing 'le mot de Cambronne' (i.e. *merde*), and contains other sequences of dialogue distinctly redolent of the opening night of *Ubu Roi*. And Loubet's trip to North Africa – 'Loubing the Loub' – while highlighting the ubuesque resonances of the president's name, has him featuring in 'turqueries' which, though Molièresque in origin, are pure Ubu in manner and execution (JOC, 429–32). Jarry's hostility to the Church – except when its institutions are in conflict with the crass anticlerical policies of Prime Minister Combes – produces some notable exercises in blasphemous verve, as in 'L'Existence du Pape' (July); and 'La Vierge au Mannekin-Pis' (September), in which he borrows the rumbustious, Ubuesque character of l'Abbé Prout, scabrous inventor of 'la vaseline de l'Immaculée Conception', from his *confrère* Paul Ranson (JOC, 915).

Among the most famous of Jarry's sacrilegious pieces is 'La Passion considérée comme course de côte', which appeared in number 4 of 11–17 April and married religious ritual to that suddenly more contemporary one of cycle racing.[44] But here other factors may be seen at work, offering insights into interconnections between what Jarry and Philippe wrote for *Le Canard sauvage*. At this time the review had not yet introduced its thematic format, and Philippe, for his part, had presumably been simply following the calendar in devoting two of his three contributions during the preceding weeks to 'Mi-Carême' and 'Dimanche des Rameaux'. Though number 4 of *Le Canard sauvage* does not have an overall theme, its contents uniformly reflect Easter, which fell on 12 April that year; the idea of this convergence, like the subsequent ones which began systematically in number 6, may have been suggested by Philippe. Or perhaps inspiration came to Jarry independently, when he realized where his co-contributor was heading from week to week: his piece appeared alongside one from Philippe entitled, precisely, 'La Passion'.

It might be argued that Philippe's religiosity cried out for some form of antidote. Though not always pious in a conventional sense, his treatment of these subjects did skirt dangerously close to his ever-present sentimental or lachrymose side.[45] It is true that with hindsight we can discern a whiff of *avant-garde* sacrilege on Philippe's part: certain words he attributes to Christ here are taken from, or later put into, the mouth of his hero Jean Rousset in a crucial scene of *Marie Donadieu*, the novel he was working on.[46] But this perspective was not available to Jarry, who may deliberately have sought to administer a corrective called for by what on the face of it is a fairly routine, if *anarchisant*, piety. Perhaps Philippe got the message anyway, whether it was intended or not: Jarry's cavalier approach certainly makes his own seem the more strait-laced in contrast.

Thus, when in June *Le Canard sauvage* announced 'Turf!' as its theme, it contained an item by Philippe called 'Les courses'. The title echoes Jarry's earlier piece, and the opening lines contain an allusion to Jarry's article in the preceding number of *Le Canard sauvage*, a text mocking the 'agent de mœurs' which ends with the phrase, 'c'est là un cercle vicieux . . . ou moral' (POC, 448). Moreover the tone and technique are clearly imitated from

Jarry: uncharacteristically, Philippe proceeds by abrupt aphoristic statements whose cumulative effect resembles that of Jarry's mad satirical syllogisms:

> Les courses servent à l'amélioration de la race chevaline. Or, on élève les chevaux de courses pour servir à l'amélioration des courses. Et c'est ainsi que le *Petit Journal* sert à former l'esprit des masses en même temps que les masses servent à former l'esprit du *Petit Journal*. Et ceci n'est pas un cercle vicieux. Le cercle vicieux contient l'erreur, l'erreur contient la mort. Or, nous sommes toute une société vivante ainsi conçue. (POC, 39)

In apparent tribute to Jarry,[47] Philippe inscribes a circular, mathematical logic into his text as he catalogues the reciprocal dependencies into which are locked that class of society which celebrates its status by ranking its heroes – poets, millionaires or jockeys: 'Il suffit d'y voir clair et de savoir compter.' Even though he ultimately veers more characteristically towards a celebration of those humble souls who escape *their* closed circles, such as 'l'obscur employé qui, du fond d'un bureau bien clos, franchit les plus épaisses murailles, s'ouvre à la vie' (POC, 40), the article retains something of Jarry's remorselessly arbitrary mock-logic as it produces its one-line conclusion: 'Les courses entretiennent l'esprit de sacrifice.'

One of Philippe's standard techniques when dealing with *faits divers* is to adopt the artless style of a teller of simple tales. 'Voici des hommes qui ont fait un choix' (POC, 12) he begins his treatment of two murderers; 'Un homme s'est éveillé, un matin' (POC, 22) is the start of his text on the execution of a criminal; his account of the assassination of the Head of State begins with the words: 'Il y eut une fois un homme très simple que rien ne put empêcher d'aller voir le Président de la République' (POC, 56). The effect of this approach varies, depending on the context. Where the title – 'Deux crimes', 'Un condamné à mort', 'Un drame chez les folles' – signals the extreme nature of the subject, the opening gambit invites us to bracket out the instinctive response, to suspend the strong emotion that impairs our judgement; it suggests that the horror arose from a perfectly normal, humdrum sequence of events and that we would do well to consider it as such. One of Philippe's most telling denunciations in the *faits divers* collection he wrote for *La Revue Blanche*, of the negligence which led to a frenzied killing in a lunatic asylum, begins, 'La chose est si simple, si naturelle, qu'elle vaut à peine d'être contée' (POC, 100). The stance of childlike innocence we are invited to adopt may enable us to see the truth of small detail more clearly than the conditioned, convention-bound emotional reaction would permit; but it may equally usher in a more intense revulsion if it contributes to our being unsuspectingly brought face to face with an outcome that contrasts brutally with the apparent innocuousness of its antecedents. Conversely, this style of presentation, with its emphasis on banal everyday detail, may serve to obstruct the rationalization, in terms of a higher order of discourse – historical, political, ideological, administrative – of the scandal in question. At the same time, however, it runs the risk of glossing over important issues by smothering them in a meretricious air of candour.

Many of these points apply to the treatment of the murder by Serbian army officers of King Alexander I and his wife Queen Draga, on 11 June 1903. *Le Canard sauvage* ran an issue on it headed 'A l'Abbatoir' for 28 June – 4 July. Philippe's reaction comes in an article entitled 'Un meurtre', whose opening line reads: 'Voici un enfant qu'on élève pour être roi'; later the text contains phrases such as 'On a conté l'histoire d'une émeute . . .' The climax of the account is the description of the assassination: 'Il ne reçut qu'une quarantaine de blessures. Il était roi par nature, on le respecta un peu, en somme. Mais elle, on l'assomma, on la tailla, on l'ouvrit . . .' (POC, 47–9).

The brutal episode provoked hostile reactions throughout France. Jarry, for his part, evidently resisted the temptation to draw parallels with Ubu. His article, which appeared alongside Philippe's, is entitled 'Les contes de l'histoire', and begins, in *guillemets* thus, '«Il y avait une fois un roi et une reine dont le royaume était arrosé par un fleuve bleu . . .»' After two paragraphs in this vein, Jarry breaks off and writes: 'Voilà un conte de fées propre à bercer suffisamment n'importe quel enfant au sommeil de facilité moyenne. / C'est comme cela qu'on écrit l'Histoire. / C'est sur le modèle des contes de fées, aussi, que se déroulent ou que des gens tâchent de dérouler les événements de l'Histoire' (JOC, 470). The rest of his text is a bitter, sardonic denunciation of the contrast between the bloody reality and the expectations conditioned by the fairy-tale approach to history. After the Queen had been violated and disembowelled, a post-mortem[48] purported to reveal that she had not been pregnant after all, contrary to her suspect claims which had been one of the grievances held against her: indubitably, therefore, she was a '"méchante reine"', since 'Si c'eût été "une bonne reine", il va sans dire que le conte ne pouvait avoir d'autre fin que la forme attendue:". . . Et ils eurent beaucoup d'enfants"' (JOC, 471). In a contemporary article, 'Livres d'enfants', published in *La Plume* of 1 July, Jarry refers to *Le Canard sauvage* and its presentation of 'le conte de fées qu'est le coup d'Etat serbe [. . .] puisque l'Histoire, avec un grand H, n'est que le ressouvenir des contes d'enfants, mis à la portée des grandes personnes' (JOC, 473).

Jarry's target is clearly the narratives and ideologies exploited by 'cette bonne vieille reine de bibliothèque bleue, nommée République ou même Société' to explain away such outrages to her subjects, the 'petites créatures puériles' who take all her tales on trust (JOC, 471). But could there also be an implied warning of the dangers in Philippe's excessive fondness for story-telling, and in particular for the style of the 'conte d'enfants'? Or do both writers share an ironic view of the form and its relevance to the society of their day? Like Jarry in *La Plume*, Philippe pokes fun in the next number of *Le Canard sauvage* at the mentality of the 'mouvement repopulateur': 'Ils nous disent: "Faites des enfants"' (POC, 50). We may be tempted to deconstruct the slogan as an invitation to propagate not infants but infantilism. Certainly there is something insistent about Philippe's frequent recourse to the style of the *conte d'enfants* following this issue of *Le Canard sauvage*. The evidence is purely circumstantial, but two issues later, Philippe begins another evocation of the murder of a head of state with words we have already quoted: 'Il y eut une fois un homme très simple que rien ne put empêcher d'aller voir le Président de la République' (POC, 56). And among the titles of his subsequent articles we find the following: 'Histoire d'après la distribution des prix';[49] 'Histoires de chasse'; 'Histoire de Paris'; and 'Histoires d'enfants'. If nothing else, this makes the point that for Philippe the form was by no means ideologically unsound or necessarily inappropriate when dealing with current affairs.

From *fait divers* to fairytale may seem like a long way to travel: but since both deal in deceptively unassuming ways with issues of fundamental human importance, the path that links them may be slightly more than a diversion.

Notes

1. See Claude Bellanger *et al.*, 'L'Apogée de la presse française (1880–1914)', in *Histoire générale de la presse française*, vol.3, *De 1871 à 1940*, Paris, Presses Universitaires de France, 1972, pp.277–405.

2. The significant development, in newspaper terms, was the move away from the political broadsheet towards the newspaper proper – the 'journal d'information' – which became evident from the third quarter of the nineteenth century onwards. See Roger Clausse, *Le journal et l'actualité*, Paris, Marabout Université, 1967, pp.95–7; Bellanger, *Histoire générale de la presse française*, p.278.

3. Jacques Wolgensinger, *L'Histoire à la une*, Paris, Gallimard, collection Découvertes, 1989, pp.79, 88.

4. Ibid., pp.89–90; see also Bellanger, *Histoire générale de la presse française*, pp.300–16.

5. The point is made in Bellanger, ibid., p.279.

6. Ibid., p.277.

7. See Félix Fénéon, *Nouvelles en trois lignes*, edited, with an introduction, by Patrick and Roman Wald Lasowski, Paris, Editions Macula, 1990.

8. Marcel Proust, *Contre Sainte-Beuve*, précédé de *Pastiches et mélanges* et suivi de *Essais et articles*, Edition établie par Pierre Clarac avec la

collaboration d'Yves Sandre, Paris, Pléiade, 1971, pp.154–5. See Georges Auclair, *Le 'Mana' quotidien: structures et fonctions de la chronique des faits divers*, Paris, Editions Anthropos, 1970, pp.209–13 on the 'plaisir sadique' evinced by Proust's narrator here.

9. See *Les Pastiches de Proust*, Edition critique et commentée par Jean Milly, Paris, Librairie Armand Colin, 1970.

10. One could list Marcel Schwob (see *Mœurs des Diurnales, traité de journalisme* [published under the pseudonym of Loyson-Bridet in 1903], Editions des Cendres, 1985), Alphonse Allais, Laurent Tailhade, Raoul Ponchon, Willy, Tristan Bernard, Franc-Nohain and others.

11. Foucault applies the term to radical journalists of the mid-century and suggests that their true heirs were indeed the anarchists of the second half of the century who presented crime as a political issue, 'la forme la plus combative du refus de la loi' (*Surveiller et punir*, Paris, Gallimard, 1973, pp.292–9).

12. Jarry announces it in *La Revue Blanche* of 15 March as an 'hebdomadaire satirique et illustré, fondé par M. Franc-Nohain' (Alfred Jarry, *Œuvres complètes*, vol.2, edited by Henri Bordillon with the collaboration of Patrick Besnier and Bernard Le Doze, Paris, Pléiade, 1987, [hereafter JOC] p.674. The rich contemporary documentation contained in this volume has contributed much to my own discussion in the present chapter). However, the *éditeur* was Edmond Chatenay, and it is clear that Philippe himself played a significant organizational role. (Letters to Emile Guillaumin in *Charles-Louis Philippe, mon ami*, Paris, Grasset, 1942, pp.93–101; quoted in JOC, p.799.) It had thirty-one issues and Jarry appeared (sometimes twice) in thirty while Philippe featured in twenty-nine. Jarry needed the money on the disappearance of *La Revue Blanche* where Fénéon had proved particularly supportive: this accounts perhaps for the greater volume of his texts in *Le Canard sauvage* (as well as for others that appeared concurrently elsewhere). Philippe, who had a modest office job and who thus found time was the resource he lacked above all, was at pains to complete his novel *Marie Donadieu* in 1903 and so, while only contributing one item at a time, went so far as to protect his August holiday by reusing for that month's issues four pieces he had published in the anarchist-inclined *L'Enclos* during 1898. Moreover, in addition to isolated paragraphs here and there, four more of his contributions during September and October come substantially from the novel he was working on at the time.

The article by Franc-Nohain, quoted below, is transcribed from the unpaginated original of *Le Canard sauvage*; all quotations from articles by Jarry and Philippe refer to texts reproduced in the modern editions of their work.

13. Président Loubet's trip to North Africa was covered in '*Le Canard*

sauvage en Algérie'; Edward VII's first official visit (as king) was commemorated in 'La Promenade des Anglais' and that of Victor Emmanuel III of Italy in 'Ententes cordiales'; 'Vive la Liberté' greeted debates on the anticlerical policies of Prime Minister Emile Combes; 'V'là les flics' opened its columns to comment on the police; while other issues focused on the Army, the death of the Pope, hunting, exploration, traffic accidents, repopulation and a variety of affairs, catastrophes, scandals and incidents such as the assassination of the King of Serbia and his wife and the extension of Russian domination in Finland.

14. Henry Poulaille, the doyen of proletarian literature, was to indicate this as a criterion of excellence in the field. See his *Nouvel âge littéraire*, Bassac, Plein Chant, 1986, p.71.

15. *Marie Donadieu*, Paris, Bibliothèque Charpentier, Fasquelle Editeurs, 1951, p.144.

16. Alain Monestier *et al.*, *Le Fait Divers*, catalogue of an exhibition organized at the Musée national des arts et traditions populaires, Paris, Editions de la Réunion des musées nationaux, 1982, p.56.

17. *La Plume*, 15 December 1903.

18. See David F. Bell, '*La Chandelle verte* and the *fait divers*', *L'Esprit Créateur*, vol.24, 1984, pp.48–56, especially pp.52–3.

19. *Le Canard sauvage*, 18–24 April 1903: 'A la Chambre, soucieuse de n'éparpiller point ses efforts, il n'y a, n'y eut et n'y aura qu'une Affaire, une!' (JOC, 425).

20. See JOC p.884, note to p.417.

21. *Le Canard sauvage*, 4–10 April 1903.

22. *Art poétique*, chapter 3, line 48.

23. Stéphane Mallarmé, *Œuvres complètes*, edited and annotated by Henri Mondor and G. Jean-Aubry, Paris, Pléiade, 1945, p.319.

24. Ibid., p.318.

25. Ibid., p.1577.

26. Ibid., p.319.

27. See JOC, pp.802–4.

28. De Quincey's precision about 'ce que nous entendons de façon confuse et embryonnaire quand nous disons: un "beau" crime' can not have been far from Jarry's mind when he himself set about defining 'une "bonne" affaire' in *Le Canard sauvage* in August 1903: 'Entendons par bonne affaire un "bon" crime – le bon crime se reconnaît à la couleur: il doit être bien noir – ou une "bonne" affaire de mœurs – bien sale, et qui se lave en famille, à huis-clos' (JOC, 497–8). Other similarities emerge from Jarry's discussions of *faits divers*. The twin crimes of the 'affaire Humbert-Dreyfus', as he baptizes his cod hybrid, have about them exactly what it takes to 'satisfaire à la formule d'Aristote: horrifier

d'abord, apitoyer ensuite' (JOC, 531). This is a reminiscence of de Quincey: 'The final purpose of murder, considered as a fine art, is precisely the same as that of tragedy in Aristotle's account of it; viz., "to cleanse the heart by means of pity and terror."' Thomas de Quincey, *On Murder as a Fine Art*, London, Philip Allan, 1925.

29. De Quincey, *On Murder*, p.7.

30. André Gide, *Journal 1889–1939*, Paris, Pléiade, 1951, p.658.

31. Charles-Louis Philippe, *Œuvres complètes*, vol.5, Moulins, Editions Ipomée, 1986 [hereafter POC], p.102.

32. *Literature and the Left in France*, London and Basingstoke, Macmillan, 1983, p.58.

33. Another example which illustrates the same point can be found in the two writers' contrasting treatment of Honoré Ardisson, the 'Vampire du Muy'. Jarry commented on the story in *La Revue Blanche* of 15 October 1901, Philippe in *L'Ermitage* in November. See JOC, pp.320–1 and p.844; POC, pp.112–13, respectively.

34. *La Revue Blanche*, 15 July 1901.

35. For a brief résumé of this episode, see Albert Camus, 'L'Homme révolté', in *Essais*, Paris, Pléiade, 1965, p. 571. More detailed coverage is provided in Jean Maitron, *Le Mouvement anarchiste en France*, vol.1, *Des origines à 1914*, Paris, François Maspéro, 1975.

36. Executed in May 1894; he had bombed the commissariat in the rue des Bons Enfants in 1892 and the café at the Gare Saint Lazare in 1894.

37. Executed in February 1894 for the bombing of the Chamber of Deputies in 1893.

38. He stabbed Empress Elisabeth of Austria in 1898.

39. He assassinated Umberto I of Italy in July 1900.

40. The first anarchist bomber to be executed, in July 1892.

41. This is a strategy Fénéon's editors see at work in his *Nouvelles en trois lignes*, p.20.

42. Letter to André Ruyters, in Charles-Louis Philippe, *Œuvres complètes*, vol.1, *Charles-Louis Philippe, la vie et l'œuvre*, by David Roe, Moulins, Editions Ipomée, 1986, p.248.

43. Cf. 'Deux crimes', March; 'Le condamné à mort', April; 'Leur Science', May; 'Le Crime de la rue Chalgrin', May. Even 'Leur Science' echoes the antimedical/sociological establishment line of the earlier *fait divers* 'L'éducation hypnotique'.

44. The first Tour de France was run in July 1903; Jarry prides himself on having been among those who had 'tenu sur ses fonts baptismaux le cyclisme,' (JOC, 406).

45. David Roe discusses Philippe's religion in his biographical survey, *Œuvres complètes*, vol.1, pp.228–46.

46. 'Il n'y a pas de souffrance humaine . . . Vous avez créé un équilibre plus

grand que le calme et l'amour. Vous avez créé, pour la juste balance, un effrayant bonheur qui goûte à la vie tout entière et peut en apprécier les deux versants,' POC, 19; cf. *Marie Donadieu*, p.202.

47. The 'cercle de la mort', a variant on *looping the loop*, the death-defying cycling feat, was all the rage in Paris during the spring of 1903: so much so that after reviewing an exponent of it for the *Revue Blanche* of 15 March 1903 Jarry had gone on to write a typically eccentric [!] piece on 'Les cercles' to accompany his essay linking cycling with the Passion in *Le Canard sauvage* for early April, and another portraying President Loubet's international diplomacy as 'Loubing the Loub' in the April–May number. It is clear that the feat appealed to Jarry's sense of the absurd in human affairs: it inspires an article in *La Plume* of 15 March on 'La mécanique d'*Ixion*' (JOC, 405–7). Furthermore, in a review of Félicien Fagus's *Ixion* that appeared, appropriately enough, on the same page of *La Revue Blanche* as his evocation of *Looping the loop*, he highlights the phrase 'un esprit bête de manège' as well as evoking what he terms 'le beau dans la fusion d'une mathématique inexorable avec un geste humain' (JOC, 676).

48. To which Jarry took particular exception, cf. JOC, 469.

49. Altered from the title 'Un pion' which it bore in *L'Enclos* in 1898.

3

Cultivating the *Fait Divers*: *Détective*

Albert Thibaudet was ostensibly looking back a century from the mid 1930s when he wrote in his *Histoire de la Littérature Française* of the generation which, from *Le Rouge et le Noir* to *Les Misérables* via *Vautrin*, had found in 'les tribunaux, les prisons, les bagnes, les échafauds [. . .] des exemples de l'énergie humaine'.[1] The fact is, though, that his own generation was no less intrigued by the same phenomena. This interest manifested itself retrospectively as publishers launched collections aimed at meeting the public demand for stories of the classic 'affairs' of the past. In the late 1920s and early 1930s, Armand Praviel, to take a prolific and representative example, published *L'Histoire tragique de la Belle Violante* and *L'Assassinat de Monsieur Fualdès* among others in Perrin's 'Enigmes et drames judiciaires d'autrefois'; *L'Egorgement de la Duchesse de Praslin* and *Les Evasions de Latude* and others in 'Secrets d'autrefois' of Editions de France; *L'Incroyable Odyssée de Martin Guerre* in Gallimard's 'Les histoires extraordinaires'; *L'Affaire Chambige* and *La Grand'mère de Mme Lafarge* in Les Œuvres libres; *Le Radeau de la Méduse* with Flammarion: and this is merely a selection. The period 1930–4 also saw *Paris-Soir*, under Pierre Lazareff, move from sales of 60,000 to over a million thanks to its exploitation of sensational contemporary news.[2] Not surprisingly, there was a simultaneous upsurge in the creation of magazines such as *Police Magazine*, *Drames* and *Faits divers* to cater for this taste in the market.[3]

In the main, of course, such developments were aimed at the lower strata of the reading clientele. But intellectuals were not all disposed to sneer. Most notably, perhaps, André Gide had anticipated the fashion when he called for a systematic and serious consideration of *faits divers* in a special rubric of the *Nouvelle Revue Française* which he ran between 1926 and 1928; and in 1930 he published two books containing accounts of striking cases, *La Séquestrée de Poitiers* and *L'Affaire Redureau*. In the course of 1928, probably as a result of Gide's example, Gaston Gallimard set Georges Kessel (brother of Joseph) the task of creating a periodical for this niche in the market. Kessel assembled an editorial team and under a title invented by Gallimard[4] launched the first number of *Détective* at the end of October

1928. By its sixth issue its print run was around three hundred thousand copies,[5] after six months it claimed half a million readers[6] and before the decade was out it was credited with a readership of over 800,000.[7] It was still selling 250,000 in 1939.[8]

The impact of *Détective* was thus very significant indeed. It became a byword for lurid reports of crime, investigations into the underworld and *reportages* on the seamier side of society. Henry Robert, the president of the bar association, described it as 'ignoble' and called for its suppression.[9] The often blatant sensationalism of its cover pictures drew the disapproval of many others and led Chiappe, Prefect of the Paris Police, to ban posters advertising it in 1932.[10] But it generated the income which enabled Gallimard to continue publishing Valéry, Gide, Claudel and other luminaries of French literature: he freely admitted that the *NRF* lost money while *Détective* made large profits, and that it was the latter periodical which maintained his publishing business on a sound financial footing.[11] The cultural position of this organ is therefore telling: it stands as a revealing example of the material and moral relations between 'high' and 'low' culture. This is nowhere more evident than in the list (and photographs) of its contributors. Leading lights from the world of the judiciary – Maîtres Maurice Garçon (later of the Académie Française), César Campinchi and Henry Torrès – wrote for it, as did distinguished reporters from the mainstream press: Paul Bringuier, Henri Danjou and Louis Roubaud. Alongside these figured prominent literary names: Francis Carco, Pierre MacOrlan, Marcel Achard, Philippe Hériat, Joseph Kessel, Albert Londres, André Salmon, Jean Cocteau (whose photograph appears, though no texts by him were published) and Georges Simenon (under the pseudonym of 'G. Sim'). Numerous other up-and-coming writers in the late 1920s and mid 1930s published novels while contributing to *Détective*.[12]

The magazine's editorial policy manifests ambivalence as to its intended readership as well as in its editorial team. 'Partout, pour tous' is the formula that heads its first editorial.[13] The novelty of its format is that it intends to pursue its own investigations on behalf of its readers: 'Pour vous, lecteurs, il épiera, il poursuivra la trace du criminel, la piste du policier.' It will call upon the skills of specialists and experts: '*Détective* sera savant, puisqu'il sera chimiste, physicien, psychiatre, juriste.' These are serious and ambitious aims, and will involve the magazine in controversial investigations and criticisms of judicial procedure, in respect of the Falcou affair of 1932–3, for instance, and in connection with psychiatric opinion on the Papin sisters in 1933–4. At the same time, however, it will take readers 'au cœur des drames de la vie: les nuits de Chicago, les bouges de Singapour, tous les ghettos, Whitechapel'. Here it is in danger of following less worthy paths into a dubious 'exotisme de la pègre'. Already in Joseph Kessel's features, 'Les Nuits de Montmartre', which appeared in 1928, we are invited to savour the *frisson* which comes of complicity with squalor and criminality enjoyed from the safety of respectable lives:'dans un restaurant de la place Blanche, avec des amis d'un tout autre milieu que celui que je fréquentais à l'ordinaire à Montmartre', the off-duty reporter thinks idly of the 'peuple mystérieux et louche qui rôdait autour de ce restaurant classé et dont aucun des convives ne soupçonnait la présence ni les secrets [. . .] je goûtais une étrange saveur de vie dédoublée'.[14] This aspect of vicarious slumming will be made all the more telling by virtue of advances in photographic reproduction. The advent of photogravure is possibly the chief reason for the impact of magazines like *Détective* in the 1930s,[15] and the first editorial singles this out as a significant feature: never before had 'les plus belles photographies' been available in mass-circulation magazines, offering the chance to communicate the faces of criminals and the aftermath of bloody crimes with unprecedented immediacy. Well-considered words and rational analyses were bound to take second place to the shock effects that such images permitted. The lure of the dramatic picture was to prove a draw not just for the readership; ultimately it drove the editorial policy, pushing the magazine in search of the ever more spectacular at the expense, sometimes, of intellectual credibility.[16]

Perhaps the most invidious equivocation in *Détective* is the way it blurs the boundary between document and fiction. '*Détective* sera romancier: il vous fera participer à des épopées merveilleuses,' the readers of the first number were told. 'Vous aurez votre film hebdomadaire à domicile et vous vous apercevrez que les inventions des conteurs ont souvent aiguillé la police vers des procédés nouveaux. C'est ainsi que la fiction ramène à la réalité. Vous serez au cœur de l'imagination', continues the editorialist with remarkable inconsistency – or honesty. Often thereafter the reader of *Détective* will have opportunities to ignore the line that divides fact from fantasy, and the writers themselves will not scruple to use their reportages as a springboard into literature.[17]

This emerges, along with other aspects of the magazine's strategy for constructing its readership, from the advertising and other promotional material it carried. The campaign to defend Louis Falcou, wrongly accused in October 1932 of murdering the wife of a business associate and of burning her body, met with success after some five months of exemplary crusading journalism involving both *Détective* and the *Journal de Rouen*. The triumphant issue of 16 March 1933 carried an advert for the NRF announcing: 'Pour éclairer les dessous de l'Affaire Falcou, quelques romans de mœurs rouennaises' (which included *Le Septième Jour*, by Trintzius), and adding 'Il faut lire aussi *Rouen*, par André Maurois; *Villes*, par Pierre MacOrlan.'[18] Regular publicity for NRF books is a standard feature, however strange it may seem for the prestigious imprint to be associated with a mere crime magazine. An advertisement for *La Condition humaine* appears alongside stories on the Violette Nozières affair in 1933;[19] the issue for 3 August 1933 carries a large advertisement for Gallimard authors including Aymé, Kessel, Maurois, MacOrlan, Lacretelle, Conrad, Bloch and Gide.[20] Books by contributors to *Détective* or by 'nos excellents confrères de la presse judiciaire' are frequently plugged on the editorial page under headings such as 'Littérature et journalisme'.[21] In April 1933 pride of place is given to publicity for '*Angèle*. . .le titre du dernier livre du docteur Henri Drouin', author of 'émouvantes enquêtes' and a 'pathétique reportage romancé qu'il donna à *Détective*', which indicates the fuzziness of the magazine's journalistic practices. Alongside copy on a book by *chroniqueur judiciaire* Géo London relating '*Les grands procès de l'année 1932*' one finds a panel concerning a forthcoming number of *Marianne* (another of Gallimard's periodicals) which will contain, among other items, a 'nouvelle inédite de D.H. Lawrence, l'auteur de *L'Amant de Lady Chatterley*' and texts by André Gide and André Maurois.[22] Taking into account the scandal and attempted suppression that had attended the publication of Lawrence's novel the previous year,[23] this page provides fascinating insights into the assumed interests of the readership *Détective* was addressing. Titillation and sensationalism alongside icons of high literary culture: could this have been a viable mixture? Certainly it may be considered an unstable combination of elements, and it is evident that a certain settling occurs with the passage of time. But still Gallimard is capitalizing on the vast readership he has at his disposal in these pages: his collection 'Les chefs-d'œuvre du roman d'aventures' is frequently advertised,[24] as are authors such as Marius Larique (who took over from Kessel as editor of *Détective* in 1932), Henri Danjou and Noël Vindry whose features in *Détective* subsequently appear as NRF volumes.[25] The logical outcome of this process is the collection 'Détective' created by Gallimard in 1933 initially under the editorship of Maurice Sachs, to publish in book form the writings of contributors to the magazine, among others: eighty-six volumes appeared between 1934 and 1939.[26]

Other advertisements promoted hair restorer and bust enhancers as well as private detective agencies, home educators, schools for detectives, clairvoyants, aphrodisiacs, systems for winning at roulette, sex manuals and remedies for infections of the urinary tract. This only makes the more significant the editorial attachment to a range of quasi-literary values. It may be judged that these reflected little more than the incestuous, mutually self-supporting literary ambitions of its contributors; the vast majority of those who read the magazine presumably made little or nothing of references to what Francis Carco would have done with a given *fait divers*[27] or to the novel that a former contributor has since made of one.[28] It seems likely that the mass readership derived their sustenance from reports on notable crimes and trials, plus features on illegal immigrants, international drug trafficking, the white slave trade, the criminally insane, *les bagnards*, *la pègre, les irrégulières, les mœurs des quartiers réservés*, and so on. Nonetheless, the persistence of literary allusions does seem to have conferred a certain *caution* or cachet upon *Détective*, for, however disreputable it may have become in later, post-War guises when in the hands of different publishers it was virtually equated with pornography,[29] the fact remains that there is plenty of evidence to indicate that it was read and taken fairly seriously by writers and intellectuals throughout the 1930s. To the extent that this was so, the magazine served as a mirror for the preoccupations of the intelligentsia as well as the phantasms of French society at large.

A case in point is the stance adopted on the *fait divers*, the staple fare of *Détective*. From the outset, the magazine, claiming it is 'le premier hebdomadaire des faits divers',[30] stresses its pioneering approach to these items. An editorial by Maître Maurice Garçon in the third issue points out the weaknesses in the crime reporting offered by the daily press and promises that *Détective* will provide more: 'On jette le journal lorsqu'il est lu [. . .] on aimerait à relire, groupés avec exactitude, les détails des affaires qui se sont échelonnés parfois pendant plusieurs mois dans les colonnes des quotidiens.' The reader of this magazine will be enabled to 'connaître le détail complet des grands procès, suivre les modernes procédés de la police scientifique, voir évoquer par l'image fidèle, les lieux du drame et les traits des acteurs'. The ultimate aim, though, will be to air 'les grands problèmes sociaux de la criminalité et ses remèdes': *Détective* will have a social conscience. This is not to say that it will be unremittingly solemn: the amusing, trivial dimension intrinsic to reporting the *fait divers* features regularly under the rubric 'Grands procès . . . petites causes' with headlines such as 'Un procureur général en correctionnelle', 'Les fantaisies du facteur',[31] 'Un extincteur d'incendie qui met le feu' and 'Il volait . . . pour créer un parachute'.[32] However, the courtroom dramas the magazine exists to report are not to be viewed in isolation from the broader context, as a later editorial emphasizes: they provide evidence of 'les terribles drames de l'existence quotidienne [. . .] les conflits nés de circonstances particulières à une époque', and call to mind 'certaines obligations sociales, dont la Société, parfois, s'est désintéressée'.[33] The meditation on the sociocultural role of the *fait divers* continues intermittently in this and related veins. The memoirs of the reporter Alain Laubreaux, 'Souvenirs du "'chien écrasé"', serialization of which began in the 31 August 1933 number, provide an insider's perspective on this aspect of journalistic culture. In an article on the fringe figures of the Violette Nozières affair, Luc Dornain takes up a similar theme: the discipline and the challenge of the *fait divers* is an essential part of any cub reporter's apprenticeship, for 'le fait divers, c'est la vie; la vie descendue des théories et de l'absolu, la vie saignante, douloureuse, l'éternelle leçon.' As often as not the rookie learns to bow dutifully to the news editor's instruction 'Six lignes, dont trois drôles!' On some days, however, an item from the same source can push the economy and international relations from the front page: 'C'est un mystère que tel fait divers suscite une frénésie de savoir, de *tout* savoir; alors, on fouille des profondeurs insoupçonnables.' Society seems on occasion to need the release of instinctual impulses that a telling *fait divers* can articulate: 'C'est aussi le bienfait de la publicité faite aux faits divers par les journaux spécialisés.' Without this safety valve, the writer argues, the crime rate at large can rise – as he alleges was the case in Italy when measures were taken to limit the coverage given to the so-called *cronaca nera*. Once again a certain equivocation is in evidence none the less: among those who seek the reflected notoriety of being a 'figurant' in a *fait divers* one finds the 'inquiets, désaxés, en marge', but never 'des bourgeois tranquilles, des ouvriers réguliers [. . .] des "Français moyens"'. For these latter, it would appear, vicarious complicity is quite enough.[34]

The telling ambivalences that emerge despite the magazine's ostensible good faith and commitment to serious analysis can be seen reflected in the reactions of its intellectual readers. Among the most vociferous of these were the surrealists. In an article considering the links between surrealism and modernism and lamenting the decline of the latter under the influence of police censorship and repression, Louis Aragon refers to *Détective* as an example of 'cette presse photographique dont l'essor est encouragé' and which contributes to 'l'exaltation du flic'.[35] In the same number of *La Révolution surréaliste*, *Détective* is violently taken to task by Georges Sadoul, for much the same reason. His critique begins with *ad hominem* arguments, blackening the editorial team by indicating that contributors to the periodical include journalists from *Le Quotidien*, socialize with Chiappe (while toadying to him in servile articles) and support the politics of the ruling class. He quotes the initial editorial, to the effect that *Détective* 'poursuivra la trace du criminel': but, by cutting the words 'la piste du policier' which follow in the original text, he makes the aim seem more one-sided than it is. Sadoul also reproduces extracts focusing on police brutality, implying a degree of collusion between the authors and the miscreants they are reporting on. Quoting from a number of editorials, he alleges that the magazine is in favour of severe sentences on minors and capital punishment for women, and that it encourages criminals to become police informers. All of this, based on passages quoted out of context, grossly oversimplifies the intentions of the writers even when these latter are not entirely blameless. For Sadoul *Détective's* contribution to public life is as follows: 'On nous fait l'éloge du régime des prisons, on crée un Détective-Club qui est une école de policiers, on demande d'interner impitoy-ablement les enfants et les fous, on accable des accusés manifestement innocents, on recrute des engagements pour la légion étrangère [. . .] on pleure sur la misère de la police, on demande une loi qui punisse ceux qui ont refusé de se faire indicateurs [. . .] on fournit enfin à la police la piste des criminels présumés.' He concludes: 'On nous prépare une belle génération de petits salops,' linking the magazine's success with the vogue for the *roman policier* and seeing them together as a symptom of the ideological promotion of the policeman to be the equal of the priest and the general.[36]

This type of hostility will manifest itself in other guises subsequently, amply testifying to the fact that the surrealists continued to read *Détective*, just as they attached importance to *faits divers* and advertising, for example, as manifestations of the modern. But while in matters of cultural analysis they proved open-minded and eclectic, they appear to have remained scathing about the intellectual betrayals which in their eyes *Détective* embodied. In October 1930 *Le Surréalisme au Service de la Révolution* carried among its plates a photograph featuring the periodical. A man in a trilby hat, face hidden behind an open copy of *Détective* he is reading, is clearly intended as a spoof portrayal of the typically furtive, duplicitous individual associated with the title and its readership. The magazine's cover, announcing its price and title in the characteristic bold lettering, is immediately recognizable. However, while the 'Rien que la vérité' on the back page may be taken tongue-in-cheek, the picture adorning the title page is clearly a surrealist photomontage inviting derision: it depicts a female with a gag over her mouth and nose. The caption, neatly killing two ideological birds and one intellectual reputation with the same stone, reads: 'Une évolution singulière. M. Parain, ancien gérant de *Détective*, est actuellement chargé de la rubrique des *livres* à *L'Humanité*.'

If the surrealists were so touchy about *Détective*, this can be attributed to the fact that they resented its appropriating crime and *faits divers* for its own purposes, while Aragon, Breton, Eluard, Péret and their colleagues were set on making these phenomena yield up meanings more in line with their own ideas. In this sense, *Détective* represented a form of competition. It is perhaps significant therefore that at the time of the affair of the Papin sisters, *Le Surréalisme au Service de la Révolution* reproduced the same photographs of the maids as had been published in *Détective*.[37] *Détective* presented on its front cover a picture of the sisters in their domestic livery; inside, on page 3, the reader encountered a photograph taken on their arrest following their brutal and inexplicable murder of their mistress and her daughter. These two pictures, the neat and demure image contrasting dramatically with that depicting them wild-eyed, with bedraggled hair, were presented on the same page in *Le Surréalisme au Service de la Révolution*, with the words 'avant' and 'après'. *Détective*'s highly novelized, conventionally literary reconstruction of the case as a horrific descent from normality into bestiality is implicitly challenged by Eluard and Péret, who recount the story in two brief paragraphs and characterize the pair as 'Sorties tout armées d'un chant de Maldoror' – a phrase which is repeated as the caption for the photographs, and which enlists the sisters as nothing less than surrealist heroines.

This ongoing dialogue is not the only point of intersection between *Détective*'s columns and the concerns of the intellectuals at large. Jean Paulhan, editor of the *Nouvelle Revue Française*, quotes a headline from 'le dernier numéro de *Détective*' in the course of his *Entretien sur des faits divers*: 'Assassin d'une vielle dame qu'il tua pour 60 francs, quel châtiment mérite Jean Ecorce?'[38] Paulhan uses the case to illustrate the way headlines misrepresent the facts and imply quite wrongly – *post hoc ergo propter hoc* – that the criminal knew this was all he would get out of the crime. No doubt this example caught Paulhan's attention precisely because the case features in two successive issues under the rubric *Détective* created for supposed instances of this kind, 'Grands procès . . . petites causes.'[39] It enables Paulhan to diagnose one of the reflexes whereby humans impose sense by tying disparate facts together to produce what he calls the 'illusion de la totalité'.[40]

At the same period, others of the intelligentsia were reading the magazine for reasons of their own. As *Détective* was seen to command a vast readership, and as left-wing intellectuals began increasingly to concern themselves with the relationship between the working class and culture, theoreticians of revolutionary literature could not avoid references to it. In *La Revue des Vivants* for September–October 1932, Paul Nizan pointed out: 'Si l'on définit une littérature par le public qui la lit, la littérature prolétarienne en France comprend *Fantômas* [. . .] *Détective*, *Police Magazine* et *Le Petit Parisien*.'[41] Meanwhile, there is evidence of a readership it commanded at the opposite end of the political spectrum. The case of Violette Nozières, as is well known, generated much interest and controversy when she was arrested in August 1933 on a charge of poisoning her mother and father. The affair gave rise to a kind of moral panic, and was exploited by the press as a symptom of the 'jeunesse pourrie' of the times. *Détective*'s initial coverage extended from August to October, involving a survey of the views of various types of expert, features on the people and milieux Violette had frequented, and notably two reports on her by Henri Danjou in the 31 August and 7 September numbers.[42] Meanwhile, readers of Emmanuel Berl's *Marianne* were presented with an article by Drieu la Rochelle, entitled 'Le cas Violette Nozières', in the September 1933 issue.[43] Drieu can explain how the case gratifies the unacknowledged fantasies of the public, but confesses himself bewildered by the ease with which people take sides on the issues it raises: 'Je me renseigne, je me retourne, j'écoute, j'interroge. Policiers, juges, avocats, psychiatres et autres me paraissent tout de suite partagés. Tout d'abord rêveurs et soudain tranchants. Et je suis épouvanté de voir que je reste seul, ou presque, avec Danjou, qui me pilote, qui en sait plus que moi sur toutes ces choses et qui tâche de me dépêtrer.' This is a testimony to the quality and seriousness of *Détective*'s coverage.

Further evidence of the magazine's influence on some of the leading minds of the generation is provided by Simone de Beauvoir. In *La Force de l'Age*, she recounts how she and Sartre often studied *faits divers* to provide themselves with material on which to test and develop their evolving philosophies.[44] In particular, she says, 'J'achetais souvent *Détective* qui s'attaquait alors volontiers à la police et aux bien-pensants.' She clearly did not see in it the pernicious proestablishment propaganda denounced by Georges Sadoul and the surrealists. But she and Sartre had their ideological prejudices: the Falcou affair, viewed by the editorial team as one of *Détective*'s great campaigning triumphs,[45] left these two unmoved. Perhaps this was because it happened on de Beauvoir's doorstep in Rouen, which diminished the aura of exoticism; but her explanation is revealing enough as it stands – 'Falcou [. . .] jouissait dans la ville d'une grande popularité.' What the two existentialists *en herbe* were looking for was the kind of story which unsettled the public, 'qui mettait à nu les tares et les hypocrisies bourgeoises' as well as the 'partis pris de classe' of the judicial system. Hence their attraction to the Papin sisters: and once again the impact of the photographs is manifest, as de Beauvoir refers to them 'avec leurs cheveux ondulés et leurs collerettes blanches [. . .] sur l'ancienne photo que publièrent certains journaux' and compares this with 'ces furies hagardes qu'offraient à la vindicte publique les clichés pris après le drame'. Reading the background reports to the case, she says, 'Nous rêvâmes à leurs nuits de caresses et de haine, dans le désert de leur mansarde': the *fait divers* as a pretext for vicarious fantasizing is clearly in evidence here. Though she and Sartre were somewhat dismayed to learn that one of the murderesses displayed signs of clinical paranoia, de Beauvoir says, they were sufficiently confirmed in their view of the sisters as avenging angels of the exploited underclass when in photographs of the trial in September 1933 'nous vîmes sur *Détective* les visages des gros fermiers, des commerçants patentés, sûrs de leur morale et de leur santé, qui eurent à décider du destin des "brebis enragées."'[46] In fact this latter phrase quotes the headline of the February 1933 issue reporting the crime – and reproducing the contrasting photographs of the pair de Beauvoir refers to – while photographs from the trial appeared in October 1933.[47] Similarly, when the Violette Nozières case arose at the same time that the Papin sisters were being tried they were inclined to view her 'bien plus comme une victime que comme une coupable'. In Sartre's work the clearest trace of his reading of *Détective* occurs in 'Erostrate', one of the stories in *Le Mur*. The narrator Paul Hilbert speaks of his fascination for 'les photos de ces deux belles filles, ces servantes qui tuèrent et saccagèrent leurs maîtresses'. 'J'ai vu leurs photos d'*avant* et d'*après*,' he adds, commenting on the contrasting details we have already mentioned. Though the terms *avant* and *après* are borrowed from the presentation in *Le*

Surréalisme au Service de la Révolution, the effect stems from *Détective*'s publication of the photographs in question, as we have seen.[48] Perhaps an acknowledgement of this source can be gleaned from the fact that when Louis Le Guillant published 'L'Affaire des Sœurs Papin' in Sartre's *Les Temps Modernes* in 1963, the study was accompanied by a reproduction of the cover of the 9 February 1933 issue of *Détective*.[49]

Jean Genet is on record as denying that his play *Les Bonnes* owes anything to the Papin sisters, but their situation is so similar as to make the connection indisputable.[50] Moreover, Solange refers to the court reports she habitually follows, and explicitly attributes her knowledge of judicial procedures to her reading of *Détective*, which is referred to twice in the play.[51]

Genet is the writer who is perhaps most extensively affiliated to *Détective*. After all, he had direct and sometimes intimate dealings with criminals who peopled its pages.[52] Furthermore, a feature such as that of 22 April 1937 on life inside Mettray, for example, awakened personal memories.[53] Harry E. Stewart provides evidence that Genet was 'an ardent and consistent reader' of the magazine from at least as early as 1929.[54] In fact Genet had already signalled his debt to the magazine some time before writing *Les Bonnes*. In *Notre-Dame-des-fleurs*, Divine is depicted reading the magazine as a way of communing with the condemned criminal and thereby emulating, it is said, Saint Catherine of Sienna.[55] More significantly, we note that once again *Détective*'s legacy to its literary progeny is the motif of the photograph. Indeed, *Notre-Dame-des-fleurs* quite explicitly draws its entire inspiration from photographs of criminals culled from the sensational press, and in this respect represents a homage to the format of *Détective*. 'J'ai découpé dans des magazines ces belles têtes,' Genet writes, and he explains that he has made a collage of some 'vingtaine de photographies' stuck together with bread paste. Fantasies deriving from these pictures will be the stuff of his narrative: 'Mes héros ce sont eux, collés au mur, eux et moi qui suis là, bouclé.' The text begins with an evocation of a photograph of Eugen Weidmann, taken when the serial murderer, his head bandaged following wounds inflicted in the course of his arrest the previous day, was brought before the examining magistrate on 9 December 1937. 'Weidmann vous apparut dans une édition de cinq heures, la tête emmaillottée de bandelettes blanches, religieuse et encore aviateur blessé, tombé dans les seigles, un jour de septembre (sic).' This is obviously a reference to a daily paper (though the photograph was also reproduced in *Détective*).[56] However, once the narrator has explained about the sources from which he draws his narrative, he gives pride of place among his iconic 'monstres' to Maurice Pilorge, who was executed for murder and to whose memory Genet actually dedicates the novel: 'Plus qu'à un autre, je songe à Pilorge. Son visage découpé dans *Détective* enténèbre le mur de son rayonnement glacé.'[57]

In Genet's work the reader finds an authentic flavour of the pages of

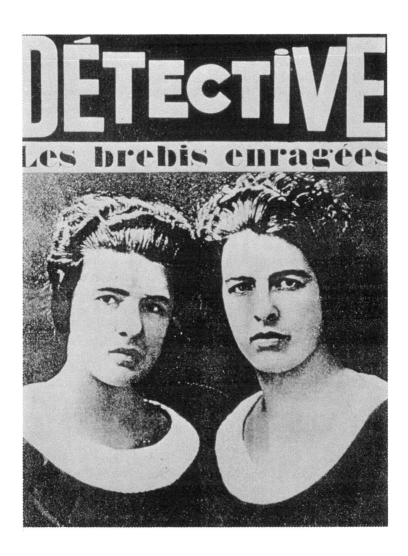

Figure 1 The Papin Sisters. © David H. Walker.

Détective.[58] The *demi-monde* of pimps and whores, thieves, *bagnards*, murderers and drug pedlars is common to both, and Genet's writings spontaneously resonate with reminiscences – whether intended or not. This can be concisely demonstrated through one example: the 24 May 1934 issue of the magazine starts the serialization of a *reportage* on drug traffickers by Paul Bringuier. Entitled *Notre-Dame-des-ténèbres*, it begins: 'Nijinski sauta par la fenêtre de la Loggia et le rideau tomba sur le miracle du *Spectre de la Rose*.'[59] Other specific instances have been noted by Harry E. Stewart, who traces Genet's reference to Louis Ménesclou in the epigraphs of *Querelle de Brest* to two particular numbers of *Détective* in 1929 and 1930, demonstrating that *Haute Surveillance* also draws on the same source.[60]

Writing at the end of the decade to whose cultural climate *Détective* must be accounted a significant contributor, Genet can presuppose a familiarity on the part of his reader – without which, indeed, his own work would not have had the impact it did, especially on *Détective* devotees such as Cocteau and Sartre. It is true that after 1936 sales of the magazine had fallen slightly and it had gone perceptibly down-market owing to the effect of competition; respectable intellectual readers had found themselves distracted from its pages by compelling news and controversies in the sphere of domestic and international politics.[61] But Genet's references to the magazine in play and novel are signals to his audience – reminders of more dubious reading habits which he expects them to acknowledge. The audience response may initially be one of ironic condescension, but already at that point Genet has achieved his initial aim. He can then proceed to undermine that comfortable voyeuristic distance and unsettle the certainties which permitted the vicarious dabbling in vice that *Détective* vouchsafed.

When Genet writes on the first page of *Notre-Dame-des-fleurs*: 'Weidmann vous apparut dans une édition de cinq heures [. . .] révélant aux bourgeois attristés que leur vie quotidienne est frôlée d'assassins enchanteurs,' the reader is both directly implicated in the dubious enchantment and presented with the spectacle of himself being thus implicated. Genet provocatively takes the lead, going further than the respectable citizen would expect to go, declaring his admiration for murderers: 'Quels monstres continuent leur vie dans mes profondeurs? [. . .] Je reconnais leur influence, le charme de leurs drames feuilletonesques.'[62] Then, developing the narrative fantasy inspired by his heroes, he draws in the reader, capitalizing on the joint recognition that the latter's reveries too are peopled by such squalid figures: 'Mes aimés seront ce que vous appelleriez: des voyous de la pire espèce. [. . .] Je vous laisse libre d'imaginer le dialogue. Choisissez ce qui peut vous charmer. [. . .] Faites ce qu'il vous plaira.'[63] Thus is the reader compromised by his own imagination, nourished as it is on *Les dessous de Paris* and the like: all the *immonde* which actually sustains the *monde*. The glory of the criminal is created, Genet suggests sardonically, to feed the appetite for sensations of 'les écoliers et les petites vieilles [. . .] au fond des provinces'. (We might add the characters in *Les Bonnes*.) Thus the ten brief lines of a *fait divers* announcing the hero's impending trial 'firent battre tous les cœurs des vieilles femmes et des enfants jaloux. Paris ne dormit pas. Elle espérait que, demain, Notre-Dame serait condamné à mort; elle le désirait.'[64] The indictment of this collusion in criminality comes when Genet points out that the criminal who merely spends his time in prison may actually be less familiar with the details of criminal activity than the respectable citizen who habitually devotes his time and freedom to savouring the *chronique judiciaire*. The narrator speaks of the disappointment felt by his cellmate Clément Village, who murdered his wife and walled up the body: 'Il fut chagrin que je ne me souvinsse pas de cette histoire, que vous lûtes dans les journaux.'[65]

With this impudent reversal Genet incriminates his audience. Thus, if the early readers of *Détective* could regard themselves as detached observers dabbling in moral exoticism, Genet's work, with its blending of the literary and the infraliterary, demonstrates that ten years or so later they were, to all intents and purposes, accessories after the fact.

Notes

1. Albert Thibaudet, *Histoire de la Littérature Française de 1789 à nos jours*, Paris, Stock, 1936, p.206.
2. Jacques Wolgensinger, *L'Histoire à la une*, Paris, Gallimard, collection Découvertes, 1989, p.101; Claude Bellanger *et al.*, *Histoire générale de la presse française*, vol.3, *De 1871 à 1940*, Paris, Presses Universitaires de France, 1972, pp.476–7, 479.
3. See Alain Monestier *et al.*, *Le Fait Divers*, catalogue of an exhibition organized at the Musée National des arts et traditions populaires, Paris, Editions de la Réunion des musées nationaux, 1982, p.140.
4. Versions vary: cf. Pierre Assouline, *Gaston Gallimard*, Paris, Balland/ Seuil, Collection Points, 1985, p.227; Yves Courrière, *Joseph Kessel, ou sur la piste du lion*, Paris, Plon/Presses-Pocket, 1986, p.407. There seems general agreement that the title was purchased from a private detective who also received in exchange the right to cut-rate publicity for his agency in the magazine.
5. Assouline, *Gaston Gallimard*, p.228, says it printed 350,000 at the outset; Courrière, *Joseph Kessel*, p.409, says sales rose above 250,000 with the sixth issue.
6. Announced in no.28, 9 May 1929, p.2.
7. Georges Sadoul, 'Bonne année! Bonne santé', in *La Révolution surréaliste*, no.12, 15 December 1929, p.46.

8. See Dominique Borne and Henri Dubief, *Nouvelle Histoire de la France Contemporaine*, vol.13, *La crise des années 1930*, Paris, Seuil, 1989, p. 261. After the war, Gallimard proved reluctant to relaunch the title when the erstwhile editor Marius Larique put the idea to him in 1945. It was sold for five million francs and was revived by another publisher. See Assouline, *Gaston Gallimard*, p.434.

9. Quoted in Courrière, *Joseph Kessel*, p.409.

10. Assouline, *Gaston Gallimard*, p.237.

11. Ibid., p.230; Courrière, *Joseph Kessel*, p.409.

12. They include Jean Desbordes, Louis Blanc, C.L.A. Gonnet, René Jouglet, Emmanuel Bove, René Trintzius and André Beucler. As a rough-and-ready indicator, they all feature in the relevant sections of René Lalou, *Histoire de la Littérature française contemporaine*, Paris, Presses universitaires de France, 1953.

13. No. 1, 1 November 1928, p.2.

14. Quoted from *Nuits de Montmartre*, Paris, Christian Bourgois, collection 10/18, 1990, p.41.

15. See Wolgensinger, *L'Histoire à la une*, pp.105–13; Bellanger *et al.*, *Histoire générale de la presse française*, p.479, stress that the prominence of *faits divers* in the mainstream press was also enhanced by virtue of photographic coverage.

16. See Romi, *Histoire des faits divers*, Paris, Editions du Pont-Royal, 1962, p.171. For an analysis of the photomontage techniques in *Détective*, see Adrian Rifkin, *Street Noises, Parisian Pleasure, 1900–1940*, Manchester and New York, Manchester University Press, 1993, pp. 120–34. Rifkin reproduces numerous photographic spreads from *Détective*; and on the popular impact of the magazine, as opposed to the responses of its intellectual readership which concern us here, his book contains, *passim*, many invaluable insights.

17. Louis Roubaud, for example, after writing a series of features on 'Démons et déments' which ran in 1933, drew on this material for a novel *J'avais peur*, published in 1935. Louis Francis builds *reportage* and *fait divers* material from *Détective* into his novel *Blanc* (1934), as Marius Larique points out in a plug in no.312, 18 October 1934, p.5.

18. No.229, 16 March 1933, p.15. The novels recommended are: René Trintzius, *Le Septième Jour*; René Bloch, *Les Rats*; Louis-Raymond Lefèvre, *Le Royaume de ce Monde*.

19. No.256, 21 September 1933, p.15.

20. No.249, 3 August 1933, p.10.

21. No.231, 30 March 1933, p.2.

22. Id.

23. See Assouline, *Gaston Gallimard*, p.237.

24. E.g. no.1, 1 November 1928, p.10; no.221, 19 January 1933, p.10.

25. No.249, 3 August 1933, p.10; no.232, 6 April 1933, p.6; no.312, 18 October 1934, p.15.

26. Assouline, *Gaston Gallimard*, p.230. By 1939 advertisements for the collection featured novels by Alice Alexandre, Anthony Gray, Means Davis and Louis Latzarus (9 and 16 February 1939).

27. No.3, 15 November 1928, pp.4, 9.

28. Louis Francis, whose novel *Blanc* is plugged under the heading 'Du fait-divers au roman' in no.312, 18 October 1934, p.5.

29. It was the object of a controversial legal intervention in 1978: see Maurice Lecerf, *Les Faits Divers*, Paris, Larousse, collection Idéologies et Sociétés, 1981, pp.31–7. See also Romi, *Histoire des faits divers*, p.171; Alain Monestier *et al.*, *Le Fait Divers*, catalogue of an exhibition organized at the Musée national des arts et traditions populaires, Paris, Editions de la Réunion des musées nationaux, 1982, p.140. It reappeared in the 1990s as *Nouveau Détective*.

30. No.1, 1 November 1928, p.2.

31. Ibid., p.9.

32. No.2, 8 November 1928, p.8.

33. No.220, 12 January 1933, p.2.

34. 'Figurants de drames', in no.255, 14 September 1933, p.7.

35. 'Introduction à 1930', *La Révolution surréaliste*, no.12, 15 December 1929, pp.57–64, at p.64.

36. 'Bonne année! Bonne santé!', *La Révolution surréaliste*, no.12, 15 December 1929, 45–7. Sadoul's conclusion fits well with an analysis provided by Lucien Goldmann, who sees confirmation of the phenomenon in Genet's play *Le Balcon*. See 'Le Théâtre de Genet et les études sociologiques', *Cahiers Renaud-Barrault*, no.57, November 1966, pp.90–125, at pp.106–11.

37. *Détective*, no.224, 9 February 1933, cover and p.3; *Le Surréalisme au Service de la Révolution*, no.5, 15 May 1933, pp.27–8 and plate. See below, p.93.

38. No.6, 6 December 1928, p.8. This enables us to date the conversation in question. The original text in *Détective* specifies 'une vieille dame charitable'. See Jean Paulhan, *Œuvres complètes*, vol.2, Paris, Cercle du Livre Précieux, 1966, p.41.

39. Cf. *Détective*, no.7, 13 December 1928, p.9. Paulhan raises the topic elsewhere in his *Entretien sur des faits divers*, pp.27–8.

40. Paulhan, *Entretien sur des faits divers*, pp.17–18.

41. 'Littérature révolutionaire en France', in Paul Nizan, *Pour une nouvelle culture*, Paris, Grasset, 1970, p.268.

42. 'L'enfant gâtée', no.253, 31 August 1933, pp.4–5; 'La fille aux poisons', no.254, 7 September 1933, pp.3–5. For further discussion of this case, see pp.94–9 below.

43. *Marianne*, 6 September 1933, p.10. For a further discussion of this item, see below, p.97.

44. Simone de Beauvoir, *La Force de l'Age*, Paris, Gallimard, 1960, pp.135–8.

45. The first articles on the case, 'Le châtiment infernal' and 'Je suis innocent', appeared in the 20 October 1932 number; 'Le bâillon' followed on 3 November and 'Les partisans' on 10 November, by which time the *Journal de Rouen* had joined the campaign. *Détective*, no.228, 9 March 1933, p.3, and no.229, 16 March 1933, pp.12–13 reported the successful outcome of the trial and the vindication of their efforts.

46. De Beauvoir justifiably castigates the judicial system for producing the verdict it did. However, in stressing the class-based institutional conspiracy against the Papin sisters and Gorguloff, condemned to death for his murder of the President of the Republic – 'l'assassin n'était pas jugé: il servait de bouc émissaire' – she omits to mention that a significant number of reports on the Papin trial highlighted the dubious nature and extreme inadequacy of the psychiatric evidence presented to support the judgement that the sisters were not insane, and argued the case for a *supplément d'enquête médicale*: see Etienne Hervier, 'L'Abattoir', *Détective*, no.258, 5 October 1933, p.7; Jérôme Tharaud and Jean Tharaud, 'L'affaire Papin et les experts', *Paris-Soir*, 8 October 1933, p.2; Louis Martin-Chauffier, 'Les mauvaises brebis du bon pasteur', *Vu*, no.290, 4 October 1933, pp.1521–2. It is not unlikely that the doubt cast on the psychiatric reports is what prompted Jacques Lacan to write his essay 'Motifs du crime paranoïaque: le crime des sœurs Papin', which appeared in *Minotaure*, no.3, December 1933. See below, p.92.

47. No.224, 9 February 1933, cover and p.3; no.258, 5 October 1933, p.7.

48. Cf. Jean-Paul Sartre, *Œuvres romanesques*, Paris, Pléiade, 1981, pp.272–3. Though the notes (p.1843) identify the Papin sisters as the source of the reference, the channels through which it comes are overlooked.

49. Cf. *Les Temps Modernes*, no.210, November 1963, pp.868–913 (facing page 880). Another feature which may owe something to *Détective* is the Autodidact in *La Nausée*. An advertisement carried in no.223, 2 February 1933, p.15, reappears regularly: 'Voulez-vous réussir dans la vie? Etudiez L'Encyclopédie Autodidactique Quillet . . . Les matières contenues dans ces 4 volumes dépassent de beaucoup le bagage des gens réputés instruits. Celui qui les possédera entièrement pourra occuper avec succès les emplois les mieux rétribués dans le Commerce, l'Industrie, les Travaux Publics, etc . . .'

50. Hélène Tournaire, 'Jean Genet, évadé de l'enfer cherche la clé d'un

paradis défendu', *La Bataille,* 10 March 1949, p.5. For more discussion of the connection, see p.94 below.

51. *Les Bonnes,* in *Œuvres complètes,* vol.4, Paris, Gallimard, 1968, p.160, p.165, p.169.

52. The case of Maurice Pilorge is mentioned below. In *Le Journal du Voleur* Genet tells how he has just read in *Détective* an article (including a photograph) announcing the condemnation to *la relégation* of Rasseneur, 'un casseur avec qui je travaillai vers 1936', and who is an important protagonist in *Miracle de la Rose.* His comments establish an insider's knowledge which make of him a privileged reader of *Détective*: 'Le journaliste, ironique, affirme qu'il paraissait très content d'être relégué. Cela ne m'étonne pas. A la Santé, c'était un petit roitelet. Il sera caïd à Riom ou à Clairvaux.' (*Journal du Voleur,* Paris, Gallimard, 1949, pp.53–4.)

53. See the picture spread on Mettray taken from *Détective* which is reproduced in Albert Dichy and Pascal Fouché, *Jean Genet, essai de chronologie,* Paris, Bibliothèque de littérature française contemporaine de l'Université Paris 7, 1988, between pp.112 and 113.

54. See Harry E. Stewart, 'Louis Ménesclou, assassin and source of the "Lilac Murder" in Genet's *Haute Surveillance',* *Romance Notes,* vol.26, no.3 (Spring 1986), pp.204–8. Cf. also Harry E. Stewart and Rob Roy McGregor, *Jean Genet: a biography of deceit,* New York, Peter Lang, 1989, p.97 n.4.

55. *Notre-Dame-des-fleurs,* in *Œuvres complètes,* vol.2, Paris, Gallimard, 1951, p.36.

56. See no.541, 9 March 1939, p.2. Colette, who covered the Weidmann trial for *Paris-Soir,* refers obliquely to this issue of *Détective* which headlined 'La vie de Weidmann en prison'. She alludes to its front cover photograph of 'Le Weidmann prisonnier, sa joue enfumée de barbe. Sa tête inclinée a essayé de fuir le déclic photographique, car il a honte d'être vu sans cravate'. Furthermore, in her comments on the notebooks of 'Philippe, émule ambitieux de Weidmann', she indicates that she has read a feature on this latter murderer, 'Le Weidmann Lyonnais' in the same number (pp.6–10). See Colette, *Œuvres complètes de Colette,* vol.13, Paris, Le Fleuron, chez Flammarion, 1950, pp. 435, 438. See below, pp.104–6.

57. Genet, *Œuvres,* vol.2, pp.10, 11, 12, 9, 55. In a note to the poem 'Le condamné a mort', also inspired by Pilorge's death, Genet indicates that he was executed on 17 March 1939 at Saint-Brieuc, on the day Desfourneaux took up his function as public executioner, and quotes from a report in *L'Œuvre* about him (p.186). The article is reproduced in Dichy and Fouché, *Jean Genet. Essai de chronologie 1910–1944,* p.198. It reveals two errors: the date of Pilorge's execution was 4 February

1939, and the line Genet misquotes reads 'L'homme, certainement, valait mieux que son destin.'

58. It is significant, for example, that Philip Thody draws on articles in the magazine to provide background on Genet's work: see his *Jean Genet, a study of his novels and plays*, London, Hamish Hamilton, 1968, pp.245, 248, 255.

59. *Détective*, no.291, 24 May 1934, pp.3–5.

60. See Stewart, 'Louis Ménesclou, assassin'; and Stewart and McGregor, *Jean Genet: a biography of deceit*.

61. Assouline, *Gaston Gallimard*, p.238.

62. In *Œuvres*, vol.2, p.54.

63. Ibid., p.56.

64. Ibid., pp.148, 149.

65. Ibid., p.84.

PART II

Culture and Criminality

4

Old Masters: Trials, Tales and Sequestration in Gide and Mauriac

After the death of Boris at the end of *Les Faux-Monnayeurs*, Edouard, the novelist who earlier has expressed his ambition to put into his *Faux-Monnayeurs* whatever reality dictated to him, declares that he will not use the child's suicide. He finds this incident incomprehensible, classifying it among the "'faits divers'", which have about them 'quelque chose de péremptoire, d'indéniable, de brutal, d'outrageusement réel'.[1] We recognize here a retreat before fact he has previously shown when a companion confronted him with an actual counterfeit coin, saying, 'Je vois, hélas! que la réalité ne vous intéresse pas. — Si, dit Edouard; mais elle me gêne' (RRS, 1086). The narrator in *Les Caves du Vatican* shows a similar unease when his hero Lafcadio sets out to rescue a family trapped in a fire: 'Lafcadio, mon ami, vous donnez dans un fait divers et ma plume vous abandonne'(RRS, 723). Both texts, then, articulate reservations about the *fait divers*, suggesting there is no place for it within the work of art. In this they satirize the reactions of those *fin-de-siècle* writers for whom the *fait divers* was frequently a point of reference in attacks on the literary ambitions of the realists and naturalists: by transcribing raw fact, these latter were demonstrating themselves to be not artists, but mere *faits-diversiers* furthering what Mallarmé dismissed as 'l'universel reportage'.[2]

Gide himself was very interested in the phenomenon. Taking his lead from Dostoyevsky whom he admired greatly in this as in other respects,[3] Gide had friends and acquaintances track down press cuttings for him on the swindle which inspired *Les Caves du Vatican*;[4] and *Les Faux-Monnayeurs* arose directly from newspaper reports in 1909 of a schoolboy named Nény who committed suicide in his school in Clermont-Ferrand in circumstances which the story of Boris replicates.[5] Moreover, the counterfeiting ring in the latter novel is based on a case reported as a *fait divers* in 1906: Gide actually reproduces the relevant press cuttings in *Le Journal des Faux-Monnayeurs*.[6]

Gide's preoccupation with the way the press deals with such matters is reflected within the fictional texts themselves. *Les Caves du Vatican* recounts the stuff of a *fait divers* when Lafcadio pushes Amédée Fleurissoire to his death from a train; subsequently the text enables us to read, over the shoulders of Lafcadio and the novelist Julius de Baraglioul, examples of what the newspaper makes of the incident. Lafcadio is unnerved at the prospect of seeing his action described in the press as a 'crime', precisely because for him this *acte gratuit* falls outside the bounds of the conventional meanings reporters are accustomed to reading into events. Moreover, the main text of the two reports we read from highlights that effort to make sense of bizarre facts, while simultaneously generating an air of mystery, which characterizes the *fait divers*: 'la victime à laquelle appartenait sans doute la veste retrouvée hier [. . .] aucun papier qui permette d'établir son identité [. . .] la mort a dû suivre la chute, car le corps ne porte pas la trace de blessures [. . .] semble indiquer la préméditation de ce crime [. . .] semble indiquer tout au moins que le crime n'aurait pas eu le vol pour mobile' (RRS, 839–41). The underlying purpose of this speculative tone – typical of the press reports it pastiches – is to offer the facts reported as fragments of a narrative which, if all the details could be retrieved and assembled in order, would explain the events in question, fitting them into recognizable patterns of causality and motivation. At the same time, and with a self-consciousness which is typically Gidean, *Les Caves du Vatican* presents, in Julius, a novelist who has hit upon the idea of using this *fait divers* as an element in the novel he is planning. His superior theory of the *acte gratuit*, with its departure from stereotyped psychology, will enable him to 'explain' the bizarre facts of Amédée's death, in a transposed fictional version. But when he realizes that the reality confirms his audacious theory, he is seized with panic and retreats into more comfortable modes of explanation, clutching at the preposterous story of the plot to kidnap the Pope which he had earlier refused to believe. Both these instances show humans seeking to fit the facts to narrative patterns of plausibility, which serve as a refuge from raw reality.

Immediately after completing *Les Faux-Monnayeurs*, Gide initiated a rubric in the *Nouvelle Revue Française*, in which, from 1926 to 1928, he regularly published newspaper accounts of *faits divers* sent in by readers or discovered by himself.[7] In his commentary he points out that too often the approach adopted in newspaper reports reflects conventional views on human nature which in fact explain nothing. Normal newspaper style keeps readers in a state of ignorance about the true depths of human psychology and responsibility. For Gide the real value of a *fait divers* is that it 'bouscule certaines notions trop facilement acceptées, et [. . .] nous force à réfléchir'.[8] But in order that it may do so, those whose job it is to record these phenomena must be prepared to avoid the easy path of resorting to the picturesque, the macabre, or the sensational (NJP, 145). The interest of the *fait divers* lies precisely in the evidence it provides of deviations from easily-understood motivation (NJP, 143). Even doctors were compelled to admit defeat in the 'Affaire Redureau', concerning a boy of fifteen, well-behaved, docile, healthy in mind and body, brought up by normal, respectable parents, who hacked to death his employer and his employer's wife, mother and housemaid, plus three small children (NJP, 143–4, 99–136). Gide inaugurated with an account of this latter case the publication of a series of volumes collectively entitled 'Ne Jugez pas'; and in a preface he announces it will be a forum for cases which 'échappent aux règles de la psychologie traditionnelle, et déconcertent la justice humaine'. The traditional legal axiom *Is fecit cui prodest*, earlier called into question by Julius de Baraglioul in *Les Caves du Vatican* during his phase of toying with the *acte gratuit* (RRS, 818), can lead into serious errors in legal proceedings, Gide points out – indicating the intimate connection between the preoccupations which inform his fictional narratives and those which draw him to the *fait divers* and legal procedure.

In 1912, in fact, he had interrupted his work on *Les Caves du Vatican* to serve for two weeks as a juror at the Assize Court in Rouen. His reflections on the cases he heard were published in 1914 as *Souvenirs de la Cour d'Assises*. Again and again Gide notes details illustrating the extent to which legal procedure is fundamentally bound up with the mechanisms of narrative.[9] 'Combien il est rare qu'une affaire se présente par la tête et simplement' (NJP, 48), he remarks; and it can be a painful process to 'recompose' (NJP, 13) a coherent story from jumbled, disjointed, often incomplete or unreliable information. A trial consists, indeed, of the construction of two stories, one for the defence and one for the prosecution; and the verdict will go in favour of the one which is the more convincing. Gide points out how frequently the prosecution's representation of the facts is an artificial simplification (NJP, 48). Essentially, the courtroom is the arena for a contest between different narratives, and weaknesses in one side's account will be denounced by the other. The rules of this contest relate to verisimilitude, essentially a convention enabling us to assess propositions about reality rather than to grasp reality itself. Hence what is at issue is an appearance of truth, rather than actual truth; so the criteria which operate in the courtroom are the same as those by which we judge fiction. The juror's only guide is plausibility, which as Barthes remarks is largely a matter of opinion (NJP, 15, 68).[10] Gide points out, however, that when it comes to convincing the audience with a story, 'la version la plus simple est celle qui toujours a le plus de chance de prévaloir; c'est aussi celle qui a le moins de chance d'être exacte' (NJP, 44).

This leads us on to the aesthetic questions faced by the novelist who seeks to preserve the authentic effect of the *fait divers* in his narratives and avoid forcing them into reductive conventional models of intelligibility. What emerges from a reading of *Souvenirs de la Cour d'Assises* is Gide's concern for the process whereby a story is established as much as for the story itself. He repeatedly expresses doubts as to whether the reconstruction on which the verdict was based is in fact true. (Equally often he notes that the jury is obliged to vote against what they consider the truth in order to secure justice, or vice versa.) What the juror is faced with is a number of different – often mutually contradictory – versions of events, in the testimony of the defendants and witnesses, which he or she is left to collate. At the end of the hearing the juror may be merely perplexed by details which do not fit any overall pattern, by events which defy verisimilitude, by unexplained but irrefutable contradictions between corroborative depositions. The courtroom has been the scene of a narrative process: the product is what the listener makes of it. The judicial procedure embodies that presentation of a multiplicity of points of view which Gide had only recently, in 1910, declared the hallmark of the novel as he saw it.[11] The reader of a text by Gide, like the judge or juror in a court case, must never forget that a critical stance is required if we are to get at the facts behind the statements of the protagonists.

The succession of *faits divers* Gide published in the *Nouvelle Revue Française* culminated in the volume *La Séquestrée de Poitiers*, published in 1930 in his collection 'Ne Jugez Pas'.[12] In his preface to the collection, Gide claims to eschew interpretative and rhetorical strategies in the interest of suspending judgement and obliging the reader to work for a conclusion: 'Nous ne nous préoccuperons pas de l'effet. Nous présenterons, en nous effaçant de notre mieux, une documentation autant que possible authentique; j'entends par là non interprétée, et des témoignages directs' (NJP, 98). Here then is a writer seeking impartiality in order to let reality speak for itself. It is an obvious point to make that this in itself constitutes a narrative strategy, and in fact *La Séquestrée de Poitiers* may be seen, in some respects at least, as a development and validation of the narrative technique Gide devised for *Les Faux-Monnayeurs*. In it, Gide recounts events which occurred in Poitiers between the 1870s and 1901, when one Pierre Bastian was accused and tried for the role he played in keeping his sister shut up in the same room for twenty-five years. She had lived thus in conditions of unspeakable squalor, naked and covered only by a filthy blanket, lying in her own excrement and the remains of her food, amidst an infestation of vermin. The epigraph quoted from *Les Faux-Monnayeurs*, suggesting that a 'total monstrueux' can be brought about by 'l'addition d'une quantité de petits faits très simples et très naturels, chacun pris à part' (RRS, 960), indicates that Gide sees the same contingent logic at work in this *fait divers* as in his novel. In Barthes's analysis of the *fait divers*, 'les troubles de la causalité' are a major ingredient: grotesque effects from trivial causes, the intervention of chance or coincidence, are the very stuff of that reality which the *fait divers* seeks to record[13] – as they are in the world of *Les Faux-*

Monnayeurs. Thus Gide gleans from the various testimonies at the trial ample evidence to show that the victim as well as her mother and father had a history of claustrophilia, a hereditary compulsion to shut themselves away; and the brother had a curious taste for filth, coupled with a defective sense of smell. The shutters of the young woman's room had had to be closed because of her tendency to exhibitionism; the windows had had to be locked and sealed up owing to her propensity for flying into demented rages and yelling obscenities. Her mental state had become unbalanced from an early age, and, rather than indicating cruelty, that her family sequestered her bore witness to an effort to care for her. Good food had always been provided for her, but she would eat only with her fingers and insisted on setting aside certain items, which she left lying on the bed beside her until they putrefied. In short, there turned out to be perfectly logical reasons for every element in the horrific picture. 'On en était arrivé là peu à peu, par une lente accoutumance' (NJP, 252, 255–6, 258). The simple truth of this conjunction of circumstances defies conventions of verisimilitude – and also of narrative logic. The appeal court, while expressing severe criticism of the passivity with which Bastian had bowed to his authoritarian mother's orders on the matter, ruled that no one had committed a crime.

In setting out the facts, Gide does resort to methods unlike those he may have used in a novel. The family history and antecedents of those involved are listed, as a catalogue (NJP, 235–6). The chronology of events is painstakingly observed. The dialogue of the cross-examinations is frequently set out in the form of a stage script, without the interpolation of 'he said' and so on. This, however, actually repeats the technique Gide uses in a conversation between Julius de Baraglioul and Lafcadio (RRS, 838–9): without the narratorial interventions, indeed, the discussions read to striking dramatic effect. They present a telling contrast with the dialogue in the introductory chapter, in which Gide presents the Police Commissioner's first visit to the victim's house according to standard narrative methods. The main effect of this sequence is in fact to highlight the very artificiality of the devices used, including the conventional past historic tense, and the familiar introduction *in medias res* followed by a strategic use of the Commissioner's questions to facilitate the insertion of background information on Bastian himself (NJP, 205–7). Elsewhere, a chapter recounting the death of the victim's mother, which ends with the lines, 'Quelques minutes avant l'arrivée du docteur, Mme Bastian s'était écriée: "Ah! ma pauvre Mélanie!"' (NJP, 222) is seeking to present more, it may be felt, than a dispassionate chronicle of events. It is true that the description of the victim's room is presented via the Examining Magistrate's formal report, and the catalogue of its contents comes from the official statement of the Commissioner responsible for seizing these items. Subsequently much of the text will consist of extracts from depositions, as well as from newspaper articles and records of cross-examinations. In all of this, however, while departing from traditional narrative methods, Gide is actually evolving techniques out of those already used in *Les Faux-Monnayeurs*, where quotation from letters, diaries and other documents is a staple ingredient. Of equal interest is the narrative voice, which as Gide declares, aims to avoid being intrusive in *La Séquestrée de Poitiers*. In fact it has an editorial function, guiding us through the material. 'Nous écouterons d'abord les accusés' (NJP, 213), he announces, or 'Ecoutons à présent Mme Bastian mère' (NJP, 220). The potentially manipulative nature of such interventions is made slightly clearer, however, when we read: 'Interrompons un instant le témoignage de Juliette Dupuis pour intercaler cet ahurissant fragment de déposition de Virginie Neveux, dont je donnerai plus loin d'autres parties également sensationelles' (NJP, 243). The effect is to foreground the practical process of assembling the stuff of the story, but the ostensibly neutral editor openly appeals to the reader's interest with this sample of 'astounding' material and the promise of more to follow shortly. The novelist, who is free to imagine the fictional reality for his story, can manipulate the plot so as to maintain the reader's interest; as documentary writer he has to stick to the facts and the temptation is all the greater to find ways of injecting interest into the telling. It is true that he can have overt recourse to a narrative enigma to maintain suspense: 'Comment cette affaire [. . .] put-elle aboutir à un acquittement des inculpés? C'est ce que l'on comprendra sans doute en lisant tout ce qui va suivre' (NJP, 204). But in the main it is by editing his material to make it centre on a succession of specific facets of the case that Gide guides and concentrates the reader's attention. In this, of course, he is selecting and shaping his material, in fact imposing an interpretation upon it despite his disclaimers. The most striking illustration of this, to the reader familiar with the rest of Gide's work, is his insistence on 'l'inconséquence des caractères' (NJP, 241) – a phrase straight from *Les Faux-Monnayeurs* (RRS, 1201) and redolent of a theme which also looms large in *Les Caves du Vatican* and elsewhere.[14] The psychological discontinuity implied by Mélanie Bastian's simultaneously revelling in the cleanliness and care to which she has been removed and expressing regret for the darkness and squalor of what she called her 'chère petite grotte' (NJP, 277) makes of her a Gidean character par excellence.[15] The intrusion of Gidean preoccupations in the narrative is also evident when the narrator remarks, after transcribing the Commissioner's enumeration of the items removed from the Bastian household, 'Nous aurions aimé connaître, par exemple, les titres des trente-sept volumes saisis, et la nature de ces "notes écrites au crayon" signalées dans ce rapport' (NJP, 212). This, from the author who has Julius de Baraglioul conspicuously fail to see the significance of the writing in Lafcadio's notebook, or of the presence in his otherwise sparsely furnished room of the *Novelle* of Anton Francesco Grazzini in Italian, and a copy of

Moll Flanders with only two-thirds of the pages cut (RRS, 715–17), demonstrates the extent to which the documentary reconstruction of the *fait divers* overlaps with the exploitation within the fictional narrative of the techniques of the judicial enquiry, making potential 'pièces à conviction' of the smallest detail. In both instances, Gide, like the other authors who resort to such techniques, is seeking to convey something of the unsettling mystery of reality, the disturbing significance of the trivial, the limitless possibilities of a world which is as it is only by chance.

In 1926–7, as Gide was developing his *faits divers* rubric in *La Nouvelle Revue Française*, Mauriac was publishing *Thérèse Desqueyroux*, a novel which incorporates reminiscences of 'La Séquestrée de Poitiers' grafted onto a *fait divers* of 1906 which had set tongues wagging in the *bordelais* region where Mauriac grew up. In 1930, when Gide published *L'Affaire Redureau* and his version of *La Séquestrée de Poitiers*, Mauriac wrote an account of 'L'Affaire Favre-Bulle', in which a married woman was found guilty of murdering her lover and his other mistress.[16] Certain aspects of the case linked with Thérèse Desqueyroux's story – and encouraged Mauriac to write some brief sequels culminating in the novel *La Fin de la Nuit* of 1935.[17] Meanwhile, in *Le Nœud de Vipères* of 1932, Mauriac has his lawyer–protagonist earn a commendation from Freud for his profound comprehension and subtle advocacy in the fictitious 'affaire Villenave' concerning a wife who, out of love for her husband, accuses herself of attempting to murder him rather than have their son pay the price for a jealous impulse.[18]

Whereas Mauriac's fiction pursues the possibilities of a genuine understanding of *faits divers* such as these, numerous features of the real trial of Madame Favre-Bulle confirmed Gide's most distressing findings in *Souvenirs de la Cour d'Assises*. The defendant's interests are ignored in the histrionic contest of narratives into which the lawyers enter for their own greater glory. No one in the courtroom will give proper consideration to 'la bourgeoise placide qui, pendant [. . .] vingt années, couvait, portait en elle l'adultère et deux assassinats' in an effort to explain the emergence in her of 'la créature forcenée qu'elle était déjà à son insu'.[19] Mauriac feels the authorities should start from her 'enfance mystérieuse [. . .] pour tout comprendre':[20] that was the treatment he had given to his own heroine Thérèse. It is clear, in fact, that the novelist is viewing the real criminal in terms of his fictional character.[21]

Thérèse Desqueyroux has attempted to poison her husband. In contrast to Madame Favre-Bulle and Mauriac's original model, Madame Canaby, the case of Thérèse 'does not come to trial. The two families have closed ranks and used their influence to protect the political reputation of her own father and the social standing of her in-laws. The novel thus begins with the examining magistrate's ruling: 'non-lieu'. In his introduction the author refers to the *fait divers* from which he started, recalling that as an adolescent he actually saw the figure who would become his character, 'dans une salle étouffante d'assises, livrée aux avocats moins féroces que les dames empanachées'. However, more than one *fait divers* underlies this novel which will seek, through creative reconstruction, to restore something of the subjective reality behind the cruel and lurid versions retailed in the courtroom and in the gossip accompanying the press reports.[22]

On the train carrying her back to Saint-Clair, Thérèse has a dream in which the case is not over, since new evidence has come to light and her acts are once more under scrutiny.[23] This expression of her continuing anxiety prefigures the confrontation she knows will take place when she is reunited with her husband Bernard. In the privacy of their home, their reputation safe from the scandal they fear above all else, the family will carry out what the judiciary have been prevented from doing. Bernard reminds her that 'Il n'y a pas prescription, Dieu merci' (T, 126): the case is not closed, and since there is no statutory limitation on the period within which new evidence may be brought forward, in effect he can keep Thérèse subject to permanent quasi-judicial restrictions and scrutiny.

The examining magistrate was persuaded of her innocence by the plausibility of the story concocted in concert with her father and the lawyer: 'une histoire simple, fortement liée et qui pût satisfaire ce logicien' (T, 14). We have seen from Gide's analysis that these are the qualities determining the outcome in the courtroom. But now that 'ils n'auront plus à construire ensemble une version avouable du drame qu'ils ont vécu,' the reality excluded by this narrative construction casts its shadow over Thérèse's relationship with her husband (T, 15). And since he too will be judging and condemning her, she must now 'préparer sa défense' (T, 28) and tackle these real events, reformulating them in a story for him. This story will be both an 'aveu' (T, 22) and a 'plaidoyer' (T, 100–1): it will ease her guilt and, by its concern to compel the credence of the listener, will make him understand and thus forgive.

However, she encounters difficulties in fitting language and narrative to the complex reality: 'Des paroles suffisent-elles à contenir cet enchaînement confus de désirs, de résolutions, d'actes imprévisibles . . .?' (T, 22). Even to begin poses problems: 'Il faudrait tout reprendre depuis le commencement. [. . .] Où est le commencement de nos actes?' (T, 25). On the other hand, the link between her mundane antecedents and the monstrous outcome appears to escape patterns of normal causality. And yet, as we have seen in the cases of *Les Faux-Monnayeurs* and *La Séquestrée de Poitiers*, an incremental accumulation, without dramatic interventions, can produce a shocking result: 'Nul tournant brusque: elle a descendu une pente insensible, lentement d'abord, puis plus vite. La femme perdue de ce soir, c'est bien le jeune être radieux qu'elle fut' (T, 27–8). Like Gide, then, Mauriac, through Thérèse, is unpicking the sensational simplifications and crude juxtapositions of the *fait divers*, as well as the professional gloss of legal parlance, in order to retrieve the enigmatic reality – even if this entails a necessary questioning of the novelist's own presentational techniques. However, as Thérèse draws near to the end of her return journey, she relives the inadequacy of her first clumsy denials when the scandal initially broke: 'Trouve autre chose, malheureuse!' she recalls her father saying then (T, 118, 10); and now, as she gets down from the train, 'Toute son histoire, péniblement reconstruite, s'effondre: rien ne reste de cette confession préparée' (T, 119). Thérèse's action in administering poison to Bernard remains beyond the grasp of conventional narrative, so that her second attempt at composing a story has come no closer to the facts than did the deliberate fabrication: despite her efforts, 'cette histoire trop bien construite demeurait sans lien avec la réalité' (T, 135).

Thérèse's crime challenges moral and psychological models and necessitates a questioning of commonplace explanations. Mauriac hints at a Freudian dimension through allusions to repressed lesbianism, but the essence of her character and story is that they unsettle the reader.[24] That, indeed, is one possible explanation for her behaviour. But it is also what motivates her to give her own account of it: she realizes her implicit aim was to make of Bernard, hitherto a member of 'la race aveugle [. . .] la race implacable des simples' (T, 38), something other than that by subjecting him to her narrative: 'Elle s'était efforcée, à son insu, de recréer un Bernard capable de comprendre' (T, 123). Her effort is eventually vindicated when a question he puts to her suggests her story has had an impact:

> Enfin! Bernard lui posait une question, celle même qui fût d'abord venue à l'esprit de Thérèse si elle avait été à sa place. Cette confession longuement préparée [. . .] cet effort pour remonter à la source de son acte [. . .] était peut-être au moment d'obtenir son prix. Elle avait, à son insu, troublé Bernard. Elle l'avait compliqué; et voici qu'il l'interrogeait comme quelqu'un qui ne voit pas clair, qui hésite . . . Moins simple . . . donc, moins implacable. Thérèse jeta sur cet homme nouveau un regard complaisant, presque maternel. (T, 173–4)

At this moment we can see that Thérèse's story meets precisely the requirement of the ideal *fait divers* as defined by Gide.

The story of Thérèse is intended to counter the stereotyped narratives on which people will otherwise base their peremptory judgement of her. Thérèse is sure Bernard will jump to a banal conclusion: 'Il s'imagine qu'un crime comme celui dont on m'accuse ne peut être que passionnel' (T, 78). Even after his certainties have been momentarily shaken he soon reaches once more for a behavioural cliché – 'comme s'il y avait quoi que ce fût à comprendre, avec ces détraquées!' (T, 177).[25]

Stories that sustain such assertions circulate throughout the novel as gossip and local legend as much as in press reports. Even Tante Clara relishes the 'anecdotes sinistres' (T, 82) about the lives of the tenant farmers in the local community, and Thérèse has been struck by tales of the solitary existence chosen by the priest (T, 105–6). Her own case has added variants to this collective repertoire, as neighbours and acquaintances absorb her story by recycling standard motifs. Both her family and Thérèse herself, each for their own reasons, are extremely sensitive to the sensational reputation this creates for her in people's minds.

The gossip had begun when Bernard was taken to hospital, leaving Thérèse alone in the house: 'Quelle que fût sa solitude, elle percevait autour d'elle une immense rumeur' (T, 117). As a result of the *instruction* the rumour grows so intense that it is suggested her father intervene through the press: 'Prenez l'offensive dans *Le Semeur* de dimanche. [. . .] Il faudrait un titre comme *La rumeur infâme*' (T, 10). But a printed *fait divers* could make matters worse: 'le silence, l'étouffement, je ne connais que ça [. . .] il faut recouvrir tout ça,' the politician responds (T, 10–11). On the other hand, lest a local editor should be tempted to feature the story, retaliation can be threatened in the form of a potentially scandalous *fait divers* concerning him: 'Dieu merci, on tient le directeur de *La Lande conservatrice*: cette histoire de petites filles . . .' (T, 13)

Scandal is above all what the family wishes to avoid: but the death of Tante Clara revives Thérèse's notoriety: '"Et qui sait si ce n'est pas elle encore qui a fait le coup?"' (T, 141). The scandal attaching to her is all-pervasive – 'A Argelouse, pas un berger qui ne connût sa légende' (T, 144) – so much so that the family has to resort to circulating counter-rumours according to which she is viewed 'sous les traits d'une victime innocente et frappée à mort' (T, 145) or 'un peu neurasthénique' (T, 147). The more people talk about her the less they understand her. This is actually more disquieting for Bernard than the direct consequences of her actions – he survived the latter, but is still vulnerable to scandal: 'Que ce fût ou non à son insu, Thérèse suscitait le drame – pire que le drame: le fait divers' (T, 163). For her part, she is aware of being the object of the self-indulgent reflex that derives a furtive satisfaction from contemplating horror and ensures an easy conscience through mechanical gestures of moral disapproval. This is made explicit when in her desperation Thérèse considers suicide and wonders whether she ought to kill her daughter too, rather than abandon her to the wretched destiny she is likely to inherit from her mother. Thérèse's reading of the *faits divers* which report such actions further sets her apart from those who are pleased to consider themselves normal: 'Thérèse a lu que des désespérés emportent avec eux leurs enfants dans la mort; les bonnes gens laissent choir le journal: "Comment des choses pareilles sont-elles possibles?". Parce qu'elle est un monstre, Thérèse sent profondément que

Figure 2 © Archives René Dazy.

cela est possible et que pour un rien . . .' (T, 139)

The fact is that Bernard is one of these people. He cannot understand, and significantly he abandons his attempt to keep her at home and resist the invidious distortions of public opinion when he becomes convinced that despite the family's efforts she has irredeemably entered the realm of the *fait divers* and risks dragging the rest of them into it after her. When he returns from a period of absence, even the knowledge that she almost killed him is eclipsed by shock as her appearance brings to mind a picture he once glimpsed as a child: 'Ce n'était pas à cause du crime de Thérèse. En une seconde, il revit cette image coloriée du *Petit Parisien* [. . .] ce dessin rouge et vert qui représentait *La Séquestrée de Poitiers*' (T, 162). This vision convinces him that she must be removed from the life of the family and the gossip of the community: 'On l'oublierait plus vite, les gens perdraient l'habitude d'en parler. Il importait de faire le silence' (T, 170). When he offers her the prospect of starting a new existence alone in Paris, Thérèse does not see that his real motivation is to banish the haunting *fait divers* from his own life: 'Thérèse l'observe [. . .] mais ne devine pas l'image que contemplent ses gros yeux [. . .] ce dessin rouge et vert du *Petit Parisien*: *La Séquestrée de Poitiers*' (T, 168).

The outcome of Thérèse's story is determined by a reworking of the story of Mélanie Bastian who at this point supersedes Mme Canaby. The motif of the sequestering of women runs through the novel, as many critics have pointed out.[26] Thérèse's sister-in-law Anne is locked away to put a stop to her love affair (T, 100); Tante Clara, being deaf, is described as 'emmurée vivante' (T, 122). Thérèse's wedding is like stepping into a cage (T, 43), and the falling rain, the pine trees, the people surrounding Thérèse will be likened to bars. She is stifled and cloistered by the family and community well before her crime, and after it she is compelled to submit to the constraints Bernard places on her existence. As the story is established that she prefers to be alone, her fate begins to impress itself upon her: 'Tout ce jour à vivre encore, dans cette chambre; et puis ces semaines, ces mois . . .' (T, 146). Gradually, unobtrusively, the text builds her situation into a replica of 'la séquestrée de Poitiers'. She refuses her food, which lies untouched beside her (T, 148,151); she omits to dress or wash or even get out of bed (T, 151), and there is no point changing her bed linen since she burns and soils it with her cigarettes (T, 152). In these conditions it becomes impossible to clean the room properly (T, 152); soon it is 'Un vrai parc à cochons!' (T, 154). The exasperated servants take away Thérèse's cigarettes for her own good, which only increases her distress; inadvertently the window is left open . . . Thérèse grows increasingly unaware of her surroundings, her weakness causing her to sink into a delirium filled with idyllic dreams of another existence.

This development is viewed from the perspective of those immediately involved, so that the reader is drawn unwittingly into sharing the aberrant logic of the situation. The experience is brusquely contrasted, on Bernard's return home, with his horrified reaction to the spectacle Thérèse presents. The shift in point of view is crucial to Mauriac's reworking of the *fait divers*, which complements Gide's forensic reconstruction with a rendering that dramatizes more directly both the day-to-day domestic reality and the scandalized reaction of the public. Bernard is tormented by this famous image of sequestration which, reactualized in the person of Thérèse, turns her from monster to victim and ultimately shames him into contriving a release for her. Though his disquiet focuses on the picture of *La Séquestrée de Poitiers*, there is another unspoken parallel, no less telling and indicative of his self-centredness. Bernard has already been a party to the incarceration of his sister Anne: what is too terrible for him to contemplate is that Bernard and his mother could find themselves tarred with the same brush as the widow Mme Bastian and her son Pierre, who won notoriety as the unfeeling custodians of Mélanie Bastian.

While sequestering is a major underlying theme of the novel, the victim who is 'cernée de toutes parts' (T, 142) experiences her condition as persecution, and dreams of escape. The connected motifs of flight and pursuit are prominent in the novel. 'Etre traquée' (T, 19) is Thérèse's fate, one which is articulated through a variety of images relating to hunted animals.[27] Thérèse's side of the picture is informed by reminiscences which draw on yet another *fait divers*, that of the fleeing murderer Daguerre, details of whose story, remembered from Mauriac's childhood, are introduced into the memory of his heroine.[28] Thérèse contemplates doing as he did:

> Autant vaudrait s'enfoncer à travers la lande, comme avait fait Daguerre, cet assassin traqué pour qui Thérèse enfant avait éprouvé tant de pitié (elle se souvient des gendarmes auxquels Balionte versait du vin dans la cuisine d'Argelouse) – et c'était le chien des Desqueyroux qui avait découvert la piste du misérable. On l'avait ramassé à demi mort de faim dans la brande. Thérèse l'avait vu ligoté sur une charrette de paille. On disait qu'il était mort sur le bateau avant d'arriver à Cayenne. Un bateau . . . le bagne . . . (T, 136–7)

Thus while Thérèse resents that tendency of public opinion to fit her story to sensational stereotypes, in fact another sensational commonplace from the rubric is seen to nourish her own vision of her fate, founded as it is on a set of associations cultivated by regular coverage in the press of the departure of convicts being transported to the penal colony. The mythology, though largely deriving from nineteenth-century sources, remained very much alive until the abolition of the penal colony in 1947.[29] Images from early in the novel anticipate this underlying motif. At the outset Thérèse recalls her maternal grandmother, all but banished from the family's memory and not even available to her descendants in the form of a 'daguerréotype' (T, 11): it may not be excessive to see an implied allusion here to the fugitive whose presence is certainly felt elsewhere. Years before, Thérèse had anticipated returning home from honeymoon like a convict heading for the *bagne*: 'Elle souhaitait de rentrer à Saint-Clair comme une déportée qui s'ennuie dans un cachot provisoire est curieuse de connaître l'île où doit se consumer ce qui lui reste de vie' (T, 48). The prospect had then been made worse with the discovery that Anne had found a lover: 'Une créature s'évade hors de l'île déserte où tu imaginais qu'elle vivrait près de toi jusqu'à la fin' (T, 56). Later Thérèse will propose to Bernard that she should disappear like the escaping convict, a plan which is linked to the fate of her grandmother's *daguerréotype*: 'Tout de suite, si vous voulez, je m'enfonce dans la nuit [. . .] brûlez toutes mes photographies; que ma fille même ne sache plus mon nom' (T, 124). When Bernard finally liberates her in Paris she still considers her fate ought more properly to be that of the convict: 'J'aurais dû partir, une nuit, vers la lande du Midi, comme Daguerre. J'aurais dû [. . .] marcher jusqu'à l'épuisement' (T, 180).

The notion is bound up with the mingled horror and envy she feels, having contemplated suicide herself (T, 61, 138–40), towards those so desperate they have taken the urge to flee to its ultimate conclusion in *épuisement* or death. Hence she wishes she could emulate Daguerre, or even, as she goes on to say, the suicidal shepherd she has heard of (presumably in one of Tante Clara's sinister anecdotes) who found 'le courage de tenir [sa] tête enfoncée dans l'eau d'une lagune' (T, 180). The image of his body lying in the *lande* is one she is tempted by, despite 'les corbeaux, les fourmis qui n'attendent pas . . .' (T, 180). In effect, her first taste of solitude in Paris brings back the same image of the outcast, combining allusions to both the suicide and the convict, who lies stretched out in the landscape she has left behind: 'Comme son corps, étendu dans la lande du Midi, eût attiré les fourmis, les chiens, ici elle pressentait déjà autour de sa chair une agitation obscure, un remous' (T, 183).

Thus we see that both the major protagonists in the novel are conceived in relation to notable *faits divers*. It is of course appropriate that the story of Thérèse, a self-confessed 'monstre', should be viewed against a background of sensational images culled from the press, though it is clearly unacceptable that those in her immediate environment should perceive her situation exclusively in these terms. Her fundamental humanity is all the more striking as the reader is able to understand that neither she nor those around her can effectively contain her experience within the lurid terms of the rubric.

Notes

1. André Gide, *Romans, récits et soties, œuvres lyriques*, Paris, Pléiade, 1958 (hereafter RRS), p.1246.
2. See M. Raimond, *La Crise du roman, des lendemains du naturalisme aux années vingt*, Paris, Corti, 1966, pp.71, 80.
3. See Introduction, p.8.
4. See Claude Martin, *La Maturité d'André Gide*, Paris, Klincksieck, 1977, pp.299–300.
5. See *Bulletin des Amis d'André Gide*, vol.10, no.55, July 1982, pp.335–46; vol.10, no.56, October 1982, p.523; vol.11, no.57, January 1983, pp.107–8.
6. André Gide, *Journal des Faux-Monnayeurs*, Paris, Gallimard, 1927, pp.91–4, 55–7.
7. Scholars have begun looking in detail at the archives Gide himself accumulated. See Emily Apter, 'Allegories of reading/allegories of justice: the Gidean fait divers', *Romanic Review*, vol.80, no.4 (1989), pp.560–70; Elizabeth R. Jackson, 'André Gide et les faits-divers: un rapport préliminaire', *Bulletin des Amis d'André Gide*, vol.20, no.93, January 1992, pp.83–91.
8. *Ne Jugez Pas*, Paris, Gallimard, 1969, p.146. This volume contains Gide's major writings on *faits divers* and is referred to hereafter as NJP.
9. Gide is the most notable of a number of writers who concern themselves with this analogy. *L'Etranger* illustrates it, as does *Thérèse Desqueyroux* (see below, pp.59–61); Barthes discusses two trials in which it is a crucial issue: see *Mythologies*, Paris, Seuil, collection Points, 1957, pp.50–3; 102–5. Legal scholars have also begun to address the same topic: see B.S. Jackson, *Law, Fact and Narrative Coherence*, Roby, Merseyside, Deborah Charles Publications, 1988; W. Lance Bennett and Martha S. Feldman, *Reconstructing Reality in the Courtroom*, New Brunswick, Rutgers University Press, 1981.
10. 'L'effet de réel,' in Barthes, Bersani, *et al.*, *Littérature et réalité*, Paris, Seuil, collection Points, p.88.
11. See François Mouret, 'Gide à la découverte de Browning et de Hogg, ou la technique romanesque de la multiplicité des points de vue', *Cahiers André Gide*, vol.3, Paris, Gallimard, 1972, pp.223–39.
12. Apter, 'Allegories of reading', p.563, points out that Gide's archive includes a collection of *faits divers* under the heading 'séquestrés'.
13. Roland Barthes, 'Structure du fait divers', in *Essais critiques*, pp.188–97, especially at pp.191, 194, 195.
14. See David Walker, *André Gide*, London and Basingstoke, Macmillan, 1990, pp.110–18, 140–3.
15. Celia Britton discusses the links between Mélanie's situation and that

of Alissa in *La Porte étroite* and Gertrude in *La Symphonie pastorale*, tellingly relating them to the madwoman in the attic in *Jane Eyre*. She concludes that Gide refuses to 'hear' Mélanie's mad discourse, labelling it unintelligible, and thereby relegates her to a conventional male stereotype of femininity. I would argue to the contrary, that in classifying her as an *être d'inconséquence* in the way I have indicated he gives her a subversive psychological identity of a kind that challenges orthodox constructions of the subject as do his other fictional creations. See 'Fiction, fact and madness: intertextual relations among Gide's females characters', in M. Worton and J. Still, eds., *Intertextuality: theories and practices*, Manchester, Manchester University Press, 1990, pp.159–75.

16. *Les Nouvelles littéraires*, 6 December 1930, reproduced in François Mauriac, *Œuvres romanesques et théâtrales complètes*, ed. Jacques Petit, vol.2, Paris, Pléiade, 1979, pp.887–94.

17. 'Thérèse chez le docteur' appeared in 1932; 'Thérèse à l'hôtel' in 1933.

18. *Le Nœud de Vipères*, chapter 6.

19. Mauriac, *Œuvres romanesques*, pp.890–1.

20. Ibid., p.890.

21. He virtually quotes from *Thérèse Desqueyroux* in calling her 'brûlée vive' (p.893), in suggesting 'curiosité' as a motive (p.891) and in stating that 'cette criminelle n'est pas une autre femme que celle [d'autrefois]' (p.890–1). A remark made by his son Claude Mauriac tends to confirm the connections these examples point to (p.924).

22. For details of the Canaby case, see the Introduction to *Thérèse Desqueyroux*, ed. Cecil Jenkins, London, University of London Press, Textes Français Classiques et Modernes, 1964, pp.22–6.

23. *Thérèse Desqueyroux*, Paris, Livre de Poche, 1974 (hereafter T), pp.20–1.

24. See William Kidd, 'Oedipal and pre-oedipal elements in *Thérèse Desqueyroux*', in J. E. Flower, B. Swift, eds., *François Mauriac, Visions and Reappraisals*, Oxford, Berg, 1989, pp.25–45.

25. Which Thérèse's father had used earlier: 'Toutes des hystériques quand elles ne sont pas des idiotes' (T, 79).

26. See John Flower, *Intention and achievement. An essay on the novels of François Mauriac*, Oxford, Clarendon Press, 1969, p.73; Maurice Maucuer, *Thérèse Desqueyroux*, Paris, Hatier, collection Profil d'une œuvre, 1970, p.58; Toby Garfitt, *Mauriac: 'Thérèse Desqueyroux'*, London, Grant and Cutler, 1991, pp.54–5.

27. See Garfitt, *Mauriac*, pp.53–4.

28. See *Œuvres romanesques et théâtrales complètes*, vol.2, pp.923–4.

29. In 1794 Guyana became a place to which convicts were transported from France and in 1852 a penal colony was installed at Cayenne, where

it continued until it was closed down in 1947. A notorious penal colony existed on Devil's Island, off Cayenne, from 1854 to 1938. Hugo's *Les Misérables* draws on the imaginative tradition, as do portrayals of other famous convicts such as Fedka in Dostoyevsky's *The Devils* and Abel Magwitch in Dickens's *Great Expectations*. Foucault, in *Surveiller et Punir*, traces the evolving role of transportation within the range of penal measures developed during the nineteenth century. Genet's *Le Miracle de la Rose* contains a testimony to its abiding exoticism. In the 1920s and 1930s the issue of conditions in the penal colonies was a subject of intense public interest owing to frequent journalistic denunciations. See Gordon Wright, *Between the Guillotine and Liberty. Two Centuries of the Crime Problem in France*, New York and Oxford, Oxford University Press, 1983, pp.184–9 and p.255 n.36.

5

Young Iconoclasts: Surrealism and the Scene of the Crime

Guillaume Apollinaire, inventor of the term surrealism, exemplifies the modern spirit in his poem 'Zone' (in *Alcools*, 1913) where he celebrates the urban environment:

Tu lis les prospectus les catalogues les affiches qui chantent tout haut
Voilà la poésie ce matin et pour la prose il y a les journaux
Il y a les livraisons à 25 centimes pleines d'aventures policières
Portraits des grands hommes et mille titres divers

André Breton pays appropriate tribute to his predecessor's insight in 'Une maison peu solide' (*Mont de Piété*, 1919), a poem in the form of a *fait divers* in which a child is rescued from the ruins of a collapsed house by one Guillaume Apollinaire.

Breton and his fellow surrealists made use of the *fait divers* in many of their creative activities.[1] They notably appropriated the technique of listing *faits divers*[2] as a means of drawing attention to 'l'envers du réel', the disturbing violence, accidents and irrational impulses below the surface of the everyday. *La Révolution surréaliste* regularly catalogued press reports of suicides, sometimes headed 'Les désespérés',[3] sometimes leaving the hollow accumulation of the explanatory cliché 'chagrins intimes' to speak for itself.[4] In one instance Eluard and Péret, denouncing insensitive remarks made by a judge, adduce three *faits divers* to illustrate the visceral and moral distress undergone by society's victims:'Après un long voyage dans l'ombre, les fous, les assassins et, comme l'on dit, les désespérés abordent à la lumière vorace.Voici qu'eux-mêmes ils sont les flammes et voici qu'ils laissent derrière eux des cendres.'[5]

The surrealists were eager to declare their solidarity with criminals against the authorities.Their stance is exemplified in *Anicet ou le panorama*, Aragon's novel of 1921.[6] Much of the book takes the form of a *rocambolesque* pastiche drawing on Fantômas, Judex, the criminal conspiracy in Gide's

Les Caves du Vatican, and so on.[7] The text is replete with allusions to the 'bande à Bonnot', the 'bandits en auto' (A, 60, cf. A, 58),[8] and to the journalistic speculation that their exploits and contemporary *faits divers* gave rise to.[9] Anicet joins a gang of aesthetic subversives, bent on stealing the major paintings from the art galleries of Paris, which is modelled on these famous renegades; and the 'célèbre détective Nick Carter' (A, 61), seeking to forestall their activities, elects to disguise himself as an art critic, declaring: 'la mission du critique d'art est de rechercher les artistes qui par leurs théories et leurs œuvres pourraient troubler la paix publique. [. . .] C'est, somme toute, une façon de détective, un policier de l'art' (A, 72). Challenging artistic tradition is bound up with breaking the law. Anicet strangles a deceitful hag who had seduced him into believing she could be a muse of modernity: the crime is dealt with in a fantastical succession of explicitly theatrical *scènes* adding a further dimension to the analogy as the aftermath of the murder is played out in a scenario of judicial procedures:

> Le Commissaire et le gendarme s'avancent et procèdent à l'arrestation du jeune libertin. [. . .] A ce moment, la scène est envahie par les machinistes qui le transforment en tribunal [. . .] les juges font leur apparition. [. . .] Anicet se félicite d'un jugement rendu au lieu même du crime, et, si l'on peut dire, au milieu de ses circonstances atténuantes [. . .] (A, 34)

The scene of the crime, the scene of the arrest and the scene of trial and judgement are packed into the one space: the text becomes the stage on which the metaphorical interaction of artistic and judicial law and order is performed. Elsewhere, two areas are singled out for attention: the nature of the criminal's experience at the scene of the crime, and the way in which the affair is 'set up', then mediated and put into public circulation through the *faits divers*.

Anicet is induced to steal paintings for the gang from the studio of a famous artist. As Anicet effects his entry to the premises 'comme un personnage de féerie', the narrator intervenes in order both to convey the sensations his hero is undergoing and to compromise the reader by presenting these illicit feelings as familiar features from a widely-shared pool of references and experiences:

> Vous savez quel merveilleux attrait donnent à l'amour le secret et le mystère. Le crime porte un charme analogue. La prudence exigerait qu'on l'exécutât rapidement. Mais les voluptés fortes sont les plus lentes, et l'assassin sensible, le cambrioleur délicat s'attardent au lieu même qu'ils devraient fuir. J'ai souvenir d'avoir lu, il y a de cela dix ans, l'histoire de ce voleur qui avait pénétré dans la cave d'une banque, ouvert le coffre-fort, en avait vidé le contenu, mais ne pouvait se décider à partir . . . (A, 133)[10]

Equally interesting is the fact that criminal activity provokes in Anicet a heightened state of consciousness in which he spontaneously enacts certain surrealist tenets. He is 'comme un dormeur qui veut parler', but the words he seeks to utter 'avaient perdu leur sens en route, on ne reconnaissait plus leur visage coutumier. Ou bien c'étaient d'autres phrases qui venaient, absurdes exhalaisons de l'esprit, trahisons déguisées de secrets intimes: "*Les fuchsias m'ont encore fait des propositions*, ou, *j'aimerais bien manger des femmes de couleur*"' (A, 133). Automatic writing, the language of dreams become available to him, as do the hallucinatory properties of memories from childhood which return to him next. Then, as he proceeds by torchlight through the dark to seek out the artist's studio, the experience resembles the trajectory through a surrealist painting: 'Dans cette pièce ignorée où toute chose semblait précisément surgir à l'endroit qu'on ne l'attendait point, le jeune homme à chaque heurt saisissait dans le pinceau lumineux de sa lampe un aspect de cet univers paradoxal, et ne savait comment relier ce nouveau phénomène à ses précédentes découvertes' (A, 134–5).[11] Finally, confronted by the intimidating artworks he has come to steal, Anicet is prompted to a deeper insight into his own creative potential (A, 139–40).

It is possible to argue, then, that the evocation of the scene of the crime is used here as an instance of the hero passing over to 'the other side', as it were. The experience fixes the attention, as Breton would later put it, 'non plus sur le réel, ou sur l'imaginaire, mais, comment dire, sur *l'envers du réel*'. We perceive here, to pursue the quotation from Breton, 'l'étrange vie symbolique que les objets, aussi bien les mieux définis et les plus usuels, n'ont pas qu'en rêve.'[12] I shall come back to this point shortly. For the moment, another feature of *Anicet* calls for comment.

The striking conclusion of the novel consists of the *chronique judiciaire* reporting the trial of Anicet and his accomplices. This is not quoted verbatim, but is picked out from among the other *faits divers* in the newspaper *Le Parisien*, by a customer in the *Café du Commerce* who reads the highlights aloud at the request of another customer. The criminal exploits of the hero are thus inserted into that curious mode of circulation adopted by the *fait divers*, both textual and paratextual, both *reportage* and hearsay, crossing over between different types of discourses. This mediation of the crime is an illustration of the cultural space which surrealists seek to infiltrate and use as the site on which to operate their artistic and other subversions. To quote Breton again, 'Cette disposition de l'esprit que nous nommons surréaliste [. . .] je ne m'oppose pas à ce que les chroniqueurs, judiciaires et autres, la tiennent pour spécifiquement moderne.'[13] The *chronique* is the stage on which they will explore and experiment with infringements of the law.

Of course the *fait divers* is only a poor approximation of surreality. The *chronique* rarely rises by its own dynamic to the required level of expressive consciousness or stylistic sophistication, and merely reiterates the censorship practised by orthodoxy upon incursions of the absurd, the outrageous or the irrational. This point is illustrated when Anicet's defence counsel is reported to have pleaded diminished responsibility on account of certain *avant-garde* writings found on the accused when he was arrested: 'Il y avait si peu de logique entre les mots qu'il lut que nous n'avons pu les reproduire pour nos lecteurs. [. . .] L'avocat général fit observer que si les criminels n'avaient qu'à porter sur eux des poèmes futuristes pour être déclarés irresponsables, cela serait tout de même trop commode' (A, 195).

Nonetheless, the *fait divers* does maintain within public consciousness, if only obliquely, certain notions that challenge rationality and propriety, and as such its subversive potential is acknowledged by the surrealists. For example, Roger Vitrac's play *Victor ou les enfants au pouvoir*, which portrays the invasion of the bourgeois family by sexual scandal, madness and other manifestations of irrationality, shows how the respectable are vulnerable to the allure of that which challenges decorum. He echoes *Anicet* in using the device of a couple sharing the *faits divers*, here read aloud from *Le Matin*, 12 September 1909, by Charles Paumelle to his wife Emilie. She interrupts his renderings of polar exploration, a fly-past, a 'singulière histoire du bagne', a report on sexually-transmitted disease and the arrest of an anarchist:

EMILIE: Enfin, lis-moi un crime. Y a-t-il un crime, il y a bien un crime?

CHARLES: Non, il n'y a pas de crime. Et puis je ne lirai pas de crimes. Tu les liras seule.

EMILIE: Bon, je me retiens . . . Je me retiens . . . Tu remarques que je me retiens, n'est-ce pas?[14]

This repressed fascination is clearly ripe for exploitation. It is no doubt for such reasons that Breton, though on occasion he could be scathing about them, declared: 'Il n'est pas un fait divers pour lequel nous ne donnerions toute la critique d'art.'[15]

Though Breton famously encouraged acolytes to take their guns into the street and 'tirer au hasard, tant qu'on peut, dans la foule',[16] writers who had not themselves committed any crime were necessarily restricted to imaginative projection, reconstruction or fantasizing from secondary sources. To this extent their texts typically constitute a *return* to, a reconstitution of, the scene of the crime. This notion recalls the link in *Anicet* between art and criminality. A brief comment from Breton, on the subject of illustrations for books which have ceased to be read, underlines the point. Such pictures, argues Breton, are exemplary surrealist art. Having been separated from the text that gave rise to them, they have a disconcertingly enigmatic quality; they 'représentent pour nous une somme de conjectures tellement déroutantes qu'elles en sont précieuses, comme la reconstitution incroyablement minutieuse d'une scène de crime à laquelle nous assisterions en rêve, sans nous intéresser le moins du monde au nom et aux mobiles de l'assassin'.[17]

The scene of the crime, for someone other than the criminal – and sometimes even for him – is an enigma of the same kind, a scene of banality which frames horror, a norm which has contained transgression; and as such it has further potential for surrealist subversion of the the everyday. As ordinary objects become potential *pièces à conviction*, they evoke *l'éventuel*,[18] *le merveilleux*, the contingency of the ordinary.[19] A *topos* characterized by all these elements is the hotel room, 'où se dénouent les faits divers' (A, 149) as Aragon puts it. Joë Bousquet agrees with Breton in declaring that such a location typifies the disquieting universe of dreams of which he in turn writes: 'L'événement et l'objet y sont rigoureusement interchangeables, comme dans ces aventures accomplies et toutes jugées où une chambre d'hôtel raconte intégralement un crime que l'imagination policière est incapable de réinventer sur-le-champ'.[20] Robert Desnos (who was a reporter for *Paris-Soir*), in his 'Aventures du Corsaire Sanglot', provides a further apposite commentary as his eponymous hero accompanies Louise Lame to a similar hotel room. Its furnishings, 'méconnus par les copistes surannés' (that is to say, by previous generations of literary returnees to the scene of the crime), have witnessed one of Jack the Ripper's murders. This past event hangs in the air as it hovers, by virtue of the special communicative status of the *fait divers* it constitutes, in the mind of the protagonists. Its remembered presence imbues the ordinary objects with an other-worldly strangeness conforming to Breton's definition quoted earlier: 'Mobilier magnifique. Le pot à eau blanc, la cuvette et la table de toilette se souvenaient en silence du liquide rouge qui les avait rendus respectables.'

These 'accessoires modestes' have featured at the Assize Court as 'pièces à conviction'; Desnos's characters thus 'considèrent avec respect [. . .] les reliefs d'une aventure qui aurait pu être la leur'.[21] Later in the same text, Desnos shows how domestic discord between the couple 'leur met dans la main de jusque-là inoffensifs couteaux de table [. . .] et transforme la paisible salle à manger en un lieu d'effroyable tuerie, le sang jaillissant des carotides tranchées, souillant tour à tour la soupière en porcelaine de Limoges, la suspension à gaz et le buffet imitation de la Renaissance . . .'.[22] The return to the scene of the crime engenders a revival of the criminal within the everyday, produces a further example of the *dépaysement* whereby unassuming domestic accessories become receptacles and propagators of horror, to constitute another décor for another crime.

A well-documented return to the scene of a crime is that which Breton records in *L'Amour fou*. In July 1936, passing, without realizing it, beside the house near Lorient in which Michel Henriot had murdered his young wife in May 1934, Breton and his companion temporarily experienced an unaccountable sense of despair and isolation from each other, as if affected by a maleficent aura emanating from the site. This was a real return to the scene of an actual crime, unlike the fictional elements in previous cases considered; moreover, the instance is one in which the awareness of the murder comes after the event, to explain a sensation which appeared gratuitous until then – unlike other cases in which prior knowledge of the crime seemed the source of whatever vibrations were experienced by visitors to the place. Breton acknowledges in humans a compulsion to inspect such sites[23] and analyses paintings by Cézanne whose purpose seems to be to depict something of the eeriness or horror these locations inspire. Recalling how he was eventually reminded that the area he had been walking in had been the 'théâtre antérieur d'une tragédie des plus particulières',[24] Breton comments: 'toute cette affaire criminelle [. . .] se reconstituait sous mes yeux'.[25] He returns there in his imagination, this time on the basis of the information to hand. Georges Auclair compares Breton's treatment of the 'affaire du Loch' to the tourist's visits to, say the *Auberge sanglante*, and suggests that Breton is indulging in a version of the so-called 'pensée naturelle', evoking what Mauss refers to as the 'mana', the contagious emanation that certain communities attribute to calamitous events or ill-starred places.[26] However, Breton's presentation aims to establish that the 'halo' exists independently of human volition. Moreover, through his allusions to the coincidence linking the 'renards argentés' raised by Henriot and the two books *La Renarde* and *La Femme changée en renard*, which the couple had brought with them and were reading at the time, he makes of the incident a case of 'le hasard objectif', an inexplicable conjuncture of objective and subjective determinisms.

Opinions vary on interpretations that may be advanced. Victor Crastre is not wholly convinced by the author's own,[27] though we could apply to this case what Jacqueline Chénieux-Gendron says: 'Ce qui séduit Breton, c'est l'équivalence toute métaphorique de cette oscillation entre réel et virtuel, et le battement propre de la vie.'[28] Breton's detailed discussion of the Henriot affair makes clear the extensive attention he paid to the press coverage. As has already been suggested, the text of the *chronique judiciaire*, like the literary text itself, becomes a site on which a crime is committed, a law is infringed, a norm challenged. Hence Breton, rereading the reports on 'l'affaire du Loch,' finds in them 'une belle page à la gloire de la famille bourgeoise' as well as evidence of the authorities' regrettable failure to pursue some investigations which were clearly called for, in particular a psychoanalytic examination of the criminal.[29]

Other surrealists carried out similar operations on *faits divers*. We have examined earlier the way in which Georges Sadoul attacks the coverage of crime stories in the popular magazine *Détective*.[30] While the mainstream press presented criminal cases in manners conforming to the dominant ideology, the surrealists were obviously intent on making them yield up meanings more in line with their own iconoclastic ideas. The conventional *méthode policière* as an approach to crime is anathema to the young artists. Aragon, like Sadoul, complains that the end of the 1920s was marked by the 'exaltation du flic'; and Breton too, in his second manifesto which dates from the same year (1929), denounces the appropriation of Edgar Allan Poe by the same phenomenon. Thus *Le Mystère de Marie Roget*, 'composé loin du théâtre du crime' and hence a classic instance of the creative return to the scene of the crime by means of imaginative projection nourished by newspaper reports, is fatally vitiated by the fact that it has made Poe the 'maître des policiers scientifiques. [. . .] N'est-ce pas une honte de présenter sous un jour intellectuellement séduisant un type de policier, *toujours de policier*, de doter le monde d'une *méthode policière?*'[31] Breton confirms this ostracism in 1932, underlining its ideological or strategic significance: 'Les maîtres que se choisit la police moderne, vous admettrez que ce ne puissent être les nôtres'.[32]

These denunciations owe their critical edge to the political situation at the time; the surrealists' adherence to the Communist party, itself beleaguered and subject to police hostility as a result of the 'mots d'ordre suicidaires' imposed on it by the Sixth Congress of the Comintern in 1928, generated a certain ideological paranoia which colours these writers' treatment of the *fait divers*.[33] This factor also comes into play as the surrealists took the side of the criminal in opposition to the authorities – construed as those in official positions or their toadies in the press. Thus Lacenaire and Landru featured notably among their heroes.[34] That their interest had clear ideological overtones can be seen from the cover of the first number of *La Révolution surréaliste* featuring Germaine Berton, the anarchist militant who on 22 January 1923 entered the premises of *L'Action française* and shot the *camelot du roi* who was its editorial secretary. In the same issue she was praised by Aragon as 'en tout admirable'.[35] A similar point emerges from the remarks on the execution of Sacco and Vanzetti among the press reviews in October 1927.[36] Moreover, a rift was to occur with the *Grand Jeu* group who were condemned among other things for having placed Landru above Sacco and Vanzetti in the criminal hierarchy.[37] For the surrealists, by 1929 the *criminel de droit commun* was already losing ground to the individual whose case carried overt political connotations.

Eluard provides a case in point. In the third issue of *Le Surréalisme au Service de la Révolution* he discusses a report by Géo London in *Le Journal* of 8 November 1931, concerning the trial of a *valet de chambre* accused of murdering his brother-in-law, a *professeur agrégé* at the *lycée de Dijon*. The butt of Eluard's criticisms is the presiding magistrate, whom he condemns as a social parasite, profiting from the class-based system he helps to police.[38] It appears that the prosecuting attorney was driven to intervene in the face of intemperate remarks made by the magistrate:'La balance n'est pas égale. Je veux bien faire condamner les gens, mais je veux les faire condamner justement et équitablement.' The original newspaper headline read:'Un étonnant incident met aux prises le président et l'avocat général.'[39] For Eluard this is merely one capitalist lackey bringing an accomplice into line. However, he ignores crucial references to the wife of the accused, a key prosecution witness, who had recently left her husband in a state of despair which may have motivated his crime. Because of this she was 'traitée sans aucun ménagement par le représentant même de l'accusation'. It is to correct *this* excess that the president stepped in, earning the above-mentioned riposte from the prosecutor, who is reported as openly admitting:'Il est douloureux pour moi de requérir dans une telle affaire!' Eluard's version actually reverses the thrust of the proceedings, which in fact hinged on open animosity towards the wife. It would appear that in re-presenting the circumstances of this alleged judicial crime Eluard is allowing his Marxist convictions to override the surrealists' commitment to 'la femme, seule capable de surmonter les puissances du néant', as Marie-Claire Bancquart puts it.[40]

Such an omission is all the more surprising, of course, in that some of the most notable surrealist provocations have as their inspiration the defence of criminal women. Germaine Berton was surrounded by photographs of the surrealists themselves on the front cover of number 1 of *La Révolution surréaliste*; issue number 5 of *Le Surréalisme au Service de la Révolution* carried photographs of the Papin sisters and an account of how the maids had murdered their mistress and her daughter, with a caption by Eluard and Péret which states they are 'sorties tout armées d'un chant de Maldoror'. Most notably of all, perhaps, December 1933 saw the publication in Belgium of the brochure *Violette Nozières*, to which seventeen members of the group contributed poems and illustrations aimed at vindicating the eighteen-year-old's poisoning of her mother and father. Such publications involve a subversive recycling of elements from the *fait divers* rubric: press photographs are built into collages, circumstantial details appropriated from news reports are written provocatively into poems.[41] These works exemplify the text as the site of an offence against *la bienséance* and recall Breton's discussion of the 'délits de presse' in the first Manifesto, in which he lists the criminal possibilities available to surrealist writers:'atteinte à la morale publique','diffamation','injures à l'armée, provocation au meurtre, au viol, etc'.[42] He illustrates the theory in his own incitement to murder in the second Manifesto:'L'acte surréaliste le plus simple consiste, revolvers aux poings, à descendre dans la rue et à tirer au hasard, tant qu'on peut, dans la foule.'[43] In Breton's mind, such actions, if carried out in the surrealist spirit, pose important legal conundrums: 'Comment seront jugés les premiers actes délictueux dont le caractère surréaliste ne pourra faire aucun doute?'[44] Hostile *littérateurs* were untroubled by such scruples: *Liberté*'s literary reviewer recommended the firing squad for Benjamin Péret, author of 'Vie de l'assassin Foch' in the second number of *Le Surréalisme au Service de la Révolution* in 1930. In the third number of the review Aragon denounces the police harassment he and other members of the group underwent even before the publication of his 'Front Rouge'. As is well known, this poem rendered its author eligible for a prison sentence of five years: and Breton's arguments for the irresponsibility of the surrealist caused him some difficulty in the aftermath of the group's protests against the legal action 'Front rouge' gave rise to, since the ensuing 'affaire Aragon' complicated matters with its politico-ideological ramifications.[45]

There are more subtle approaches to colonizing and subverting the scene of the crime in print. In his *Traité du Style*, Aragon quotes news items from *L'Intransigeant* and *Paris-Soir*, in September 1927, concerning thefts of porcelain objects and church furnishings carried out by one Louis Aragon. He highlights inconsistencies in the reports, thereby undermining their authority: 'Pour *L'Intransigeant* j'ai été pris à Moisenay, sur le fait. Pour *Paris-Soir* c'est mon exploit de Mormant qui me vaut l'incarcération, et quelque doute plane, albatros de probabilité, sur mes rapts autant de Moisenay que de Mormant. Qui croire. Voilà donc comment sont faits les journaux. Inexacts jusque dans les puces de rat.' Insofar as 'Le merveilleux, c'est la contradiction qui apparaît dans le réel,'[46] the reality of events reported begins to give way to something more elusive, comprising contradiction, uncertainty, the 'air of eventuality'.[47] In response to the comment in *Paris-Soir* that the same offender 'est également croit-on, l'auteur de vols commis dans les églises de Mormant et de Moisenay', Aragon writes: 'Je dois prévenir le rédacteur de *Paris-Soir* que je suis *aussi* l'auteur de plusieurs livres capitaux non seulement à l'échelle des jardinières en porcelaine ancienne, mais à celle de l'histoire future de l'esprit humain.'[48] Punning on the term, the *auteur* links together criminal acts and literary creations, simultaneously claiming the identity of the law-breaker which is made available by the coincidence of the name, thereby declaring his solidarity with the criminal – in keeping with what we have seen already in other instances. The sense of *dédoublement* provoked by this coincidence highlights the convergence of two distinct realities which again is congenial to 'l'esprit surréaliste'. Furthermore, as Chénieux-Gendron puts it: 'Ces actes à vrai dire réalisables témoignent qu'autour d'une personnalité quelle qu'elle soit certains comportements possibles restent comme suspendus.'[49]

This is not an isolated instance. Joë Bousquet reports a news story headed 'drame passionnel', in *Le Surréalisme au Service de la Révolution*.[50] The *Dépêche de Toulouse* of 9 February 1933 tells, he says, how a Bulgarian shot his wife and was eventually arrested in a shop owned by a certain M. Bousquet. Here, as in the example Aragon offers, the coincidence of names appears to wrench the story from its strict referential status, while on the other hand Bousquet's own apparent presence on the scene gives his account the spoof credibility of eye-witness testimony. He relates the facts given in the paper, adding (presumably) a host of extravagant details on the bizarre sexual practices which he alleges led to the shooting. By highlighting the contingency of the real the coincidence authorizes the kind of embroidery that Bousquet indulges in. Further grounds for Bousquet's elaborations stem from the horizon of transgression which the reported incident opens up in the first place.

These two items, along with Breton's account of his experiences at the scene of 'l'affaire du Loch', confirm a 'second-level' confluence between the surrealist spirit and what we can call the spirit of the *fait divers*. For the *fait divers* as *chronique judiciaire* is not the whole of the rubric; it also concerns itself with strange conjunctions of circumstance troubling our conception of the norm. We can see that in reworking the text of the crime reports they start from, these writers effectively transform them into *faits divers* of the broader type challenging not just the codes of legality but the very basis on which reality is codified or perceived.

Aragon's *Le Paysan de Paris* usefully corroborates the perspective emerging from the other works we have considered. It is characteristic of Aragon in that the construction of Paris as a fantastical cityscape, scene of crimes as well as arena for the 'merveilleux quotidien' and the 'insolite' (PP, 15–16) in general, is a fairly consistent feature of his writing over a long period.[51] In 'Le Passage de l'Opéra' Aragon categorizes the décor as 'un grand secret dans un décor de lieu commun' (PP, 25). The stress here, of course, lies on the detailed reality of the location, not its evocation as the setting for a fictional adventure. But Aragon's aim, clearly stated at the outset of this later text and repeated throughout, is to explore the notion of 'lieux sacrés', to elaborate a 'métaphysique des lieux' (PP, 19). Yvette Gindine develops this motif with some thoroughness, but fails to emphasize the importance of the 'lieu sacré' as the scene of a crime.[52] The fact is that the surreal qualities of a given location stem in large part from the criminal associations it awakens. Aragon explicitly seeks out 'le trouble des lieux [. . .] où se poursuit l'activité la plus équivoque des vivants' (PP, 20) and speaks of 'le paysage fantomatique des plaisirs et des professions maudites' (PP, 21). Such sites generate the 'mythologie moderne' which is Aragon's goal; but they are significantly bound up with illegality, since they are described as 'recéleurs de plusieurs mythes modernes' (PP, 21). A typically evocative one 'rappelle les opérations de police les plus basses et les poursuites au cœur même de leurs amours de ces assassins sentimentaux que la faiblesse des sens a livrés' (PP, 25). The café Biard is described as 'le décor du crime qui se cache, de l'attentat projeté, de la poursuite et du traquenard' (PP, 74–5).

With the arrival of the character named L'Imagination the link between crime, surrealism and news reports is made manifest: 'J'annonce au monde ce fait divers de première grandeur: un nouveau vice vient de naître, un vertige de plus est donné à l'homme: le *Surréalisme*, fils de la frénésie et de l'ombre' (PP, 82). Whereupon the conceit of artists as subversive criminal conspirators, already suggested in *Anicet*, is revived, this time with the surrealists peddling the 'stupéfiant *image*' (PP, 83):

> Bientôt, demain, l'obscur désir de sécurité qui unit entre eux les hommes leur dictera des lois sauvages, prohibitrices. Les propagateurs de surréalisme seront roués et pendus, les buveurs d'images seront enfermés. [. . .] Alors les surréalistes persécutés trafiqueront à l'abri de cafés chantants leurs contagions d'images. A des attitudes, à des réflexes, à de soudaines trahisons de la nervosité, la police suspectera de surréalisme des consommateurs surveillés. Je vois d'ici ses agents provocateurs, leurs ruses, leurs souricières. (PP, 83–4)

Another strand of associations links back to *Anicet* and points forward to the latter part of *Le Paysan de Paris*. Just as in the earlier text the tailor's shop had been the scene of a murder (A, 28), so here it is the establishment of the *Tailleur mondain* which has about it a special aura by virtue of having been frequented by Landru:[53]

> Je ne peux pas m'empêcher de penser que c'est ici que Landru, expérimentateur sensible, se faisait habiller, essayant ses costumes au milieu des bagages exposés comme autant de symboles mystérieux de son destin. J'ai retenu de cet homme auquel on a coupé la tête, qu'il avait chez lui le masque de Beethoven et les œuvres d'Alfred de Musset, qu'il offrait à ses amies de rencontre un biscuit et un doigt de madère, qu'il portait les palmes académiques.

Clearly this is not the scene of his crimes, but the association is an intimate one none the less: 'Il me semble que ce point précis du passage où je me tiens est exactement apparié à cet homme et à ses accessoires' (PP, 59). These allusions to the murderer also connect with an earlier discussion of the 'double jeu de l'amour et de la mort' (PP, 44) which gives such comments a heightened significance.

In the later part of the book, 'Le sentiment de la nature aux Buttes-Chaumont', this complex of motifs is developed to its culmination. The park itself is referred to as 'Cette grande oasis dans un quartier populaire, une zone louche où règne un fameux jour d'assassinats [. . .] où est niché l'inconscient de la ville' (PP, 167, 170). Noll, Breton and Aragon head there in the hope of finding a site where they can 'se soustraire aux lois [. . .] dans la marge la plus favorable à la liberté et au secret, qui nous semblait cette grande banlieue équivoque autour de Paris, cadre des scènes les plus troublantes des romans-feuilletons et des films à épisodes français, où tout un dramatique se révèle' (PP, 168).[54] It is clearly the equivalent, in terms of the geography of the city, of that cultural domain occupied by the *fait divers*.[55] In the park they seek out the 'pont des Suicides où se tuaient avant qu'on ne le munît d'une grille même des passants qui n'en avaient pas pris le parti mais que l'abîme tout à coup tentait' (PP, 171); the site seems to have about it the 'halo' which Breton experienced at Lorient, capable of provoking, as he puts it in *L'Amour fou*, 'un état affectif *en totale contradiction* avec nos sentiments réels'.[56] And sure enough it is Breton, in Aragon's text, who announces their arrival at the place and triggers a meditation on locations which have witnessed violent events: 'Entre les lieux sacrés qui manifestent [. . .] tout le concret de quelques grandes idées surnaturelles particularisées, j'imagine qu'un païen, je veux dire un homme qui sache éprouver la nouveauté mystérieuse d'une idole, va préférer les lieux qui sont dévolus à la Mort Violente, cette divinité qui tient la hache, à côté d'un faisceau de margotin' (PP, 206). In a passage which could apply to the relevant pages of *L'Amour fou* – which indeed it appears to anticipate – Aragon regrets the fact that the modern world seems to be losing this sense of what a *lieu sacré* is. He argues the case for the revival of the notion and provides thereby a means of conceptualizing the surrealists' fondness for such places, 'seuil de tous les mystères' (PP, 208), 'serrures qui ferment mal sur l'infini' (PP, 20). The heightened awareness they afford can be generalized and can transfigure one's existence. As he approaches the climax of his book, Aragon reaffirms that this has been his intention from the start: 'J'avais donc entrepris [. . .] d'exposer une imagination que j'avais du divin, et des lieux où il se manifeste' (PP, 226). He repudiates the role of the intelligence in such a conception of place, exhorting his readers: 'Réveillez-vous sous le couteau, condamnés à mort, mes frères,' (PP, 229) and reactivating the theme which has underpinned earlier parts of the text. 'Et je rêve, et ma tête va,' he writes, inaugurating the concluding sequence, 'Où va-t-elle, coupée?' (PP, 230). The reminiscence of the guillotined murderer Landru, hero of the *fait divers*, inspires the climactic fantasm of the poet who decapitates himself and flings his head away the better to escape the tyranny of the intellect and penetrate the mystery of the *lieu sacré*. For of course, a key *lieu sacré*, source of a powerful *mana*, was the site of public executions such as that of Landru in the square in front of the prison of Versailles.[57] The climax of the book therefore mingles reminiscences of an assassin with the aura of a *lieu sacré* which in turn serves as the scene for the surrealist transfiguration of a judicial murder. The text become the site for an execution – in the sense also of an intensely poetic realization – of a criminal:

> Celui qui s'était séparé de sa pensée quand au loin les premiers flots eurent léché les plaies du chef méprisé sortit de l'immobilité comme un point d'interrogation renversé [. . .] le corps décapité lançait à grandes saccades le triple jet de ses plus fortes artères, et le sang formait des fougères monstrueuses dans le bleu étincelant de l'espace. [. . .] L'homme-fontaine, entraîné par la capillarité céleste, s'élevait au milieu des mondes à la suite de son sang. [. . .] Et l'homme ne fut plus qu'un signe entre les constellations. (PP, 232)

Notes

1. Cf. pp.38–40 on *Détective*, pp.91–8 on the Papin sisters and Violette Nozières. Jacqueline Chénieux-Gendron has written extensively on the use to which the surrealists put the *fait divers*, particularly as an avatar of 'le merveilleux quotidien' and as a vehicle for conceptualizing a theory of the event that would permit forms of narrative other than the novel the movement was committed to decrying. See *Le Surréalisme et le Roman*, Paris, L'Age d'homme, 1983, pp.13–19, 33–100, 133–5, 151–73, 178–91, 296–9 and *passim*.

2. Deriving perhaps from Jarry, who in 'Déplacements et villégiatures' lists thirteen reports of sudden deaths as features of the holiday season (*Le Canard sauvage*, 16–22 August 1903, see JOC, pp.499–501), the device was pioneered also (though more subtly) by Félix Fénéon whom Jarry 'nominated' as his successor. His *Nouvelles en trois lignes*, items from *Le Matin* of 1906, were not published as a volume until 1948. See Patrick and Roman Wald Lasowski, eds., *Nouvelles en trois lignes*, Paris, Editions Macula, 1990, p.24, and pp.16–17 above. The same technique is used in Aragon's 'Asphyxies' (*Le Libertinage*, Paris, Gallimard, 1924), which accumulate oddities, scandals and crimes that fly in the face of decorum and common sense.

3. *Clarté*, in a survey on the apparent epidemic of suicides that troubled public opinion in 1925, had concluded this was a plausible motive: the surrealists were presumably satirizing this finding. See introduction to the facsimile reprint of *La Révolution surréaliste*, p.vii.

4. *La Révolution surréaliste*, no.1, December 1924, p.32. Other instances, listed separately, hit home by virtue of odd details: the woman who got up in the night and took her umbrella with her to throw herself down her neighbour's well, for example, or the woman who left a suitcase of initialled lingerie on the quai des Célestins from which she jumped into

the Seine (ibid., pp.13, 20).

5. *La Révolution surréaliste*, no.8, 1 December 1926, pp.1–2.

6. *Anicet ou le panorama, roman*, Paris, Gallimard, 1921. Hereafter referred to as A.

7. Y. Gindine, *Aragon Prosateur surréaliste*, Geneva, Droz, 1966, pp.17–18; Jacqueline Chénieux-Gendron, *Le Surréalisme et le roman*, Paris, L'Age d'homme, 1983, pp.111–21.

8. 'Lorsque tout est fini', a story in *Libertinage*, presents an account of the gang's exploits by one of its members. Cf. Gindine, *Aragon prosateur surréaliste*, pp.50–2; Chénieux-Gendron, *Le Surréalisme*, p.64; and Jacqueline Lévi-Valensi, *Aragon Romancier*, Paris, SEDES, 1989, pp.80–1. The 'bande à Bonnot' and its exploits, which dominated the news in 1911–12, also feature in *Les Cloches de Bâle*, Aragon's novel of 1934. For further literary echoes of the gang, by Léon Daudet and Robert Goffin, see M. Lecerf, *Les Faits Divers*, Paris, Larousse, collection Idéologies et Sociétés, 1981, pp.109–16.

9. Examples include floods in Paris, pp.171–2, and anarchists' attempts to undermine the currency, p.190; other items occur on pp.149–50. The novel as a whole also owes something to the theft of the *Mona Lisa* in 1911 – a crime which was briefly imputed to Apollinaire.

10. Magritte's painting *L'assassin menacé* presents a variant of this scenario.

11. The occurrence of the word 'pinceau' is of course significant here.

12. *Manifestes du Surréalisme*, Paris, Gallimard, collection Idées, pp.121–2 n.1.

13. Ibid., pp.79–80.

14. Roger Vitrac, *Victor ou les Enfants au Pouvoir*, Paris, Gallimard, Le Manteau d'Harlequin, 1946, p.61. The newspaper items are reproduced in facsimile in the script.

15. *Les Pas perdus*, Paris, Gallimard, 1924, p.65; cf. also pp.116, 127. For Breton's reservations, see *Point du Jour*, Paris, Gallimard-Folio, pp.108–9.

16. *Second Manifeste du surréalisme*, p.78.

17. *Point du Jour*, p.61.

18. The term is developed in *Les Pas perdus*: for a discussion of its implications, see Chénieux-Gendron, *Le Surréalisme*, pp.71–2, 81–3, 131–2.

19. For a critical view of the surrealists' construction of the scene of the crime associated with the urban marvellous, see Adrian Rifkin, *Street Noises, Parisian Pleasure 1900–1940*, Manchester and New York, Manchester University Press, 1993, p.125.

20. *Le Meneur de Lune*, quoted in Alain Robbe-Grillet, *Pour un Nouveau Roman*, Paris, Gallimard, collection Idées, p.109.

21. *Domaine public*, Paris, NRF/Le point du jour, 1953, pp.335–6.

22. Ibid., pp.337–8.
23. *L'Amour fou*, Paris, Gallimard-Folio, p.156.
24. Ibid., p.161.
25. Ibid., p.155.
26. Georges Auclair, *Le 'Mana' quotidien: structures et fonctions de la chronique des faits divers*, Paris, Editions Anthropos, 1970, pp.173–85, especially at pp.177–81.
27. *Trilogie surréaliste*, Paris, SEDES, 1971, pp.102–3.
28. *Le Surréalisme*, p.90; on the significance of the 'halo', cf. p.41. It seems worth indicating a coincidence Breton perhaps significantly omits to mention – indeed rules out: he wrote the opening section of *L'Amour fou* at the height of the press coverage of Michel Henriot's murder of his wife on 8 May 1934 and first met his own future wife during the same month, on 29 May 1934, as he points out in his text (p.63).
29. Ibid., pp.160, 159.
30. 15 December 1929, pp.45–7. See above, pp.38–9.
31. *Manifestes du surréalisme*, p.81.
32. *Point du Jour*, p.93.
33. See Dominique Borne, Henri Dubief, *Nouvelle histoire de la France contemporaine*, vol.13, *La Crise des années trente*, Paris, Seuil, 1989, pp.86–7.
34. See Jeremy Stubbs, 'From De Quincey to Surrealism: an art that kills', in *Digraphe*, special number 'Thomas de Quincey', June 1994.
35. *La Révolution surréaliste*, December 1924, p.12.
36. Ibid., October 1927, pp.63–4. Breton will refer to the 'magnifiques journées de pillage dites "Sacco-Vanzetti"' in *Nadja*, Paris, Gallimard-Folio, 1928, p.180, as will Aragon in *Traité du Style*, Paris, Gallimard, 1928, pp.117–20.
37. See M. Nadeau, *Histoire du Surréalisme*, Paris, Seuil, collection Points, 1964, pp.122–3.
38. Paul Eluard, *Œuvres complètes*, Paris, Pléiade, 1968, pp.830–1; originally published in *Le Surréalisme au Service de la Révolution*, no.3, pp.11–12.
39. *Le Journal*, 8 November 1931, p.4.
40. Introduction to the facsimile edition of *La Révolution surréaliste*, p.i.
41. Cf. José Pierre, 'Violette Nozières et les surréalistes', preface to *Violette Nozières*, St. Niklaas, Belgium, Terrain Vague, 1991, pp.9–11. See also p.98 below.
42. Breton, *Manifestes du surréalisme*, p.60.
43. Ibid., p.78.
44. Ibid., p.60. The topic recalls the evocation of the poems found on *Anicet* and adduced in his defence at his trial (see above).
45. See Nadeau, *Histoire du surréalisme*, pp.140–7.
46. Louis Aragon, *Le Paysan de Paris*, Paris, Livre de Poche (hereafter PP),

1926, p.250.

47. *Les Pas perdus*, p.115; see the article of the same title by Roger Cardinal, *Aura*, no.1, January 1993, pp.72–81.

48. *Traité du Style*, pp.165–8.

49. *Le Surréalisme*, p.55.

50. No.5, 1933, p.41.

51. The first two chapters of *Anicet* can be seen as an early version of 'Le passage de l'Opéra' in *Le Paysan de Paris* (a note of 1966 in the latter, p.53, implies as much). Anicet locates the story he tells to Arthur (Rimbaud) in 'un des passages vivants qui mènent des plaisirs aux affaires, des boulevards aux quartiers commerciaux' (A, 25). 'Décor où se complaît ma sensibilité, je te baptise Passage des Cosmoramas', he says (A, 26). It is here that various transfigurations and fantasies, notably concerning the dummies in the tailor's shop (A, 28), lead to the enactment of the murder of Lulu. The same décor will play an important role in *Les Beaux Quartiers* and *Aurélien*: see Lévi-Valensi, *Aragon romancier*, p.100. Breton refers to Aragon's propensity for fantasizing around the urban environment: see remarks quoted by Chénieux-Gendron, *Le Surréalisme*, p.49 n.92, from *Entretiens*, Paris, Gallimard 1969, pp.38–9; one critic has also compared Aragon's achievement in *Le Paysan de Paris* with that of Zola in *Thérèse Raquin*: see Auguste Dezalay, 'Commentaires' to his edition of *Thérèse Raquin*, Livre de Poche, 1984, p.255. Aragon's depiction of Paris draws on a tradition – *Habent sua fata loci* – adumbrated by Louis Chevalier, *Classes laborieuses et classes dangereuses à Paris pendant la première moitié du XIXe siècle*, Paris, Plon, 1958, pp.52–9, 77–85, 98–113, and highlighted by Walter Benjamin in *Paris, capitale du XIXe siècle*: see Rifkin, *Street Noises*, chapter 1. See also Peter Collier, 'Surrealist city narrative: Breton and Aragon', in E. Timms, D. Kelley, eds., *Unreal city: Urban experience in modern European Literature and Art*, New York, St Martin's Press, 1985, pp.214–29.

52. See *Aragon Prosateur surréaliste*, pp.57–74. André Gavillet, in *La Littérature au Défi. Aragon surréaliste*, Neuchatel, Editions de la Baconnière, 1957, pp.165–80, also devotes a chapter to the theme but similarly omits the element of criminality and *fait divers*.

53. Following his execution in February 1922, Landru's personal effects had been publicly auctioned off in January 1923. A book entitled *L'Affaire Landru*, by Béraud, Bourcier and Salmon was published by Albin Michel in 1924: he was therefore a *figure d'actualité* at the time.

54. These lines fit precisely into the criminal geography of Paris as outlined by Chevalier, *Classes Laborieuses*, and Rifkin, *Street Noises*. See note 51 above.

55. Cf. what Genet has to say about *fait divers* as the Barrios Chinos of the

newspapers: see below, p.156.

56. *L'Amour fou*, p.163.

57. On the historic relevance of, and the sentiments inspired by, sites of execution in Paris, see Chevalier, *Classes Laborieuses*, pp.78–85, 98–101. The *mana* associated with such sites is discussed in Auclair, *Le 'Mana' quotidien*, pp.175–8.

PART III

Literature, History and 'La Factidiversialité'

6

Literature, History and Factidiversiality

The twentieth century is commonly held to be an era in which the existence of the individual is invaded by or subsumed under the wider collective adventure – or calamity. Hélène in Simone de Beauvoir's *Le Sang des Autres* exemplifies the experience as she contemplates the occupation of France by the Nazis: 'Comme si je n'existais pas. [. . .] Je ne compte pas. [. . .] Je regardais passer l'Histoire! C'était mon histoire. Tout ça m'arrive à moi'.[1] However, despite the advantage of hindsight the lived experience of historical forces swamping the individual often eludes our retrospective grasp. This is in part because even as history is being lived, it is encountered in mediated forms, chiefly through the news: soldiers who have fought on the battlefields, when interrogated for first-hand testimony, as often as not quote the news reports back at the investigator.[2]

Meanwhile, for those not directly involved in great cataclysms there is another arena where private experience is transfigured by being expropriated and projected into the public domain. Turandot, in Raymond Queneau's *Zazie dans le Métro*, becomes aware of it when, having come close to being accused of indecent assault, he trembles at his narrow escape – not from 'l'histoire', but from 'la factidiversialité'.[3] For ordinary French mortals, the *fait divers* is notoriety enough. It does not normally entail appearances on the front page, in due deference to the march of history which has its place reserved there. In fact one of the features of the *fait divers* is systematically to commemorate the recurrent, rather than ongoing, patterns in current affairs: the *crime passionnel*, varieties of other crimes and scandals, the curious accidents and paradoxes of everyday life, all are reported in their stark challenge to common sense and ordinariness, so as to reassure us nonetheless by confirming our belief that 'there's nowt so queer as folk.' or 'it's a funny old world.' It is through this material that people relate to their own existences as much as, if not more than, through representations of history on the march.

It is clear, however, that these two types of experience converge in the newspaper. Social and ideological undercurrents and tensions frequently find in the *fait divers* a pretext for expression.[4] The process can be recognized at work when a *fait divers* becomes an *affaire* and draws the attention of artists and intellectuals as well as of journalists and the judiciary. This seems to occur most readily when explicit sociohistorical pressures as such are not at their most acute. It is appropriate, in a sense, that when history appears to be going nowhere in particular, attention should turn to the cyclical or timeless patterns in human existence.

For example, the late 1920s and early 1930s have been characterized as a period of historico-political stagnation in France: traditional political parties were in disarray, the unions were divided, the Communist party ghettoized through the 'mots d'ordre suicidaires' imposed on it by the Sixth Congress of Comintern in 1928, and Hitler was not yet perceived as the threat he would soon become.[5] These years saw an intense interest in *faits divers*.[6] It is as if the rubric provides a framework within which sociopolitical anxieties can be articulated in displaced forms during a time of political transition and uncertainty. To quote Edgar Morin on the way in which such periods are conducive to *la rumeur*, they correspond to 'une phase d'incertitude, d'inquiétude qui, puissamment refoulée hors de la conscience politique, aurait dérivé vers les bas niveaux inconscients'.[7] An examination of some noteworthy cases commented on by writers and intellectuals shows how social and political concerns penetrate the journalistic aura of triviality or sensationalism.

In an article in *Le Jour*, in the autumn of 1933, Montherlant singled out three *faits divers* of a kind which, as he puts it, have not had the impact they should have had on 'la sensibilité française'.[8] They all concern suicide.[9] The stories, he says, had received the standard *fait divers* treatment in the newspapers, highlighting the discrepancy between modest cause and dramatic effect as a technique to 'accrocher le lecteur', and underlining the enigma at the heart of the incident: '"Comment expliquer ce désespoir mortel?" écrit notre confrère.' Provoked by the apparent incomprehension, even cynicism, of the press reports, Montherlant argues that the instances he highlights contain an important lesson in honour. This can be illustrated through his comments on one case, that of Serge Dimitrief, a former sub-lieutenant in the Russian cavalry, reduced to washing dishes in a Paris restaurant, who killed himself on 7 May 1932, on learning that President Doumer had been murdered the previous day by another Russian, Gorguloff. 'Je meurs pour la France,' his suicide note read. Now the assassination of the president between the two *tours de scrutin* of the elections was obviously a sensitive matter. By common consent Gorguloff was insane, but in a climate where his Russian nationality gave rise to partisan reactions, his guilt and execution were foregone conclusions: as Simone de Beauvoir puts it in her recollection of the case, 'l'assassin n'était pas jugé: il servait de bouc émissaire.'[10] Montherlant, for his part, laments the poverty of responses to what is in effect an attempt to atone on Dimitrief's part: press coverage of routine murders and conventional thieving bankers crowded it from all but the most modest *entrefilets*. 'Sacrifice inutile,' responds an anonymous interlocutor. 'Bref, il ne s'agit jamais que de rabaisser,' concludes Montherlant, who considers it a serious matter for the country at large that such acts which he calls 'honorables' and even 'sublimes', should elicit only 'indifférence, dénigrement et ricanement'. In wartime they would have received 'l'audience, l'émotion et l'admiration qui leur sont dues'; for the sake of the peace, argues Montherlant, it is important to recognize them for what they are, 'toute la dignité de l'homme'.

Journalists were sharper to respond to Motherlant's rebuke than to the details of the original stories. The writer in *Le Temps* adduces Corneille and Hugo in support of his view that people have always complained that the sense of honour is not what it once was. Dismissing Montherlant's three examples, he proposes a lesson to the self-appointed 'professeur d'honneur à la génération nouvelle': 'M. de Montherlant a raison: on ne doit jamais rabaisser ce qui est noble. Il faut pourtant choisir la noblesse authentique. Comme M. Mauriac souhaite la résurrection du mot "gloire" dans l'éducation des jeunes filles, souhaitons celle du mot "honneur", pour éviter l'atonie, la dégénérescence et l'asphyxie de l'humanité. M. de Montherlant, même si ses exemples persuadent mal, a raison de sonner l'alarme.'[11] Not entirely pleased at being thus damned with faint praise, Montherlant chose to see in this riposte only further proof of defective powers of discernment. In a follow-up article he sardonically quotes the journalist to the effect that Dimitrief was exploiting an opportunity to disguise his desperate act as heroism: 'Le voici bien des nôtres. Il ne gênera plus personne.' And in the journalist's proposal to resurrect honour, he seizes on the unfortunate phrase 'S'il est un snobisme bienfaisant, n'est-ce pas celui-là?' to conclude: 'Définition 1933 de l'honneur: snobisme et mythomanie. Nous voici fixés.' If civilian suicides such as these are mocked and discredited, says Montherlant, small wonder that young men turn to war where self-sacrifice in the interest of a higher ideal wins admiration and praise. In all of this, the *fait divers* is made a pretext for a debate on the moral state of the country. The assassination of the President of the Republic is linked with the idiosyncrasies of the *chiens écrasés* to make important points about the links between the individual and national politics, between private impulses and historic events.

The Papin sisters, the notorious maids who murdered their mistress and her daughter and featured in the news between their arrest in February 1933 and their trial in October of the same year, similarly generated much public soul-searching on questions such as social hierarchies, criminal responsibility, and the involvement of psychiatrists in the judicial process. We have seen how their violence opened up perspectives on human reality that the surrealists chose to link with the provocations of Lautréamont.[12]

Simone de Beauvoir, on the other hand, was familiar with many typical bourgeois households where servants were treated in a cavalier manner, and the story, though horrible, to her was 'tout de suite intelligible'; responsibility lay with 'tout cet affreux système à fabriquer des fous, des assassins, des monstres qu'ont agencé les gens de bien'.[13] Sartre has his protagonist–narrator in 'Erostrate' comment on the famous photographs: for the antihumanist Paul Hilbert the contrast between *avant* and *après* reveals above all the fragility of the sisters' 'ressemblance si bien pensante, qui mettait tout de suite en avant les liens du sang et les racines naturelles du groupe familial'.[14] In this view then, the horror poses a challenge to notions of blood ties and the ideological construction of the family as a natural organism.

Sartre's interest was to prove enduring: his review *Les Temps Modernes* gave pride of place in November 1963 to a major study of the psychiatric implications by Dr Louis Le Guillant. This issue had been a major bone of contention in the case: the so-called psychiatric experts at the trial denied that the accused were suffering from any mental defects. De Beauvoir and Sartre had actually been disappointed to perceive clear signs of paranoia in the girls, since this weakened their favoured interpretation of events as the product of social injustice and their instinctive view of the maids as avenging angels: 'Nous répugnions à le croire et continuâmes sourdement à les admirer,' de Beavoir writes. Besides, they were wary of Freud's ideas in general, since the theory of the unconscious seemed to diminish individual freedom and responsibility. However, Sartre's Paul Hilbert actually endorses an approach that sees in the sisters' action 'un forfait où le hasard a la plus grande part'. His refusal to credit them with the initiative for their actions accommodates – and of course highlights – his wish to go one better and carry out a crime which would express conscious hostility to the system and thereby achieve the notoriety he aspires to: 'que ne puis-je espérer d'un crime entièrement conçu et organisé par moi?' Hilbert therefore embodies an attempt to realize the fantasy Sartre and Beauvoir had had about the sisters.[15] In reality, so far as Sartre's and Beauvoir's reactions to the actual Papin trial were concerned, their reservations about psychoanalytic method were immaterial: 'Cela ne nous empêcha pas de nous indigner quand les psychiatres de service les déclarèrent saines d'esprit.' Indeed the psychiatrists' contribution to the proceedings generated a wide range of counter-analysis in the press – largely from those of a literary turn of mind. Louis Martin-Chauffier, director of the magazine *Vu* but also, at this time, engaged in editing Gide's *Œuvres complètes* for Gallimard, highlights the confusion among the officially-appointed psychiatric experts, castigating 'incompétence du responsable, légèreté des autres' and concluding: 'Toutes les questions essentielles sont demeurées sans réponse, non peut-être parce qu'elles

Figure 3a

Figure 3b

The Papin sisters. Photographs reproduced in *Le Surréalisme au Service de la Révolution*, with the captions *avant* and *après*. (See pp.39–40.)

étaient insolubles, mais parce qu'elles n'ont pas été posées.'[16] Martin-Chauffier goes on to develop an argument prompted by the extraordinary, almost autistic intimacy of the relationship between the two maids (at one point Christine said of Léa, 'C'est drôle, j'ai l'impression d'avoir été autrefois le mari de ma sœur.'). 'On imagine combien, chacune ressentant plus vivement encore que les siennes les humiliations de sa sœur, devaient se multiplier en se réfléchissant les rancunes de ce couple qui, en quelque sorte, constituait un troisième et monstrueux personnage.' Credit for perceiving the significance of this phenomenon must go to Dr Logre, the psychiatric expert who was brought in by the defence to testify, and whose contribution was largely ignored – chiefly because its subtlety escaped the jury and most of the rest of those present. He alone, says Martin-Chauffier, had 'posé l'existence de ce troisième personnage qui est, je pense, le véritable meurtrier'.[17] When Jean Genet wrote his play *Les Bonnes*, which derives from the same case, he seems, either consciously or instinctively, to have had this interpretation in mind. The blurring of the boundaries of the human subject, the interpenetrability and interchangeability of the maids' identities and their dissolution in a third, joint persona, lies at the heart of the work. Sartre's own interpretation of Genet's play, in *Saint Genet, comédien et martyr*, specifies its source in the Papin sisters, and moreover seems to echo Martin-Chauffier's analysis of the case. Writing of the lack of differentiation between the sisters, he says: 'leurs dissemblances sont des rêves qui dissimulent mal une identité foncière. [. . .] En réalité Genet a mis en scène *un seul objet* mais profondément truqué, ni un ni deux, un quand nous voulons le voir deux, deux quand nous voulons le voir un: le couple ancillaire comme pur chassé-croisé d'apparences. Et le lien qui unit ces deux reflets est lui-même un rapport truqué . . . etc.'[18] Something similar might be advanced, *mutatis mutandis*, about the collaborative interpretation of the Papin case that emerges from this interchange, over almost twenty years, between these literary commentators.

If the case of the Papin sisters sent a shudder through the ranks of the servant-employing classes while a corresponding thrill excited the champions of the oppressed, an analogous polarization was provoked when Violette Nozières was arrested in August 1933 on suspicion of poisoning her parents. This time, however, it was not a simple question of the servants rising up to attack the citadel of bourgeois privilege; the threat came from within the very ranks of the respectable classes and crystallized around the spectre of female sexuality within the family (Violette, admitting her promiscuity, counter-attacked by accusing her father of having abused her sexually). As an editorial in *Détective* put it: 'On constate avec tristesse, avec effroi, que ce qui était l'ordinaire destin d'êtres voués à l'infamie tend désormais à gagner un rang plus élevé de l'échelle sociale, comme une vague de boue qui monterait peu à peu.'[19]

One reaction was expressed in the slogan 'jeunesse pourrie' : the *bien pensant* press, having as they put it 'mainte fois fustigé' this phenomenon, was at pains to place the culprit at arms' length.[20] The complexity of the ideological situation, however, can be seen in the disarray of the arguments adduced. On the one hand, Violette is portrayed as a victim of circumstances which had taken her out of her depth; on the other hand an editorial in *Détective* calls for extreme severity in dealing with 'ce jeune monstre' whose respectable background gave her no excuse for falling into crime, as opposed to the less fortunate offspring of jailbirds and prostitutes whose misdemeanours habitually brought them 'travaux forcés à perpétuité'.[21] On the one hand, she has allegedly been 'envoûtée, *contrainte au parricide*' by manipulative decadents, while on the other hand she is vilified as a systematic and devious liar who 's'est édifié un astucieux système de défense' designed to 'tirer un bénéfice du trouble qu'elle a semé dans les esprits'. But again, she is 'une pauvre fille qu'un changement trop brusque de milieu avait déséquilibrée' and it would be scandalous if the upper-class young predators who battened on her should remain 'libre, eux, de fonder paisiblement un foyer'.[22]

The unsavoury sexual components of the scandal were put down to the spread of a certain *freudisme de mauvais aloi* which meant that it was fashionable in bohemian student circles to boast about sexual particularities and to bring a certain relish to the analysis of psychological idiosyncrasies.[23] That other element of the story, the so-called 'pègre latine' which was a contributory factor in leading Violette astray, receives its own analysis. Extensive features on the students and hangers-on in the bars, *boîtes de nuit* and *dancings* of the Montagne Sainte Geneviève and the Boul'Mich' produce a strikingly faithful reworking of the plot of *Les Déracinés*. Petit-bourgeois provincial parents send their sons to Paris in pursuit of diplomas and entry into careers as lawyers and doctors, without proper consideration of the material or moral implications, on the assumption that the youngster 'se débrouillera'. The argument is supported by quotations purporting to be from the students themselves: 'Les "paternels" nous lâchent ainsi, avec quelques centaines de francs par mois, dans le quartier le plus cher de Paris, dans l'atmosphère la plus dissolvante et la plus exaltante à la fois, où tout brûle, la peau et la volonté. [. . .] Sans blague, croyez-vous que la plupart d'entre nous ne seraient pas mieux dans leur province?'[24] This constitutes a telling testimony to the tenacity of Barrès's influence, despite his death in 1923 and the attacks on him by Gide and the surrealists alike.

Clearly the details of the affair of 'la fille aux poisons' touch numerous raw nerves in society, and indeed the press mobilized many spokespersons and commentators in a multiplicity of surveys and *enquêtes* which sought the views of policemen, pathologists, psychiatrists, lawyers, the famous 'sexologist' Magnus Hirschfeld, housewives, intellectuals and so on. The impenetrable enigmas presented both by the facts (which remained in dispute) and their interpretation were bound to prompt a rich crop of interpretative hypotheses. The deep-seated significance of the case is testified to by the fact that even after her imprisonment (her death sentence commuted to twenty years' hard labour) Violette continued to command wide coverage at every juncture of her life right down to her rehabilitation in 1963 and her death in 1966.

It seems likely that these incidents and the background from which they arose nourished – whether directly or through the press coverage – literary texts portraying the generally-perceived decadence of the 'youth culture' of the era: texts such as Nizan's *La Conspiration* (1938) and Drieu la Rochelle's *Gilles* (1939), as well as 'L'Enfance d'un chef' in Sartre's *Le Mur* (1939) (we have already seen that the Papin sisters feature in 'Erostrate' in this latter collection). At a trivial level, we have only to look at photographs of Sartre and Nizan taken at the time to see that they too subscribed to the fashionable image embodied by Violette's *comparses*: 'des jeunes gens aux lunettes cerclées d'écaille, aux cravates énormes, aux cheveux huilés'.[25] For both Sartre and Beauvoir this was one of many *faits divers* of the early 1930s that provided ammunition for social criticism. 'Nous accordions un prix particulier à toutes les turbulences qui mettaient à nu les tares et les hypocrisies bourgeoises, abattant les façades derrières lesquelles se déguisent les foyers et les cœurs,' she says.[26] She recalls that Violette Nozières was arrested while the Papin trial was proceeding, and that 'il se trouva un chroniqueur judiciaire pour rapprocher les deux affaires: il réclamait une impitoyable sévérité à l'égard de "toute cette jeunesse dévoyée."'[27] For Beauvoir and Sartre the chief similarity consisted in the fact that Violette too was above all a victim of social forces which despite being unsettled by the case, 's'employèrent à étouffer la vérité'.[28]

Other literary commentators were similarly drawn to the troublesome aspects of the affair that the mainstream press clearly had difficulty dealing with and sought to resolve with cultural and journalistic clichés. Jean Paulhan wrote a short story entitled 'La petite Violette', included in his *Les Causes célèbres*, in which he focuses on the adolescent's sexual awakening, dating it from her first kiss on 6 March 1927 (she would be twelve at the time). Paulhan locates the source of her subsequent misfortunes 'dont il serait injuste de faire grief aux parents Nozière [sic]' in 'le plaisir qu'elle avait longtemps attendu et qui ne se montra guère', concluding that 'Comme elle était froide et ne se résigna pas à l'être, elle avait chaque jour davantage à rattraper.'[29]

Georges Duhamel, asked for his opinion by *Détective*, offered psychosocial comment, stressing the unconscious complicity the public manifests towards criminals of this kind: 'J'ai senti combien les criminels rendent service à la majeure partie des êtres, en commettant pour eux un acte qui les obsèderait. Comme il est triste de voir les gens, même dans leur réprobation, assouvir leur besoin de crime! Ceux qui agissent les libèrent. [. . .] Quand je pense aux passions que cette affaire a déchaînées dans le cœur d'honnêtes gens qui se croient très tranquilles, je me sens plein d'indulgence pour cette malheureuse.'[30]

Drieu la Rochelle approached the subject from a similar angle, in a major article he wrote for *Marianne* shortly after the arrest.[31] For him the story touches the great themes – family, love, money, death – which unite individuals who in other respects live solitary or fragmented existences: people are therefore 'plus touchés dans leur rêverie que dans leur morale'. But the unanswered questions it raises turn the *fait divers* into an *affaire* because people are uncomfortable when perplexed, and feel compelled to take up positions and pass judgement on the issues. 'Il s'agit [. . .] ma foi, je risque le mot [. . .] d'une espèce de politique.' The political interest for Drieu lies in the fact that the reaction cuts across social divisions, 'ne range pas les gens selon leur intérêt, la classe ou la culture'. Moreover, while those around him are jumping to crude conclusions he dwells on the uncertainties and complexities involved, confessing himself mystified by the ineptness of the parents, the thoughtlessness of the young people involved, the apparent impenetrability of the facts. But finally, for Drieu, the salient fact is the unsettling effect of the case on the public at large, highlighting as it does in them a capacity for something other than the banal prejudice and the 'sadisme des concierges' into which, however, they inevitably fall once more: 'Quelque chose remue, saute en eux – lors d'un tel événement – et puis, tout de suite, cela retombe, cela se couche, cela rampe vers le repos, vers le parti pris . . .' In all this, we can see, perhaps with the benefit of hindsight, the incipiently fascistic attraction for Drieu of the shock of the irrational as a means of rousing the population from its torpor. His indignation at the complacency and decadence he laments in his other works underpins his final challenge here: 'Mais si vous êtes du jury, par hasard? Alors vous verrez, une fois dans votre vie. Tout d'un coup, on vous forcera à entrer dans le détail, dans le terrible détail [. . .] peuple songeur.'

When the *instruction* was drawing to a close, Colette published a commentary in which, among other things, she permitted herself to speculate on the resemblances she discerned in photographs of the father and the daughter. Both had faces that expressed 'le reproche des faibles, le mécontentement de ceux qui n'ont jamais lutté contre eux-mêmes'. Drieu too had written of the 'épouvantable capacité des êtres qui ne peuvent se gouverner eux-mêmes et à qui il vient des enfants. Et puis cette enfant unique qu'on charge d'égoïsme dès la plus tendre enfance.' But for Colette what in the father can be 'de séduisants travers virils, transmis à un être féminin, subissent un décantage propre à épouvanter'. However, lest she be construed as pleading on behalf of a criminal she knew nothing about,

Colette restricts her comments to general observations on matters she does claim knowledge of: 'La jeunesse la plus compliquée, la plus mal connue peut-être, est celle de notre bourgeoisie modeste.' The wretched constraints of maintaining a threadbare respectability, keeping up appearances while struggling to make overstretched ends meet can, she says, be an 'école d'héroïsme': but it can also provoke desperate unseen surges of revolt and impulses to escape: 'Tout, mais plus jamais l'odeur du ragoût et du gaz, ni celle du lit camouflé en divan!' Colette's imaginative projection into this miserable petit-bourgeois existence is compelling. She looks to the trial as an occasion when 'deux étrangères, deux ennemies, la mère et la fille, vont affreusement combattre. [. . .] Mais du moins la fille mettra fin au rêve confus, atroce, qu'elle mûrit si longtemps, entre sa mère l'étrangère et son père l'inconnu.'[32]

While therefore Duhamel, Drieu and Colette all see in her case the stuff of reverie and fantasms, it is typically the surrealists who projected those phantasms in the harshest light. For them Violette was a heroine: like Germaine Berton and the Papin sisters she was a woman who had risen up against her particular oppression. She embodied the force of sexual desire and scandal, and posed a challenge to patriarchal authority and to the family, to respectability and social propriety. The group published a brochure in her honour, which was printed in Brussels in December 1933 and seized by French customs officials at the frontier, as the surrealists had feared (or hoped). It contained contributions from sixteen of their number, including poems by Breton, Eluard and Char, and artwork by Magritte, Max Ernst, Man Ray and Salvador Dali. Breton calls Violette 'Mythologique jusqu'au bout des ongles', and in a poem containing (like many in the collection) numerous allusions to details which had nourished the *faits divers*, he refers to her father having 'choisi pour sa fille un prénom dans la première partie duquel on peut démêler psychanalytiquement son programme'. He affirms: 'Devant ton sexe ailé comme une fleur des Catacombes [. . .] toute hiérarchie finit'; and he is even prepared to forgive her boyfriend who had allegedly been a supporter of *Action française*, saying he 'Cesse d'être mon ennemi puisque tu l'aimais'. In another poem Gui Rosey indicates the solidarity that binds the artists to the criminal as he writes of 'la personnalité inconnue/ poétique/ de Violette Nozières meurtrière comme/ on est peintre'. He also shows how she embodies timeless psychological undercurrents that challenge respectability: 'On voit le bras d'Œdipe toujours vert le long des siècles/ fendre la foule des amours endimanchés.' Paul Eluard's lines have a similar resonance:

Violette a rêvé de défaire
A défait
L'affreux nœud de serpents des liens du sang.[33]

It can be seen, once again, that there are ideological and political strands entwining with the poetic, psychological or sensational in all these responses. As history evolved, the former tended to predominate. Certainly, foreign and domestic politics and international tensions visibly reduced the prominence accorded by the newspapers to the Papin trial in September 1933. The derisive rejoinder to Montherlant from which we started, printed on the front page of *Le Temps* on 8 October 1933, used in its parting shot a maxim gloatingly cited from one of Motherlant's own works: 'Les dictateurs naissent dans les maisons où l'on ne sait pas donner un ordre à la bonne.' 'Elle est fameuse,' remarks the journalist – presumably because he considered it put Montherlant in an ironic position *vis-à-vis* the trial of the Papin sisters whose outcome the paper had reported in precisely the preceding week, on 1 October 1933 in particular. The maids' murderous frenzy had indeed apparently been triggered by an ill-judged comment from their mistress. But more tellingly, the journalist is connecting it to developments in Germany following Hitler's election as Chancellor in January 1933 and his seizure of power in March of the same year.[34] In the month that saw the Papin trial Drieu is asking in his article on Violette Nozières whether her trial will clarify the confusion about her motives – but adds a parenthesis: 'Mais serons-nous encore là pour le procès? Hitler ou Roosevelt auront peut-être repris la vedette, et sérieusement.' It is striking, however, that even as this shift of attention is under way, political anxieties are injected explicitly into reports on *faits divers* rather than kept separate from them. Anxieties about political prejudice linked with procedural improprieties in the Gorguloff trial in France obviously carried through to intellectuals' views on the Papin and Nozières cases: but perhaps just as pertinent in the evolving climate was the arrest of Dimitroff and other suspects following the Reichstag fire in Nazi Germany in February 1933, and their notorious rigged trial in March 1934. In any case, with the end of 1933 and the eruption of the Stavisky affair in France, politics subsumed the *fait divers*. The riots of February 1934 and their consequences were followed by the assassination of Foreign Minister Louis Barthou and King Alexander of Yugoslavia by a Croatian nationalist acting on orders from Mussolini. This last incident occurred on 10 October 1934 – the very day that Violette Nozières' trial began. Much as Drieu la Rochelle had predicted, such events brought about a revision of news values, with the effect that the *fait divers* as such commanded less attention and ideological debate crystallized around more explicitly political material. This state of affairs could only be intensified by Stalin's show trials, and by general historical trends in the late 1930s.[35]

Notes

1. *Le Sang des Autres*, Paris, Gallimard-Folio, 1945, pp.296–7.
2. Gide makes the point after interviewing survivors from the First World War: see *Journal 1889–1939*, Paris, Pléiade, 1951, pp.913–4. Camus reports a similar situation in respect of soldiers from the Second World War: 'Ils répètent les journaux. Ce qu'ils y ont lu les a bien plus frappés que ce qu'ils ont vu de leurs yeux' (*Carnets I*, Paris, Gallimard, 1962, p.234).
3. See Raymond Queneau, *Zazie dans le Métro*, Paris, Gallimard-Folio, p.36.
4. For a case-study of this process, see Edgar Morin, *La Rumeur d'Orléans*, Paris, Seuil, collection Points, 1969.
5. See Dominique Borne, Henri Dubief, *Nouvelle Histoire de la France contemporaine*, vol.13, *La crise des années 30, 1929–1938*, Paris, Seuil, collection Points, 1989, pp.73–103. For the more highly-politicized elements among the surrealists the situation quickly became more sharply defined: see above, pp.76–8.
6. See above, pp.33–45 on the creation of *Détective* during this period; and pp.53–66 on the interest shown by Gide and Mauriac. Romi, *Histoire des faits divers*, Paris, Editions du Pont-Royal, 1962, pp.104–6, comments that 1933 was particularly 'favorable aux chroniqueurs'.
7. *La Rumeur d'Orléans*, p.29. Similarly, Roger Clausse points out that the need for contact with the news varies in nature and intensity 'sous l'influence de facteurs individuels, collectifs ou sociaux' (*Le journal et l'actualité*, Paris, Marabout Université, 1967, p.18).
8. 'Service inutile' in *Mors et Vita. Service Inutile*, Paris, Gallimard, 1954, pp.274–7. Unless otherwise indicated, all quotations in the following discussion are taken from these pages.
9. Suicide was a topic of intense debate during the 1920s and 1930s. Marcel Arland sounded a warning in his article 'Sur un nouveau mal du siècle' in *La Nouvelle Revue Française*, no.125, February 1924, p.156. In March 1925 the review *Clarté* published an editorial on the subject 'Le suicide est-il une solution?'; later the same year *Le Disque vert* published the responses to a questionnaire it had addressed to certain prominent figures. (See Marie-Claire Bancquart, '1924–1929: une année mentale', introduction to *La Révolution surréaliste*, pp.vi–vii.) Gide documented many suicides in the *Nouvelle Revue Française* during 1926–7. *La Révolution surréaliste* made a particular point of reproducing press reports of suicides, to begin with as part of the surrealists' own survey launched in the first number, December 1924. Jacques Rigaut and André Gaillard were to enact their own answer to the question in 1929; René Crevel followed suit in 1935. See above, p.82 n.3 and 4.

10. *La Force de l'Age*, Paris, Gallimard, 1960, p.137.
11. *Le Temps*, 8 October 1933, p.1.
12. See above, pp.39–40.
13. She speaks of them and the case in *La Force de l'Age*, pp.136–7.
14. *Œuvres romanesques*, Paris, Pléiade, 1981, pp.272–3.
15. That the sisters were an object of fantasy for them is evident in Beauvoir's comment, 'Nous rêvâmes à leurs nuits de caresses et de haine, dans le désert de leur mansarde', *La Force de l'Age*, p.137. See above, pp.39–40.
16. Jérôme Tharaud and Jean Tharaud, who covered the Papin case for *Paris-Soir*, cast serious doubt on the personnel and the procedures available for forensic psychiatry and remarked: 'Qu'il reste un doute très grave sur la responsabilité des sœurs Papin, c'est l'évidence même. Qu'un supplément d'enquête médicale fût nécessaire, j'en suis aussi persuadé' (8 October 1933, p.2). The forensic psychiatrist was of course a *bête noire* of the surrealists. Breton in particular, after some hostile critical responses to comments on the subject in *Nadja*, had taken the forensic psychiatrists to task in 'La médecine mentale devant le surréalisme' of 1930, in which he had referred to a number of miscarriages of justice, spoken of 'le croissant abus de pouvoir de gens en qui nous sommes prêts à voir moins des médecins que des geôliers, et surtout que des pourvoyeurs de bagnes et d'échafauds', and declared that 'le médecin qui consent . . . à se prononcer devant les tribunaux, si ce n'est systématiquement pour conclure à l'irresponsabilité complète des accusés, est un crétin ou une canaille, ce qui est la même chose' (*Point du Jour*, Paris, Gallimard-Folio, pp.90–1). These circumstances no doubt account in part at least for the fact that it was in the surrealist review *Le Minotaure* that Jacques Lacan published in December 1933 his essay 'Motifs du crime paranoïaque: le crime des sœurs Papin' (*De la psychose paranoïaque dans ses rapports avec la personnalité*, Paris, Seuil, 1975, pp.389–98), taking his authority from Dr Logre: 'elle nous couvre du reproche de porter un diagnostic sans avoir examiné nous-même les malades' (p.391). The dispute over psychiatric evidence at the Papin trial focused on the career of Dr Truelle, the prosecution's expert witness. 'Quand le chef de l'Etat fut assassiné par Gorguloff, qui choisit-on, dans une affaire aussi grave, pour examiner l'assassin? . . . Et dans cette affaire Nozières, qui affole aujourd'hui l'opinion, qui donc le tribunal de la Seine a-t-il désigné encore comme expert?' The Tharaud brothers, noting this courtroom statement on the subject, record that the barrister adds: 'La cour d'assises, c'est le guignol' (*Paris-Soir*, 8 October 1933, p.2). Certainly there is something grotesque in the recurring presence of this so-called expert who had clearly become the butt of anti-establishment forces in the course of a saga of

miscarriages of justice.

17. *Vu*, no.290, 4 October 1933, p.1521.

18. Paris, Gallimard, 1952, p.567.

19. *Détective*, 7 September 1933, no.254, p.2.

20. *Détective*, 31 August 1933, no.253.

21. *Détective*, 14 September 1933, no.255, p.1.

22. Ibid., p.3.

23. *Détective*, 21 September 1933, no.256, p.3. The sensitivity about psychiatric interventions resurfaces in the case of Violette Nozières in the form of fears that facile Freudianism will get her off: 'Des experts vont examiner la meurtrière: des rapports vont être écrits sur sa psychopathie. On va discuter à perte de vue sur sa mentalité de monstre. S'il est prouvé que la fille du cheminot a été victime de la passion criminelle de son père, elle bénéficiera des circonstances atténuantes . . .' (Id.) See above, note 16.

24. 'La Pègre latine', *Détective*, 21 September 1933, no.256, p.8.

25. Ibid.

26. *La Force de l'Age*, p.135.

27. Ibid., p.138.

28. Id.

29. *Les Causes célèbres*, Paris, Gallimard, 1950, pp.27–30.

30. *Détective*, 2 November 1933, no.262, p.2.

31. *Marianne*, 6 September 1933, p.10.

32. *Œuvres complètes*, vol.14, Le Fleuron, chez Flammarion, 1950, pp.268–70.

33. An echo of the title of Mauriac's *Le Nœud de Vipères* (1932) can be discerned here. The *plaquette* was reprinted in 1991: *Violette Nozières, Poèmes, dessins, correspondence, documents*, preface by José Pierre, Paris, Editions Terrain Vague, 1991.

34. *Le Temps*, 8 October 1933, p.1.

35. We have seen (p.44) that sales of *Détective* fell away in the second half of the decade, appearing to confirm this hypothesis.

7

The News and the War

The relative importance of the *fait divers* appears to decline as people experienced the invasion of their lives by politics and history in the slide to the Second World War. To enable us to understand a little of what this means in practice, we might pay attention to the page layout of the newspapers which reported this process. Certainly there is evidence that some writers of fiction approach the reconstruction of historical experience in this way.[1] As an illustrative example we will consider the case of Eugen Weidmann, the serial killer who was arrested near Paris in December 1937 along with his accomplices and confessed to having murdered six people. The first wave of interest following Weidmann's arrest coincides with the agonies of the Front Populaire, thus providing more evidence that political disorientation and anxiety can interact with the sensationalism of the *fait divers* rubric.[2] The run-up to the Christmas holidays perhaps also accounts in part for the huge amount of front-page news space the story was accorded. It dominated the papers from 10 December 1937, when the arrest was first reported, through to the New Year.

The position this story occupied in the following year is fairly precisely noted by Sartre in *L'Age de Raison*, the first volume of *Les Chemins de la Liberté*, which alludes to events in mid-June 1938.[3] The hero Mathieu, conscious of hovering on the brink of the historical maelstrom and tormented by the social and political responsibilities that his freedom entails, buys a copy of the newspaper *L'Excelsior*, and finds it emblazoned with front-page headlines about the fascist bombing of Valencia. 'Mathieu tourna la page, il n'avait pas envie d'en savoir plus long,' we are told. What does he come across? 'Du nouveau sur l'affaire Weidmann', among other things.[4] Here the texture of immediate experience, including the recoil from history towards the *fait divers* even while the former shoulders the latter aside in the news, is explicitly bound up with turning the pages of a newspaper; the process becomes the very stuff of the literary narrative.

Weidmann again occupied the front pages at the time of his trial, in March and April 1939, and once more on 17 and 18 June 1939, marking his execution. But by the time Weidmann came to trial, Hitler had annexed

Austria and there was increasingly little doubt about his intentions. During the trial Franco defeated the Republicans in Spain and Hitler invaded Czechoslovakia. These events did not eclipse the *fait divers*, however. The cataclysms of history and the drama of the courtroom were actually reported side by side on the front pages. In the newspaper *L'Œuvre* the second day's court proceedings appeared on 12 March alongside the headline 'La révolte communiste serait enfin vaincue à Madrid.' On 16 March the headlines read 'Quatrième épisode de l'affaire Weidmann: l'assassinat du chauffeur Couffy' and 'Hitler a fait son entrée à Prague. Fin de la Tchécoslovaquie.' On 17 March it was 'La Slovaquie à son tour subit le sort de la Bohême. Elle est pratiquement rattachée au Reich'; and 'Weidmann l'assassin et Million le fossoyeur de Jeanine Keller'. The sentence of death was passed on Weidmann and Million on 1 April, two days after Poland rejected German demands and the day after Britain guaranteed its support of the country against the Nazi threat. The reasons why the *fait divers* remained on page one despite the urgency of the broader political situation are complex, but it seems clear that while the international situation seemed increasingly beyond the control of ordinary French people (and even of French politicians), at home here was a German who could be dealt with. It is of course quite possible to see a parallel between the two sets of reports. The story of how the German psychopath – 'le monstre allemand' as *Détective* called him[5] – crossed the frontier into France and massacred a number of French citizens (as well as a German and an American) might have been read as a fable for what the German war-machine was doing (would do) across Europe. It is true that at the outset, the reporter in *L'Œuvre* of 16 March comments, 'On a un peu honte à parler longuement de cette affaire Weidmann, quand d'autres drames plus angoissants, qui se déroulent en Europe, occupent les esprits.' But the *fait divers* forces itself into the limelight regardless of this acknowledged inappropriateness, and the connection between the two sets of events was not lost on the defence lawyer. Maître Maro-Giafferri also apologized for pleading on behalf of Weidmann while terrible crimes were being perpetrated in Spain and Central Europe: but in so doing he was acknowledging the hostility felt towards the German as a perceived representative of the fascist aggressors. Moreover, he exploited this perception when he sought to explain Weidmann's barbaric instincts by referring to the history of the German people.[6] In the event his remarks came close to sparking an international incident, since German radio took the barrister violently to task for suggesting that Weidmann's German origins explained his murderous conduct.[7]

The Weidmann case took on a literary dimension independently of intervention by the *littérateurs*. Maître Renée Jardin, reports *Paris-Soir* of 30 March 1939, 'chercha avec beaucoup d'émotion la "vérité psychologique" de Weidmann. Elle emprunta la voix de Ludmilla Pitoëff pour faire des remarques qui évoquaient tantôt Mauriac, tantôt Dostoievsky, quelquefois Eugène Sue.'[8] But this was not the only instance of its kind, since Colette had been commissioned to write 'les impressions d'audience du procès' for *Paris-Soir*. Parts of these reports, in modified form, were later published in her *Œuvres complètes* under the title 'Monstres'.[9] Among other remarks, she refers to Weidmann's physical appearance as having the allure of the vampire in *Le Docteur Caligari*.[10] But in *Paris-Soir* of 2 April, in a text printed after the death sentence had been pronounced and not subsequently reproduced, she explores in more telling detail the nature of this monster's charm. This text, which merits extensive quotation because of its intrinsic interest as well as its comparative inaccessibility, is the more audacious and significant for being written against a background of intense anti-German feeling:

> Délivrons-nous d'abord d'un malaise qui allait grandissant. Malaise qui n'était point la nausée banale, la banale horreur qu'inspire un criminel rebutant, mais un étrange vacillement, dangereux pour l'équilibre de notre raison. Notre sens du social et du moral qui luttait contre un parti pris favorable formé, fortifié en nous au cours du très long procès. Nous n'acceptions pas sans nous débattre qu'un assassin hideux ait, d'un bout à l'autre des audiences, conservé la dignité corporelle, la mesure dans les mots, le refus de s'apitoyer sur lui-même, qu'il ait pris soin de ne jamais en appeler à notre compassion, voire à notre intérêt; mais, en nous débattant, nous l'acceptions. Un accablant dossier, la répétition du geste homicide, ses motifs bas, nous retenaient – j'allais écrire: heureusement – dans ce glissement vers la faveur, que nieront, seuls, ceux qui n'ont pas assisté à l'affaire Weidmann.
>
> Que devons-nous appeler un criminel horrible? Celui qui nous remplit d'effroi, non par ce qu'il nous présente de bestial et de grossièrement terrifique, mais par ce qui le rapproche de nous, nous rend sensible sa ressemblance avec nous. Quoi, ce 'monstre' qui a sauté la barrière, mis entre lui et nous un espace aussi incalculable que la fallacieuse étendue répercutée par deux miroirs en face l'un de l'autre, il était hier notre semblable? Bien plus, il est encore aujourd'hui, sur le banc de chêne tout paré des doux dehors humains, de l'humaine chaleur persuasive? Quoi, il dépendait d'un moment effréné, d'une ivresse, d'une erreur, que nous nous précipitions vers une ressemblance avec lui plus profonde? Cela fait trembler – et nous avons tremblé.[11]

Colette's insights cut through the highly-charged atmosphere to actualize the physical magnetism of the man and convey something of the unsettling experience of confronting a monster who was so patently a human being too. They lay the foundations for subsequent literary identifications with

Weidmann, as we shall see.

The time and date of Weidmann's execution were announced on the radio and published in the press, with the result that an unruly crowd gathered round the guillotine in the course of the night, and police and troops had to drive them back at dawn for the execution to take place. So repugnant was the spectacle, reported (with copious photographs) in the papers on 18 June 1939, that on 26 June it was decreed that executions would no longer be carried out in public. This was thus the last execution at which the condemned man could, if he felt so inclined, 'souhaiter qu'il y ait beaucoup de spectateurs le jour de [s]on exécution et qu'ils [l]'accueillent avec des cris de haine', as Meursault puts it at the end of *L'Etranger*. Camus had sketched this ending as early as 1938[12] – thus before the Weidmann trial – though he did not complete the novel till 1940, to see it published in 1942. Its concluding lines had thus already been overtaken by events at the time they appeared in print, and represented an anachronism. We know that Camus had an almost obsessive interest in the death sentence, having been haunted from an early age by a story his mother told about his father's reactions after having attended a public execution. He has Meursault recall such a story[13] and regret that he had not taken more interest in capital punishment when he had the opportunity: 'rien n'était plus important qu'une exécution capitale', Meursault realizes, and he tells how he resolved that, 'Si jamais je sortais de cette prison, j'irais voir toutes les exécutions capitales.'[14] Clearly this will not be possible for him: he has himself been condemned to death and it is part of Camus's purpose to denounce capital punishment by stressing its irrevocable nature. But now we see that even if this had not been the case the option was not available to anyone, let alone Meursault, after 18 June 1939. Of course when the novel was published in 1942, under the German Occupation, such quibbles would have appeared inappropriate, even unseemly: perhaps this is one reason why Camus felt he could maintain the conclusion despite the fact that he knew as well as anyone how its significance had altered. It is also of interest to consider how Meursault attempts to rectify the general ignorance about what happens at a beheading. He had been the victim of a popular misconception, he points out, stemming from the iconography of the French Revolution which tends to suggest that the condemned person climbs to the guillotine up steps to a platform (from which, for example, s/he can make noble speeches to the crowd).

> Mais un matin, je me suis souvenu d'une photographie publiée par les journaux à l'occasion d'une exécution retentissante. En réalité, la machine était posée à même le sol, le plus simplement du monde. Elle était beaucoup plus étroite que je ne le pensais. C'était assez drôle que je ne m'en fusse pas avisé plus tôt.

Cette machine sur le cliché m'avait frappé par son aspect d'ouvrage de précision, fini et étincelant [. . .] la machine est au même niveau que l'homme qui marche vers elle. Il la rejoint comme on marche à la rencontre d'une personne.[15]

Here Meursault highlights the way in which the glamour of historical representations falsifies the physical reality. The perception works in the same way that Colette's remarks do, and will be ratified by Tarrou's denunciation in *La Peste* of the images that travesty the brutal facts of political and judicial execution: 'vous en êtes resté aux estampes et aux livres'.[16] The photograph Meursault refers to is almost certainly one taken at the execution of Weidmann. It was published widely in the newspapers and in particular in *Alger-Républicain*, on which Camus was a reporter, in June 1939.[17] In his *Réflexions sur la guillotine* of 1957, Camus actually recalls the tasteless press coverage of the execution in *Paris-Soir*, indicating that the photographs enabled the 'bon peuple parisien' to 'se rendre compte que la légère machine de précision dont l'exécuteur se servait était aussi différente de l'échafaud historique qu'une Jaguar peut l'être de nos vieilles de Dion-Bouton'.[18] 'Ouvrage de précision', 'machine de précision'; the echo, though perhaps unconscious, is telling, as is the common nature of the revelation involved. By the time he wrote this latter essay, however, Camus could complain that the reasons for the 'mesure relativement récente' making this the last public execution had been wiped from people's memories by the intervening years. Perhaps a part of his irritation stemmed from the irrevocable effect this now forgotten measure was to have on the significance of *L'Etranger*. What is certain is that the immediacy of the *fait divers* and the accompanying photograph impressed themselves enduringly upon Camus even while the greater forces of history were overtaking him and millions like him with dizzying speed.

At the height of the German Occupation of France, Camus wrote a series of articles entitled *Lettres à un ami allemand*, addressed to an anonymous misguided German who had given way to nihilism to the extent of furthering the Nazi cause. It is unlikely, however, that Camus had Weidmann in mind, given that he is clearly not susceptible to the glamour of the criminal *de droit commun*. In his specific reference to Weidmann of 1957, Camus calls him slightingly the 'auteur de plusieurs meurtres, que ses exploits avaient mis à la mode'.[19] His detachment is perhaps partly explained by the fact that being a newspaperman himself, he is more conscious than most of the way in which such glamour is manufactured by the press. A journalist will tell Meursault, 'Vous savez, nous avons un peu monté votre affaire.'[20] But it is equally well worth pointing out that by 1957 Camus had built on the thesis of the *Lettres à un ami allemand* by completing that critical scrutiny of the criminal impulse and its intellectual apologists which is an important feature of *L'Homme révolté*. He had done

Figure 4 © AFP Document Photo, France.
Execution of Eugen Weidmann.'Je me suis souvenu d'une photographie publiée par les journaux à l'occasion d'une exécution retentissante' (see p.106).

this quite deliberately in an effort to free himself as well as his contemporaries from the spell of such individuals as Weidmann. An important theme of *L'Homme révolté* is that the distorted construction of history by which the twentieth century has been blighted is in no small measure due to the misplaced sympathy for the criminal that inspired early rebels.[21] In other words, Camus's purpose was to purge history of its contamination by the *fait divers*. Thus the detachment he shows towards Weidmann twenty years after the case has perhaps been hard won.

Be that as it may, an aspect of Meursault's trial appears to link it to another notable feature of the Weidmann affair. Both Colette and the *Paris-Soir* staff reporter remarked on the detachment from the proceedings which the defendant showed at his trial: '[. . .] il s'éloigne de nous',[22] she wrote; and her colleague noted: 'Feint ou sincère, son détachement paraissait absolu. Il était impossible de n'en être point frappé.'[23] After the announcement of the sentence, when his lawyer mentioned the possibility of an appeal, Weidmann is reported as saying: 'Merci, maître, mais je suis déjà plus loin que cela.'[24]

Meursault evokes this process from the point of view of the defendant. Particularly in chapter 4 of the second part of the novel, he indicates how his involvement in matters wanes as the court procedures seem to acquire their own momentum and exclude him. In fact, Camus derives considerable satirical effect from Meursault's distanced presentation of the barristers' rhetoric. When this culminates in the defence lawyer's usurping Meursault's own first person pronoun to speak on his client's behalf, the hero is briefly surprised, but accepts the situation with the comment, 'J'étais déjà très loin de cette salle d'audience'[25] – an echo, perhaps, of Weidmann's phrase (which as we shall see drew the attention of at least one other novelist of note).

We have seen that Sartre evokes the Weidmann case as an ingredient in the history of the period. Another significant if less obvious reference occurs in *Les Mouches*. This play, which was of course staged under the German Occupation, contains a piece of tongue-in-cheek social criticism by Jupiter which seems to refer back to the impact on the populace of the suspension of public executions following the guillotining of Weidmann. The King of Mount Olympus explains that this was how Agamemnon lost his grip over the people of Thebes, allowing them to decline into a state where they stood by and welcomed his assassination by Egisthe: 'Agamemnon était bon homme, mais il eut un grand tort, voyez-vous. Il n'avait pas permis que les exécutions capitales eussent lieu en public. C'est dommage. Une bonne pendaison, cela distrait, en province, et cela blase un peu les gens sur la mort. Les gens d'ici n'ont rien dit, parce qu'ils s'ennuyaient et qu'ils voulaient voir une mort violente.'[26] An allusion to the guillotine here would have been too anachronistic, but the wry implication is nonetheless evident, and fits appropriately with the play's allegorical concern for resistance in the face of oppression and Occupation: had public executions been maintained, the cynic suggests, the French people would not have accepted so passively the defeat of their rulers by the Germans.

In the light of the evidence so far assembled, we can better appreciate the impact of the opening lines of *Notre-Dame-des-fleurs*, which make it clear that Jean Genet was especially struck by the case: 'Weidmann vous apparut dans une édition de cinq heures, la tête emmaillotée de bandelettes blanches, religieuse et encore aviateur blessé, tombé dans les seigles, un jour de septembre pareil à celui où fut connu le nom de Notre-Dame des Fleurs.'

In fact the whole book is summed up here. The novel's climax when Notre-Dame achieves notoriety as hero of the *fait divers* is exactly prefigured and exemplified in the serial murderer. The allusion is to a famous photograph, published in *Paris-Soir* on 10 December 1937, of Weidmann's appearance before the examining magistrate after having sustained head wounds during his arrest.[27] That Genet is precisely recalling *Paris-Soir*'s coverage of the arrest is made explicit when he indicates that 'Sous son image, éclataient d'aurore ses crimes: meurtre 1, meurtre 2, meurtre 3 et jusqu'à six.'[28] A noteworthy feature in Genet's presentation of the photograph is that though it predates the outbreak of the war, Genet, evoking it in 1942, can retrospectively read into it an expression of the hostility between France and Germany that as we have seen was latent in 1937–9, but existed for real as he wrote (and glorified in it, especially in *Pompes funèbres*). Hence Weidmann's bandaged head gives him the appearance of an aviator and produces in Genet 'une ferveur comparable à celle qui me tordit, et me laissa quelques minutes grotesquement crispé, quand j'entendis au-dessus de la prison l'avion allemand passer et l'éclatement de la bombe qu'il lâcha tout près.'[29] What Camus appears to have shied away from is made manifest here: Weidmann is associated with the Nazi invasion of France – which Genet welcomed as retribution visited on the society that had condemned Genet himself.

At the outset of his novel, Genet catalogues the sources from which he culled clippings and photographs of his criminal idols' exploits and stuck them to the cell wall; he then integrates their notoriety into his autobiography, as he announces his intention to 'écrire une histoire [. . .] ma propre histoire' of which they and he will be the heroes.[30] In contrast to Queneau's Turandot, Genet seeks precisely to project his life not into 'l'Histoire' with a capital 'H', but into 'la factidiversialité'. Certainly, as he concludes his book and appears to accept the prospect of a life in prison, Genet quotes verbatim a second time, and makes his own, a sentence he has highlighted in the opening pages of the novel: he reproduces those

Figure 5 © AFP Document Photo, France.

'Weidmann vous apparut dans une édition de cinq heures, la tête emmaillotée de bandelettes blanches . . .' (see p.110)

words Weidmann spoke to his lawyer after receiving his sentence: 'J'ai résigné mes désirs. Moi aussi, je suis "déjà plus loin que cela" (Weidmann).'[31] Both Genet's biographer, and the most recent chronicler of the Weidmann case on whom he relies, cast unjustified doubt on the authenticity of this quotation, mistakenly seeing it as a distorted citation from a different source: but the evidence of the *fait divers* report is clear enough.[32]

Genet's prose work is a spiritual autobiography modelled on the lives of the criminals who have inspired him. His fascination for Weidmann is a constant of this perverse enterprise. Perhaps finding inspiration and authorization in Colette's reports on the powerful charisma of the murderer, Genet identifies closely with him. Indeed, it is probably not by chance that he gives the date of Weidmann's first appearance in the papers, erroneously, as September rather than December 1937: that was the date when he himself made his début in the *fait divers* rubric of *Le Petit Parisien* on receiving his first prison sentence. Nor would it have escaped his notice that Weidmann was executed on the same day Genet was jailed in Châlon-sur-Saône.[33]

As late as the *Journal du Voleur* Genet returns to the photograph of Weidmann alluded to at the start of his first book, and analyses its qualities. Second-rate villains whose photos he compares this with look unimpressive, and not just because of the nature of the print, the angle of the photograph: 'Ils avaient la mine de gens pris au piège, mais à celui qu'ils se sont tendu, au piège intérieur.' Weidmann is a different case altogether, since he defies the image-appropriating machinery of the media: 'Sur la très belle photo qui le montre dans ses bandes Velpeau Weidmann blessé par le flic qui l'arrêta, c'est aussi une bête prise au piège, mais à celui des hommes. Contre lui, sa propre vérité ne se retourne pas pour enlaidir sa gueule.'[34] As Colette had put it, despite their notoriety and personal magnetism criminals like Weidmann remain essentially elusive since they are 'pour notre esprit, hors de portée'.[35] For this reason, Weidmann has a fundamentally aesthetic, timeless value for Genet, standing as a precursor of Saïd in *Les Paravents*.[36] On the copy of the photograph cut from *Paris-Soir* which Genet dedicated to Olga Kechelievitch in November 1944, he wrote: 'j'offre éternellement l'image d'un archange ensanglanté pris au piège de la police des hommes.'[37]

Genet therefore begins by glorifying in Weidmann the bloodthirsty invader who wreaks havoc among the French people and in the imagination of those respectable bourgeois whom Genet hated because their society excluded him. Through the establishment of chronological and other correspondences, the hero of the *fait divers* becomes the embodiment of a personal vengeance which takes on historic dimensions. Ultimately, however, he progresses even beyond history to become a constellation in Genet's poetic heaven.

While Genet relished the French public's inability to comprehend, appropriate or assimilate this irredeemable monster, Michel Tournier also invokes Weidmann, in *Le Roi des Aulnes* – but makes of him more a victim of the mediocre society he terrorized. Abel Tiffauges, the narrator–hero whose 'Ecrits sinistres' constitute the first part of the novel, sets the Weidmann affair against a background of the disreputable politics of the dying days of the Third Republic.[38] His personal narrative is interspersed with allusions to both the historical information and the *fait divers* he reads concurrently in the newspapers. He is thus a clear example of the phenomenon of interaction between the two which we are concerned with.

In all likelihood taking his inspiration from Genet, Tournier structures this part of his novel around an identification that develops between Abel Tiffauges and Eugen Weidmann. Furthermore, in order to establish a close connection between this process and the historic decline into war, Tournier alters the chronology, for example having Tiffauges read of Weidmann's arrest on 9 December 1938.[39] This is precisely a year later than in reality: but it locates the whole affair in the period following Munich and Ribbentrop's visit to Paris on 6 December 1938 and presents it thereby as an integral part of that inglorious phase of history. (Tournier also increases the number of murders from six to seven, in keeping perhaps with the pseudo-cabbalistic patterning which Tiffauges will increasingly perceive at work in his existence.) At a practical narrative level, however, this chronological alteration entails the compression of allusions to the *instruction* into the period between December 1938 and March 1939 (RA, 155, 162, 164); the trial is said to be in progress on 3 June 1939 (RA, 183), whereas in fact it began in March and was over by 2 April. President Lebrun's refusal of clemency and the subsequent execution, reported on their true dates of 16 and 17 June, thereby seem to come with unseemly speed: but this has the effect of underlining Tiffauges's view that Weidmann is being ignobly treated by a régime whose characteristics amounted to 'ce tour de force: allier l'insignifiance à l'abjection' (RA, 166).

Tiffauges lives out the identification with Weidmann that Genet's novels are built on. He records a series of coincidences that make this identification seem fateful: 'On dirait que le destin s'acharne à le rapprocher de moi' (RA, 184), he says on discovering that Weidmann is left-handed like himself, that the murderer's crimes are *sinistres*, like Tiffauges's writings. He has noted earlier that the German's height and weight are precisely the same as his own (RA, 155), and elsewhere that they were both born on the same date: 'Ce sont des rencontres qui me blessent plus que je ne saurais le dire', he writes (RA, 164). This is because he feels immense sympathy for the accused, as he says, in the face of 'le spectacle du corps social tout entier attaché à la perte de cet homme seul, accablé de crimes' (RA, 183–4).

Weidmann is seen to be a victim insofar as the forces ranged against him, and particularly the institution of capital punishment, are even more despicable than his crimes, however numerous these latter are. Having read that 'l'abject Lebrun' has refused to commute Weidmann's death sentence, Tiffauges declares indignantly: 'Y a-t-il un crime plus abominable que celui de cet homme chamarré, assis derrière son bureau monumental, libre de toute pression, qui refuse d'accomplir le petit geste qui arrêterait la perpétration de l'assassinat légal?' (RA, 185)

Tournier has carefully prepared the ground for this *prise de position*. Tiffauges's intimate interest in the subject has been prefigured by an earlier reflexion on capital punishment (RA, 65) and by a passage referring to a jet of cold water which 'comme un couperet de guillotine m'est tombée sur la nuque' (RA, 75). Tournier has previously had his hero attack the moral basis of the judicial system in 'la société effrayante où nous vivons'(RA, 82–3). Prompted by statistics he reads in the press for the number of people who disappear without trace, and assuming that so-called 'normal' deaths conceal a fair proportion of disguised murders, Tiffauges concludes that the vast majority of murders go undetected and the cases that come to court are purely symbolic, intimating a respect for life which is quite spurious. Moreover, echoing Benjamin Péret's notorious denunciation of 'l'assassin Foch', Tiffauges notes the 'culte des assassins qui fleurit à la lettre à chaque coin de rue, sur les plaques bleues où sont proposés à l'admiration publique les noms des hommes de guerre les plus illustres, c'est-à-dire des tueurs professionnels les plus sanguinaires de notre histoire'. He concludes: 'notre société a la justice qu'elle mérite' (RA, 82–3).

The epitome of this morally bankrupt society and judicial system is the account of Weidmann's execution which Tournier/Tiffauges chronicles at length and with notable fidelity to the facts as set out in contemporary reports. The climate of 'ignoble fébrilité' (RA, 185) hanging over the crowds and the atmosphere of 'complicité crapuleuse' (RA, 186) in which the grotesque deed is carried out leave Tiffauges nauseated. However, his companion Mme Eugénie cries out at the striking physical resemblance she sees between Weidmann and Tiffauges himself: 'Ma parole, on dirait votre frère! Mais c'est vous, Monsieur Tiffauges, c'est tout à fait vous!' (RA, 190). As the culmination of allusions previously indicated, the overall effect of the experience is to leave Tiffauges unable, as he puts it, to 'recouvrer l'équilibre que m'a fait perdre l'assassinat de Weidmann' (RA, 192).

Soon after, Tiffauges is arrested on a charge of raping the young girl Martine he has been attracted to. Like Meursault, he finds that his previous innocuous existence is reconstructed in a judicial perspective to prove 'avec une rigueur implacable' (RA, 199) that he is necessarily a criminal. Though he begins by disputing the facts, one thing does emerge: Tiffauges, with his 'vraie tête d'assassin' (RA, 200)[40] – a reminder of the Weidmann parallel

– is about to fulfil his 'destin' as an object of the hatred of the mob, earlier hinted at when he mentioned his fear of being lynched (RA, 127, 202). 'Le Destin était en marche, et il avait pris en charge ma pauvre petite destinée personnelle' (RA, 200), he says. However, this destiny, encompassing the connections with Weidmann as we have seen, from being a projection into 'la factidiversialité' quickly becomes a matter for 'l'histoire': Tiffauges's fate is bound up with 'l'Histoire' with a capital 'H', which he is convinced is also 'en marche' (RA, 201). It is therefore with considerable serenity that he reads the *Code pénal* in prison, confirming and reiterating his view that the judicial system is a 'pesant magma de bêtise, de haine et de cynique lâcheté' (RA, 203). The declaration of war leads to the release he has come confidently to expect, and in the confusion of mobilization he sees the fulfilment of a hidden purpose only he understands.

Sure enough, some twelve months later, Tiffauges is able to witness the fall of France and to indicate that this 'cauchemar de fin du monde', occurring 'une année jour pour jour après l'assassinat de Weidmann à Versailles' is in effect 'le châtiment prévu et mérité de la plèbe veule et cruelle' (RA, 234).

Like Genet, Tiffauges's story exploits retrospectively the historic confrontation of two nations implicit in the Weidmann affair. Maître Maro-Giafferri had sought to explain Weidmann's crimes with reference to the history of the German people. Tiffauges, alienated from France by the hostility he experienced there towards those of his kind, and identifying in his feelings of persecution with the victimized Weidmann, lives out a compulsion to explore the mentality and mythology of the murderer's nation.

Tournier's novel is a complex and subtle work and I am considering merely a small corner of it. But it seems reasonable to suggest, on the basis of this evidence, that the dynamic of the narrative, seeking as it does to espouse and illuminate the broader sweep of history itself, achieves this end in part at least by constructing an imaginative discourse midway between 'l'histoire' and 'la factidiversialité'. In so doing it continues a dialogue which seems in turn to be a significant part of literary history, as our examination of the fortunes of this and other news items has sought to indicate.

Notes

1. A good example would be Aragon, who adopts this strategy towards the period before the First World War in *Les Beaux Quartiers* (1936), which is also visibly informed by current affairs in the early 1930s when it was being written. Similarly *Les Cloches de Bâle*, published in 1934,

had introduced into its portrayal of Doumer's political role in 1911 a reference to his assassination twenty-one years later while Aragon was writing the novel (Edition Folio, pp.355–6).

2. See Dominique Borne and Henri Dubief, *Nouvelle Histoire de la France Contemporaine*, vol.13, *La crise des années 1930*, Paris, Seuil, 1989, pp.186–7.

3. This is the date arrived at on the basis of textual evidence by Contat and Rybalka, in their edition of Sartre, *Œuvres romanesques*, Paris, Pléiade, 1981, p.1940.

4. *L'Age de Raison*, Gallimard-Folio, 1945, pp.140–1.

5. *Détective*, 2 March 1939, no.540, p.8.

6. *L'Œuvre*, 30 March 1939, p.5.

7. *Paris-Soir*, 1 April 1939, p.3.

8. *Paris-Soir*, 30 March 1939, p.3.

9. *Œuvres complètes de Colette*, Vol.13, Paris, Le Fleuron, chez Flammarion, 1950, pp.435–41.

10. Ibid., p.440.

11. *Paris-Soir*, 2 April 1939, p.3, cols. 4 and 5: 'Le dernier jour, Weidmann a souri à la mort.' This item is omitted from the bibliography in the latest volume of the Pléiade edition: Colette, *Œuvres*, vol.3, ed. Claude Pichois, Paris, Gallimard, Bibliothèque de la Pléiade, 1991. According to chronology, it should appear in the forthcoming volume 4 in the series. It would appear that Colette was not the only woman to acknowledge such sentiments. *Détective*, no.540, 2 March 1939, has a report that refers to 'Ce monstre, que certaines «piquées» ne craignent pas de déclarer non antipathique (elles n'osent pas encore dire sympathique) . . .' Colette's comments on Weidmann assume their full significance when read as part of her remarkable ongoing, long-standing meditation on the criminal in articles such as those she devoted to Landru and Mahon.

12. See Camus, *Carnets I*, Paris, Gallimard, 1962, pp.143–4.

13. Albert Camus, *Théâtre, récits, nouvelles*, Paris, Pléiade, 1962, p.1203.

14. Ibid.

15. Ibid, p.1204.

16. Ibid., pp.1422, 1424.

17. This is indicated by Jacqueline Lévi-Valensi in a review of a thesis by André Abbou: *Albert Camus 14*, *Revue des Lettres Modernes*, 1991, p.202.

18. Albert Camus, *Essais*, Paris, Gallimard, Bibliothèque de la Pléiade, 1965, p.1025.

19. Ibid.

20. *Théâtre, récits, nouvelles*, p.1185. See below, pp.139–53.

21. Similarly, Camus appears to have had little time for the cult that surrounded Genet. See my 'Le criminel chez Camus', in *Albert Camus*,

les extrêmes et l'équilibre, proceedings of the Keele colloquium, edited and presented by David H. Walker, Amsterdam, Rodopi, coll. 'Faux Titre', 1994, pp.17–32.

22. *Paris-Soir*, 19 March 1939, p.4.
23. *Paris-Soir*, 1 April 1939, p.3.
24. *Paris-Soir*, 2 April 1939, p.3.
25. Camus, *Théâtre, récits, nouvelles*, p.1199.
26. Jean-Paul Sartre, *Huis Clos suivi de Les Mouches*, Paris, Livre de Poche, p.86.
27. The photograph is referred to in similar terms later in the novel. See *Notre-Dame-des-fleurs*, in *Œuvres complètes de Jean Genet*, vol.2, Paris, Gallimard, 1951, p.67.
28. Edmund White neglects to mention this, drawing instead, for his assessment of Weidmann's presence in the text, exclusively on the coverage in *Détective* which appeared almost a week later: see *Genet*, London, Chatto and Windus, 1993, pp.181–2.
29. *Œuvres complètes de Jean Genet*, vol.2, p.10.
30. See my 'Antecedents for Genet's persona', in *Existentialist Autobiography*, ed. T. Keefe and E. Smyth, Liverpool, University of Liverpool Press, 1995.
31. *Œuvres complètes de Jean Genet*, vol.2, p.174: the initial, full quotation is on p.12. The source, as indicated above, is *Paris-Soir*, 2 April 1939, p.3.
32. See White, *Genet*, pp.182–3, and p.748, n.49. The erroneous supposition to which White gives credence is in Roger Colombani, *L'Affaire Weidmann*, Paris, Albin Michel, 1989, p.259.
33. See Harry E. Stewart and Rob Roy McGregor, *Jean Genet: a Biography of Deceit 1910–1951*, New York, Peter Lang, 1989, pp.93–4; Albert Dichy and Pascal Fouché, *Jean Genet. Essai de chronologie 1910–1944*, Paris, Bibliothèque de littérature française contemporaine, 1988, pp.159–60.
34. Jean Genet, *Journal du Voleur*, Paris, Gallimard, 1949, pp.159–60.
35. *Œuvres complètes de Colette*, vol.13, p.438.
36. See Walker, 'Antecedents for Genet's persona'. White, *Genet*, pp.294, 368, provides evidence to show that the picture of Weidmann was transformed into a veritable icon: Genet gave copies to his friends and hung it in rooms he inhabited.
37. White, *Genet*, photographs between pp.372 and 373. White's translation of this text on p.294 is inaccurate: he appears to have misread the handwriting.
38. I shall be considering only 'Les Ecrits sinistres' in my discussion of *Le Roi des Aulnes*. The material covered in this section constituted the whole of the novel in an early version written by Tournier some ten

years before the final full text. See *Le Vent Paraclet*, Paris, Gallimard-Folio, pp.193–4.

39. *Le Roi des Aulnes* (hereafter RA), Paris, Gallimard-Folio, 1970, p.151.

40. The severed head links Weidmann and Tiffauges with the headless child referred to later in the novel, and with a significant series of allusions to wounded flesh: see Emma Wilson, 'Tournier, the body and the reader', *French Studies*, vol.47, no.1, January 1993, pp.43–56, especially at p.45 and p.54 n.7.

8

The Aftermath of Calamity

The state of French culture in the immediate post-War years can be gauged from the literary history of the time as mirrored in the Prix Goncourt winners. On the face of it the picture is as we might expect: 1944 – Elsa Triolet, *Le premier accroc coûte deux cents francs*; 1945 – Jean-Louis Bory, *Mon village à l'heure allemande*; 1947 – Jean-Louis Curtis, *Les forêts de la nuit*. The pattern is clear, predictable and representative of literary endeavours in the country (indeed the continent) at large: these novels – like *Le Sang des autres* of 1945 and *La Peste* of 1947 – all emerge from the attempt to come to terms in one way or another with the experience of the Second World War and the Occupation.

But if these texts singly and in sequence reflect the recent experience of history, is there not a crack in the mirror? Amidst this understandable consistency, what are we to make of the Goncourt winner of 1946: Jean-Jacques Gautier, *Histoire d'un fait-divers*? The exception to the pattern indicates the persistence of our second dimension of history.

Such was the case in reality. Looking back in a work published in 1978, Georges Perec would write: 'Je me souviens qu'après la guerre il y eut une "affaire Petiot" qui ressemblait à l'affaire Landru.'[1] The 'affaire Petiot' arose following the discovery in March 1944, in a house in Paris, of the remains of a large number of murder victims. The arrest of Dr Marcel Petiot in October 1944 and his eventual trial in March and April 1946 received enormous press coverage, due no doubt to the fact that France was occupied by the Nazis when the case first broke. The collaborationist newspapers exploited the investigation as a means of boosting circulation, and the occupying forces looked upon it benignly as a useful diversion from the evolution of the war. Liberation in August 1944 changed the picture somewhat: when Petiot was arrested in October 1944 – at a time when the *épuration* of former collaborators was officially beginning – it was an episode right-thinking people preferred to shun. Albert Camus's newspaper *Combat* poured scorn on the trivial-minded individuals who took an interest in such matters. Camus himself complained about them in an editorial on 8 September,[2] and, on 1 November, the paper acknowledged its duty to communicate the facts as news, but announced to its readers that it would not be seeking to exploit the details of so sordid a case at a time when too many tragic and urgent problems demanded the attention of the nation.[3]

Roger Grenier, the novelist and critic who worked as a journalist on *Combat*, would later recall this high-minded proclamation and its aftermath, in an article entitled 'Utilité du fait divers' published in *Les Temps Modernes* in 1947. Without naming the newspaper, he notes its principled opposition to *faits divers* and all that panders to the 'goût dépravé du public': and reveals that when Petiot came to trial 'ce journal fut celui qui accorda le plus de place au compte rendu des audiences.' Why should this be so? Grenier thinks he has the answer: 'Parce que ses rédacteurs avaient compris que le fait divers, dont ils avaient raison de rejeter le côté sordide, contenait une riche matière humaine qui valait la peine d'être révélée. Et il n'y avait rien de bas dans ce qu'ils ont publié sur le docteur [. . .] .'[4] Indeed, as Grenier points out, *Les Temps Modernes* itself featured a study on the case in July 1946 (shortly after Petiot's execution in May). Its author was Albert Palle, who had actually covered the trial for *Combat*, and who in this article tries to explain why a society which is still overshadowed by the monstrous aftermath of the Second World War can take an obsessive interest in a squalid, apparently trivial matter.[5] After all, when the prosecuting counsel referred at the trial to the sanctity of human life, the spectators in the gallery, having endured or witnessed ordeals at the hands of the Nazis, could only laugh.[6] Following the First World War the case of the mass murderer Landru (who had spent the war killing women) had provided a diversion: 'La guerre est décidément finie, on va pouvoir parler d'autre chose,' one commentator put it.[7] As well as a welcome change of obsession, the Landru case marked a return from the exposed terrain of History to the more comfortable familiarity of the private domain, the abnormal psychology of an individual. But for Palle, Petiot presented an instance of a different type: 'L'affaire Petiot semble au contraire, non plus la revanche du drame privé sur le drame social, mais la manifestation pathologique de ce dernier.'[8] Palle goes on to argue that, far from being a distraction, the case actually lent itself to the elaboration of a myth enabling the public to direct at Petiot the sense of outrage they felt at all the murders committed during the Occupation: 'Petiot pouvait être l'occasion d'une purification. Il était tentant de le charger de tous les crimes inexpliqués et absurdes de toute une époque.'[9] Petiot claimed to have connections with the Resistance, with the result that the public's need to establish in black and white the contours of an era most notable for its shades of distressing grey expressed itself in an intense vilification: 'Petiot est le traître qui ne saurait être trop épouvantable d'une histoire dont le héros, celui de la résistance, ne saurait être trop merveilleux. Mais ni l'un ni l'autre ne sont aussi purs qu'on le voudrait.'[10] Just as Weidmann catalysed anxieties when war loomed, so Petiot is a focus for the traumatized psyche of a society which has just emerged from the troubling illegality of the Resistance: 'Les meurtres de Petiot plongent leurs racines dans l'état pathologique d'une société contrainte d'encourager l'assassinat et le pillage, par conséquent de saper les fondements mêmes de son existence pour survivre.'[11] Ultimately, Petiot becomes a monstrous emblem of an even more general metaphysical disorder: 'Ce criminel du vingtième siècle dont on a pu parler; démesuré jusqu'à la démence, sans individualité, témoignage d'une société marquée par le nihilisme et qui ne sait plus engendrer que la mort.'[12]

If a vulgar *fait divers* can serve in this way to map the mentality of an era and a society in crisis, there is evidently more to it than meets the eye. It is on this basis that Grenier argues the usefulness of the form.[13] But he also suggests that its role is variable over time. Looking back to Thomas de Quincey, he repudiates the purely aesthetic perspective, the equivalent of art for art's sake: 'Dans les sombres forêts du crime, l'assassinat considéré comme un des beaux-arts n'est qu'un genre étrange et maladif. Appartenant de nature à la littérature vécue, le fait divers éveille comme elle les sentiments intéressés de l'homme avide de se connaître. L'émotion artistique est en supplément, comme le couronnement.'[14] Arguably this reflects the sentiments of a period when Sartre's *Qu'est-ce que la littérature?* codified the notion of the committed writer. Nevertheless, Grenier's approach to his subject remains substantially literary, as he suggests that *faits divers* can be categorized in the same way that plays can: just as we have 'un théâtre de caractère et un théâtre de situation', so we have 'deux genres de faits divers: les faits divers psychologiques et les faits divers de situation'.[15] Furthermore, since 'le génie de l'époque', as Grenier puts it, favours theatre of situation (and we will recall that the writings of Sartre confirm the point), so the spirit of the age 'met également en valeur l'espèce correspondante de faits divers, à la fois parce qu'elle répond mieux aux problèmes de l'heure et bénéficie ainsi d'une attention particulière du public, et parce que ses protagonistes sont "embarqués" dans le siècle et en portent la marque dans leur chair.' This provides an echo of Palle's views on the Petiot case as opposed to that of Landru, though that is not to say the 'fait divers psychologique' has no constituency; on the contrary, it offers insight into the behaviour of others and 'un témoignage rassurant' 'pour celui qui est effrayé par ce qu'il entrevoit en lui-même'.[16] But if there exists an analogy between literary taxonomy and that applicable to *faits divers*, is there a distinction to be drawn between the two domains? No, says Grenier: he has referred to the *fait divers* as 'littérature vécue', and he asserts that the reader of both derives the same experiences from the process – to the extent of defying the would-be taxonomists: 'Si l'amateur de littérature ne se contente pas de l'art et cherche une réponse à ses problèmes humains, l'amateur de faits divers ne se cantonne pas dans une attitude de curiosité humaine, et finit par éprouver une émotion esthétique. Les personnages dont il lit les aventures dans les colonnes des journaux se parent à ses yeux des qualités magiques des héros de romans.'[17]

We need not follow Grenier through all the subsequent details of an analysis in which he rapidly evokes classicism, the picaresque, romanticism and so on to suggest a history of these paraliterary forms that culminates in the modern heroes of the absurd and the avant-garde *à la* Genet to show how each movement in culture finds its counterpart in the *fait divers*. Suffice it to say that in 1948 these deliberations will reappear under the chapter heading 'Le Mythe du fait divers' in *Le Rôle d'Accusé*, a volume published in the collection 'L'Espoir' which Camus edited for Gallimard; and that 1953 saw the publication of Grenier's first novel, *Les Monstres*, bearing epigraphs from Proust and Baudelaire, including the line: 'Je ne comprends pas qu'une main pure puisse toucher un journal sans une convulsion de dégoût.'[18]

This novel depicts the *fait divers* industry, focusing on the staff of a weekly magazine. Alluding to some of the issues outlined above, Grenier evokes the state of numbed cynicism in which, having lived through ten years of massacres, torture, hunger and slavery, the hard-bitten habitués of the newsroom go about their business in 1950: 'Nous ne sommes que des survivants, à titre précaire. Dieu sait quelle fin nous attend.'[19] The hero of the novel is a *fait-diversier* who chases up his sensational stories with due professional ruthlessness, but with growing disquiet: 'Ces choses qui, pour l'immense majorité des hommes, n'existent que sous forme de papier imprimé, étaient, pour le reporter, des réalités écrasantes' (M, 49). In the course of his work he also lends himself to monsters whose stories he is ghost-writing: a mass murderer and an executioner's assistant, 'à la place de qui il disait "je"' (M, 49, 231). The narrative thus traces out the effects on a man of a close involvement with the reality behind the *fait divers*, an involvement that causes him to question the news industry's relation to human mortality: 'Qu'avaient donc les journaux, et qu'avait donc le public, à courir ainsi après le malheur des autres, comme si leur mort et leur sang pouvait [sic] adoucir notre agonie?' (M, 214). He had started out cynical, manipulative, uninvolved, we learn: 'J'ai accepté cet état de journaliste pour rester spectateur et ne jamais être "engagé". Je m'aperçois que je me suis trompé. Les événements commencent à agir sur moi', he tells a colleague (M, 81). The gesture in the direction of Sartrean commitment will develop into a critique of the magazine's treatment of the *fait divers*. A climactic argument with the news editor offers an extended analysis. This latter maintains that the reporter's role is to take a horrific incident and 'rendre ce sujet acceptable, d'en faire quelque chose propre à intéresser, à émouvoir, à divertir le grand public, sans choquer aucune de ses idées. On peut choquer ses sens, par une information extraordinaire, mais pas ses idées [. . .] il ne faut jamais s'attaquer aux moules étroits de sa pensée.' Just as the reporter must make his story fit the space allocated to it on the page, so he must not exceed the ideological space determined by the magazine's editorial style and the prejudices of its readership. The purpose of the rubric, argues this old pro, is to 'ordonner, simplifier, schématiser la réalité, lui donner la cohérence qu'elle n'a jamais'. The *fait divers* therefore is not an incident as it occurs – which is merely banal, 'un fatras incompréhensible et sans intérêt' – but a reworking in accordance with a more consistent, more conventional view of the truth (M, 124–5). The reporter, however, is forced to acknowledge that constant exposure to what he will term 'ces *faits* qui n'avaient rien de *divers*' (M, 214) has caused him to lose 'le sens de la mesure': 'Je ne sais plus où j'en suis,' he confesses, but he denounces 'cette accumulation de sottises et d'ignominie' that the magazine serves up to its 'imbéciles de lecteurs' (M, 125). Ultimately the editor admits that he shares his reporter's reactions to the brute facts he encounters every day, but that cowardice motivates him to sustain the veneer his journal puts on them.

The reporter thus becomes a figure of the alienated hero of the time, succumbing to moral relativity and even nihilism, that supreme twentieth-century sickness. Confronted on a daily basis with murderers and the other 'monsters' of the novel's title, his powers of judgement have been undermined and he feels merely a generalized weary pity for humankind: 'Mon Dieu [. . .] comment condamner ces hommes, si monstrueux soient-ils. C'est si compliqué, et si terrible, la situation d'homme. On est si démuni, si dépourvu de connaissances et de certitudes que toutes les erreurs, toutes les aberrations sont permises. Il n'y a pas de salauds, seulement de pauvres êtres qui cherchent ou qui croient avoir trouvé. Il faut leur pardonner.' But the narrator does not go all the way with this desperate assessment. He intervenes in the hero's meditation to point out: 'Il oubliait qu'il existe de purs gredins, des individus qui sont comme des bêtes nuisibles. Il eut un attendrissement d'ivrogne pour la condition humaine, suivi aussitôt d'une pointe d'agressivité envers ses contradicteurs éventuels . . .' (M, 123). The reporter's malaise is thus diagnosed as an indulgence, requiring to be corrected by a more discriminating perspective. His colleagues will point out that in giving way to the brutality which he transcribes he has lost his own humanity and his capacity to write. The copy he turns in is 'atroce', adopting a 'ton froid, presque rigolard, pour parler de la souffrance et de la mort'. At this reaction he realizes how far he has travelled from the norm in writing up the memoirs of an executioner: 'C'était vrai qu'il n'était plus capable d'éprouver de l'horreur en relisant ces notes. Il ne pouvait plus y discerner ce qui était insoutenable. Il eut exactement ce vertige qui saisit un grimpeur débutant, au milieu de l'escalade d'une paroi, s'il vient à se retourner et à se dire: "Comment, je suis déjà si loin au-dessus du vide!'" (M, 144). But he will not capitulate to the conventional propriety in horror required of the magazine: Grenier uses him to pursue a dialogue with representations of the unspeakable. The novel addresses what Grenier himself has said about the quasi-fictional way *faits divers* are perceived, by portraying the reporter's dealings with the actual individuals whose distress will subsequently fuel the rubric. In one section the reporter's notes are presented in fragmentary form, setting out the stark data from which he is to write up the memoirs of the executioner's assistant (M, 127–43). Now the character launches into a tirade setting these horrors alongside modern brutalities in comparison with which the *Maître des Hautes Œuvres* appears positively quaint, merely a picturesque artisan (M, 144–50). So effective are these sequences of the novel, and so striking the documentation they evoke, that Grenier's own journalistic and literary colleague Albert Camus, having first ascertained from Grenier that the facts are indeed authentic, adduced them in his essay against capital punishment, 'Réflexions sur la guillotine' of 1957.[20] Within the novel their effect on the erstwhile self-denigrating news editor is significant: 'Galiani s'était repris. [. . .] Le moment des confidences où il avait parlé de ses limites et de sa lâcheté paraissait maintenant très loin' (M, 150). Faced with the risk of contagion by a desperate vision, even this cynic reacts spontaneously by distancing himself from such an extreme. His response will be vindicated in the finale of the novel, during which the reporter, while on an assignment, is caught up in an avalanche which disables him and causes the death of a colleague. The experience restores to him the sense of self he had lost by lending his voice to monsters (M, 231), and distances him from his previous torments. It also stirs the news editor out of his 'apathie mêlée d'ironie nihiliste' (M, 231). The novel ends as the reporter, having changed his job, 'dans sa survie sans but et sans espoir, engourdie par la morphine des gestes quotidiens' realizes that 'il ne sentait plus rien de l'agonie du monde' (M, 236). Thus, in keeping with Grenier's argument in 'Utilité du fait divers', the encounter with the form is depicted as an experience with moral and metaphysical overtones that parallel the philosophical debates of the age.

Grenier's novel of course concentrates on an insider's view, not so much drawing specific inspiration from an isolated *fait divers* as showing what is involved in their production. But it does serve to illustrate the striking prominence of the form at a time when, arguably, matters of much greater import might have been expected to monopolize minds.

It was in the closing years of the decade we are considering that Nathalie Sarraute wrote two major articles setting out the theory underpinning what she had put into practice in her first two texts of fiction, *Tropismes* (1939) and *Portrait d'un inconnu* (1948).[21] A striking feature of these two essays –

striking if we recall that their author's novels concern themselves with the elusive, intimate psychological phenomena she calls 'tropisms' – is that the starting point of both is crude fact of the kind we have been dealing with. 'De Dostoïevski à Kafka' actually begins with specific reference to and discussion of Grenier's thesis in 'Utilité du fait divers'. Quoting Grenier's text somewhat approximately, Sarraute takes up his point that the contemporary era favours the 'fait divers de situation'. She argues that the alleged superior relevance of the depiction of an absurd world, exemplified by the novels of Kafka to the detriment of the psychological realm of which Dostoyevsky is the patron saint, is based on a false opposition between the two.[22] The fact that her argument quickly leaves behind all reference to the *fait divers* in pursuit of her tropistic thesis makes it all the more telling that she should mention it in the first place. She adopts a similar strategy in 'L'Ere du soupçon'. Here she broaches the subject of the reader's mistrust of the novelist's imagination by alluding at the outset to an article in *La Table ronde* of January 1948 in which Jacques Tournier bemoans the contemporary narrative's fear of admitting that it is an imaginary invention. 'Le document seul importe, précis, daté, vérifié, authentique. L'œuvre d'imagination est bannie, parce qu'inventée . . . [. . .] Plus rien ne compte que le petit fait vrai,' he had complained.[23] Sarraute, however, is only too willing to take the suspicious reader's part: '"Le petit fait vrai", en effet, possède sur l'histoire inventée d'incontestables avantages. Et tout d'abord celui d'être vrai. De là lui vient sa force de conviction et d'attaque [. . .] , cette désinvolture qui lui permet de franchir les limites étriquées où le souci de la vraisemblance tient captifs les romanciers les plus hardis et de faire reculer très loin les frontières du réel.'[24] Despite appearances, this is not a reversion to the nineteenth-century polemics of realism and naturalism. For Sarraute, documentary fact disrupts conventions of verisimilitude and propriety, liberates the novelist from accepted tenets of realism, takes her and her reader into unknown regions and unexplored depths of experience where they would not have thought to go otherwise. 'C'est donc pour de très saines raisons que le lecteur préfère aujourd'hui le document vécu (ou du moins ce qui en a la rassurante apparence) au roman,' she concludes.[25] Sarraute sees in this mistrust of convention a licence to break away from the traditional techniques of the novel – consistent characterization, impersonal omniscient narrator – which in turn enables the novelist to address a hitherto neglected kind of psychological material, to 'rendre compte des états complexes et ténus qu'il cherche à découvrir'. For Nathalie Sarraute, then, the 'document humain' furnishes the pretext for her narrative experiments. But it is far from evident what the specific connection with her own work might be: she composes virtually plotless texts in which intimate psychological tropisms with their ebbs and flows, their surges and swells, relegate to the margins any coherent sequence of external events, whether documentary or invented. André Allemand, tracing the 'facts' in *Le Planétarium*, highlights 'la discontinuité du récit' and points out that 'l'événement est trop mince'.[26]

However, a clue to the connection resides in the example Sarraute cites of a 'document humain' with the appropriate 'richesse' and 'subtilité' to serve as a starting point for a new kind of novel: 'Quelle histoire inventée pourrait rivaliser avec celle de la séquestrée de Poitiers?' she asks.[27] This notorious story, brought to prominence by Gide and Mauriac, is referred to as a 'document admirable' by Grenier, who presents a digest of it in *Le Role d'Accusé* of 1948.[28] The story was clearly in the air: the motif of involuntary reclusion struck a chord in an era which had known Occupation and imprisonment at the hands of the Nazis. Stifling enclosure is crucial to the symbolic representation of Oran in Camus's *La Peste* of 1947; Sartre was to acknowledge a direct debt in his play *Les Séquestrés d'Altona* of 1960, and the wartime sequestering of the heroine in Duras's *Hiroshima mon amour* (1960) provides another likely echo. 'La Séquestrée de Poitiers' therefore provides a perfect instance of Grenier's 'fait divers de situation', a story mirroring a collective experience.[29]

However, Nathalie Sarraute provides a striking exception to this pattern in treating the same 'document humain' very much as a 'fait divers psychologique' in her first novel *Portrait d'un inconnu*, published in the same year as Grenier's book. The link between the novel and the *fait divers* is not a humdrum matter of influence or vague inspiration. In this respect *Portrait d'un inconnu* owes much to *Eugénie Grandet*, as Sarraute has pointed out. What is worthy of remark is the way she derives crucial textual and thematic detail from the story of Mélanie Bastian, 'La Séquestrée de Poitiers'.[30] Gide's version, as we have seen, highlights the theme of claustrophilia, and the fact that the brother had a bizarre taste for filth coupled with a defective sense of smell. The extreme avarice of the parent (NJP, 240–1) and an unhappy love affair that unsettled the daughter and created tension in the household (NJP, 255), are also key ingredients which reappear in Sarraute's novel (it shares them with *Eugénie Grandet*, of course). The most obvious borrowing, however – though not explicitly acknowledged as such in the text – is a recurrent phrase widely associated with Mélanie Bastian, who after her rescue repeatedly asked to be taken back to what she referred to as her 'chère petite grotte', or less intelligibly as 'cher bon fond de moulin en piâtre' (NJP, 225) or, most famously of all, her 'cher grand fond Malampia' (NJP, 227).

Sarraute's novel presents an unnamed narrator speculating on the relationship between a father and daughter who are apparently neighbours of his. He approaches other neighbours to test his suspicions as to why the daughter apparently submits to her father's miserly domination. The narrator himself is insecure and highly-strung: he is in search of shared experience, which he acknowledges is a weakness in him. He embarks on a drama of intersubjectivity typical of Sarraute's work, seeking out a common ground – a *lieu commun*, as Sartre puts it – on which to interact psychologically with others. Aspiring to the comforting complicity of gossip, he begins, 'Ne trouvez-vous pas . . .'[31] His comments initially awaken no significant echoes, his first interlocutors proving unwilling to meet his speculations halfway: their views are trenchant and definitive – the father is 'un vieil égoïste' and 'un grippe-sou' and the daughter 'une maniaque' (PI, 19). With other neighbours, however, he finds a more congenial reception, which emboldens him to advance further: 'Alors vous aussi vous trouvez cela? [. . .] Franchement, quelle est votre impression?' (PI, 23). The question elicits an answer which is both substantial and in the event disastrous for him. This neighbour has visited their home: 'Il me semble qu'ils habitaient un vieil appartement avec des meubles 1900. [. . .] On devinait de vagues grouillements dans les coins, des choses menaçantes. [. . .] Elle faisait penser, avec sa tête un peu grosse, à un énorme champignon poussé dans l'ombre [. . .] elle devait aimer cela: leur grand bon fond de Malempia' (PI, 23). It is of course the last phrase that confirms the other elements as an allusion to Mélanie Bastian's squalid incarceration. The narrator recognizes it too, and he is gripped by panic at the position this puts him in: 'Je sens que, par ce mot, ils viennent de faire un bond subit qui les rapproche de moi. Ils ont vu comment j'ai compris, tout de suite, trop vite . . . et mon léger recul.' The complicity he was pitching for has rebounded on him. He has been caught out as a familiar of that shaming territory, the *fait divers*, in which people vicariously entertain their sordid, inadmissible fantasies through ruminating on the unseemly behaviour of others. His interlocutors continue, repeating with delectation their reminiscences of the Poitiers case, presenting in their turn a spectacle that disturbs the narrator: '"Ils devaient jouir de cela, elle et le vieux, tous les deux enfermés là sans vouloir en sortir, reniflant leurs propres odeurs, bien chaudement calfeutrés dans leur grand fond de Malempia." Ce mot a l'air de les chatouiller un peu, de les exciter' (PI, 23). He is then subjected to whispered suggestions about other insalubrious features the two households might have in common; and gradually the scatological fantasizing gathers all the participants in its repugnant embrace:

Ils rient, l'air enchanté, ils prennent et ils me jettent, de plus en plus excités, des racontars stupides, de vieilles réminiscences de faits divers, de grosses 'tranches de vie' aux couleurs lourdes, trop simples, absolument indignes d'eux, de moi, mais ils se contentent maintenant de n'importe quoi, ils prennent n'importe quoi et ils l'étalent sur moi, ils m'empoignent n'importe comment, ils nous empoignent, moi, elle, le vieux, ils nous tiennent tous ensemble, pressés les uns contre les autres, ils se serrent contre nous, nous étreignent. (PI, 24–5)

Sarraute has developed here a conception of the *fait divers* as the site or currency of a surreptitious commerce between private and collective fantasizing. It fits perfectly within the context of her tropistic experimentation as it triggers a prime illustration of the way in which inner space can be invaded and colonized by the Other. At the conclusion of the chapter the narrator evokes his interlocutor's coarse laugh and feels himself being dragged helplessly into this grubby territory by 'un rire râpeux qui vous accroche par en dessous et vous traîne . . .' (PI, 25).

Reminiscences of the 'Séquestrée', having been thus provoked in him against his will, will constitute an unwelcome component of the phantasms through which he tries – and naturally fails – to understand the relationship between the couple who preoccupy him. They surface as he imagines the daughter showing him into her apartment: he admits to 'un tremblement d'excitation pénible et douce' as he anticipates the sight of the dirty wallpaper in the hall and the 'vague odeur de poussière et d'urine, peut-être des relents de lavabo' emanating from the bathroom. He visualizes her turning to him mockingly, spotting in him the claustrophilia that attracts him to her situation: 'Elle me narguerait sûrement maintenant [. . .] : "Ah! c'est donc cela? [. . .] Les intérieurs sinistres donnant sur des cours sombres?" Elle sourirait sûrement, comme les autres, [. . .] quand ils me taquinaient, me chatouillaient, quand ils voulaient m'exciter un peu avec leur grand bon fond de Malempia' (PI, 36). Coprolitic motifs return unbidden to colour his vision and betray his own intimate compulsions as he sees the old man at the railway station, breathing in the sulphurous smoke and other smells: 'C'est pour [. . .] humer cela, avec cette volupté équivoque, au goût douceâtre, qu'on ressent à renifler ses propres odeurs, qu'il est venu ici, comme j'ai fait moi' (PI, 103–4).

Above all, the model of enclosure deriving from the *fait divers* of the *Séquestrée de Poitiers* informs his ruminations.[32] The daughter's supposed attempts to escape containment by her father culminate in a fierce quarrel which the narrator embroiders in detail. For him, this very expression of their mutual hostility is made possible by the privacy and seclusion in which it is worked through: 'Ils sont arrivés au fond, ils sont seuls tous les deux, ils sont entre eux, tout à fait entre eux ici [. . .] seuls dans leur *grand bon fond*, où tout est permis, où il n'est plus besoin de rien cacher' (PI, 187: emphasis mine). Far from being a manifestation of forcible confinement, the 'grand bon fond' is here an ideal of intimacy and psychological freedom in security. It is again indicative of the narrator's own predilections that he perceives at the heart of the relationship between father and daughter a fundamental ambivalence. That ambivalence, intrinsic to the phantasm of sequestering deriving from the *fait divers*, is brought out at the climax of the quarrel, which weaves into the portrayal of the couple a complex set of reminiscences from the Poitiers source:

Dans ce monde obscur et clos de toutes parts où ils se tiennent enfermés tous deux, dans ce monde à eux où ils tournent en rond sans fin. [. . .] L'odeur familière, fade et un peu sucrée, de leur intimité . . . Elle la sent, j'en suis sûr, elle hume avec volupté, calfeutrée ici avec lui, quand il la serre si fort [. . .]. C'était cette même saveur, cette même odeur secrète qu'elle goûtait déjà, dont elle se délectait – je le sentais confusément – autrefois, quand ils marchaient [. . .] blottis l'un contre l'autre sous les regards indiscrets, insolents des étrangers, sa menotte moite pelotonnée dans la grosse main chaude, serrée . . . *Leur fond. Leur grand bon fond* . . . [. . .] il va la tenir bien serrée tout contre lui, collés l'un contre l'autre, dans leur fade et chaude odeur, tout enveloppés de lourdes vapeurs [. . .] (PI, 189–90; emphasis mine)

The narrator corrects himself: 'Mais non. [. . .] Je ne sais pas à quoi je pensais [. . .]' (PI, 190–1). It is evident that his *fait divers* based fantasies are running away with him, colouring his construction of reality, as will be made clear in the episode in the art gallery when the daughter warns him, in effect, of his tendency to see everything in terms of his obsessions.

The fact is that the story of Mélanie Bastian is especially congruent with the tropistic undercurrents to which the narrator is susceptible. His concern is with the enclosure of the intimate self, which he needs to protect even while making overtures to others. The notion of the *fond*, central to the text of the 'Séquestrée de Poitiers', becomes therefore a key motif in Sarraute's depiction of tropistic interactions. The narrator's starting-point in respect of his 'paysage intérieur' is expressed in his 'J'ai touché le fond' (PI, 27). This explains his equivocations towards others, whom he sees ensconced in their own *fond*, their own private world, where they are 'calfeutrés', 'bien à l'abri' (PI, 40, 43, 150, 174), both impervious to his timid bids to make contact and potential threats to his own private sanctuary. In effect, he dramatizes his own insecurity through his vision of the father's intimacy being disrupted: 'arraché à son monde malléable et douillet où il se tenait calfeutré [. . .] il a été projeté brutalement dans son monde à elle [. . .] sur lequel il n'a pas de prise' (PI, 156). The fear of psychological eviction is reiterated in his image of the daughter, expelled by the father and pleading from behind the door to be readmitted to their home (PI, 194–7).

It is clear then that Sarraute succeeds in demonstrating how the *fait divers* infiltrates the intersubjective consciousness and imagination. At the same time, we can see that *Portrait d'un inconnu* is in large measure constructed out of literal and metaphorical variations on the thematic material made available in the *fait divers* of *La Séquestrée de Poitiers*. This novel stands therefore as further testimony to the importance of the form in cultural life.

The examples of the two novels we have adduced so far throw a particular light on the cultural history of the immediate post-War years. But what of the Goncourt winner of 1946: Jean-Jacques Gautier, *Histoire d'un fait divers*? For one thing, we can place it alongside the articles by Grenier and Palle which we have considered, and which appeared in the same year. This now little-known novel can also be seen to take its place in that sequence which is embodied in *Portrait d'un inconnu* and *Les Monstres*. But while these two texts are about the *fait divers* as a cultural phenomenon, reflecting as they do on the background to it, its mode of diffusion and its impact on individuals, Jean-Jacques Gautier's novel, as its title implies, purports to be more of a direct transcription of a *fait divers*. As such it sets out to restore the reality behind the constructions of the journalist and the fantasies of the reader. It also enacts an effort to promote the humble, anonymous but nonetheless intense and tragic drama of private life into an appropriate frame for public consideration. As a *fait divers*, the title and the novel seem to say, this item might attract only casual attention: by being given an *histoire*, it calls for consideration.

Its chief protagonist is Louis Cappel, who cut his wife's throat and following controversy over whether or not he was in a state of diminished responsibility, went on trial for murder. The novel begins with an account of the actual killing, by way of a prologue at the end of which the narrator declares: 'Le fait-divers est terminé. Mais un fait-divers ressemble à un fait-divers, à tous les faits divers. Il faut savoir ce qui s'est passé avant, comment on en est arrivé là, connaître l'histoire du fait-divers.'[33]

Here we see a standard theme: the *fait divers* is intensely singular, and yet falls readily into familiar categories which habitually blur our perception of the individual instance. The aim of this narrative will be to retrieve the specificity of its content from the banality of its categorization. At the same time, it will restore a narrative, and thus an explanation, to what habitually bursts into the public domain from out of the blue, its effect all the more shocking because at first sight at least it is a rupture in the continuity of the everyday norm.

An additional dimension of this novel is the bid for verisimilitude entailed by this integration within its structure of the relationship between fact and representation. The reader cannot verify whether the events in question actually did occur or were reported – whether the author is working from a real or imagined *fait divers*. The difference between the two is a matter of literary self-consciousness and degrees of irony, but either way the same strategy is brought into play. The novel lays claim to a particular credibility since it offers a model of representation that goes beyond the shortcomings which habitually attend on such cases. It points both to journalistic and other discursive mediation, and to the newspaper reader's customary casual mode of apprehension of the *fait divers*: and it ostensibly thereby establishes itself as more reliable and more serious than these.

The flashback which occupies the first three-fifths of the novel after the prologue, is pronouncedly deterministic and teleological in its approach. We are presented with insistent pointers to Cappel's character and temperament: he is naïve and easily manipulated, but subject to severe headaches and uncontrollable rages when he has been drinking; he comes from a poor background, having been raised by insensitive and somewhat unbalanced parents in an unstable marriage; he has had two marriages of his own that ended unhappily prior to the third which ended in murder; all of this presents a recipe for the almost inevitable disaster.

However, it is possible to discern elements which run counter to the apparently inexorable logic embodied in these details. For instance, Cappel's second, very happy marriage (which produced two children and ended with the untimely death from tuberculosis of a wife he loved) bears a striking parallel to the disastrous third one. He met both wives, in the street and the park, quite by chance. The encounters and subsequent relationships evolve very much along contingent lines. The suggestion is that he could just as well have been happy, fulfilled, and normal had it not been for bad luck.

Furthermore, when the third relationship acquires a sexual dimension – and intense eroticism, sexual infidelity and jealousy are major components in the story from this point on – the narrative suddenly breaks down. Suspension points across the page break the text up into discrete blocks; gaps appear in the diegesis. The narrator records one of the wife's disappearances:

> Dans les romans, l'auteur a toujours une explication prête, il a plus de chance que celui qui veut raconter une histoire vraie, et tous les rapports de police trouvés dans le dossier ne sont pas parvenus à me fixer sur ce que Fernande Cappel avait pu fabriquer dans Paris pendant ces dix jours. (FD, 182)

The dimension of the unexplained and unsubstantiated is thus inscribed into the text: the story will contain unresolved enigmas; and in a strategy that underscores precisely this point with a bid for greater verisimilitude through the multiplication of voices, the narrator's text at this stage tends to give way to the testimony of police witnesses and reports of the official investigation. Extracts from judicial interrogations are inserted into the narrative, often without warning – 'Alors en quoi avait-il changé, interrompait le juge?' (FD, 137) reads one such – and the text frequently proceeds via passages like the following:

> Le tenancier d'un débit de boissons voisin assurera que si 'Cappel était un bon gars pas compliqué pour un sou, sa femme, une gonzesse tout ce qu'il y a de

coquette et de plus, vicieuse, faisait ce qu'elle pouvait pour le rendre jaloux!' (FD, 140)

Quand, plus tard, on interrogera Mme Culotin, la concierge . . . (FD, 137)

The narrative, then, begins to both authenticate and problematize the story, presenting a series of fragmentary points of view, explicitly becoming an edited reconstruction rather than an authoritative seamless chronicle. Something of the influence of Gide's technique in *La Séquestrée de Poitiers* and *L'Affaire Redureau* can be seen in evidence – which reinforces the fiction's bid to be read as documentary. At the same time, we note what Peter Brooks calls an 'anticipation of retrospection'[34] in the cases quoted above, as well as elsewhere in 'D'après les renseignements que l'on put recueillir dans la suite . . .' (FD, 146). The narration announces its own closure: but simultaneously it adopts a technique foregrounding the openness to interpretation of the facts as available, even as it evokes the exponents of official explanation bearing down on the material.

We know from the prologue that Cappel is going to murder Fernande, and the text highlights this with references such as: 'Dès lors, l'histoire va s'accélérer [. . .] quelque chose comme le décrochage d'un des derniers crans du destin' (FD, 199). Destiny appears to operate its teleological influence: but the nature of the determinism driving events forward is left open and enigmatic.

At the last moment preceding the murder we find an evocation of an alternative, as Lucien has arranged with Fernande a meeting which might have reconciled them: 'A 7 heures, expliquera Cappel [which in itself anticipates the need for an explanation], on aurait dîné ensemble et puis elle serait partie après' (FD, 213–4). The interplay of tenses here catches us up in a web of intersecting chronologies between which the ontological status of the events evoked hangs uncertainly.

This treatment of the *fait divers*, then, has a different emphasis from the outsider's fantasizing and trading in sensation that is the stuff of *Les Monstres* and *Portrait d'un inconnu*. Rather, what we see here is another line of approach which, while highlighting the irremediable, accentuates the problematic causality and anguishing contingency of events as viewed from a perspective close to the participants. The private drama, ill-understood, ultimately incommunicable, offers little definitive purchase to the formal interpretative frames of outsiders, and something essential is lost in official reconstructions of events. With Cappel's arrest after the murder, and the first police report telegraphed to 'M. le Procureur de la République', the novel comes to an end. With 'Ça fera quatre lignes sans titre dans certains journaux du lendemain' (FD, 217) the text signals the entry of the private facts into the public domain – which ironically consecrates them as anonymous. Indicating the point at which the data is appropriated by judicial and psychiatric discourses, the narrator tells us: "'L'affaire Cappel" est commencée' (FD, 219).

This narrative thus claims temporarily to have withdrawn the events from the distorting glare of publicity, inquisitorial investigation, journalistic speculation and vicarious fantasizing which transform them into an *affaire*. In declining to pursue matters further as the case is taken up by others, the text is implicitly establishing a distinction between the experience of the protagonist on the one hand, and the rest, which is a matter of public record, on the other. In the final analysis, the novel has failed to make the events themselves cohere into a story: rather it has traced the preliminaries, showing how such a case is destined to become a story, a *fait divers*, an *affaire*, in the hands of others. The ambiguity of 'histoire' in the novel's title furnishes a reminder that, as Camus puts it: 'L'histoire n'est pas tout'.[35]

Notes

1. *Je me souviens. Les Chose communes*, I, Paris, Hachette, 1978, p.63n.230. It is noteworthy that in fact the recollection of the two *faits divers* together characteristically denies history insofar as the two cases are grouped into the one type of the monstrous mass murderer.
2. See Albert Camus, *Essais*, Paris, Pléiade, 1965, p.266.
3. See Thomas Maeder, *The Unspeakable Crimes of Dr. Petiot*, London, Penguin Books, 1990, p.155. See also p.140 below.
4. 'Utilité du fait divers', *Les Temps Modernes*, no.17, 1947, p.950.
5. Albert Palle, 'Petiot "faux résistant"', *Les Temps Modernes*, no.10, July 1946, pp.157–62.
6. Maeder, *The Unspeakable Crimes*, p.206.
7. Emmanuel Bourcier, in Béraud, Bourcier, Salmon, *L'Affaire Landru*, Paris, Albin Michel, 1924, p.26.
8. Palle, 'Petiot "faux résistant"', p.158.
9. Ibid., p.159.
10. Ibid., p.160.
11. Ibid., p.162.
12. Ibid. Cf. the status of the modern criminal touched on with respect to *L'Homme révolté* and to Genet: pp.107–8;158. Georges Bataille includes a reference to Petiot in the context of a quasi-mystical meditation on crime in *Sur Nietzsche*, published in 1944–5, between the arrest and the trial: see his *Œuvres complètes*, Paris, Gallimard, vol. 6, pp.52, 75. I owe this detail to John A. Baker, in 'L'humanisme noir de Georges Bataille,' paper presented at a conference on 'Surrealism, the scene of the crime' at the University of Manchester, April 1993.

13. For his part, Grenier had established a rubric 'Les faits divers du mois' in *Les Temps Modernes*, where from early 1946 – see nos. 9 and 10 – he had presented lists somewhat akin to those we have seen used by Jarry, Fénéon and the surrealists.

14. Grenier, 'Utilité du fait divers', pp.950–1.

15. Ibid., p.951.

16. Ibid., pp.952–3.

17. Ibid., p.953. Grenier will reiterate some of these considerations forty years later: see his article 'Le pays des poètes. Le fait divers: de l'acte à la parole', *Nouvelle Revue de Psychanalyse*, vol.31, 1985, pp.19–27.

18. The Baudelaire extract is *Mon cœur mis à nu*, LXVIII. The full text had earlier been quoted, with relish, by Marcel Schwob, writing as Loyson-Bridet, in *Mœurs des Diurnales. Traité de journalisme* in 1903, and republished by Editions des Cendres (1985, pp.164–5). Grenier's other epigraph is from Proust's 'Souvenirs d'un parricide' to which we have referred above, p.16.

19. *Les Monstres* (hereafter M), Paris, Gallimard, 1953, p.101.

20. Camus, *Essais*, p.1036; cf. R. Grenier, *Soleil et Ombre*, Paris, Gallimard-Folio, 1987, pp.332–3.

21. The articles in question are 'De Dostoïevski à Kafka', which appeared in *Les Temps Modernes* of October 1947, and 'L'Ere du soupçon' (later to provide the title of the 1956 volume it appeared in), which was first published in *Les Temps Modernes* of February 1950.

22. Grenier himself had of course argued the equal relevance of the second.

23. Quoted in *L'Ere du Soupçon*, Paris, Gallimard, collection Idées, 1966, p.74.

24. Ibid., pp.81–2.

25. Ibid.

26. *L'œuvre romanesque de Nathalie Sarraute*, Neuchâtel, Editions de la Baconnière, 1980, p.339.

27. Sarraute, *L'Ere du soupçon*, p.82.

28. The relevant section of the book, 'Notes sur la justice vue par un juré: André Gide', commemorates Gide's contribution to the literature of the *fait divers*.

29. See, Sartre, *Les Séquestrés d'Altona*, Acte 2 Scene 8; and *Un Théâtre de Situations*, ed. M. Contat, M. Rybalka, Paris, Gallimard, collection Idées, 1973, p.356, where Sartre acknowledges the influence of Gide's *fait divers* on his play. Camus makes notes on the story in his *Carnets II*, Paris, Gallimard, 1964, p.14, while writing *La Peste* during the Occupation years. For fuller consideration of the theme of reclusion in this period, see Mary Ann Frese Witt, *Existential Prisons. Captivity in Mid-Twentieth-Century French Literature*, Durham, Duke University Press, 1985. In fact, Robert Brasillach had compared Sartre's *Le Mur*

with *La Séquestrée de Poitiers* in a review in *L'Action française* as early as 1939 (quoted in *Œuvres romanesques*, p.1816), and the theme of sequestering, so frequent in Sartre's work, has been described as the prototypical metaphor of existentialist literature; so the collective experience in question is not exclusively historical. See Marie-Denise Boros, *Un Séquestré, l'homme sartrien*, Paris, Nizet, 1968.

30. Sheila Bell, in *Nathalie Sarraute: 'Portrait d'un inconnu' and 'Vous les entendez?'*, London, Grant and Cutler, 1988, identifies the allusions to the 'Séquestrée' in the opening section of the novel and in the climactic quarrel (pp.20–4, 46) and also discusses the function of *Eugénie Grandet* (pp.26–8).

31. Nathalie Sarraute, *Portrait d'un inconnu* (hereafter PI), Paris, Union Générale d'Editions, collection 10/18, 1956, p.17.

32. Sarraute indicates, without specifying 'La Séquestrée', that this was her point of departure for the novel: 'Cela se présentait comme un espace entièrement clos avec une agitation intérieure' ('Comment travaillent les écrivains', presented by J.-L. de Rambures, *Le Monde*, 14 January 1972).

33. Jean-Jacques Gautier, *Histoire d'un fait divers* (hereafter FD), Paris, Julliard, 1946, p.17.

34. Peter Brooks, *Reading for the Plot*, Oxford, Clarendon Press, 1984.

35. Camus, *Essais*, p.6.

PART IV

Facts, Fictions and Rumours

9

Albert Camus: The Eye of the Reporter

Among the many jobs Camus tried as a young man, that of *fait-diversier* was prominent. It proved, in fact, to be the start of a progression that established him as an eminent newspaper editor and editorialist on *Combat* and Servan-Schreiber's *L'Express*, among others. This distinguished career began with his announcement towards the end of 1938, in a letter to Jean Grenier: 'Je fais du journalisme [. . .] – les chiens écrasés et du reportage.'[1] His work as a 'chroniqueur judiciaire' for *Alger Républicain* involved him reporting on several trials, the experience of which, as he says himself, was crucial to the writing of *L'Etranger*.[2] The intensely-staring journalist whom Meursault singles out from the audience at his trial, and Tarrou's story in *La Peste* of the 'hibou effarouché' whose trial he attended to watch his father at work,[3] can doubtless be traced to the same source. Similarly, the job Camus has Rambert come to do in Oran – an enquiry on living conditions among the Arabs – carries echoes of Camus's own features, 'Misère de la Kabylie', in 1939. Arguably, indeed, the eye of the journalist is ever present in Camus's work. An initial idea of the extent to which his world-view and sense of identity are bound up with newspapers can be indicated by considering some of his remarks on the subject. For example, in 'Amour de vivre', a section of the early work *L'Envers et l'Endroit* which recounts the disturbing experiences he underwent while travelling for the first time in Central Europe in 1936, he writes: 'Sans les cafés et les journaux, il serait difficile de voyager. Une feuille imprimée dans notre langue [. . .] nous permet de mimer dans un geste familier l'homme que nous étions chez nous, et qui, à distance, nous paraît si étranger' (E, 102). His use of this last word seems significant: the ritual of reading a newspaper might be seen as a shield against the absurd. In an article written much later Camus speaks of 'le monde où nous vivons [. . .] qui nous saute du journal aux yeux tous les matins' (E, 793). In his *Carnets* he also refers to 'cette folie du monde [. . .] qui vous assaille au lever dans le journal'.[4] Here we have an acknowledgement that the world we inhabit is as good as constructed through our reading of the press.

But these points are not specific to *faits divers*, about which Camus could actually be rather scathing. Mersault, the hero of his first novel, *La Mort Heureuse*, in a moment of weariness, almost gives in to his 'envie de me marier, de me suicider, ou de m'abonner à *L'Illustration*. Un geste désespéré, quoi'.[5] (*L'Illustration* specialized in *faits divers* accompanied by melodramatic pictures.) However, for a few months in 1940 Camus himself worked on *Paris-Soir*, notorious for its lurid *faits divers* of crimes and catastrophes (though he was doubly glad not to be actually writing for it under the Occupation, just doing the page layouts).[6] He evidently had, or conceived, an abiding disdain for *Paris-Soir*, considering it to be the embodiment of all that was trivial and tasteless in press terms.[7] At the Liberation, when as editorialist on *Combat* he was campaigning among other things in favour of a genuinely informative press and what he termed 'le journalisme critique', he lamented the 'retour à [. . .] *Paris-Soir*' (E, 1542) as an unmistakable harbinger of a general return to the poor journalistic standards of the inter-War years (E, 1564–6). He detested 'les appels à cette sensibilité de midinette' (E, 265) that characterized such organs, and waxed indignant, for example, at the way the liberation of Metz by Allied troops was quickly replaced in the headlines by stories on Marlene Dietrich's entry into the town (E, 266–8). Surely the public could be educated to take an interest in more serious matters, he asked, referring to a widespread fascination for other *faits divers* of the day: 'Puisque le lecteur s'intéresse au docteur Petiot et à l'escroquerie aux bijoux, il n'y a pas de raisons immédiates pour que le fonctionnement d'une agence internationale de presse ne l'intéresse pas. L'avantage serait de mettre en garde son sens critique au lieu de s'adresser à son esprit de facilité' (E, 266). But no, the commentator endeavouring to awaken political consciences to the scandal of the Nagy affair, for instance, has to contend with 'un monde préoccupé seulement d'aller dans la lune ou de marier des altesses' (E, 1788). Things even reach a point where Jonas, the painter hero in *L'Exil et le Royaume*, expresses mild astonishment that society people should show an interest in his pictures 'quand ils eussent pu, comme chacun, se passionner pour la royale famille d'Angleterre ou les relais gastronomiques' (TRN, 1643). A further reference to Princess Margaret's unfortunate love life which fuelled the *faits divers* in the mid-1950s also appears as a variant in the manuscript of *La Chute*, in which Jean-Baptiste Clamence sardonically bemoans his inability to match up to Group Captain Peter Townsend (TRN, 2023). Such is the decadence of contemporary society, says Clamence: 'Une phrase suffira pour l'homme moderne : il forniquait et lisait des journaux' (TRN, 1479).[8]

Leaving fornication to one side for as long as propriety dictates, we might see this statement as Camus's definitive dismissal of a futile press in which the *fait divers* has triumphed over quality critical journalism and which has thereby condemned itself and its readership to triviality and insignificance. Such would presumably have been the conclusion of Camus's projected *Comédie sur la presse* for which he jotted down an outline in his *Carnets* in 1952 (CIII, 43–4).

However, there are other instances in which Camus's allusions to the *fait divers* lead one to quite different conclusions. For example, during the widespread strikes which affected France in the winter of 1947, the newspapers reported, so he tells us, that the state executioner in Paris would also be withdrawing his labour. 'Il demandait naturellement une prime pour chaque exécution, ce qui est dans la règle de toute entreprise. Mais, surtout, il réclamait avec force le statut de chef de bureau. Il voulait en effet recevoir de l'Etat, qu'il avait conscience de bien servir, la seule consécration, le seul honneur tangible, qu'une nation moderne puisse offrir à ses bons serviteurs, je veux dire un statut administratif' (E, 400–1). One recognizes here a classic example of a *fait divers*. But why should this particular instance of a man on strike be singled out for publication, precisely at a time when being on strike was the commonplace state of millions? The fact is that there is something unusual about an executioner being on strike. It is rather like an accountant pining from a broken heart, an estate agent telling the truth, or an archbishop having the misfortune to suffer a heart attack and die in a brothel. Such instances appear regularly in the *fait divers* rubric: and the reason they appear, like the story of the executioner, is that they fly in the face of our customary presuppositions and stereotypes concerning the professions they evoke.[9] Though it is only by implication that such notions are present, it is possible to infer them from the story that finds its way into print. Camus does just that in his commentary on the *fait divers* he highlights:

> Dans les temps barbares, une auréole terrible tenait à l'écart du monde le bourreau. Il était celui qui, par métier, attente au mystère de la vie et de la chair. Il était et il se savait un objet d'horreur. Et cette horreur consacrait en même temps le prix de la vie humaine. [. . .] Dans une civilisation où le meurtre et la violence sont déjà des doctrines et sont en passe de devenir des institutions, les bourreaux ont tout à fait le droit d'entrer dans les cadres administratifs. [. . .] Un peu partout dans le monde, les exécuteurs sont déjà installés dans des fauteuils ministériels. Ils ont seulement remplacé la hache par le tampon à encre.

Now I would not wholly subscribe to the view of the contemporary world which Camus derives from this *fait divers*: if the state of affairs he satirically denounces were in fact the case, the instance in question would not have made its way into the *fait divers* rubric because it would have nothing odd about it to 'accrocher le public', as the *faits-diversiers* put it. Nevertheless, what Camus has to say about the traditional stereotype of the executioner underlying the story seems accurate enough, and would justify a comment made by one analyst of the *fait divers*: 'Ce sont des anecdotes futiles qui renvoient à l'essentiel.'[10] The *fait divers* does articulate, in its way, fundamental truths – or widely-held beliefs – about society and the world.

As is well known, the role and function of the executioner constitute a recurring theme in Camus's work. 'Ce qui m'intéressait, c'était la condamnation à mort,' says Tarrou in *La Peste* (TRN, 1423). Camus's meditations on the subject are clearly nourished by what he encountered in the 'chronique des fait divers', in which this is also a characteristic motif. To judge by a note in his *Carnets*, he planned to include a related fictional *fait divers* in *La Peste*, using a rich irony intrinsic to the form as a means of highlighting the absurd conditions to which the plague-stricken community is condemned: 'C'est à ce moment en effet qu'on apprit les suites d'une affaire qui avait soulevé en son temps la curiosité des connaisseurs. Un jeune meurtrier avait été gracié. Les journaux pensaient qu'il s'en tirerait avec dix ans de bonne conduite et qu'ensuite il pourrait reprendre sa vie de tous les jours. Ce n'était vraiment pas la peine' (CII, 101). He also starts his *Réflexions sur la guillotine* by recalling one of the few memories he had of his father, who followed a celebrated murder case in the papers, saw it through to its conclusion, and was nauseated by what he witnessed at the execution. The rest of this essay derives extensively from newspaper reports on unusual murder cases, trials, sentences and *erreurs judiciaires*. Camus acknowledges in a note Roger Grenier's novel *Les Monstres*, an extensively-documented narrative about the life and work of a *fait-diversier* which contains a chapter based on the memoirs of an executioner the hero is ghost-writing.[11] From this and other sources Camus quotes grotesque and bloody details of what is involved in the use of the guillotine. On his experience of being exposed to such material, Camus concludes: 'Pour qui vient de passer des semaines dans la fréquentation des textes, des souvenirs, des hommes qui, de près ou de loin, touchent à l'échafaud, il ne saurait être question de sortir de ces affreux défilés tel qu'on y était entré' (E, 1062). Nothing trivial or insignificant here. Sensational perhaps, beyond the realm of the commonplace or of *bienséance*; but far from being without wider relevance.

In a letter to a historian of the nineteenth-century *canards* of which the *fait divers* is a direct descendant, Camus recalls that it was while reading an Algiers newspaper one day in the late 1930s that he came across a *fait divers* he was to make much of subsequently: 'Il faisait particulièrement chaud, ce qui me fait supposer que nous étions en été, saison, comme vous le savez, propice au serpent de mer.'[12] This particular silly season threw up what is a commonplace of the *canard*, going back into the mists of time: 'L'Auberge sanglante'.[13] The fact that it is a journalistic chestnut doesn't mean it never actually occurred: the 'Rapport sur les Assises de l'Ardèche' for the second term of 1833 relates the 'Affaire de l'Auberge de Peyrebeille', an out-of-the-way inn whose proprietors were found guilty of systematically increasing their turnover by murdering their guests and keeping their money.[14] The case has inspired novels and a film by Autant-Lara starring Fernandel, and Camus certainly knew it since he refers to it in a denunciation of those so-called progressives who saw fit to condone totalitarian regimes in the USSR and Eastern Europe in the 1950s: 'Trop de nos intellectuels et de nos artistes [. . .] ont fini par ressembler à ces filles qui, devant l'auberge de Peirebeilhe [sic], chantaient de toute leur gorge pour couvrir les cris des voyageurs égorgés par leurs vertueux parents' (E, 1805). Indeed it is perhaps no coincidence that Camus wrote his play *Le Malentendu* in 1942 – since at that time he was living in the Ardèche, at Le Chambon-sur-Lignon, which is less than thirty miles as the crow flies from the Auberge de Peyrebeille itself (TRN, 1789).

However, it is clear that Camus did not actually need a further prompt, since he had already used the *fait divers* we started from in *L'Etranger*, begun in Algeria and completed in Paris in 1940. It will be recalled that Meursault finds beneath the mattress in his prison cell a newspaper cutting telling the story of a mother and daughter who have taken to killing guests at the hotel they run. The son, who left home years before, returns unrecognized, puts up at the hotel without disclosing his identity, and is murdered in his turn. 'J'ai dû lire cette histoire des milliers de fois,' says Meursault. 'D'un côté, elle était invraisemblable. D'un autre, elle était naturelle' (TRN, 1182). As a *fait divers*, the story commands credence because it is a record of something that actually happened. But the events so depart from normal expectations that they offend against our sense of what is plausible. Our sense of the plausible in turn is what Barthes calls 'opinable',[15] deriving from that accumulated, largely communal fund of precedents in which the boundary between reality and fiction is extensively blurred by memory and rhetoric. The conflict between the *vrai* and the *vraisemblable* will be taken up during the trial of Meursault himself: the norms applied to the judgement of his case will be shown to exclude the essential reality, so that Marie will cry out that 'ce n'était pas cela' (TRN, 1192) at the prosecuting counsel's interpretation of events. The *fait divers* is assessed by the judicial machine in terms of conventional (chiefly narrative) criteria which by its very nature it calls into question. To return to Meursalt's *fait divers* and its development in *Le Malentendu*, it is worth reflecting on the sense in which the story may be considered 'naturelle'. In the play especially, the excruciating ironies that are generated by the failure of communication which occurs between Jan on the one hand and his mother and sister on the other, produce an agonising sense of the contingency of events. 'If only . . .', we may be induced to murmur. Drugged tea – the first phase of the murder plan – is served to Jan on the basis of a misunderstood message from the aged servant; the revelation of the comatose victim's identity is delayed until too late, by the trivial fact that his passport falls from his pocket and slips unseen behind the bed while the women are preparing to carry him outside and drop him in the river. If Camus's plot is a reconstruction of the *fait divers*, his interpretive strategy is geared to demonstrating sod's law in action: if this is all perfectly 'natural', it is because chance presides over human affairs and the worst is just as likely to occur as is any other sequence of events. Contingency is in fact a common feature of the *fait divers*. Barthes, Auclair and numerous others have brought out the way the rubric tends to specialize in cases where causality is stretched to the limit, where a trivial instance can provoke catastrophic consequences, where there is a huge disproportion of scale between cause and effect: 'Un Anglais s'engage dans la Légion,' begins a headline Barthes picks out: 'il ne voulait pas passer Noël avec sa belle-mère.'[16] A historian of the *fait divers* selects a title which runs 'La baignoire fuyait: le bateau coule'.[17] According to Meursault, the tragedy in his *fait divers* stems from a trivial error of judgement: 'Il ne faut jamais jouer,' he concludes (TRN, 1182). Something of the same logic is in operation in Meursault's own story, of course: a random succession of banal, unexceptional events leads up to a murder and capital punishment. One may draw from this narrative the conclusion Gide drew from *La Séquestrée de Poitiers*: 'Il suffit, bien souvent, de l'addition d'une quantité de petits faits très simples et très naturels, chacun pris à part, pour obtenir un total monstrueux.'[18] We can see both Meursault's narrative and the constructions placed on events by the prosecution at the trial in an identical light: where Meursault and his witnesses see 'le hasard' leading up to the disaster, the prosecuting counsel takes the accumulation of trivial details to constitute the picture of a premeditating villain (TRN, 1193). Meursault's story too is at one and the same time natural and monstrous. The *raison d'être* of the *fait divers* rubric is precisely to single out events which make that point about existence in general.[19]

One of the things Camus is doing in *L'Etranger* is showing the events behind a published *fait divers*: for that is what Meursault's case will become, as we learn at the outset of the trial. The journalists are there in force, and one of them says to Meursault, 'Vous savez, nous avons monté un peu votre affaire. L'été, c'est la saison creuse pour les journaux. Et il n'y avait que votre histoire et celle du parricide qui vaillent quelque chose' (TRN, 1185). Sure enough, in *La Peste*, we hear of the shopkeeper who, in conversation with Cottard, 'avait parlé d'une arrestation récente qui avait fait du bruit à Alger. Il s'agissait d'un jeune employé de commerce qui avait tué un Arabe sur une plage. "Si on mettait toute cette racaille en prison, avait dit la marchande, les honnêtes gens pourraient respirer"' (TRN, 1262–3). By means of this intertextual cross-reference, Camus dramatizes the mode of circulation of *faits divers*, simultaneously bringing out the important fact that they are not restricted to textual manifestations. In the universe of Camus's literary works, we similarly recognize Meursault's press cutting as an allusion to *Le Malentendu* and vice versa. The *fait divers* can become a form of common currency of shared understanding, transmitted by gossip and hearsay and becoming in the end a kind of modern myth, part of the repository of common knowledge, cultural references and collective and individual fantasies on which we can all draw as aids to communication.[20] 'Le parricide' of which the journalist speaks to Meursault, the exophoric article calling it up from (but for the reader placing it in) the stock of common knowledge, is likewise exploited by the prosecuting counsel in the courtroom. Alluding to it as the next case to be tried, he uses the presuppositions it carries with it to clinch the sleight of hand whereby he incriminates Meursault on the grounds of his apparent insensitivity on the death of his mother. The lawyer thus confirms a set of values the jury will acknowledge as their own and will apply to Meursault. 'Selon lui, un homme qui tuait moralement sa mère se retranchait de la société des hommes au même titre que celui qui portait une main meurtrière sur l'auteur de ses jours' (TRN, 1197). Again, this is a feature of the *fait divers*, relating each new horror, outrage or scandal to precedent. Each new assassin is attached to a lineage for which the stereotype is Landru, Violette Nozières, Doctor Crippen or Jack the Ripper, as circumstances dictate; and each time the force of the shared knowledge is strengthened.[21] Neutrality is not possible in the face of the *fait divers*, says one commentator: its function, he points out, is to 'compromettre psychologiquement et moralement'.[22]

In at least one instance Camus as journalist operates a subversive variant within the circuit of common knowledge which generates so many interconnections across the world of the *fait divers*. In an editorial in *L'Express*, dated 8 November 1955, he breathes a mock sigh of relief that the story of Princess Margaret and Group Captain Peter Townsend has been resolved by 'la déchirante séparation d'un Titus et d'une Bérénice de magazine' and connects this long-running 'calvaire' with two other *faits divers*.[23] One illustrates 'un problème peu connu, je crois, à Clarence House, celui de la retraite'. The incident of two roofers who fell several storeys to their deaths became a *fait divers* by virtue of the odd detail that one of them was aged seventy-three and the other over sixty. In another case building workers digging out the foundations of a new construction site were buried when the earth collapsed back on top of them. Resorting to the kind of irony frequently relished by the *chronique*, Camus points out: 'Ils creusaient en réalité leur propre fosse.' He performs two significant operations here. First he takes the unusual or ironic detail that determines these items as *faits divers* – the 'scandale logique' as Auclair calls it[24] – and makes it into a matter of socio-economic scandal. Why were old men so poorly provided for in retirement that they had to risk their lives going back onto the roofs in this way? Why was the building contractor using unqualified immigrant workers on a job like this, and why were the walls of the excavation not properly shored up? The sensationalism typical of the rubric is here turned into a sort of counter-sensationalism. Secondly, Camus suggests a connection which the *chronique*, normally so prompt at tying things together, had omitted in these cases to make, between on the one hand, 'ce vieillard jeté dans le vide, ces morts à la bouche pleine de terre, rapidement enterrés' and on the other, 'les éditions spéciales et les photos royales'. The moral or political point (the two are so rarely separate for Camus) need hardly be expanded. But the demonstration that *faits divers*, used in a certain way, can be made to yield such points is significant, as I shall endeavour to show.

Camus was travelling in Italy in December 1954 when, reading a newspaper as we have seen was his wont while *dépaysé*, he learned that the Prix Goncourt had been awarded to Simone de Beauvoir's *Les Mandarins* and noted: 'Il paraît que j'en suis le héros,' along with some disobliging reflections about the contents of the book (CIII, 146–7). Obviously this opened up old wounds going back to the polemics and break with Sartre in 1952. Two days later appears in the *Carnets* the first of a series of remarks on existentialism which will find their way into *La Chute*. There seem to be grounds for suggesting that this novel was informed in some way by the news report he read. Certainly the sense of self and the world, of self *in* the world, as coming into being through the circuit of gossip and tittle-tattle, of *potins* and *entrefilets*, is very marked in the text.

Like Tarrou in *La Peste*, Camus had always been in the habit of noting anecdotes and incidents in his *Carnets*. In the absurd universe as Camus formulates it, every case is an exceptional case, every phenomenon equally futile and equally paramount: in this respect the modest miscellanies associated with the *fait divers* rubric seem to have proved particularly congenial for his world view – as is confirmed by the tongue-in-cheek introduction, 'De l'insignifiance' (E, 1903–5), to a projected anthology. The notebooks for the Occupation years are particularly rich in details of the 'petits faits vrais' type, dispassionately cataloguing large numbers of *faits divers* with a reporter's eye for telling juxtapositions of the banal with the monstrous.[25] In 1953 he published twelve other such anecdotes under the title 'Notes empruntées à l'actualité' in the review *Démenti* (CIII, 66). In 1956, in an interview in which he speaks of both *La Chute* and his stage adaptation of Faulkner's *Requiem pour une nonne*, he stresses that a great author 'n'a jamais répugné à chercher ses personnages dans les *faits divers* rapportés par les journaux' (TRN, 1880). Here he had Faulkner in mind; he could just as easily have made the point about Dostoyevsky's *The Devils*, which he was adapting also during the gestation of his own novel. But it is striking how much *La Chute* owes to the *fait divers*. Firstly, at least one of the 'notes empruntées à l'actualité' finds its way into the novel: the story of the beggar who is discouraged from importuning the well-heeled clients eating lobster in a restaurant and is thrown out by the proprietor with the words: 'Mettez-vous à la place de ces messieurs-dames' (CIII, 66; TRN, 1522). Secondly, a feature central to the plot is the notorious theft of Van Eyck's *Just Judges*. Clamence finds himself having to explain to his interlocutor, who, disappointingly, is not surprised when confronted with *Les Juges intègres* which the narrator has concealed in his room. 'Votre culture aurait donc des trous? Si vous lisiez pourtant les journaux, vous vous rappelleriez le vol, en 1934, à Gand, dans la cathédrale Saint-Bavon, d'un des panneaux du fameux retable' (TRN, 1542). But the irony of the case emerges from a note in Camus's *Carnets*: in July 1956, after the publication of *La Chute*, a correspondent wrote to him with the 'véritable histoire du Van Eyck'. It was actually a priest who came under suspicion and confessed that he had stolen this panel of the polyptych because he couldn't bear the sight of the judges next to the Lamb of God. He was absolved on the strength of his good intentions and on condition that on the day of his death he would reveal where he had hidden the picture. But at the last minute his voice failed him and the secret accompanied him to his grave (CIII, 189).[26]

This seems a striking instance of the way Camus's use of the *fait divers* generates a special collusion in the reader, plugging into the newspaper world we live in and thereby eliciting corroboration of at least one element in Clamence's judgement on modern man: 'Il forniquait et lisait des journaux.' The procedure is employed systematically: when Clamence describes himself as 'moitié Cerdan, moitié De Gaulle' (TRN, 1503) he is trading upon a familiarity with the popular press which regaled its readers with tales of Edith Piaf's world-champion boxer boyfriend, the untimely victim of an air crash in 1949; De Gaulle, for his part, was at this point in the mid-1950s the recluse at Colombey-les-Deux-Eglises, a hero of the 'chronique' and not yet President of the Republic. Elsewhere, an allusion to Einstein (TRN, 1506) calls to mind the scientist's death in 1955 and the ensuing controversy as to which of several competing agencies should have access to his brain for scientific investigation.[27] In such ways as these, Clamence compels the reader's connivance. They are an important aspect of that strategy of his which includes, among other things, the cynical trick maxims and definitions he invites us to agree with: 'Le charme: une manière de s'entendre répondre oui sans avoir posé aucune question claire' (TRN, 1504); 'Nul homme n'est hypocrite dans ses plaisirs, ai-je lu cela ou l'ai-je pensé?' (TRN, 1509); 'La honte, dites-moi, mon cher compatriote, ne brûle-t-elle pas un peu? Oui? Alors, il s'agit peut-être d'elle, ou d'un de ces sentiments ridicules qui concernent l'honneur' (TRN, 1510). It is with good reason that Clamence can say 'Je n'ai plus d'amis, je n'ai que des complices' (TRN, 1513): that certainly is what he is seeking.

The key elements of Clamence's life are in effect a series of *faits divers*. During an incident at the traffic lights, Clamence receives a clout on the ear when himself about to 'frotter les oreilles' of an ill-mannered motorcyclist (TRN, 1501–2). By a curious coincidence, the year 1965 saw a moral panic arising precisely from a rash of fights like this between motorists, which proliferated in the *fait divers* rubric to the accompaniment of solemn commentaries from psychiatrists and sociologists on this disturbing new feature of modern civilization.[28] This may perhaps be taken as evidence of the extent to which *La Chute* draws on the reporter's instinct for a good *fait divers*. But the intention is beyond doubt in that other incident which is a crux of Clamence's narrative: the story of the woman who commits suicide by throwing herself from the Pont Royal, and of his failure to retrace his steps to try to rescue her. Contrary to his ingrained habit, he says, 'Ni le lendemain ni les jours qui suivirent, je n'ai lu les journaux' (TRN, 1511). To come across this incident as a *fait divers* would compel his acknowledgement of his involvement, his complicity in misfortune, in precisely the way he wishes to avoid for himself while seeking to subject his interlocutor to it.

It is thus appropriate that in order to 'éviter personnellement le jugement' and to 'étendre la condamnation à tous' (TRN, 1543), Clamence should have recourse to *faits divers* which illustrate the shortcomings and crimes of others just as those in which he was a protagonist illustrate his own. 'Mes histoires', as he calls them, represent in effect an anthology of *faits divers* intended to illustrate 'l'homme du jour', a composite of 'traits communs', 'expériences que nous avons ensemble souffertes', 'faiblesses que nous partageons' (TRN, 1547), constructed in such a way as to force the interlocutor's assent to Clamence's view that mankind in general is beyond redemption. The *fait divers* is, as we have seen, an integral part of the world we inhabit, it is the air we breathe, it is a common culture that cuts across hierarchies and ensures that we are all implicated, 'dans le bain' (TRN, 1546) as Clamence desires. His career as a judge has brought him into contact with a wealth of examples involving criminals who only committed their crimes, according to him, in order to see their names in the newspapers (TRN, 1488–9). Like the expert *fait-diversier* he is, Clamence draws on these and other instances, selecting for inclusion the cases which best call into question comfortable assumptions about norms of behaviour and human nature: 'désorienter [. . .] l'opinion' (TRN, 1524) is his express aim. So that through the fragmentary and heterogeneous character of his text – and in this too, as we have seen, *La Chute* mimics the rubric – he marshals a world view which is profoundly dispiriting. He offers anecdotes about life under the Nazis, in particular the 'Sophie's choice' instance of a woman forced to select which of her sons was to be executed (TRN, 1481), or that of the Frenchman at Buchenwald protesting that his case is exceptional because he is innocent (TRN, 1516–17). But Clamence also evokes the industrialist who kills his wife because her very qualities exacerbate the guilt he feels at having been unfaithful to her (TRN, 1485). He speaks too of the girl who commits suicide to avenge herself on her father for preventing her from marrying the man she loved (TRN, 1513). He resorts to cases from history: a trusting individual who declared his house open to all during the wars of religion and who was massacred in it by passing militiamen (TRN, 1481); a Russian landowner who had his serfs whipped if they did not greet him and had them whipped for their presumption if they did (TRN, 1522).[29] He quotes bizarre devices as triumphs of humanity's depraved ingenuity: the 'malconfort', a prison cell too small to stand up in and too narrow to lie down in (TRN, 1531); the 'cellule des crachats', in which the prisoner is immobilized so he can be spat on by prison warders (TRN, 1532). Such examples of the 'strange but true' are presented as often as not as if they come from the domain of common knowledge: 'Avez-vous au moins entendu parler de . . .?' 'On m'a parlé d'un homme . . .' (TRN, 1491). The circuit of hearsay is itself a kind of proof of the collective nature of the human existence – which suits Clamence, of course, because he wishes to generalize guilt through these channels in order to achieve his own form of domination. So that in the final analysis *La Chute* makes the point firstly that the world is fragmented and chaotic and that to give an account of it conventional linear narrative must give way to a jumble of assorted anecdotes; and secondly that such coherence as the world may have for human beings is achieved through the derisory avenues of the *bouche à oreille* and the complacent connivence of gossip. 'Compromettre psychologiquement et moralement': such is indeed the effect of this text.

In one sense, Camus's work is based on the creation of myths. The very titles of his prose fiction – *L'Etranger, La Peste, La Chute, L'Exil et le Royaume* – suggest that he is seeking to concentrate the detail of reality into a certain number of representative figures and general statements about existence and experience. This tendency could be related to Camus's interpretation of Nietzsche's 'Eternal Return' as he notes in his *Carnets*: it is a matter of 'une répétition des grands moments – comme si tout visait à reproduire ou faire retentir les moments culminants de l'humanité.[. . .] Toutes les défaites ont quelque chose d'Athènes ouverte aux Romains barbares, toutes les victoires font penser à Salamine, etc., etc.' (CII, 28). This is one aspect, as I hope to have indicated, of the *faits divers*:[30] every mass murderer is a Landru – and this is one effect Camus derives from exploiting them as he does. They highlight the recurrent, weighty, significant truths about human experience. But in their perceived triviality they also enable one to appreciate a dimension which is equally crucial, and which goes directly against the 'Eternal Return'. Milan Kundera highlights it, when he takes issue with Nietzsche: it is not the fixity of human experience – which can be comforting, gratifying, fulfilling – that should concern us, so much as 'The unbearable lightness of being'. By this token, the important characteristic of life is its fleeting, unrenewable nature: the fact that the past does not return is what condemns us to weightlessness, contingency, insignificance, futility. We do not in fact get a second chance, and on this basis 'Our day-to-day life is bombarded with fortuities . . . Chance and chance alone has a message for us. Everything that occurs out of necessity, everything expected, repeated day in and day out, is mute. Only chance can speak to us.'[31] It can be argued that something of this insight lies at the heart of Clamence's world-view, and motivates his use of *fait divers* rather than a sustained narrative for his monologue. A lengthy narrative lends accumulating weight to incidents it chronicles, establishing explanation, justification, extrapolation, and so on. But the *fait divers* is in essence a one-off, characterized as an exception, as often as not the product of chance or freak elements. It does not cohere into patterns of significance, it cannot be rerun. Clamence wishes it could: witness his reaction to the traffic incident: he goes over it again and again in his mind, rehearsing what he should have done – but it is too late. 'Je tournai cent fois ce petit film dans mon imagination, mais il etait trop tard, et je dévorai pendant quelques jours un vilain ressentiment' (TRN, 1503). The same happens in the incident of the woman throwing herself from the Pont Royal: 'Trop tard, trop loin . . .' murmurs Clamence as he contemplates the impossibility of doing anything about it (TRN, 1511). But he has since developed a compulsion to repeat the story to people he meets in the Mexico-City bar. *This* is what he has to come to terms with, *this* is what his strategy is designed to help him live with: the sense that on the one occasion when he might have done something, he did not – or did the wrong thing. The unbearable triviality and absurd fleetingness of life is at the centre of the text: not for nothing, I think, does the crucial incident involve a fall into a river which carries the victim off. At his weakest moment, Clamence cries out 'les mots qui n'ont cessé de retentir dans mes nuits': 'Oh jeune fille, jette-toi encore dans l'eau pour que j'ai une seconde fois la chance de nous sauver tous les deux!' The freak occurrence offers no chance to prepare for it, to implement a well-ordered, so-called contingency plan: and afterwards it is too late, the event is irreparable – or at least unrepeatable. In typical fashion, Clamence concludes by stifling his anguish, reversing the *données* and seeking comfort in the impossibility of a second chance: 'Mais rassurons-nous! Il est trop tard, maintenant, il sera toujours trop tard.

Heureusement!' (TRN, 1551). But the ironic tone of the text makes it possible to suggest that it is the agonizing contingency of events which retains its power to torment. This is a message which would not carry the force it does were it not for the fact that it is articulated within a text which presents itself as a tissue of miscellanies, a collection of anecdotes that hinge on the same logic.[32] They may indeed be viewed as trivial, but they do go to the heart of matters.

Notes

1. Albert Camus and Jean Grenier, *Correspondance 1932–1960*, Paris, Gallimard, 1981, p.33.

2. Ibid., p.53, letter of 5 May 1941; *Fragments d'un combat*, edited, introduced and annotated by Jacqueline Lévi-Valensi and André Abbou, Paris, Gallimard, Cahiers Albert Camus 3, 1978, vol.2, pp.351–596; Paul-F. Smets, 'Camus chroniqueur judiciaire à *Alger Républicain* en 1939', in *Albert Camus, dans le Premier Silence et au-delà*, Brussels, J. Goemaere, 1985, pp.142–88.

3. Albert Camus, *Théâtre, récits, nouvelles*, Paris, Pléiade, 1962, pp.1186, 1421. Subsequent references to works in this edition will be indicated by TRN in the text. References to works contained in Albert Camus, *Essais*, Paris, Pléiade, 1965, will be indicated by E in the text.

4. Albert Camus, *Carnets III, Mars 1951–Décembre 1959*, Paris, Gallimard, 1989, p.77. Subsequent references to this volume will be indicated by CIII in the text. CII in the text refers to *Carnets II, Janvier 1942–Mars 1951*, Paris, Gallimard, 1964.

5. Albert Camus, *La Mort Heureuse*, introduction and notes by Jean Sarocchi, Paris, Gallimard, Cahiers Albert Camus 1, 1971, p.68.

6. Camus and Grenier *Correspondance*, p.37.

7. See H. Lottmann, *Albert Camus*, Paris, Seuil, 1978, pp.236–7. Camus was not alone in his view of *Paris-Soir*, of course.

8. As for the modern woman, Clamence remarks at one point, 'Elle avait si bien lu la presse du cœur qu'elle parlait de l'amour avec la sûreté et la conviction d'un intellectuel annonçant la société sans classes' (TRN, 1526).

9. See Georges Auclair, *Le 'Mana' quotidien: structure et fonctions de la chronique des faits divers*, Paris, Editions Anthropos, 1970, pp.42–3, 56–9.

10. Alain Monestier *et al.*, *Le Fait Divers*, catalogue of an exhibition organized at the Musée national des arts et traditions populaires, Paris, Editions de la Réunion des musées nationaux, 1982, p.56.

11. Camus had earlier selected Grenier's first book, *Le Rôle d'Accusé: Le*

Mythe du Fait Divers (1948), for publication in the collection 'Espoir' which he ran for Gallimard. See above, pp.122–4. On Camus's interest in executions, see pp.106–9.

12. Quoted in Jean-Pierre Séguin, *Nouvelles à sensation: Canards du XIXᵉ siècle*, Paris, Armand Colin, 1959, p.207.

13. See, ibid., pp.187–90, and Monestier *et al.*, *Le Fait Divers*, pp.104–8. Roger Grenier reproduces the texts of the news items Camus refers to: see his *Soleil et Ombre*, Paris, Gallimard-Folio, 1987, pp.155–6.

14. See Monestier *et al.*, *Le Fait Divers*, pp.104–8.

15. 'L'effet de réel', in Barthes, Bersani *et al.*, *Littérature et réalité*, Paris, Seuil, collection Points, 1982, p.88.

16. Roland Barthes, 'Structure du fait divers', in *Essais critiques*, Paris, Seuil, 1964, p.193. See also Auclair, *Le 'Mana' quotidien*, pp.41–3.

17. Romi, *Histoire des Faits Divers*, Paris, Editions du Pont-Royal, 1962; quoted in M. Lecerf, *Les Faits Divers*, Paris, Larousse, collection Idéologies et sociétés, 1981, p.153. See also Monestier *et al.*, *Le Fait Divers*, exhibition catalogue, p.53.

18. André Gide, *Ne Jugez Pas*, Paris, Gallimard, 1969, p.200. Gide was actually quoting his own *Les Faux-Monnayeurs*, itself based on a *fait divers*: see above, p.56.

19. Auclair, *Le 'Mana' quotidien*, pp.109–11.

20. Cf. Monestier *et al.*, *Le Fait Divers*, pp.110–41; Auclair, *Le 'Mana' quotidien*, p.153–4: 'Papotage et commérage sont désormais à l'échelle planétaire'. For a systematic sociological analysis of the phenomenon, see Edgar Morin *et al.*, *La Rumeur d'Orléans*, edition supplemented by *La Rumeur d'Amiens*, Paris, Seuil, collection Points, 1969.

21. See Auclair, *Le 'Mana' quotidien*, pp.89–90, 299.

22. Monestier *et al.*, *Le Fait Divers*, pp.14–15.

23. *Albert Camus, éditorialiste à 'L'Express'*, Introduction, commentary and notes by Paul-F. Smets, Paris, Gallimard, Cahiers Albert Camus 6, 1987, pp.90–2.

24. Ibid., p.41.

25. Some examples may be found in CII, pp.37–8, 132–3, 192, 218, 235–6, and *passim*. Cf. Jean-Pierre Rioux, 'Camus et la Seconde Guerre Mondiale', in *Camus et la Politique*, ed. Jeanyves Guérin, Paris, Editions L'Harmattan, 1986, pp.97–106, at p.100.

26. For more detail on this story, see my 'Le criminel chez Camus', in *Albert Camus, les extrêmes et l'équilibre*, proceedings of the Keele colloquium, edited and introduced by David H. Walker, Amsterdam, Rodopi, 1994, pp.17–32, especially at pp.29–30.

27. Barthes poked fun at this particular folly: see 'Le cerveau d'Einstein', in *Mythologies*, Paris, Seuil, collection Points, 1957, pp.91–3.

28. See Auclair, *Le 'Mana' quotidien*, pp.119–20. Simone de Beauvoir

alludes to this episode in *Les Belles Images*: see below, pp.179–80.

29. CIII, p.107, reveals that this was actually Dostoyevsky's father.
30. See note 21.
31. Milan Kundera, *The Unbearable Lightness of Being*, London, Faber and Faber, 1985, pp.52, 3–6, 48.
32. Cf. Auclair, *Le 'Mana' quotidien*, pp.253–4.

10

Jean Genet: Life Among the
Faits Divers

In the *Journal du Voleur*, recounting the period when he lived in Spain, Genet speaks of the room of his lover Stilitano, where he acted out many of his most telling fantasies. In the silence of early morning, he listens to 'le bruissement mystérieux de la feuille de journal jauni qui remplaçait la vitre absente'. He struggles to decipher the sound, entranced by its subtlety and unsettled by his inability to understand its meaning. 'Je découvrais beaucoup de mots nouveaux,' he says. '"C'est un journal imprimé en espagnol, me disais-je encore. Il est normal que je ne comprenne pas le bruit qu'il fait"' (JV, 56).[1]

This curious evocation, so perversely at odds with common sense – why should he expect to derive a meaning from the rustling sound of a sheet of newspaper replacing the broken glass in a window, and why should the language it is printed in make any difference one way or the other? – is all the more susceptible to figurative interpretation. The window pane which normally affords a view of the outside world, is here substituted by newsprint, which speaks in its own language about the reality outside. The suggestion seems to be that newspapers mediate Genet's view of reality. In fact this incident can be read as an echo of the opening pages of his first novel, *Notre-Dame-des-fleurs*. Here, similarly enclosed within his prison cell, the narrator's only window on the world is constituted by the press cuttings and photographs he has culled from newspapers and magazines and stuck on the wall, and around which he elaborates the fantasies which are the stuff of the book itself (NF, 9–12). In the novel's first words, the reader is also reminded how s/he views the world through newsprint: 'Weidmann vous apparut dans une édition de cinq heures.' Both texts, then, afford news reports an important place in Genet's creative strategies.

A dominant theme of these strategies is the transfiguration of a squalid existence into a glorious essence through the intervention of writing. Though present in the earlier texts, it appears at its most highly-developed in *Journal du Voleur*. Referring to the possibility of simply enumerating the incidents in his life, he writes:

> Je refuse de vivre pour une autre fin que celle même que je trouvais contenir le premier malheur: que ma vie doit être légende c'est-à-dire lisible et sa lecture donner naissance à quelque émotion nouvelle que je nomme poésie. Je ne suis plus rien, qu'un prétexte. (JV, 125–6)

For present purposes the key element in this passage is the importance Genet attaches to what he calls the 'poésie' of his 'légende'. It is evident that Genet sees his life as something to be read about; moreover the reading must have the effect on the reader of a particular type of poetry.

The kind of poetry – the kind of legend – he has in mind are specifically associated with the *fait divers*. The rubric is the informing source of the criminal legends which, in effect, Genet is emulating. Thus, for example, he involves himself in fantasies of Joseph Vacher, the mass murderer of the late 1890s who stalked the countryside massacring children (JV, 47, 51). He relishes the 'atmosphère de sourde rancœur, de crapuleuse infamie' which he associates with the police files of similar cases (JV, 209–10). A major attraction for him in these instances are the 'décalages moraux' which they provoke, particularly where the stories of crime involve unexpected reversals of fortune and macabre coincidences which defy reason and belie the careful calculations of perpetrators and investigators alike. He refers to 'les découvertes grandioses du hasard, dont la décapitation d'un homme est le but' (JV, 209–10): the convergence of the contingent and the catastrophic, so typical of the rubric, proves a heady mixture for Genet. The plot of *Notre-Dame-des-fleurs*, for example, will trace the manner in which 'la plus légère imprudence' can lead a man to the guillotine (NF, 37), how seemingly trivial and inconsequential gestures can suddenly usher in 'l'univers de l'irrémédiable' (NF, 135) so that a minor delinquent can find himself 'voué à la guillotine comme Jésus-Christ à la passion' (NF, 125). Genet envies the police inspector who can consult the record of such items, 'd'un casier sortir un meurtre ou un viol, s'en gonfler, s'en repaître, et rentrer chez soi' (JV, 210): the *fait divers* is the stuff on which Genet's imagination sustains itself. Clearly his interest is far from conventional. In *Miracle de la Rose* he writes of a news item he has heard:

> Que l'on ne confonde pas avec le sadisme cette joie que je connais quand on m'apprend certains actes que le commun appelle infamie. Ainsi mon plaisir quand j'appris le meurtre de cet enfant de quinze ans par un soldat allemand me fut causé par le seul bonheur de cette audace qui osait, en massacrant la chair délicate des adolescents, détruire une beauté visible et établie pour obtenir une beauté – ou poésie – résultant de la rencontre de cette beauté brisée avec le geste barbare. (MR, 375)

As well as providing material for Genet's perverse poetic meditations, the *fait divers* rubric furnishes an important pretext for his biographical and autobiographical recreations, and one which bulks extremely large in his work. *Notre-Dame-des-fleurs* starts with several *faits divers*, and the reverie of which the book is entirely made up arises, as we have seen, from a series of newspaper clippings and photographs stuck on the narrator's cell wall. *Miracle de la Rose* alludes repeatedly to items from the *chronique* and in its closing lines Genet confesses a compulsion to 'fouiller les vieux journaux' and speaks of an article on the death of Maurice Pilorge (which we know inspired his first poem, 'Le condamné à mort'). Indeed he refers elsewhere to the production of a 'héros déjà idéalisé puisque mort et réduit à l'état de prétexte à l'un de ces poèmes brefs que sont les faits divers' (MR, 225): a statement which can be construed as indicating that the rubric precisely exemplifies Genet's own aesthetic.

Genet's texts contain further allusions which enable us to consider more closely the place of the *fait divers* in the mechanisms his work brings into play. The murder by Notre-Dame-des-fleurs of an old man appears in the newspapers as just such an item. His name thereby becomes known 'de la France entière', we are told. Certain kinds of readers merely pass over it, but Genet's preferred readers, 'les écoliers et les petites vieilles, [. . .] ceux qui vont tout au fond des articles, flairant l'insolite et l'y dépistant à tout coup' (NF, 148), tremble with delight – and envy – as they read. Their reaction, Genet stresses, is that of the 'voyageur taciturne et fébrile' who on arriving in a new town, heads for the 'bouges, quartiers réservés, bordels', guided by 'des mots de passe échangés par les subconscients et qu'il suit de confiance'. The reports they savour, of murder, theft, rape, armed attacks – these, says Genet, are the '"Barrios Chinos" des journaux' (NF, 149). Now the Barrio Chino, as he points out in *Journal du Voleur*, is that *quartier réservé* of Barcelona, inhabited by an extraordinary rabble of disreputable and dangerous low-life characters, where Genet himself elected to live and whose lifestyle he chose to espouse in the early 1930s (JV, 26). It is in fact an essential part of his mental landscape: 'Mon aventure si, géographiquement elle s'arrêtait à Barcelone s'y devait poursuivre profondément, de plus en plus profondément, dans les régions de moi-même les plus reculées' (JV, 33). A series of spatial references superimposing the regions of the self and the psyche, the map of cultural landmarks and the geographical distribution of a readership produces an implicit figure of the position occupied by the *fait divers* rubric within the page layout of the newspaper.[2]

At the same time, Genet is putting in place a significant series of correspondences which underlines his own identity as a denizen of the *fait divers* while highlighting the collusion of certain kinds of readers seeking exotic thrills within this autobiographical space. 'Pour me comprendre une complicité du lecteur sera nécessaire,' as he puts it (JV, 17). The nature of this complicity hinges not infrequently on a mutual familiarity with the *fait divers*. We have seen that the thirties saw a tremendous vogue for the *fait divers*, not just among the mass public but also among intellectuals, from Gide and the surrealists onwards.[3] We misunderstand the initial impact of Genet's work if we overlook the way it played on its first readers' fascination for *faits divers* and related disreputable domains of the popular press. Genet draws directly on it, for example, when he evokes Fontevrault in *Miracle de la Rose*. Contrary to what he asserts, he was never incarcerated in this prison, and much of what he writes of the life of its inmates and of its origins as a monastery, burial place of Plantagenet monarchs, would already be familiar to readers of a series of features by Gilbert Rougerie and Georges Oubert, run by *Paris-Soir* in the latter half of September 1933.[4] Similarly, reports and books by Henri Danjou, Alexis Danan and Albert Londres ensured that the authentic details on Mettray in Genet's text (including mockery aimed at the crusading zeal of the latter two: MR, 264, 308) found a ready echo in a public already primed to recognize them.[5]

To return to a passage quoted above, Genet's strategies seem designed to make of himself a 'héros déjà idéalisé puisque mort et réduit à l'état de prétexte à l'un de ces poèmes brefs que sont les faits divers' (MR, 225). As we have seen, his own writing reduces him to 'plus rien qu'un prétexte' (JV, 126); and we should also take account of Genet's complementary assertion that he is already dead,[6] and hence implicitly eligible to fulfil the role of hero of the *fait divers*. To understand this claim, we need to consider the status of Genet *vis-à-vis la Relégation perpétuelle* in the works we are considering. At the time of *Notre-Dame-des-fleurs* and *Miracle de la Rose*, Genet, convicted as a persistent offender, had the threat of a life sentence hanging over him, the 'condamnation à la Relègue' having a 'goût funèbre', evoking 'l'office des morts' and plunging him into a despair from which he sought refuge in his imagination (MR, 322–3; cf. 395). It is in fact a condition of the '*sainteté*' to which he aspires (MR, 215). In *Notre-Dame-des-fleurs* he explains that, following the recent abolition of transportation, people in his position are condemned to virtual entombment in a prison cell: 'Personne ne peut dire si je sortirais d'ici [. . .] Les Relégués demeurent jusqu'à la fin de leurs jours dans les massives Centrales [. . .] j'y commence une existence de vrai mort [. . .] J'accepte d'y vivre comme j'accepterais, mort, de vivre dans un cimetière' (NF, 12, 95, 97). Genet insisted in later life that he began writing because he did not know whether he would ever get out of prison.[7] Here then, his writing is a *post mortem* exercise, his references to the construction of his *légende* having a Mallarmean ring – 'Tel qu'en lui-même enfin l'éternité le change.'

Hence, at the time of these earlier texts, as he indicates in *Journal du Voleur*, 'l'ennui de mes journées de prison me fit me réfugier dans ma vie d'autrefois' (JV, 115): but the 'autrefois' of these earlier works is of a different character, and is used in different ways, from what is the case in *Journal du Voleur*. When he wrote this latter work, he could recount his life in the certainty that, thanks to the efforts of Cocteau, Sartre, Marc Barbezat and others who signed a petition to the President of the Republic on his behalf, this past had already acquired an aura of notoriety – or 'gloire infâme'. He had a myth on which to embroider his legend, the relationship with a public that this presupposes being an essential ingredient in that aggressive, subversive, disorienting dialogue with the reader that animates so much of his texts.

In *Notre-Dame-des-fleurs* and *Miracle de la Rose* he does not have the same kind of past of his own which has been thus determined by a public reputation. As a result the construction of antecedents, simultaneously determining a relationship with the public and underlining his challenge to moral values, evokes an 'autrefois' of a different, even anachronistic, kind. At this stage in Genet's career, his autobiography is bound up inextricably with meditations on representations of criminals, on 'la gloire qu'ils secrètent et que j'utilise à des fins moins pures', as he will put it in *Journal du Voleur* (JV, 117). There is a characteristic perverseness in the way he undertakes this exercise. In a world where the figure and exploits of the common-law criminal have been eclipsed by those of dictators and totalitarian régimes, Genet is seeking to revive the profile of the romantic criminal. Though his models are authentic enough in the main, they are as out of place in sociopolitical or ideological terms as the figure of Lacenaire which Hugo evokes in *Les Misérables*. One could say of them what Louis Chevalier does of this latter case: there is a striking and problematic contrast between the monstrous glorying in a spectacular individualism such a criminal represents and the diffuse, anonymous or bureaucratic nature of much of the criminality which the author cannot conceal as the real background to his narrative.[8]

Philippe Lejeune remarks: 'Une histoire de l'autobiographie aujourd'hui devrait être l'histoire des résistances aux modèles de récit (et de vies) qu'imposent à la fois la tradition littéraire et scolaire et le jeu des médias.'[9] Given his delinquent posture, Genet's resistance to models is most acute in the case of institutional ones; and his concern with aspects of the *légende* and notions of notoriety, even when anachronistic as has been suggested, can be construed as forms of resistance to modern administrative conceptions of criminality. Michel Foucault links these issues with the rise, in the development of modern penal systems, of an apparatus to define and circumscribe criminality in an urban industrial society. 'Le châtiment légal porte sur un acte; la technique punitive sur une vie,' he writes; and he continues: 'L'introduction du "biographique" est importante dans l'histoire de la pénalité. Parce qu'il fait exister le "criminel" avant le crime et, à la limite, en dehors de lui.'[10] Furthermore, while the official mechanisms for documenting the delinquent existence are specifically aimed at diminishing 'la gloire douteuse des criminels', Foucault highlights the *fait divers* as that section of the media working in its equivocal fashion to reveal the everyday criminality of the modern world 'à la fois comme très proche et tout à fait étrangère'.[11] All these points are borne out by the example Genet presents.

Genet confronts simultaneously both institutional models of behaviour and official representations of the self. As a vagabond with a criminal record he fell foul of the ruling concerning the 'carnet anthropométrique', a document containing details of his civil status, physical characteristics and general description, which he was required to present to the authorities at regular intervals. He recounts how he first learned about it on returning from Spain to France, in the course of a brutal interview with local gendarmes: 'J'apprenais l'existence de l'humiliant carnet anthropométrique. On le délivre à tous les vagabonds. A chaque gendarmerie on le vise. On m'emprisonna' (JV, 97). Albert Dichy and Pascal Fouché record that Genet was 'inculpé de défaut de carnet anthropométrique' in June 1939:[12] but he had been living with aspects of this phenomenon from an early age, having been subject to the state's inquisitorial attentions since childhood.[13] *Miracle de la Rose* comments on it: 'Tous les gars qui passent par Fontevrault doivent laisser leur signalement anthropométrique aux archives de la Centrale. On me fit donc sortir de la salle vers 2h pour monter au greffe, afin d'être mesuré (les pieds, les mains, les doigts, le front, le nez) et photographié' (MR, 313). The prisoner therefore, becoming aware of his 'criminal identity' in his encounters with the penal system, is at pains to construct his self and life, the 'autobiographical', as a form of resistance to this officially-sanctioned biography. Genet refers thus to the process – signalling in passing how it flies in the face of popular received opinion about a criminal's moral or intellectual capacities, something else to commend it in his eyes: 'Construire sa vie minute par minute en assistant à sa construction, qui est aussi destruction à mesure, il vous paraît impossible que je l'ose prêter à un voleur sans envergure. On ne voit capable de cela qu'un esprit sévèrement entraîné. Mais Harcamone était un ancien colon de Mettray, qui avait là-bas bâti sa vie minute par minute . . .' (MR, 224–5). This self-construction resists the institutional version, as often as not by appropriating and subverting it. Legal records show that time and again Genet falsified his own identity, and his criminal career consisted substantially of trafficking in forged identity papers.[14] Moreover for the writer he aimed to be, the possibility of a criminal autobiography 'avant le crime et à la limite en dehors de lui', as Foucault puts it, is not without interest. Thus Genet can write of the prison warders and officials and the 'formative' discipline they imposed: 'Ils écrivaient mon histoire. Ils étaient mes personnages. Ils ne comprenaient rien à Mettray. Ils étaient idiots' (MR, 264). Similarly, he takes to task more than once the campaigning journalists who wrote reports on prison conditions, expressing wonderment at 'ce qui provoquait l'indignation d'un Albert Londres, d'un Alexis Danan' (MR, 264, 308). The culmination of this latter stance will occur in *L'Enfant criminel*, in which he more or less tells would-be reformers to mind their own business and leave the delinquent children to see to it that reformatories carry on performing their proper function, i.e. producing criminal youngsters . . .[15] Similarly, in his evocation of the criminal–heroes of his novels, Genet makes a point of indicating that the *fait-diversiers*, through their conventional, stereotyped approach to reporting, misconstrue the true sense of what they evoke. Thus he purports to show us the poetic reality of Harcamone while indicating that 'Les journaux l'avaient enlisé sur ces épithètes:"Le Tueur","le monstre"' (MR, 303); and in evoking his execution he remarks: 'Il ne fit aucun humour, comme on l'osa écrire dans les journaux' (MR, 389). The efforts of the 'Ideological State Apparatuses', or of the Benthamite 'Panopticon' analysed by Foucault, can be commandeered or subverted by the resolute creations of the criminal himself, and give way to a particular meaning.

Genet creates the criminal–heroes of his books with systematic reference to the standard procedures of forensic documentation – which are in turn common features of the *fait divers* as *chronique judiciaire*. In his heroes Genet creates an image of himself, of course: his aim in *Notre-Dame-des-fleurs*, for example, is to 'refaire à ma guise [. . .] l'histoire de Divine que je connus si peu, l'histoire de Notre-Dame-des-Fleurs, et n'en doutez pas, ma propre histoire'. Significantly, his starting point is as follows: 'Signalement de Notre-Dame-des-Fleurs: taille 1m. 71, poids 71kg., visage ovale, cheveux blonds, yeux bleus, teint mat, dents parfaites, nez rectiligne' (NF, 12). The description has been lifted – stolen, as it were – straight from the prison records. Elsewhere, Genet will refer to his own 'photographies de l'identité judiciaire' in *Journal du Voleur*, commenting on them to revive the experience and the character behind, and belying, 'la fixité que m'imposait le photographe officiel' (JV, 90–2). He tells how he fell in love with the newspaper photograph of Marc Aubert, executed for treason and referred to at the start of *Notre-Dame*, saying that he still carries it around with him (NF, 29; JV, 77). In both *Notre-Dame-des-fleurs* and *Miracle de la Rose*, he enthuses about the beauty and compelling charm of Maurice Pilorge as evidenced in a mug shot reproduced in, and cut out lovingly from, the crime magazine *Détective* (NF, 53–5; MR, 327).[16]

A related exploitation of mock-forensic methods can be seen in the way the autobiographical element in Genet's texts mimics the movement of testimony under interrogation or the inquisitorial gaze of the tribunal – which it invites, or rather provokes. The tribunal constitutes one of the schemas of Genet's spiritual existence: in *Journal du Voleur* God is defined as 'mon tribunal intime', and sainthood as the moment 'quand va cesser le tribunal, c'est-à-dire que le juge et le jugé seront confondus' (JV, 261). The narrative of *Notre-Dame-des-fleurs* reaches its climax in the report of the trial of the hero, and is intercut with allusions to the narrator's own appearances before the examining magistrate: confrontations during which, in his own words, he practices 'la ruse des aveux partiels. Spontanément, j'avoue un peu, afin de mieux celer le plus grave' (NF, 103–4). He then reflects on the complex strategies by which he and the magistrate attempt to outwit each other, thereby providing a commentary on the text's own labyrinthine anticipations of the reader's scrutiny. Notre Dame in court, required to recount to the jury what he has already retailed numerous times to the police and the examining magistrate, 'décida de raconter autre chose. Pourtant, dans le même temps, il racontait exactement cette histoire qu'il avait dite avec les mêmes mots aux policiers, au juge, à l'avocat, aux psychiatres. [. . .] Il relisait son crime comme une chronique se relit, mais ce n'était plus vraiment du crime qu'il parlait' (NF, 156). Repetition produces an effect of distance akin to reading the story of one's crime second-hand among the *faits divers*. This reiterative function further problematizes the autobiographical project, along lines Arnaud Malgorn sees operating consistently in Genet's writing as he repeats and rewrites texts – and even rumours and anecdotes he himself put into circulation in the first place: 'L'autobiographie chez Genet n'est pas tant une œuvre de faussaire que le palimpseste d'autres textes, sans cesse effacés et réécrits.'[17] However one looks at it, this is a strategy to unsettle the gaze of the inquisitor and reassert the peculiar integrity of the prisoner's evasive confession. 'Les prisons sont pleines de bouches qui mentent,' Genet warns. 'Chacun raconte de fausses aventures où il a le rôle de héros' (MR, 217). The *procès-verbal* is contaminated by the vagaries of the *fait divers* with its secondary dimension of unverifiable rumour and gossip.

Further implications of the topos of interrogation are developed in *Miracle de la Rose* when the prison governor seeks to get to the bottom of Harcamone's murder of a warder. Genet reports through rumour and hearsay a story at the heart of which is the defeat of the officer's probing:

> La scène du prétoire, qui précéda les interrogatoires de la Police Judiciaire et du juge, me fut connue grâce à des recoupements traîtres, faits dans la conversation silencieuse des gâfes. Harcamone comparut devant un directeur affolé d'être en face d'un mystère aussi absurde que celui que propose une rose dans tout son éclat. Il voulait savoir ce que signifiait ce meurtre, [. . .] mais il se heurtait à l'ignorance d'Harcamone, et il ne pouvait non plus compter sur une explication mensongère car l'assassin était plus fort . . . (MR, 309)

The enigma presented by the criminal constitutes the core of the text, as the allusion to the rose, linking it with the book's title, indicates. It is the essence of Genet's counter-biographies and of his own autobiographical enterprise. The criminals' beauty is a 'beauté en creux' inaccessible to the respectable reader (JV, 117). 'Les crimes d'Harcamone [. . .] apparaîtront des actes idiots' (MR, 216), Genet writes. But they are not supposed to make sense – they are intended to unmake it. Like certain words which 'sont un danger pour la compréhension pratique du discours', these acts 'font surgir la poésie' (MR, 217). It is perhaps an obvious thing to say, but Genet is not confessing so that we may condemn or understand him. When he writes 'A chaque accusation portée contre moi, fût-elle injuste, du fond du cœur je répondrai oui' (JV, 186), he is seizing the initiative and claiming responsibility for his guilt, while denying the reader the capacity to comprehend and thus to judge.

The crux of the matter is highlighted in the narrator's references to his lover Bulkaen. He actually started writing *Miracle de la Rose* 'pour jouir par les mots du souvenir de Bulkaen' (MR, 214). However, when the two went through a phase of exchanging secret notes, a furtive correspondence 'où nous parlions de nous', Genet says, Bulkaen signed himself 'Illisible' and Genet in turn addressed him as 'Mon Illisible'. Quite apart from the further subversive parody of official documents contained in these allusions, Genet makes the point that 'Pierre Bulkaen restera pour moi l'indéchiffrable' (MR, 232). The text concludes with a reprise of this theme, underlining the impenetrability of what it is seeking to glorify: the book will transmit his heroes' reputation, Genet says, but so far as knowing who they are is concerned, there can be no explanation. 'Si je quitte ce livre, je quitte ce qui peut se raconter. Le reste est indicible' (MR, 395). The hero's biography – the narrator's autobiography – is the aura around an ungraspable truth. Put another way, the attainment of being *lisible*, having a *légende*, is conditional upon the preservation of the existential self as *illisible*.

The use of features from and allusions to the *fait divers* can be seen as a technique intended to draw the reader in towards the contemplation of such unsettling enigmas. The fact is that although Genet prizes squalor and criminality above all that normal society (addressed as 'vous') can offer, he simultaneously needs and must seek out 'votre reconnaissance, votre sacre', to validate his legend.[18] Certain aspects of Genet's work stem from his having come to understand and colonize or assert his place in the world – on the margins of society – by exploiting the arm's-length but fascinated collusion with it that society adopted as a posture, and which he could see exemplified in the role it accorded to *faits divers*. This is the domain where society's repressed impulses are contained and observed, where *l'immonde* ferments to sustain *le monde*.

The *fait divers* therefore provided Genet with a particularly appropriate

– because insidious – means of penetrating the society which excluded him. His writing entered through the back door as it were, via the ill-acknowledged and inadequately policed collective subconscious. At the same time, however, the *fait divers* rubric also provided him with role models, the stuff from which to create a persona.[19]

The opening line of *Notre-Dame-des-fleurs* provides an effective illustration of these points: 'Weidmann vous apparut dans une édition de cinq heures [. . .] un jour de septembre pareil à celui où fut connu le nom de Notre-Dame des Fleurs.'

As Genet steals furtively into the lives of 'bourgeois attristés', the voice which he finds to articulate his presence is at its very origin a challenge to the hypocrisy of these readers whose 'vie quotidienne est frôlée d'assassins enchanteurs, élevés sournoisement jusqu'à leur sommeil qu'ils vont traverser, par quelque escalier d'office qui, complice pour eux, n'a pas grincé' (NF, 9).[20] Genet affirms his identity only indirectly as the one who unveils that complicity linking the first two characters to feature in the text: Weidmann and 'vous'. He will trace his presence obliquely, and will speak of himself to his reader through the intermediary of his heroes. Thus the text continues:

Un peu plus tôt, le nègre Ange Soleil avait tué sa maîtresse.

Un peu plus tard, le soldat Maurice Pilorge assassinait son amant [. . .] vous vous le rappelez . . .

Enfin, un enseigne de vaisseau, encore enfant, trahissait pour trahir: on le fusilla.

The infamy of these criminals is invidiously constructed by the reader's own recognition of their names, recollection of their exploits, or acknowledgement of the celebrity presupposed by the exophoric article. It is only after listing them thus that Genet declares his hand: 'Et c'est en l'honneur de leurs crimes que j'écris mon livre.' He places himself at the bottom of a systematically-arranged hierarchy descending from the most notorious to the unknown: the implication is that he proposes to ascend it.[21] Genet's autobiographical project progressively absorbs into the author's life the notoriety of the criminals who have inspired him. 'J'envie ta gloire,' he says in *Notre-Dame*, apostrophizing Pilorge. 'J'irais bien facilement à la guillotine, puisque d'autres y sont allés, et surtout Pilorge, Weidmann, Ange Soleil, Soclay [. . .] ces créations forment tout mon concert spirituel passé' (NF, 54). Elsewhere he refers to himself as 'moi qui recrée ces hommes, Weidmann, Pilorge, Soclay, dans mon désir d'être eux-mêmes' (NF, 141).[22]

Here we rejoin once again the *légende* from which we started. As Sartre puts it, Genet's dream is to 'venir à soi comme un autre, sous l'aspect légendaire d'un criminel'.[23] It is in the nature of the denizens of the *fait divers* that their renown circulates as rumour and gossip as much as in printed form. While press cuttings as such play a substantial role in Genet's texts, it is also notable that his heroes' reputations precede them via other channels. The source material for *Notre-Dame-des-fleurs* came to his attention via lawyers' chat and prisoners' conversations as well as news items (NF, 9). The *forçats* passing through Fontevrault on their way to Saint-Martin-de-Ré speak, in a casual way that leaves Genet and the other inmates stunned, 'de tous les princes du crime à qui les journaux firent un nom immense [. . .] je fus émerveillé comme on devait l'être lorsqu'on pouvait entendre Murat tutoyer Napoléon' (MR, 319). The children in Mettray trade stories of notorious villains: 'Chacune de leurs histoires [. . .] ne nous était pas connue avec une exacte précision mais, soit parce que son auteur en avait parlé à mots couverts, soit que lui-même arrivât, escorté et précédé d'une réputation qui s'était accumulée [. . .] ces histoires avaient fini par se savoir, mais dans une forme assez vague, imprécise. [. . .] Donc chaque histoire était connue sous une forme légendaire' (MR, 316–7). This is the stuff legends are made of: the *faits divers*, 'ces poèmes brefs', transmit precisely that lyrical distillation of a life that circulates independently of author, text and pretext, and which Genet seeks to achieve through his written (and oral) versions of his biography.

He aims to acquire this status at the expense of the reader, who as we have seen is drawn into the louche celebration willy-nilly, from the very beginning. Genet forces the voyeuristic complicity of the bourgeois who is invited to acknowledge that s/he reads the *chronique* for the gory bits too: 'Vous savez par *Paris-Soir* qu'il fut tué, lors de la révolte à Cayenne' (NF, 90), he says of the murderer Clément Village, and in connection with his brutal crime he alludes to 'cette histoire, que vous lûtes dans les journaux' (NF, 84).

At this juncture, however, Genet reveals that he himself did *not* read the story – much to Village's dismay when the two met in prison. 'Il fut chagrin que je ne me souvinsse pas de cette histoire, que vous lûtes dans les journaux' (NF, 84). Wrongfooting the reader, Genet indicates that he himself might be less immersed in the *fait divers* than the latter. This is an important point, as emerges from a passage of *Miracle de la Rose* which brings out the underlying thrust of the autobiographical in these early texts:

> Si j'écrivais un roman, j'aurais quelque intérêt à m'étendre sur mes gestes d'alors, mais je n'ai voulu par ce livre que montrer l'expérience menée de ma libération d'un état de pénible torpeur, de vie honteuse et basse [. . .] soumise aux prestiges, subjuguée par les charmes du monde criminel. Je me libérais par et pour une attitude plus fière. (MR, 206)

The *sujet de l'énonciation,* being distinct from the *sujet de l'énoncé,* does not share the foibles of the narrated self. In *Notre-Dame-des-fleurs* too, at the same moment as he speaks of recreating his criminal heroes from a desire to emulate them, Genet adds that 'fidélité à ses personnages' is not his strong point, since 'je me suis depuis longtemps résigné à être moi-même' (NF, 141).

Even as he subjects the reader to the prestige and dubious charms of the criminal world, Genet himself speaks as one who has, he says, broken the spell they cast on him. The mechanism enabling him to do this is his particular brand of autobiographical writing, the aesthetico-therapeutic discipline which he discusses in *Journal du Voleur.* 'Ce journal que j'écris n'est pas un délassement littéraire [. . .] à mesure que j'y progresse, ordonnant ce que ma vie passée me propose [. . .] je me sens m'affermir dans la volonté d'utiliser, à des fins de vertus, mes misères d'autrefois. [. . .] Par l'écriture j'ai obtenu ce que je cherchais. [. . .] Réussir ma légende' (JV, 65, 217–8).

Although his writing thus modifies its own character, Genet continues to draw his inspiration from news clippings featuring notorious criminals. Appropriately enough, therefore, the change in perspective associated with the prospect of escaping *la Relègue* is signalled by a reference to his having read in *Détective* news of the condemnation to 'la relégation' of his old croney Rasseneur – a prominent figure in *Miracle de la Rose* – in precisely the same week that 'une pétition d'écrivains demandait, pour la même peine, ma grâce au Président de la République' (JV, 53–4). In other words, Genet is contemplating freedom as he writes *Journal du Voleur.* Thus, rather than simply consigning his past life to a *Légende dorée* to rival that of Christ, as was the aim in *Miracle de la Rose* (MR, 256–7), he here looks to his autobiography as a basis for future strategies to undermine structures of authority. By now the systematic purpose underlying his references to *faits divers* has come to the fore. Of collaborators during the Occupation he writes, 'Ce qui m'avait fait détacher et conserver ce morceau de journal où sont leurs photographies, c'est le désir d'en tirer nourriture pour une argumentation en faveur de la trahison' (JV, 159). He returns to Pilorge, saying 'J'acceptais qu'il me fût non un exemple, mais une aide pour parcourir une route jusqu'à un ciel où j'espère le joindre (je n'écris pas le rejoindre)' (JV, 159). Ultimately, he views his autobiography as a poor substitute for those lives – and deaths – he refers to, and dismisses as an illusion the hope that he might achieve their kind of notoriety, however much his alleged acquaintance with some of them might seem to give his life a certan significance:

Soclay, Pilorge, Weidmann, Serge de Lenz, Messieurs de la Police, indicateurs sournois, vous m'apparaissez quelquefois parés comme de toilettes funèbres et de jais, de si beaux crimes que j'envie, aux uns la peur mythologique qu'ils inspirent, aux autres leurs supplices, à tous l'infamie où finalement ils se confondent. Si je regarde en arrière je n'aperçois qu'une suite d'actions piteuses. Mes livres les racontent. [. . .] J'eus tant de mal pour réussir si mal ce que font si vite mes héros. (JV, 117–8)

If he retains 'peut-etre' (JV, 159) a cult for Pilorge and his ilk, it is one from which the sentimental attachments of former times have been filtered out, one which is now sustained by a much more analytical stance, concerned critically with the nature of the criminal's image in society. Notoriety, after all, is merely a further form of subjection to society's gaze; throwing the criminal image back in the face of the bourgeoisie does not in itself achieve control over the relationship between judge and accused.[24]

The very title of *Journal du Voleur* announces that the work is engaging with this question. The text itself does not conform to the standard generic expectations it at first seems to prompt: it does not consist of dated entries. The book

contient – doit contenir – les commandements que je ne saurais transgresser: si j'en suis digne il me réservera la gloire infâme dont il est le grand maître. [. . . N] e serait-ce logique que ce livre entraînât mon corps et m'attirât en prison [. . .] par une fatalité qu'il contient, que j'y ai mise, et qui, comme je l'ai voulue, me garde comme témoin, champ d'expérience, preuve par 9 de sa vertu et de ma responsabilité. (JV, 284–5)

The reader, it is implied, will have little choice but to condemn Genet to prison for what he has written; but Genet retains the initiative, claiming responsibility as we have already seen, and continues to preside over the exercise. In fact, another genre this text plays on in order to subvert it is the criminal's memoirs from prison, a form much prized by writers and readers of the *fait divers*.[25] The criminal's own testimony, direct and unmediated, commands a special kind of attention because it speaks from beyond those bounds which the judicial system exists to confirm: the more so since, as in the particularly notorious case of Landru, the criminal's intimate record of his misdeeds might constitute the principal evidence that condemns him. Thus, the covers of *Détective* for 27 September and 4 October 1934 vaunted *Le Journal de Violette Nozières* – 'un document formidable' – while she awaited trial for poisoning her mother and father.[26] The magazine's extensive coverage of Weidmann's life in prison focused with regret on his failure to 'livrer par écrit les secrets de son étrange nature' despite the facilities made available to him to do so.[27] In the same number, however, the headline 'Le carnet d'un assassin' introduced extracts from the diary of one Louis Philippe, referred to as 'Le Weidmann Lyonnais'.

Born in 1910, the same year as Genet, he was sent to the reformatory at Mettray in 1926, the same year that Genet was sent there, after being found guilty of inflicting grievous bodily harm on his mother. He left Mettray in the same way that Genet did, by enlisting for service in the armed forces, and thereafter committed a series of murders beginning with that of the second officer of the ship on which he was serving.[28] Genet may well have encountered this criminal with whom his existence had so much in common and who achieved precisely that parallel with Weidmann that Genet's writing was to pursue. All of which gives extra point to the fact that the Philippe's writings are ironized and become the butt of that self-righteous censoriousness which seems to typify crime reports of the time. A more sophisticated commentator, Colette, refers tellingly to the function of writing in these cases: 'Ecrire est la plus grande tentation du prisonnier, qui débute dans la rédaction par le mensonge littéraire, mais glisse peu à peu vers la tentante, vers l'incroyable vérité. Un carnet, un crayon, et Philippe, émule ambitieux de Weidmann, se perd.'[29]

Genet's writing can be seen as a response to the implicit challenge here: how can the former inmate of Mettray offer his own testimony and attain the notoriety of a Weidmann without playing into the hands of his judges? The point emerges in *Journal du Voleur* when he returns, significantly, to the photograph of Weidmann alluded to at the beginning of his first book and reassesses his point of departure from the perspective he has subsequently attained. As we have seen, he now understands that the criminal's notoriety represents a 'piège' from which few, but notably Weidmann, escape. The lesson he now sees embodied in Weidmann is the possibility of exhibiting a truth about the self which 'ne se retourne pas pour enlaidir sa gueule' (JV, 159–60). By the time he writes *Journal du Voleur* Genet too is seeking ways of manifesting his truth without compromising it, without making it available for misinterpretation or misappropriation.[30] This represents a return to 'l'illisible' – what he here calls 'l'impossible nullité' (JV, 100): it is perhaps 'la transparence' (JV, 229) he might achieve if he were able to 'bondir au cœur de l'image' (JV, 229) and suppress the existential self altogether. The idea of it will continue to haunt his work, especially his theatre, where it will find perhaps its most authentic expression in Saïd of *Les Paravents*, who disappears at his moment of triumph, leaving behind him simply a suggestion of a 'chanson': an insubstantial poetic aura.[31]

Notes

1. Page references are given in the text of this chapter, with abbreviations as follows: NF – *Notre-Dame-des-fleurs*, and MR – *Miracle de la Rose*, in

Jean Genet, *Œuvres complètes de Jean Genet*, vol.2 (Paris, Gallimard, 1951); JV – *Journal du Voleur* (Paris, Gallimard, 1949).

2. The same figure is present in *Le Paysan de Paris*: see above, pp.80–1.

3. See pp.33–102.

4. Cf. Albert Dichy and Pascal Fouchet, *Jean Genet. Essai de chronologie 1910–1944*, op.cit., p.127.

5. Alexis Danan, *Maison des Supplices*, Paris, Denoel, 1936; Henri Danjou, *Enfants du Malheur*, Paris, Albin Michel, 1932. See Dichy and Fouché, *Jean Genet. Essai de chronologie 1910–1944*, p.120, and photographs between pp.112–13 showing extracts from a feature on Mettray in *Détective*, 22 April 1937; see also Harry E. Stewart and Rob Roy McGregor, *Jean Genet: a biography of deceit 1910–1951*, New York, Peter Lang, 1989, p.33.

6. The notion is elaborated on in some detail by Sartre in *Saint Genet, comédien et martyr*, op.cit., pp.9–22, 25–6.

7. See for example the interviews reproduced in Arnaud Malgorn, *Jean Genet qui êtes-vous?*, Lyon, La Manufacture, 1988, pp.163, 172. The extent to which this was true is still difficult to ascertain, despite the work of Stewart, McGregor, Moraly, and Dichy and Fouché. But certainly the possibility arose repeatedly between 1939 and 1942 (Dichy and Fouché, *Jean Genet, essai de chronologie 1910–1944*, pp.175–93), casting its shadow over the writing of *Notre-Dame-des-fleurs* and *Miracle de la Rose*. Indeed it appears that it was only via inadvertence or deliberate leniency that Genet escaped it in November 1943 (Stewart and McGregor, *Jean Genet: a biography of deceit 1910–1951*, pp.131–4): a circumstance he perhaps alludes to in an interview with Robert Poulet in 1956: 'Par chance, j'ai rencontré un juge d'instruction qui, dans un mouvement de générosité, m'a épargné la relégation, en déchirant subrepticement dans mon dossier la copie de mon casier judiciaire' (in Malgorn, *Jean Genet qui êtes-vous?*, p.161).

8. Louis Chevalier, *Classes laborieuses et classes dangereuses à Paris pendant la première moitié de XIXᵉ siècle*, Paris, Plon, 1958, pp.117–8. It is worth pointing out that the opening passage of *Notre-Dame-des-fleurs* is very reminiscent of the sequence in *Le Dernier Jour d'un Condamné* in which the prisoner deciphers the signatures on the prison wall and details the exploits of his notorious criminal predecessors who have carved them there. See Chevalier, ibid., pp.74–5. Philip Thody, *Jean Genet, a study of his novels and plays*, London, Hamish Hamilton, 1968, rightly points out how the contrast between poeticization and sordid reality runs throughout the whole of *Miracle de la Rose*. In *Pompes funèbres* Genet will bemoan the fact that having imagined he could put a gulf of scandal between himself and the society of his time by cultivating vice and criminality, he is dismayed to realize that he is indistinguishable from

the people around him who 'y sont venus facilement . . . Ils sont dans l'infamie comme un poisson dans l'eau' (*Œuvres complètes*, vol.3, Paris, Gallimard, 1953, pp.108–9).

9. Philippe Lejeune, 'Les projets autobiographiques de Georges Perec', in *Parcours Perec*, edited by Mireille Ribière, Lyon, Presses Universitaires de Lyon, 1990, p.68.

10. Michel Foucault, *Surveiller et Punir*, Paris, Gallimard, 1975, p.255.

11. Ibid., pp.114, 292–4. From a perspective which, paradoxically, is not unrelated to Genet's, Camus in *L'Homme révolté* underlines the romantic – or nostalgic – attractions of the heroic *criminel de droit commun* as a contrast to or protest against the totalitarian 'univers du procès'. See D. Walker, 'Le Criminel chez Camus', in *Albert Camus, les extrêmes et l'équilibre*, Amsterdam, Rodopi, collection 'Faux Titre', 1994.

12. Dichy and Fouché, *Jean Genet. Essai de chronologie 1910–1944*, p.173.

13. Edmund White underlines the important role played by such official scrutiny in shaping the writer's life and work: see *Genet*, London, Chatto and Windus, 1993, especially at pp.47–8, 60, 67, 182. Two critics in particular explore the juridical dimension of Genet's theatrical rhetoric which arguably stems from the same source: Jeannette Savona, 'Théâtre et univers carcéral: Jean Genet et Michel Foucault', *French Forum*, vol.10, no.2, 1985, pp.201–13, and *Jean Genet*, Basingstoke, Macmillan, 1983; and Maria Paganini, 'L'Inscription juridique dans *Les Bonnes* de Jean Genet', *Romanic Review*, vol.80, no.3, 1989, pp.462–82.

14. See the documents reproduced by Dichy and Fouché, *Jean Genet. Essai de chronologie 1910–1944*, and Stewart and McGregor, *Jean Genet: a biography of deceit 1910–1951*.

15. See 'L'enfant criminel,' in *Œuvres complètes*, vol.5, Paris, Gallimard, 1979, pp.377–93.

16. It is interesting to note the important role played by photographs in Genet's texts. They are clear instances of an item 'que présente le passé', through which the past remains strikingly present. The problematic relationship of language to the past it seeks to retrieve is overlaid by a different interaction, between the visual and the linguistic, when Genet constructs his antecedents in this way. The overlap between the public and the private is another issue they raise. It would be productive to compare Genet's case with the photographs Gide writes of in *Si le grain ne meurt*; or with the example of Barthes in *Barthes par Barthes* and *La Chambre claire*. *Le Balcon* goes further, depicting photographers who specialize in creating 'une image vraie, née d'un spectacle faux', and explicitly linking 'la lecture' with 'l'image' (*Le Balcon*, edited with an introduction and notes by D. H. Walker, London, Methuen, 1982, pp.115–18). This reminds us that in *Notre-Dame-des-fleurs* too the

referential value of photographs is dubious since the narrator is not prepared to guarantee that they depict the individuals he chooses to see in them (NF, 10). As so often in Genet's work we find ourselves dealing with effects of secondary signification arising from the evacuation of a reliable referent.

17. Malgorn, *Jean Genet, qui êtes-vous?*, pp.28–9.
18. On the readerly discomfort this supposes, and the problematics of communication it entails, see Colin Davis, 'Genet's *Journal du Voleur* and the ethics of reading', *French Studies*, vol.68, no.1, January 1994, pp.50–62, especially at pp.53–6.
19. Harry E. Stewart has done much to clarify the inspiration Genet drew from such sources. See for example his 'Jean Genet's favorite murderers', *The French Review*, vol.60, no.5, 1987, pp.635–43; 'Louis Ménesclou, assassin and source of the "Lilac Murder" in Genet's *Haute Surveillance*', *Romance Notes*, vol.26, no.3, 1986, pp.204–8. See also Stewart and McGregor, *Jean Genet, a biography of deceit 1910–1951*.
20. The 'escalier' could legitimately be seen as an image of the way the *fait divers* works. For a complementary discussion on Genet's relations with the reader, see above, pp.42–4.
21. There is a clear link here with *Haute Surveillance*, whose original title was *Préséances* and whose plot turns on the hierarchy among criminals.
22. It should be underlined that the self-projection does not respect the facts of his heroes' lives: Stewart and McGregor point out that whatever Genet knew of Pilorge he had read in the newspapers, since contrary to his numerous assertions there is no evidence of an actual acquaintance of any kind. Moreover Pilorge was not a homosexual and the man he killed was not his lover. 'Pure invention' is the judgement these researchers pass on Genet's version of events, although certain details of Notre Dame's trial do echo reports of that of Pilorge. Similarly, despite what Genet says, neither Ange Soleil nor Soclay were guillotined. See *Jean Genet, a biography of deceit*, pp.86–8, 99 n21; and Stewart, 'Genet's favorite murderers', pp.639–40.
23. Sartre, *Saint Genet, comédien et martyr*, p.480.
24. This problem will be the central element of *Les Nègres*.
25. On this genre, see Monestier *et al.*, *Le Fait Divers*, pp.147–8.
26. No.309, pp.7, 8, 9; no.310, pp.4, 5.
27. *Détective*, no.541, 9 March 1939, p.4.
28. Ibid., pp.6–10. It is noteworthy that Philippe's biography develops that nautical dimension of the Mettray experience, evoked at length in *Miracle de Rose* (e.g. MR, 226, 237, 243–4), to which *Querelle de Brest* also owes much; this latter novel may well echo the story of Philippe.
29. *Œuvres complètes de Colette*, vol.13, Paris, Le Fleuron, chez Flammarion, 1950, p.438. Colette covered the Weidmann trial for *Paris-Soir*. See

above, p.105.

30. Cf. Michael Sheringham, 'Narration and experience in Genet's *Journal du Voleur*', in *Studies in French Fiction: a Festschrift for Vivenne Milne*, ed. Robert Gibson, London, Grant and Cutler, 1988, pp.289–306, at p.295: 'Genet's quest is not so much for a new image of himself, a new hypostasis as the Thief, or the Poet, but for a flight or at least a distancing from all images.'

31. Barthes offers a meditation on the problem, using some of the same terminology as Genet, in 'L'Image', *Le Bruissement de la Langue*, Paris, Seuil, 1984, pp.389–97.

PART V

Fantasies of Violence:
Female Intuitions

11

Consuming News:
Simone de Beauvoir

The title of Simone de Beauvoir's novel *Les Belles Images*, coupled with the fact that its heroine Laurence works in an advertising agency, is enough to indicate that it is concerned with idealized representations of reality whose purpose is to attract custom or deflect disquiet. The two are combined, for example, in the case of the wood-panelling for which Laurence is trying to find a slogan: 'Le bois n'est pas plus inflammable que la pierre ou la brique: le dire sans évoquer l'idée d'incendie. C'est là qu'il faut du doigté' (BI, 23).[1]

Laurence has personal as well as professional reasons for steering clear of life's unpleasant aspects: she has had an emotional breakdown some five years before and a profound unease lies just beneath the surface of her outwardly secure and successful existence.[2] Moreover, at the point at which the novel takes up her story, her daughter Catherine is showing signs of emotional disturbance, waking in the night crying and pressing her mother to explain why there is so much unhappiness in the world (BI, 23–4).

What is less clear at a first reading – and seems to have escaped the notice of most critics[3] – is the extent to which the novel presents newspapers as the focus of the fears that threaten the consumerist myth in the society it depicts. In fact, the conjugation of consumerism and the news media which Beauvoir develops in this novel can be seen to anticipate the analysis set out by Jean Baudrillard in his book *La Société de consommation*, published four years after *Les Belles Images*, in 1970. In what follows I wish to propose a reading of the novel that does proper justice to these elements.

Both Beauvoir and Sartre had a long-standing interest in the *fait divers* going back at least to the early 1930s, when they followed the prominent cases of the day – those of Violette Nozières and the Papin sisters, for instance – in *Détective* and *Paris-Soir*.[4] In 1964 Sartre reaffirmed that for him 'l'analyse d'un fait divers peut être bien plus révélatrice de la nature d'une société qu'un commentaire sur un changement de gouvernement.'[5] It can be argued that in *Les Belles Images* Beauvoir demonstrates the truth of this remark.

Beauvoir's stance in relation to the 'société technocratique' she portrays is that though she holds it at arm's length as far as possible, 'à travers les journaux, les magazines, la publicité, la radio, elle m'investit'.[6] It may therefore be seen as a kind of revenge on her part that in her novel she contrives to have the idyllic world of her characters invaded in turn, through the same channels, by features that challenge its sanitized social fiction.[7] Indeed, an examination of this phenomenon goes some way towards validating her claim that she was less interested in the people inhabiting this world than in the sound of its discourses (TCF, 139).

Laurence's breakdown, what her insensitive husband subsequently refers to as her 'crise de mauvaise conscience' in 1962, was specifically triggered by her having read in a newspaper the story of a woman tortured to death. The likely context seems to be the Algerian War, given Beauvoir's own involvement on this issue as reflected, for example, in the testimony of *Djamila Boupacha*, which she published with Gisèle Halimi in 1962. However, as we shall see, Laurence's reading of the news tends to highlight the sensational or emotional to the exclusion of historical or political detail. The horror of this incident proved hard for her to dispel, and since her convalescence 'elle avait désormais évité de lire les journaux' (BI, 133).

At the beginning of the novel, therefore, we must understand the extent to which her own traumatic experience of the news underpins her concern to protect her daughter Catherine from the atrocities in the world.[8] Disturbed by the ten-year-old's tearful questions, she realizes that 'Le monde [. . .] s'est glissé dans la vie de Catherine, il l'effraie et je devrais l'en protéger' (BI, 26). She wonders how the child has come by such insights into unhappiness, since 'elle a défendu à Catherine de lire les journaux; elle lui a expliqué, avec des exemples, que lorsqu'on est ignorante on risque de comprendre les choses de travers; et que les journaux mentent beaucoup' (BI, 39). Her father, to whom she turns for advice, is sceptical about this strategy: 'Tu ne peux tout de même pas tout contrôler,' he remarks, and adds: 'Quelle vie est protégée, aujourd'hui, avec les journaux, la télé, le cinéma?' (BI, 39). Laurence explains that she is extremely careful about what television her daughter watches, just as she and her husband do not leave newspapers lying around the house.

Laurence is not an intellectual. She is not really concerned about any metaphysical questions her daughter may stumble across: 'Pourquoi on existe? bon, ça c'est abstrait, c'est de la métaphysique; cette question-là ne m'inquiète pas beaucoup. Mais le malheur: c'est déchirant pour une enfant' (BI, 37). Beauvoir clearly concentrates attention in this text on the particularly vulnerable points of a social class that normally copes in this robust way with ideological or philosophical dilemmas. Laurence appears to respond much more intensely, however, to emotion and sensation: and this can become the source of more far-reaching interrogations.[9] As Beauvoir says in an interview on the novel, adults as well as children are led to take metaphysical questions seriously 'par des raisons affectives'.[10]

To be more precise, Laurence's abstinence from newspaper reading has actually left her out of touch with current affairs, and, as with the other sociocultural narratives available to her on her visit to Greece, they consequently leave her cold. 'Je ne pourrais pas d'un instant à l'autre me prendre de passion pour ces histoires dont j'ignore tout' (BI, 161), she says, with a telling allusion to the emotive engagement she fears but which is her only method for getting involved. She is happy enough to defer to her husband's bluff technological optimism about the meaning of life, the fate of the world and the outcome of its present crises. For her part, finding it difficult to pick up the threads of contemporary issues when she tries to read *Le Monde*, she is in fact all the more happy to abandon the effort because of her abiding phobia: 'Elle replie le journal, soulagée tout de même, parce qu'on ne sait jamais ce qu'on risque d'y découvrir. J'ai eu beau me blinder, je ne suis pas aussi solide qu'eux' (BI, 43).

Her personal defence mechanism is called into question when she discovers how her daughter has become aware of the problems which trouble her. On meeting Catherine's friend Brigitte, Laurence learns that the little girl does not like reading novels:

> — Je m'ennuie quand un livre est trop long. Et puis j'aime mieux les histoires vraies.
> — Les récits historiques?
> — Oui. Et les voyages; et ce qu'on lit dans les journaux.
> — Votre papa vous laisse lire les journaux? (BI, 54)

Stunned at this discovery, Laurence recalls her own father's words: 'Papa a raison, ai-je pensé, je ne contrôle pas tout. Si elle apporte les journaux au lycée, si elle raconte ce qu'elle a lu dedans . . . tous ces horribles faits divers: enfants martyrs, enfants noyés par leur propre mère' (BI, 54).

The selection she makes of the imagined *faits divers* that disturb her constitutes an eloquent projection of her own guilt for what she sees as her failure as a mother in this regard. She attributes Brigitte's unfortunate worldliness to neglect on her parents' part, and reminds Catherine of the prohibition on newspapers that still applies where she is concerned. She will even go so far as to take Brigitte aside and ask her not to recount *faits divers* to Catherine (BI, 78).

She does not want to stop the two girls from seeing each other, judging the friendship potentially beneficial for Catherine, who is after all old enough to 's'intéresser à ce qui se passe dans le monde' – with the important proviso that 'seulement il ne faudrait pas non plus la traumatiser'

(BI, 57). As a former victim herself, she is only too aware of the dangers involved when the discourses of the world infiltrate the protective family cocoon.

However, Laurence now finds herself in an ironic – and potentially tragic – double bind. She feels duty-bound to read the newspapers so as to be in a position to anticipate and cope with her daughter's queries about the way of the world. But this involves subjecting herself to precisely those horrors she is seeking to protect her daughter from: and she knows which they are because she herself is so sensitive to them.

Two developments follow from this point. First, the tragedies Laurence encounters in the *faits divers* rubric exacerbate the difficulties of her own emotional situation; and secondly, as she becomes more aware of the media's input into her milieu, the text is able to articulate, through her eyes, a critique of the media's role in shaping the discourses of the society she lives in.

The starting-point of these mechanisms can be located in the following passage:

> Il faut que je sois vigilante, que je me tienne au courant, que je renseigne moi-même ma fille. Laurence essaie de se concentrer sur *France-Soir*. Encore un fait divers affreux. Douze ans: il s'est pendu dans sa prison; il a demandé des bananes, une serviette, et il s'est pendu. 'Des faux frais.' Gilbert expliquait qu'en toute société il y a forcément des faux frais. Oui, forcément. N'empêche que cette histoire bouleverserait Catherine. (BI, 57–8)

In the 'Oui, forcément' we can see a dawning sense of irony in Laurence, arising from the confrontation between her revulsion at the suicide and the heartless application to it by her mother's lover Gilbert of the discourse of accountancy.[11] But at the same time she is putting herself under the added emotional pressure of maternal guilt as, faced with the distress in her family (her mother's lover is threatening to leave her) as well as in the world at large, she acknowledges that 'c'est si rare qu'on puisse quelque chose pour quelqu'un . . . Pour Catherine, oui. [. . .] Lui faire découvrir la réalité sans l'effrayer. Pour ça je dois d'abord m'informer. [. . .] Il s'agit de Catherine. Elle ne se pardonnerait pas de lui faire défaut' (BI, 58).

The *fait divers* comes to be a point of reference in her life. It is in the nature of the form that once read it remains in the mind and circulates in conversation: hence Laurence's lover Lucien, in an effort to convince her of the enduring nature of their love, will quote the news item of an elderly doctor who took poison on the death of his wife (BI, 60). Later, Laurence will ruminate privately on the story, clearly moved by its implications as something more than literary fantasy even though it does not fully convince her: 'Les histoires d'âmes sœurs, est-ce qu'on en rencontre ailleurs que dans les livres? Même le vieux médecin que la mort de sa femme a tué: ça ne prouve pas qu'ils étaient vraiment faits l'un pour l'autre' (BI, 67). The idea of dying for love, emanating from the same source and dramatized in the notorious failed suicide of Jeanne Texcier which is on everybody's lips (BI, 8, 118), also informs her views on the crisis her mother is going through, as she considers on a number of occasions – and even goes so far as to assert – that Dominique might resort to a *crime passionnel* or suicide in her despair (BI, 72, 85, 95, 96–7).

Most telling of all for Laurence, however, is that the motif of suicide links all these elements with the news report of the boy who hanged himself in his cell (BI, 57–8: see above, p.178). The subject also engages with the unhappiness that drives people to it and that lies at the heart of little Catherine's distress and hence Laurence's concern. But more than that, it jars a raw nerve in Laurence, one she is frightened to touch on since it revives memories of precisely the *angst* she experienced during her breakdown. In other words, through the network of interconnected *faits divers* in the novel, Laurence is seen to be identifying with the child–victims, the 'enfants martyrs'. The poignant singularity of the news item on the hanged boy, freighted with all these elements, comes back to her with particular force:

> Il y a ce creux, ce vide, qui glace le sang, qui est pire que la mort bien qu'on le préfère à la mort tant qu'on ne se tue pas: j'ai connu ça il y a cinq ans et j'en garde une épouvante. Et le fait est que des gens se tuent – il a demandé des bananes et une serviette – parce qu'il existe justement quelque chose de pire que la mort. C'est ce qui fait froid aux os quand on lit le récit d'un suicide: non le frêle cadavre accroché aux barreaux de la fenêtre, mais ce qui s'est passé dans ce cœur, juste avant. (BI, 85; cf. 57–8)

Before pursuing the developments of these crucial motifs, we ought to review further evidence of Beauvoir's efforts to indicate that Laurence's sensibility is increasingly marked by the *fait divers* rubric. This material has to do with the role of the car in her family and the society of the time. We learn that on occasions the stress of his job can leave her husband Jean-Charles so highly-strung that he is almost unfit to drive. As Laurence puts it after one such experience: 'Pour un peu avant-hier les journaux auraient eu à mentionner un nouveau cassage de gueule entre automobilistes' (BI, 86). 'La psychologie de l'homme au volant' is also a current topic of conversation in Laurence's office (ibid.). These passing references contain much more contemporary relevance than at first meets the eye, since they provide specific comment on a media-induced moral panic which actually arose in November 1965. Drivers appeared to have taken to assaulting each other over minor traffic incidents: two deaths were reported, and the *faits divers* rubrics characteristically whipped up a controversy out of these and any other related episodes that came to hand for a month or so. Psychiatrists and sociologists were brought in to diagnose this sudden threat to civilization as it had been known up till then: the following month everything had blown over.[12] The allusions are thus an implied satire on the workings of the press, and the light-heartedness of Laurence's comment indicates an appropriate sense of proportion on the issue.

Of course matters soon become much more serious when she takes the wheel to spare the couple from any possibility of being involved in such an episode, and ends up wrecking the car to avoid colliding with some cyclists (BI, 101–3). Itself a form of involvement in a *fait divers*, the experience will prove to be one of the key incidents in the plot of the novel, precipitating an extended clash of values with Jean-Charles who is more concerned about the cost of repairing the damage than the welfare of other road users (BI, 103, 109, 134–5). Moreover Laurence will continue to mull over its implications to the extent of using the incident as the basis for a 'moral dilemma' party-piece with subversive ideological undertones which she envisages putting to her family and acquaintances as an expression of her incipient estrangement from their values (BI, 150). An essential part of the plot and thematics of the novel, as well as the psychology of the main protagonist, thus owes its existence to the *fait divers* rubric. It is not for nothing that, like the rooms in which the characters play out their lives, this novel is lavishly furnished with newspapers and magazines (BI, 7, 43, 74, 91, 100, 147).

Hence we note that Laurence's views on her milieu change as she resumes reading the press. In particular, she comes to see through the apparently authoritative discourses which had formerly reduced her to a passive compliance: 'Depuis qu'elle regarde les journaux Laurence a remarqué que souvent dans les conversations les gens récitent des articles. Pourquoi pas? Il faut bien qu'ils puisent leurs informations quelque part' (BI, 93). This insight provides a basis for a sequence of clichés and crypto-quotations from contemporary thinkers which, while its content most obviously stems from the narrator, is viewed with a wry detachment attributable in part to Laurence herself (BI, 93–4).[13] 'Jean-Charles et Dufrène sont d'accord (ils ont les mêmes lectures),' she notes – the parenthesis highlighting the irony (BI, 94).[14] Her detachment is not, however, a preliminary to critical engagement, as can be seen in her reaction to the topics of such newspaper-nourished discussions. She tends to view them as a random miscellany – placing upon them, in fact, the perspective of one who skims the headlines or sees things via the format of the *fait divers* rubric: 'Le féminisme: ces temps-ci on en parle tout le temps. Aussitôt Laurence s'absente. C'est comme la psychanalyse, le Marché commun, la force de frappe, elle ne sait pas qu'en penser, elle n'en pense rien' (BI, 99). While implying a criticism of Laurence's need for affective components in conversation as in her reading, this passage also constitutes a denunciation of the way that crude news values contaminate intellectual life.[15]

Laurence's stance is in keeping with her non-intellectual character, which is what Beauvoir gave herself to work with in full knowledge of the technical difficulties that entails. While it denies the author the means to articulate an explicit critique of the technocratic society she reviles, it also obliges her to 'faire parler le silence': and on this point, she indicates, she is not sure of having succeeded (see TCF, 139). Blandine Stefanson confesses to having difficulty in understanding the phrase.[16] Something of its meaning might be grasped in the ironic sense of the above examples, as well as in other instances of Laurence's ambivalent relationship to the discourses of her society. For example, she congratulates herself at overcoming her fear of the news:

> Laurence prend dans le porte-revues les derniers numéros de *L'Express* et de *Candide*. [. . .] Elle les ouvre, à présent, sans appréhension. Non. Il ne se passe plus rien de terrible – sauf au Viêtnam, mais personne en France n'approuve les Américains. Elle est contente d'avoir vaincu cette espèce de peur qui la condamnait à l'ignorance. [. . .] Au fond, il suffit de prendre sur les choses un point de vue objectif. (BI, 74)

The unconscious irony of this is surely eloquent enough. Laurence can conquer her apprehension by reducing the Vietnam war to a *fait divers* which she can dismiss by espousing the alleged indifference of her peers. She is in touch with the consensus – which means more to her than being in touch with the facts. At the same time she can feel satisfaction at being less ignorant than she was. However, she is still not as well-informed as she needs to be: 'En ce moment Catherine semble calme. Mais si de nouveau elle s'agite, je ne saurai pas mieux lui parler qu'avant . . .' (BI, 74). But she is left with the difficulty she experiences when faced with ploughing through a report on the '*Crise entre l'Algérie et la France*'.

Laurence's lack of intellectual faculties, then, leaves her ill-equipped, even if she were so inclined, to absorb and evaluate the cold facts at her disposal. But her capacity for an emotional response remains: she recoils with horror before the 'scènes peu supportables' on the television news, saying (on her own behalf as much as on her daughter's) that 'pour une enfant, les images sont plus saisissantes que les mots' (BI, 79). This propensity does enable her to formulate criticisms of some news reports. In particular, when reading *L'Express* she notes the absence of anything which might move the reader: 'débitée en minces rubriques, l'actualité s'avale comme une tasse de lait; aucune aspérité, rien n'accroche, rien n'écorche' (BI, 100). She, who is so easily disturbed by the news, is well placed to judge when the news is turned into vacuous pap for painless consumption.[17]

In her own way, therefore, Laurence is sensitive to some of the issues associated with news coverage. This sensitivity links with her professional capabilities and becomes the basis of a critical perspective on the media.[18] She is aware of what the public wants, and knows how the producers collude in gratifying its wishes: 'Les gens veulent de la nouveauté, mais sans risque. [. . .] Pour elle, c'est toujours le même problème [. . .] étonner tout en rassurant; le produit magique qui bouleversera votre vie sans en rien déranger' (BI, 42). These criteria are equally applicable to the news, as Laurence comes to recognize. The realization hits her, climactically, as she reconsiders the news from the past year in the retrospective compilations put out in print and on television at Christmas. Here she contemplates the full panoply of frightful *faits divers*, which she lists at length only to conclude that she has been mistaken all along about their potential to disturb: 'Il faut dire qu'on assiste à toutes ces catastrophes confortablement installé dans son décor familier et il n'est pas vrai que le monde fasse intrusion: on n'aperçoit que des images, proprement encadrées sur le petit écran et qui n'ont pas leur poids de réalité' (BI, 147). She finally appreciates that this material is not intended to upset the reader or viewer; that, contrary to what she had believed, its presentation does not involve invading or infiltrating the private universe in any significant way. 'La nouveauté [*les nouvelles?*], mais sans risque'; 'étonner tout en rassurant'; the news 'bouleversera votre vie sans en rien déranger'. The conjunction of these comments anticipates precisely what Baudrillard says about the 'sécurité miraculeuse' purveyed by the news media: 'L'image, le signe, le message, tout ceci que nous "consommons", c'est notre quiétude, scellée par la distance au monde et que berce, plus qu'elle ne la compromet, l'allusion même violente au réel.'[19] By seeking to protect her sensitive antennae from further traumas, Laurence has previously failed to see what is implicit here and what Baudrillard spells out: that is, the intrinsic complicity between the production and consumption of the news, and the production and consumption of commodities in the consumer society. Laurence's preoccupation with the *fait divers* has, however, drawn her to the nexus of this suspect solidarity:

Ce qui caractérise la société de consommation, c'est *l'universalité du fait divers* dans la communication de masse. Toute l'information politique, historique, culturelle est reçue sous la même forme, à la fois anodine et miraculeuse, du fait divers. Elle est tout entière *actualisée*, c'est-à-dire dramatisée sur le mode spectaculaire – et tout entière *inactualisée*, c'est-à-dire distancée par le médium de la communication et réduite à des signes. Le fait divers n'est donc pas une catégorie parmi d'autres, mais LA catégorie cardinale de notre pensée magique, de notre mythologie.[20]

Laurence draws the appropriate conclusion from her insight, expressing in the ensuing pages her most disabused criticism of those around her and of their beliefs, culminating in her giving literal expression to her psychological estrangement by agreeing to go away with her father (BI, 146–52).

Her father, of course, proves to be not the man she thought he was, and enlightenment is not forthcoming from him.[21] A form of enlightenment is vouchsafed to Laurence, however, through the intermediary of the young Greek girl who dances for them. The child, 'le visage noyé d'extase' (BI, 158), embodies the capacity for passion – the sort of capacity which Jean-Charles has mocked as excessive in Laurence, calling it her 'sensiblerie' (BI, 133, 159) and the 'côté convulsif des femmes' (BI, 44) when she was 'hors d'elle' (BI, 133) in response to the story of the woman tortured to death.[22] The evocation of this 'adorable ménade' (BI, 158) indicates that there is a place for such benign frenzy in the world. Laurence has had to suffer for her own propensity to it in the face of society's atrocities; as she travels in Greece, a psychologist back in Paris is seeking to expunge it from Catherine in order that she may maintain the so-called 'harmonieux équilibre [. . .] entre l'intelligence et l'affectivité' (BI, 43) which their society expects of its women.

In addition to this set of affinities, the Greek girl impresses Laurence as another example of a child whom society is set to destroy. It is significant that this encounter is articulated in terms connecting very precisely with the *faits divers* which gave rise to Laurence's concern earlier in the novel and prompt her most intense identification subsequently: in effect she is once more confronted here by an example of the 'enfants martyrs, enfants noyés par leur propre mère' (BI, 54) as this girl with her 'visage noyé d'extase' dances under the 'regard bovin' of the mother 'placide et grasse' she will come to resemble: 'Petite condamnée à mort, affreuse mort sans cadavre. La vie allait l'assassiner. Je pensai à Catherine qu'on était en train d'assassiner' (BI, 158). In the same vein, Laurence suddenly revolts against the idea that 'sous prétexte de guérir Catherine [. . .] on allait la mutiler' (BI, 159).

Her resistance to her husband's and father's viewpoints on her return is expressed in her vomiting and her anorexia – which can be seen also as a refusal to go on internalizing the guilt she has been made to feel, as a mother, for Catherine's problems (BI, 135). But her opposition is equally conveyed in terms of what and how people read, and this entails attitudes to narratives of information.

'Tous les jours nous lisons dans les journaux des choses affreuses, et nous continuons à les ignorer' (BI, 133), she complains to Jean-Charles. When he attributes to 'une crise de mauvaise conscience' her horror of five years earlier at the report on the tortured woman, she realizes he had betrayed her, having only pretended to 'read' it with feeling as she had (BI, 133). Now she rejects his 'bonne conscience' as a mere consumer of the news, and furthermore follows her inclination to refuse the 'fables faciles pour tranquilliser les enfants' (BI, 136), insisting on her daughter's right to read what she likes, including news reports of whatever kind. At the same time, she rejects the other alien narratives of her society's dominant ideology, 'ces histoires dont j'ignore tout', as she has put it, and for which she cannot '[se] prendre de passion' (BI, 161). While she can experience no affective response to orthodox narratives, Jean-Charles for his part finds her views on Catherine – 'Elle, on ne la mutilera pas' (BI, 181) – elude his rational patterns of reading: 'Je ne comprends rien à ce que tu racontes' (BI, 181), he admits. Having considered Catherine's situation as a 'technical' problem susceptible to professional remedy (and his wife's as one which must have a 'raison' [BI, 169]), it now dawns on him that this all means something more, and different, to his wife: 'Je ne savais pas que tu prenais cette histoire tellement à cœur' (BI, 182). Here his language touches all unwittingly on the key to her stance. For Laurence, declining to relinquish the insights she has derived from her sensibility to the *faits divers*, is refusing to have her daughter become another 'enfant martyr'. She effectively defies the rationalizations of (male) pseudo-intellectuals whom the author has in any case denied her the wherewithal to refute on their own terms. She clings to her affective, passionate reading, however distorted (or even unreliable) it may prove: 'je n'ai peut-être plus de cœur, mais cette histoire, je la prends à cœur' (BI, 182).

This can hardly be the last word on the novel as a whole. Critics agree that the ending resolves nothing, in practice. For Beauvoir the real solution in any case lies outside the class, and beyond the grasp, of the characters she depicts. But however this may be, it is clear that Laurence has won *droit de cité* for her emotions and taken a step thereby towards tackling one of her major personal difficulties.

Notes

1. Unless otherwise indicated, page numbers in this text refer to the Gallimard-Folio edition of *Les Belles Images*, hereafter BI, Paris, 1966.
2. Terry Keefe points out in detail the importance, for an understanding of Laurence, of reconstructing her past from the details available in the text. See T. Keefe, *Beauvoir: 'Les Belles Images', 'La Femme Rompue'*, Glasgow, University of Glasgow French and German Publications,

Introductory Guides to French Literature 12, 1991, pp.19–21.

3. C. Ascher, *Simone de Beauvoir, a life of freedom*, Brighton, Harvester Press, 1981, pp.177–81, stresses the importance of the mother–daughter relationship and mentions the allusions to news and newsreels, but fails to see that the former is significantly mediated by the latter. Mary Evans, *Simone de Beauvoir: a feminist mandarin*, London and New York, Tavistock, 1985, pp.85–8, concentrates on man–woman relations, on the intense but fleeting nature of emotional life, and on the bleakness of personal relationships in advanced industrial capitalism. My reading suggests that such emotional resources as exist in this world crystallize around the *fait divers* and can be tapped from there.

4. See Simone de Beauvoir, *La Force de l'Age*, Paris, Gallimard, 1960, pp. 135–8; see also pp.41–2 and 91–2 above.

5. Jean-Paul Sartre, *Situations VIII*, Paris, Gallimard, 1972, p.143.

6. Simone de Beauvoir, *Tout compte fait*, Paris, Gallimard, 1972, p.139. Page references to this text are indicated here by TCF.

7. E. Fallaize, *The Novels of Simone de Beauvoir*, London and New York, Routledge, 1988, p.128, notes most pertinently that the 'truth of the human condition' 'explodes into the "marvellous" world of *Les Belles Images* through the poster of the starving child'. It is true that various media channel the subversive information, as Beauvoir herself indicates. But Laurence cannot be sure whether the poster or 'autre chose' is to blame (BI, 29). In any event, my discussion, while seeking to highlight the special contribution of the press, is not, of course, aimed at excluding the other dimensions.

8. For Terry Keefe one of the keys to Laurence's personality is the depth of her emotional involvement with her children. But even he is hard put to to explain why in that case the second daughter Louise is paid so little attention. His suggestion is that Catherine 'becomes the principal focus of some of Laurence's own unresolved psychological difficulties' (see *Beauvoir: 'Les Belles Images'*, pp.24–5). My reading of the text indicates that exposure to the *faits divers* and the news in general is crucial in this identification between mother and daughter.

9. Keefe enables us to see that though the critique of society emerges largely through the sensitivity of Laurence she is symptomatic, rather than an exception in her world: both her husband and her mother are much more fragile than they may seem on the surface. Moreover, most of those around her take sleeping pills and other medicaments to dull their perceptions which would otherwise by implication be the same as hers. See ibid., pp.8–9, 14–16, and Beauvoir, *Les Belles Images*, p.83.

10. *Le Monde*, 23 December 1966, p.17. My interpretation of the novel brings together and endorses, in its way, the comments of Elizabeth

Fallaize that 'Laurence is able to question the language of stereotype but she can substitute no more than a fragmentary voice for its pervasive presence' and that 'her capacity for feeling [. . .] is a weapon against the indifference which traps Laurence' (*The Novels of Simone de Beauvoir*, pp.125, 131).

11. *Faux frais* are defined in the *Petit Robert* as 'Toute dépense accidentelle s'ajoutant aux dépenses principales'.

12. See Georges Auclair, *Le 'Mana' quotidien: structures et fonctions de la chronique des faits divers*, Paris, Editions Anthropos, 1970, pp.119–20.

13. See Fallaize, *The Novels of Simone de Beauvoir*, pp.125–6, and p.140 nn 13, 14, 15, on the sources and background for this passage. Such detachment as is evident here highlights the process whereby Laurence ceases to be wholly immersed in the discourses of her environment and goes beyond being a mere 'echo' of 'her immediate milieu' (ibid., p.120).

14. On the function of the parenthesis in the text see B. Stefanson's introduction to her edition of *Les Belles Images*, London, Heinemann Educational, 1980, pp.32–3, 38.

15. On the development of this phenomenon, see Gilles Lipovetsky, *L'Empire de l'éphémère*, Gallimard, Folio-Essais, 1987, pp.272–81.

16. Stefanson, Introduction to *Les Belles Images*, p.26.

17. It must be acknowledged that *L'Express* was a prime target for satire and criticism: it is the butt of running jokes in Perec's *Les Choses*, winner of the Prix Renaudot in the autumn of 1965 when Beauvoir began writing her novel.

18. Keefe points out rightly that Beauvoir's choice of profession for Laurence was an inspiration, for 'she must see through publicity images in order to exploit them commercially' (*Beauvoir, 'Les Belles Images'*, pp.35–6).

19. Jean Baudrillard, *La Société de consommation*, Gallimard, Folio-Essais, 1970, p.32.

20. Ibid., p.31.

21. See TCF, p.141, on Beauvoir's reservations about him. Keefe, *Beauvoir, Les Belles Images*, pp.17–19, 23–4, provides a subtle and pertinent analysis.

22. For a complementary discussion on the collocation of terms relating the Greek girl to Laurence's state of mind, see Fallaize, *The Novels of Simone de Beauvoir*, p.134.

12

Consuming Passions:
Marguerite Duras

Journalism represents a substantial component in the career of Marguerite Duras.[1] The volume entitled *Outside*, first published in 1981, contains a collection which is characteristic of her approach over some twenty-five years.[2] In her preface she speaks of the 'mouvement irrésistible' which prompts her to denounce injustice and to make her voice heard on 'le crime, le déshonneur, l'indignité et quand l'imbécillité judiciaire et la société se permettent de juger – de ça, de la nature, comme ils jugeraient l'orage, le feu' (O, 12). She makes it her business, then, to go behind conventional judgements and to retrieve the true character of incidents thrown up by brute nature, which necessarily occur 'en dehors des normes de la vie quotidienne'. Given that the sensibility which propels her into these regions is essentially intuitive, she claims no consistent rational reliability for her testimony: 'Je me suis pas mal trompée. Je revendique ce droit' (O, 13). Such was to be most notoriously the case when she intervened in the 'affaire Grégory', as we shall see.

Reviewing a book by Robert Linhardt on working conditions in a Citroën factory, she writes: 'Tout le monde voudrait nous *apprendre* à "penser" l'événement politique, à juger selon les normes en cours, et tout à coup [. . .] *L'Etabli* fait avancer tout l'inconnu du monde. [. . .] Il porte un coup très dur à ce facteur de plus en plus intolérable, ce choléra, qui s'appelle *l'interprétation des faits*. Qu'il s'agisse aussi bien d'un fait divers criminel que d'un fait politique quelconque' (O, 185). The writing she admires and emulates is that which makes us 'savoir qu'on ne connaît pas' and which 'rétablit les termes dans leur splendeur première' (ibid.). This echoes what she has Jacques Hold say of the eponymous Lol V. Stein: 'Moi seul de tous ces faussaires, je sais: je ne sais rien. Ce fut là ma première découverte à son propos: ne rien savoir de Lol était la connaître déjà.'[3] Duras is arguing here for a fundamental questioning of rational discourses and the epistemological models they conventionally serve. For this reason she is equally suspicious of the journalistic alternative to interpretation of the facts: the creation of an evasive aura of mystery that elides the need for further reflexion. She explains in deliberately prosaic terms, for example, why a man successively killed his wife and mistress and then committed suicide as his income diminished: 'Cet article n'a de raison d'être que de tenter de combattre la tendance qu'ont les journaux à trouver du "mystère" dans tous les crimes. Rien de moins mystérieux, à mon avis, que la logique pragmatique de Charles Clément' (O, 73).

She argues for those psychological dimensions which do not fit readily into the approved scenarios of the courtroom or the *chronique*. In particular, transgressive manifestations of love and eroticism command Duras's attention. She identifies with 'l'amour quand il devient fou, quand il quitte la prudence et qu'il se perd là où il se trouve' (O, 12). In 1961 she speaks out against the vilification of André Berthaud, a simple man who stabbed himself to death after eighteen years in prison following a passionate though by all accounts platonic affair with a young girl. 'Je crois absolument à cet amour. A. Berthaud et la petite se sont aimés,' she declares (O, 107). The inevitable sexual impulse underpinning this love fulfilled itself, according to Duras, in self-immolation: 'Qu'il y ait eu un déplacement du viol non perpétré au geste dernier d'A. Berthaud, c'est possible, c'est probable – on ne voit pas un amour aussi violent sans cette conséquence du désir – mais c'est pour moi la raison même pour laquelle le viol a été transgressé: la force de l'amour de l'enfant' (O, 107). While she adds 'que ça ne me regarde pas, que ça ne regarde personne', granting the man's right to privacy, her speculation draws on her own insights into the peculiar intensity of erotic love that links it in extreme forms with death.

Another case provides an apologia for these insights. In June 1957 Simone Deschamps and her lover Dr Evenou were arrested for the murder of his wife, and Deschamps was tried alone in October 1958 following the death in prison of her accomplice.[4] The fascination this case exercised is attested to by Jouhandeau's account, in which he acknowledges, 'Ce médecin [. . .] j'ai cru un moment que c'était moi. Je ne voyais plus tout d'un coup ce qui me distinguait de lui, comme si j'avais été là magiquement, en état de somnambulisme.'[5] His words corroborate Duras's own compulsion to lend herself to the protagonists: the desire made manifest in the story is such as to break down barriers and lead the unwitting spectator into a realm where intersubjective phantasms hold sway. However, whereas Jouhandeau addresses himself in turn to each of the protagonists – sketching with particular poignancy a profile of the victim – Duras is almost exclusively preoccupied with the role played by Simone Deschamps.

She begins by quoting, not without irony, the admonition of the *chroniqueur* in *Le Temps*, who warns of the invidious appeal of literary constructions likely to be placed upon these events: 'Soyons sourds à la complainte des esthètes sur le crime d'amour.' Observing the failure of criminological explanations she notes that the rational faculty, 'mal à l'aise [. . .] en dehors des catégories du crime', must beware of 'la jésuitique mécanique qui rend compte des faits divers en général' (O, 119). While accepting that 'il est très difficile de décanter un fait divers de son contexte émotionnel' Duras offers a quasi-rational approach to the events, evoking a peculiar 'convenance sexuelle' that must have bound the lovers. A ritualized *mise en scène* in accordance with which Deschamps carried out the murder at her lover's request seems to have been a response to obscure needs in both of them, going well beyond mere sexual infatuation.

Judicial procedure and courtroom conventions at the trial deprived Deschamps of 'les mots pour se dire' (O, 125). Duras argues against the injustice caused when official discourses appropriate the sense of the case:

> On n'explique pas les ténèbres, bien sûr, mais quand même, ce qu'on peut faire c'est de les circonscrire, de laisser aux ténèbres la part qui leur revient. [. . .] Il faut admettre la 'vérité' des ténèbres [. . .] qu'une fois pour toutes on renonce à interpréter ces ténèbres [. . .] puisqu'on ne peut pas les connaître à partir du jour. (O, 119, 121)

Once more, morality, rational discourses and epistemologies must be eschewed – which also entails the loss of a secure sense of ethical identity: 'Que la conscience accepte donc de se perdre quelquefois au lieu de se réfugier dans la duplicité de la morale dite courante' (O, 122).

This is the perspective that Duras brings to bear on events in this case. Svengali-like, Evenou induced Deschamps to perform the murder in 'l'illusion de la liberté'; he marked out each stage 'comme si elle pouvait reculer'. The 'comme si' is a recurrent note in Duras's reconstruction, alongside the repetition of the verb *jouer* – as when Deschamps 'joue l'esclave' (O, 120–1). Not for nothing does Jouhandeau categorize this as a *crime rituel*. Duras, for her part, repudiates the naïve journalistic interpretation of this pattern: '"passer du stade des jeux de l'amour pour glisser jusqu'aux profondeurs extrêmes du crime", qu'est-ce que ça veut dire?' she asks mockingly. What this view omits, and what Duras places emphasis on, is 'le stade intermédiaire, précisément crucial, qui y conduit: celui où les jeux cessent d'être des jeux, ne divertissent plus, mais hypothèquent la conscience jusqu'à la supprimer' (O, 121).

Such a mode of awareness – or to be more precise, such an oblique mode of being – has a direct bearing on much of her own writing. The enactment of behaviour while in a state where consciousness has foregone its usual autonomy will be a staple of Duras's fiction. Her narratives frequently hinge on states of consciousness altered by vicarious participation in scenarios which do not properly belong to the order of knowledge.[6]

In this sense, we can see that her commentary on *faits divers* proves to be a pretext for defining both a mode of being for her own characters and a mode of perception for her readers.

Moderato cantabile, published in 1958 and written during the period of the Evenou/Deschamps affair, is evidently not unrelated to it and other cases Duras chooses to comment on.[7] This novel traces precisely the imaginative involvement of Anne Desbaresdes and her companion Chauvin in a *fait divers*, a crime of passion willed as a lover's suicide. The opening pages establish its sociological impact, as it were: to quote Edgar Morin, we perceive the event 's'infiltrant dans l'inconscient de la ville en même temps qu'elle se [fait] digérer par les structures traditionnelles de la Polis'.[8] To begin with, a woman's cry interrupts the music lesson and arouses the curiosity of Anne and her child; soon the voices of bystanders are heard: 'D'autres cris relayèrent alors le premier, éparpillés, divers' (MC, 11). The choice of the final adjective carries an appropriate journalistic resonance, as does the ensuing sentence: 'Ils consacrèrent une actualité déjà dépassée, rassurante désormais' (MC, 11). The incident has been taken up by a familar mechanism to integrate it into and permit the continuation of normal life. It seems natural, therefore, that the next manifestation of the process should be 'la rumeur d'en bas' which 's'engouffra dans la pièce', calling to mind the particular propagation of sensational items analysed by Edgar Morin and others.[9] Further allusions to events rippling out from the drama beneath the window punctuate the lesson as it proceeds, until 'des appels maintenant raisonnables, indiquèrent la consommation d'un événement inconnu' (MC, 13), which underlines the notion of processing and consuming the shocking episode as a commodity.[10] While policemen record the testimony of witnesses, a photographer also captures the scene (MC, 14–15). 'Demain, nous le saurons bien,' remarks the piano teacher (MC, 13), in anticipation of the reports which will inevitably appear in the *fait divers* rubric of the following day's newspapers.

Anne is not alone in being drawn to the site of the killing, as the café proprietress points out: 'Ce matin, c'était un défilé' (MC, 18; cf. MC, 25). In this too the incident is made to partake of the standard characteristics of the *fait divers*.[11] A man who turns out to be Chauvin 'lisait un journal' (MC, 17) which he puts down to inform her, on the basis of the report he has clearly been reading: 'C'était un crime' (MC, 18). Noting her evident emotion he repeats the word as a means of entering into conversation with her; but he is taken aback by the intensity of her preoccupation with the crime and the construction she seeks to place upon it: 'Comme si, vivante ou morte, ça ne lui importait plus désormais, vous croyez qu'il est possible d'en arriver . . . là [. . .] ?' His response is to recoil: 'Il la ramena vers des régions qui sans doute devaient lui être plus familières' (MC, 21). Despite his defensive reflex, Anne continues her 'reading' of the *fait divers* and compels Chauvin to live out its implications in his relationship with her. Through this couple the text stages the phantasmatic experience of the *fait divers* reader. In the course of a series of dialogues which have about them something of a psychoanalytical exchange, Anne and Chauvin thus vicariously enact and ritually explore a pact which has evidently led a man to kill his lover at her request. We are clearly faced with a double 'convenance sexuelle' of a kind which, according to Duras, presided over the Evenou/Deschamps partnership. The fantasies of desiring love and death which constitute the chief motor of the novel[12] shift the action out of the world of conventional representational discourses and trace its elaboration in a 'schéma de l'entre-deux-mondes',[13] a space which takes on the obsessional repetitive characteristics associated with a primal scene.[14] The mode which Anne adopts to narrate her version of events is that of speculative hypothesis – which serves to embed events more firmly in the fantasizing consciousness, the consciousness of the 'comme si' Duras has also shown at work in the Evenou/Deschamps case. This is not a path to empirical knowledge: 'J'ai essayé de savoir davantage. Je ne sais rien' (MC, 30), Anne says. She asserts – baselessly – that Chauvin has told her things and insists that he say more, adding for herself remarks that will dictate the character of their own relationship: 'Elle a su soudainement ce qu'elle désirait de lui. Tout est devenu clair pour elle au point qu'elle lui a dit quel serait son désir. Il n'y a pas d'explication, je crois, à ce genre de découverte-là' (MC, 31–2). In their exchanges, Anne and Chauvin are party to a transaction whereby their own relationship is shaped by the *fait divers*, which in turn is given substance by the projection of their compulsions.[15] Their dialogue thus ceases to be a commentary on events and becomes a displaced performance of the events, best illustrated, perhaps, at the climax of the text when Anne compels Chauvin to say 'Je voudrais que vous soyez morte' and she can then respond 'C'est fait' (MC, 84). Not the least of the resemblances between this novel and the *fait divers* of the Deschamps/Evenou case is expressed in Tison-Braun's summary of the novel: 'Ce n'est pas une histoire d'amour, c'est un drame d'envoûtement consenti.'[16] Anne and Chauvin can properly be said to inhabit that intermediate zone illustrated in the *fait divers*, 'où les jeux cessent d'être des jeux, ne divertissent plus, mais hypothèquent la conscience jusqu'à la supprimer' (O, 121; see above).

The consummation aimed at by this 'rite mortuaire' (MC, 82) is the transvaluation of desire in an experience of 'ravissement' which will feature in the title of a later novel and become equated more widely in the works with 'anéantissement' or ultimately a state of madness.[17] It may be linked with the exasperated sensibility of Laurence in *Les Belles Images*, which identifies its culmination in the Greek girl who is 'noyée d'extase'; in both novels also, the woman possessed of this insight recoils in the act of vomiting from the conventional modes of consuming both knowledge and food she has been subjected to.

The violence implicit in this cluster of affective responses is a constant fascination for Duras, as can be seen in her reactions to a *fait divers* which first appeared in *Le Monde* of 14 January 1950:

Le crime de Savigny-sur-Orge

L'auteur est la femme de la victime

Depuis près d'un mois, les enquêteurs de la première brigade mobile cherchaient à identifier les restes d'un corps mutilé découvert à Savigny-sur-Orge. L'affaire est aujourd'hui éclaircie. La victime est un employé retraité de la SNCF, M. Georges Rabilland, 61 ans, qui demeurait 15, rue de la Paix, à Savigny-sur-Orge. Et l'auteur de ce forfait n'est autre que sa femme, âgée de 51 ans. Celle-ci, qui vivait en mauvaise intelligence avec son mari, l'assomma, le 13 décembre dernier, tandis qu'il lisait un journal. Puis pendant trois jours et trois nuits elle dépeça le cadavre avant d'aller en jeter les restes dans différents égouts et même sur le toit des wagons d'un train qui passait sous le pont de Savigny-sur-Orge.

C'est en signalant la 'disparition' de son mari aux policiers que la meurtrière mit ceux-ci sur la piste. Arrêtée, elle a fait des aveux.[18]

Duras indicates that she followed reports of the trial in *Le Monde* by Jean-Marc Théolleyre.[19] The story appears to have lodged in her imagination: as she puts it in an interview, 'Cet homme dont on a retrouvé les morceaux éparpillés aux quatre coins du pays dans des wagons de marchandise, cette femme qui l'a tué, il me fallait les interroger.'[20] A reminiscence may be discerned in her novel *Les Petits Chevaux de Tarquinia*, published in 1953. Here the elderly parents of a young man blown up while defusing a land-mine have collected together in a crate all that remains of his body, but the mother refuses to sign a death certificate allowing the remains to be removed from the scene. This episode suggestively counterpoints the doings of a group of friends on holiday on the coast below, as intense heat and the paroxysms of desire threaten to disrupt their relationships. Memories of the earlier story may also have been reactualized by another *fait divers* Duras reported in 1958, that of Charles Clément who disposed of his wife's dismembered body around the valley of Chevreuse (O, 70–3). However this may be, the 'crime de Savigny-sur-Orge' inspired Duras to write her first play, *Les Viaducs de la Seine-et-Oise*, in 1959; then a novel, *L'Amante anglaise*, in 1967; and then to turn the novel into another play of the same title which was first staged in 1968.

Duras was evidently struck by the fact that the dispersed human débris could be reassembled and identified as constituting a single individual; and by the more remarkable fact that the routes followed by the various trains in which the remains were found could be retraced by detectives to the one spot they had all passed through on their journeys, the viaduct at Savigny-sur-Orge. She draws prominent attention to these two details in all versions of her texts on the subject. The dual convergence of the 'recoupement anthropologique' and the 'recoupement ferroviaire' provides a powerful instance of rationality operating to counter the dissemination of sense implied in the initial crime, and yet the coincidence itself challenges verisimilitude, generates incredulity: 'Jamais je n'aurais cru que c'était possible', says the criminal herself (AA, 191). These ambiguities are the stuff of which the best *faits divers* are made. We have seen Duras oppose the pragmatic logic of Charles Clément to the sensationalism of the press coverage his crime occasioned: now she will have a character speak of this case in terms which recall what Meursault says of his *fait divers* in *L'Etranger*. 'Ces crimes qui paraissent tellement extraordinaires, de loin, deviennent presque . . . naturels quand on arrive à la vérité' (AA, 33).[21]

In Duras's versions of the story the head is not recovered, and the criminal refuses to divulge its whereabouts. This absent element works to resist the reductive force of the networks of meaning bearing down on the data from the investigation: the interrogation must continue as long as the head remains missing, and this object in turn becomes a metaphor for the mystery of motivation that lies at the heart of the *fait divers*. The information gap also guarantees the continuance of communication with the criminal, the suppression of whose voice in the Deschamps trial we have seen was a cause for concern to Duras. So long as the head is missing, the other pieces of the puzzle will not fall into place and the dialogue will continue: this is what lies behind Duras's repeated attempts to dismantle and reconfigure the story, in a movement that recapitulates the itinerary of the body itself. More generally the material has been shown to reproduce an important recurring phantasm in Duras's writing, that of the 'corps morcelé', which perhaps helps explain her compulsion to return to it again and again.[22] Thus, Duras writes in the blurb for *L'Amante anglaise*: 'Au départ il s'agit du même coup de dés: même crime, mêmes personnages, même lieu. Voici donc, entre beaucoup d'autres possibles, une seconde approche [. . .].' The pattern followed by Duras's attempts to permute this *fait divers* material can be examined in the successive texts.

The first thing we note is that from the outset she has altered the configuration of characters involved. Whereas the original reports have a woman attaining 'le plus haut point de l'aversion humaine' and killing her husband while he read a newspaper,[23] the initial durassian version establishes once and for all the change of victim to Marie-Thérèse, a deaf and dumb cousin, invented by Duras, whom she has living with the couple. Despite this definitive change in the scenario, Duras maintains that it is the original *données* that underpin her text – even as late as 1968, she asserts: 'Cet homme dont on a retrouvé les morceaux éparpillés aux quatre coins du pays [. . .] cette femme qui l'a tué, il me fallait les interroger.'[24] Duras wants both the married partners alive so that she can examine their personalities and the relationship between them; but she makes it clear that the murderer 'visait son mari',[25] a view that the text substantiates in remarks made by the husband himself (AA, 123). Because the victim herself is already dead and therefore physically absent from the narrative in all versions, she acts as a third pole that effectively catalyses the psychological interaction between the other characters here as elsewhere in Duras's work.[26]

The two-act play *Les Viaducs de la Seine-et-Oise* presents, in effect, a prologue to the later variants.[27] The first act is the only text to present the couple alone together, prior to the arrest, and virtually none of it will find its way into subsequent texts. This presumably was the material that Duras later found 'antipathique et faux' and caused her to refuse permission for performances or republication.[28] Moreover, in this text the married couple are accomplices in the crime; even if Claire appears to have given the lead her husband (here named Marcel) helped with the disposal of the body. He hopes that she will explain why it had to be done; but she finds their action unspeakable, and similarly cannot put her motives into words. She has had a momentary flash of insight into what drove her, but now all she is aware of is the absence of that knowledge she once had. This recalls the ungraspable '"vérité" des ténèbres' (O, 121) we have discussed, and anticipates the way in which Lol V. Stein's 'ravissement' will be evoked: 'Elle ne dispose d'aucun souvenir même imaginaire, elle n'a aucune idée sur cet inconnu [. . .] innommable faute d'un mot. [. . .] Elle a cru, l'espace d'un éclair, que ce mot pouvait exister [. . .] ce mot, qui n'existe pas, pourtant est là: il vous attend au tournant du langage.'[29] Later versions will take up this motif via the theme of madness, but it is here merely one element in the seemingly inconsequential ramblings between an elderly couple.

The journalistic origins of the work betray themselves with peculiar insistence in this text. The couple are eager for notoriety as they wait to be found out but fear that the newspapers will label them merely common or garden criminals. Claire is a compulsive reader of the news: she repeatedly borrows the vocabulary of sensational reports, and draws on her familiarity with the *fait divers* rubric to suggest ways in which they should behave. The *fait divers* element here gives precedence to themes of vulgar sensationalism and mediated gossip over the more far-reaching phantasms we have seen Duras pursuing elsewhere. This probably explains why the material will be repudiated subsequently.

Act 2 of this stage version takes place in a café where the criminals encounter precisely the trivializing misrepresentation of the murder which is going on in the news, compounded via the gossip of the locals. In the face of these competing discourses they are gripped by a curious compulsion and admit their guilt. The play as a whole, in this version, is less concerned with what motivated the crime than with what brought about the confession, so enigmatically referred to in the original news report. This perspective ceases to be directly available when the material of the original Act 2 is taken up and reworked in later versions, where it becomes the prelude to new material and is made to relate to that. The confession in the café thus stands as a transitional element between, and a constant in, the two different conceptions of the story.

In her revised presentation, Duras has Claire carry sole responsibility for the crime. Events have moved forward, and the emphasis shifts to the interrogation of the protagonists, carried out by a figure whom the author refers to as 'le juge d'instruction ou plutôt l'écrivain'.[30] The novel comprises three sections of dialogue: the café proprietor relating the episode of the confession; the testimony of the husband Pierre; and the questioning of Claire. The second stage version reduces this to the interrogation of Pierre followed by that of Claire, in texts which reproduce, in slightly abridged form, those of the novel. Two points emerge from this evolution. Firstly, the narration leaves the reported events progressively further in the past. Secondly, this movement is paralleled by an increasing emphasis on the questioning of Claire, which, though coming at the end in both revised versions, carries even more weight in the play script since the café proprietor's contribution is eliminated completely.

However, while the novel eradicates 'live' testimony from the past, the repetition–compulsion that informs this process of textual revision is dramatized strikingly through the introduction of two tape recorders (perhaps inspired by Beckett's *La Dernière Bande*, first performed in French in 1960). The interview with the café proprietor, Robert Lamy, goes over the evening of the confession first portrayed in Act 2 of *Les Viaducs de la Seine-et-Oise*; but it does so by having Lamy comment on a play-back of a tape recording allegedly made on that evening, unknown to those present: 'Quand la soirée du 13 avril aura pris, grâce à votre récit, son volume, son espace propres, on pourra laisser la bande réciter sa mémoire et le lecteur vous remplacer dans sa lecture' (AA, 9). The intention to draw the reader into this climactic scene could hardly be clearer. The device imparts a peculiar intensity to the confession, which we hear as if in a play-back of Act 2 of *Les Viaducs de la Seine-et-Oise*. A second machine records both the play-back and the ensuing commentary, imbuing events with a further obsessively repetitive dimension. The immediacy of Claire's impulsive outburst, again in response to ill-informed speculation about what really happened, is thus doubled by an acute sense of the irremediable which at the moment of reading we know she is plunging into.

We learn that it is precisely Pierre's speculative comment that the murder took place in the forest which drives Claire to confess: 'Elle n'a pas pu s'empêcher de rétablir la vérité.' His remarks in turn derive from the fact that 'les journaux parlaient du crime,' and that he 'li[t] beaucoup les journaux' with the result that he spoke with 'le style des journalistes de faits divers' (AA, 127–8). Thus once again the news reports are implicated in the dénouement; the more so as the official investigators, present in plain clothes at the time, were able to manipulate events since they were in possession of certain vital clues which 'la presse n'avait pas le droit de [. . .] dire' (AA, 47).

Duras's evolving presentation of the narrative appears to be moving away from the confession to concentrate on the testimonies following Claire's arrest. However, Duras highlights the importance of the features in question since she inserts material pertaining to them into the final stage version, in crucial adjustments which represent the only significant departures from the direction this revision otherwise pursues. Pierre's stage testimony contains newly-inserted allusions to his provocative intervention in the café (TAA, 20–1); and indeed the dramatic climax of the play is attained during the interrogation of Claire when, in a parallel departure from the text of the novel, the 'Interrogateur' plugs in a tape recorder and plays back the café conversation so as to counter Claire's more recent claim that she did not confess directly and that Alfonso had done so on her behalf (TAA, 101–2; cf. AA, p.181).

Duras's imagination thus circles round the scene of the confession with particular insistence. It is in fact the only element common to all versions of the story. Claire retains the secret of where the head is hidden, and of what happened in the cellar where the killing and dismemberment occurred. This experience of horror sets her apart from the rest of humanity and contains the inexpressible aspects of the case: 'J'avais peur à devenir folle dans la cave. [. . .] S'ils avaient été dans la cave même pendant une minute ils se tairaient, ils ne pourraient pas dire un mot sur cette histoire,' Claire says (AA, 135, 174–5).[31] But the feature which Duras draws attention to is precisely the key exception to her enigmatic and challenging silence, the one occasion on which she did speak, contrary to what she knows to be the best course for someone in her position: 'Je sais que plus les criminels parlent clairement, plus on les tue' (AA, 142). While her dumb cousin Marie-Thérèse met her death without having broken her silence, Claire's only hope will lie in reconstituting the effect of silence through her speech.[32]

If it was thus an irrational suicidal impulse that made Claire confess, this is in keeping with the reading of the murder which sees in it a displaced attempt on her own life.[33] Moreover, it was Pierre who triggered the confession by evoking news reports so as to offer an erroneous version of events which she would feel compelled to correct and thus give herself away. The interrogator diagnoses his behaviour as reflecting a wish to rid himself of Claire (AA, 129) – in other words as an urge to kill her. For his part, Pierre feels that he was the one Claire was seeking to kill through Marie-Thérèse (AA, 123). The relationship between man and wife which is Duras's starting-point in the text seems to hinge on a reciprocal death-wish not unlike the 'convenance' she has studied through *Moderato cantabile*: the more so as the couple of male and female plain-clothes police officers who eavesdrop on proceedings in the café and ultimately receive Claire's confession are specifically designated as 'Deux amants' in *Les Viaducs de la Seine-et-Oise*. Duras appears to associate this crime with that topos. The intratextual complex woven around this story thus contains suggestions of another meditation on the *crime passionnel* – or 'suicide passionnel' – as one ultimate goal of the 'rite mortuaire' which is love. All of which gives a particular resonance to Claire's declaration: 'Je sais que des gens [. . .] préfèrent ne pas lire les journaux mais ils ont tort' (AA, 186).

This analysis of Duras's creative treatment of documentary elements drawn from the *faits divers* helps us better understand the production of her notorious text deriving from the 'affaire Grégory', in which Christine Villemin came under suspicion of murdering her own son. Published in the newspaper *Libération* on 17 July 1985 alongside reports on the ongoing investigation, Duras's article thereby took on at first sight the air of a news-related feature itself. The editor Serge July provided a perceptive disclaimer: 'Ce n'est pas un travail de journaliste, d'enquêteur à la recherche de la vérité. Mais celui d'un écrivain en plein travail, fantasmant la réalité en quête d'une vérité qui n'est sans doute pas la vérité, mais une vérité quand même, celle du texte écrit.' He went on to highlight the relationship in this text between writing and the truth, which he characterizes as 'celle d'une femme "sublime, forcément sublime" flottant entre deux langages, celui de l'écrivain d'une part et celui bien réel, en grande partie non-dit, de Christine Villemin'. This remark calls to mind once again the silence effectively imposed on Simone Deschamps by judicial procedure, and which Duras had earlier attempted to remedy. July accepts that Duras is inviting scandal, 'car si elle ne vole pas son langage à Christine Villemin, elle ose rêver publiquement de la douleur de cette femme, transgressant son propre malaise et le nôtre, pour affoler le jeu de miroirs qu'offre à chacun de nous toute grande affaire criminelle.'[34]

Duras's text refers throughout to 'Christine V.' The initial eases this female out of her real context and places her in the same fictive, phantasmatic constellation as 'Lol V. Stein'.[35] Similarly, Duras refers only to 'l'enfant', 'la nourrice', 'l'homme', and so on, and locations are specified only as 'la maison [. . .] le chalet vosgien, aux toits de pentes inégales', 'la rivière', 'les collines'. These devices imbue the drama with the timeless anonymity of myth and make it available for creative elaboration. Her presentation of detail situates it less in a physical, real world than in that domain of common knowledge, of collective rumination and intersubjective imaginings, which is associated with the *fait divers*. She speaks of 'les paires de gifles de l'homme pour les beefsteaks mal cuits' (p.4), of 'le corbeau' and of 'cet autre crime, cet homme abattu'; she describes 'cette autre enfant. Pour tout le monde elle reste l'inconnu de l'enquête' (p.6). These references compromise her readers by compelling them to bring their own information to bear on the text, co-opting their visions as accessories in its speculations.[36]

Duras thus moves her writing outside the tightly-circumscribed referential registers of journalism and identifies with Christine, 'qui a peut-être tué sans savoir comme moi j'écris sans savoir'. Once again writing and murder evoke a realm beyond knowledge and express fantasies and unconscious compulsions incompatible with a conventional epistemological framework. Duras's text, like Anne Desbaresdes's reconstruction of the *crime passionnel*, makes intensive use of modal verbs – 'il se pourrait que', 'ça ne devait pas être', 'il ne devait rien avoir' – which further opens the way to conjectural musings and vicarious participation: 'Ce crime est un crime dont on ne se lasse pas. Il est insondable, très étendu, très. Souvent on le perd de vue là où on croyait le trouver. [. . .] Dans ce crime-là on est allé jusqu'à la couche dernière du mal' (p.6). Once more the *fait divers* prompts an attempt to articulate the unspeakable, to grasp the unknowable: 'La mise à mort de l'enfant par sa mère, je ne sais pas son nom, je ne sais pas appeler ce crime.' As something entirely unfounded in forensic and legal terms it must be formulated in a phrase without a verb: less an actual event than a mythologized one.

Duras travelled to the scene of the murder, replicating the behaviour of Anne Desbaresdes:[37] 'Dès que je vois la maison, je crie que le crime a existé. C'est ce que je crois. C'est au-delà de la raison. [. . .] j'essaye de savoir pourquoi j'ai crié quand j'ai vu la maison. Je n'arrive pas à le savoir.' Just as in *Moderato cantabile*, the cry bears witness to an intuitive vision beyond words, beyond knowledge. It inaugurates a 'rite mortuaire' which mingles passion, childbirth and death. Duras is possessed by the crime, as in a hallucination that excludes reason and justice: 'C'est ce que je vois. C'est au-delà de la raison. Je vois ce crime sans juger de cette justice qui s'exerce à son propos. Rien. Je ne vois qu'elle au centre du monde quant à moi et ne relevant que du temps et de Dieu. Par Dieu je n'entends rien' (p.4). The vision triggers a compulsion to go over the circumstances, as did the crime passionnel of *Moderato cantabile* and the murder in Savigny-sur-Orge. And a set of topoi linking with earlier works emerge as both the instruments and the focus of her deliberations here too.[38]

Recalling the preface to *Outside*, Duras evokes 'un amour soudain, incommensurable, devenu fou' (p.4). For the writer the mysteries of this ineffable transgressive love, 'sublime, forcément sublime', were the driving force which apparently impelled the mother to kill her own child.[39] Equally strikingly, in meditating on Christine, Duras returns to the motif of confession, so prominent in *L'Amante anglaise*. It is precisely when Christine breaks her silence that she betrays herself:

> La première personne qui a parlé de la disparition de l'enfant, c'est la mère de l'enfant, Christine V. [. . .] chose inattendue: bouleversante, je dois dire, Christine V. pose la question et aussitôt après elle parle d'elle, [. . .] de l'existence qu'elle a endurée. [. . .] au lieu de ne parler que de l'enfant, de sa disparition brutale, vertigineuse, ou de se taire, Christine V. fait une confidence profonde, intemporelle, sur sa propre existence.

For Duras there is a connection between the disappearance of the child and the wretchedness Christine is here driven to externalize. Duras presents this confession as 'cette imprudence, cette distraction': it betokens a particular kind of madness which has overtaken Christine, obliterating even her awareness of her child's death and making her disregard her own interest, as the supposed murderer, in concealing it. Language being the domain of the Other, the woman who launches into it – Christine or Claire – finds her words turn against her and accuse her.

In such ways as these, Christine becomes a durassian heroine, the embodiment of female experience, and the author repudiates 'la séparation de cette criminelle d'avec toutes les autres femmes. Ce qui aurait fait criminelle Christine V. c'est un secret de toutes les femmes, commun' (p.6). It is a secret she shares perhaps especially with Claire Lannes and other female figures from the *faits divers*.

Notes

1. For its place in her biography, see Alain Vircondelet, *Duras*, Paris, Editions François Bourin, 1991 pp.220–1, 238, 251, 255.
2. *Outside*, Paris, POL, 1984. References to this collection in the text are indicated by O followed by a page number. A second volume, *Le Monde extérieur*, ed. Christiane Blot-Labarrère, was published in late 1993.
3. *Le Ravissement de Lol V. Stein*, Paris, Gallimard-Folio, 1964, p.81. See Michael Sheringham, 'Knowledge and repetition in *Le Ravissement de Lol V. Stein*', *Romance Studies*, no.2, Summer 1983, pp.124–40.
4. The material presented in *Outside* conflates two different articles for *France-Observateur*, 'Horreur à Choisy-le-Roi' on 6 June 1957, shortly

after the arrest, and 'Deschamps, Simone' on 16 October 1958, during the trial. See the bibliography in Leslie Hill, *Marguerite Duras, apocalyptic desires*, London, Routledge, 1993, pp.181–2. Curiously, in his brief discussion of the case, p.6, Hill erroneously asserts that Deschamps killed her lover.

5. *Trois crimes rituels*, Paris, Gallimard, 1961, p.23.

6. See Sheringham, 'Knowledge and repetition'.

7. *Moderato cantabile* (hereafter MC), Paris, Minuit, collection Double, 1958.

8. Edgar Morin *et al.*, *La Rumeur d'Orléans*, Paris, Seuil, collection Points, 1969, p.12.

9. Ibid. Morin's investigation is supplemented by *La Rumeur d'Amiens*. Cf. Jules Gritti, *Elle court, elle court, la rumeur*, Ottowa, Editions Stanké, 1978; and Jean-Noël Kapferer, *Rumeurs*, Paris, Seuil, 1987.

10. A theme central to Beauvoir's *Les Belles Images*: see above, pp.182–4.

11. See Georges Auclair, *Le 'Mana' quotidien: structures et fonctions de la chronique des faits divers*, Paris, Editions Anthropos, 1970, pp.162–85, on 'le retour sur les lieux'.

12. 'Ce que veut Anne Desbaresdes de Chauvin, c'est ce qu'elle n'a jamais vécu mais ce qu'elle aurait pu vivre avec et à travers d'autres hommes: son anéantissement dans l'amour même.' Preface to the Prentice Hall edition, ed. Thomas Bishop, Englewood Cliffs, 1968, pp.9–10.

13. M. Tison-Braun, *Marguerite Duras*, Amsterdam, Rodopi, 1985, p.32.

14. On the prevalence of 'scènes originaires' in Duras's work, see Madeleine Borgomano, *Marguerite Duras, une lecture des fantasmes*, Paris, Cistre, 1987, pp.111–90, and Hill, *Marguerite Duras, apocalyptic desires*, p.78. See also Sheringham, 'Knowledge and repetition', pp.126, 138. On the multilayered interwoven temporalities underpinning the slippery epistemologies in the text, see Roger McLure, 'Duras *contra* Bergson: time in *Moderato cantabile*', *Forum for Modern Language Studies*, vol.25, no.1, January 1989, pp.62–76.

15. Hill refers to the novel as a 'transferential re-enactment or repetition of the scene by its interpreters', *Marguerite Duras, apocalyptic desires*, p.54.

16. Tison-Braun, *Marguerite Duras*, p.29.

17. Marguerite Duras, *Le Ravissement de Lol V. Stein*; and *Les Parleuses*, Paris, Minuit, 1974, pp.65–6. See also David Coward, *Duras: 'Moderato cantabile'*, London, Grant and Cutler, 1981, pp.27–8, 55; Borgomano, *Marguerite Duras, une lecture*, pp.204 *et seq*. Hill sums it up tellingly: 'That limit at which meaning falters and yields to an ecstatic otherness that no longer fits the bounds of language', *Marguerite Duras, apocalyptic desires*, p.36.

18. *Le Monde*, 14 January 1950, p.12, col.5.

19. Marguerite Duras, *Le Théâtre de l'Amante anglaise*, Paris, Gallimard,

collection L'Imaginaire, 1991, p.11. Hereafter referred to as TA in the text. AA refers to the novel version, Marguerite Duras, *L'Amante anglaise*, Paris, Gallimard, 1967.

20. *Le Monde*, 20 December 1968, p.12.
21. Cf. *L'Etranger*, in TRN, p.1182: 'D'un côté, elle [l'histoire] était invraisemblable. D'un autre, elle était naturelle.' See above, pp.143–4.
22. See Borgomano, *Marguerite Duras, une lecture*, pp.174–204: 'Le corps morcelé'; and Janine Ricouart, *Ecriture féminine et Violence: Une étude de Marguerite Duras*, Birmingham, Alabama, Summa, 1991, pp.62–72: '"Le corps morcelé": *L'Amante anglaise*'.
23. Marguerite Duras in an interview, *Le Monde*, 20 December 1968.
24. Ibid.
25. Ibid.
26. Sheringham, 'Knowledge and repetition'.
27. Marguerite Duras, *Les Viaducs de la Seine-et-Oise*, Paris, Gallimard, 1959.
28. *Le Monde*, 20 December 1968.
29. Duras, *Le Ravissement de Lol V. Stein*, p.48. Borgomano, *Marguerite Duras, une lecture*, pp.189–90, makes a pertinent link between this section of the novel and a later one in the same vein from *L'Amante anglaise*, p.192.
30. *Le Monde*, 20 December 1968.
31. See Borgomano, *Marguerite Duras, une lecture*, pp.185–6. The cellar also plays an important part in *Hiroshima mon amour*, where the sequestering of the heroine may well owe something to *La Séquestrée de Poitiers*.
32. Duras characterizes silence as the domain of women's lived experience and language as an instrument that serves men to 'arrêter le cours du silence': see remarks quoted in Hill, *Marguerite Duras, apocalyptic desires*, p.27.
33. The interrogator says, for example: 'on a tué l'autre comme on se serait tué soi . . . C'est le cas de beaucoup de crimes vous savez' (AA, 32), and Claire's suicidal tendencies are highlighted elsewhere (AA, 95). See Ricouart, *Ecriture féminine et violence*, p.63; Borgomano, *Marguerite Duras, une lecture*, pp.187–8.
34. Hill, *Marguerite Duras, apocalyptic desires*, p.34, and note 43, p.164, points out that Duras had indicated in an interview as early as April 1985 that her fascination for Christine Villemin as a potential infanticide was linked to uncomfortable memories of her own involvement in the infliction of torture during the Resistance. Hill writes: 'In the figure of Villemin therefore, it was also – perhaps even principally – her own past that Duras was accusing, in the process turning herself and Villemin into a pair of apocalyptic witnesses, martyrs to a mythic crime.' Mme

Villemin was declared innocent in July 1992; a further official chapter on the story was added in December 1993 when her husband Jean-Marie Villemin emerged from jail after receiving a relatively lenient sentence for the murder of his cousin Bernard Laroche: this was seen as confirming suspicions that Laroche killed Grégory, though the mystery remains unresolved.

35. See David Amar and Pierre Yana, '"Sublime, forcément sublime": à propos d'un article paru dans *Libération*', *Revue des Sciences Humaines*, no.202, April–June 1986, pp.153–76; pp.168–9. Similarly, the names of the characters in *L'Amante anglaise* evolve, from Georges and Amélie Rabilland (or Rabilloux or Rabilloud, as various reports spell it) to Marcel and Claire Ragon and thence to Pierre and Claire Lannes – which as Madeleine Borgomano shows, marks their progressive integration into the universe of the author's phantasms (*Marguerite Duras, une lecture*, p.178).

36. The references are respectively to details of family life in the Villemin household; the pseudonym of the author of poison-pen letters; the killing of Bernard Laroche by Jean-Marie Villemin; the incriminating testimony first given then retracted by Muriel Bolle. Readers' reactions came in the form of indignant letters; *Libération*, 20–21, 23, 27–8 July 1985. *L'Evénement du jeudi* published interviews with readers on 25 July 1985; and a special number of *Esprit*, no.116, July 1986, was devoted to the issues raised.

37. See above on the 'retour sur les lieux'.

38. See Amar and Yana, '"Sublime, forcément sublime"', for additional details.

39. On the sublime in Duras, see Hill, *Marguerite Duras, apocalyptic desires*, pp.31, 83–4, and *passim*. The irrational intensity, bordering on violence, of the mother's love for her son, is frequently associated with death in the fiction. In *Les Petits Chevaux de Tarquinia*, Paris, Gallimard-Folio, 1953, Sara's vertiginous passion for her child (p.116), sliding into phantasms of his death by beating and drowning at the hands of an unreliable maid (p.125), actually prefigures elements of Duras's version of the Villemin crime; it is also allusively linked in the novel with the mute exaltation of the old mother as she sits before the box containing fragments of her son's body (p.42), in a graphic demonstration of love's true fulfilment in death: 'Tout amour vécu est une dégradation de l'amour' (p.88), as the novel has it. Anne Desbaresdes's relationship with her infant son has a similar ecstatic, funereal quality; he accompanies her to the café where she enacts the 'rite mortuaire' with Chauvin, and the text associates him closely, both metonymically and metaphorically, with each phase of the *crime passionnel* and with the violence it involves.

PART VI

Fantasies of Violence:
Male Perversions

13

Anything Can Happen:
Jean-Paul Sartre

The first years of Sartre's appointment as a school-teacher in Le Havre (1931–3), when he began writing *La Nausée*, were a period during which he and Simone de Beauvoir became particularly interested in the *faits divers*. While history appeared temporarily to have becalmed their generation[1] they took to studying *Détective* and *Paris-Soir* for reports on 'les cas extrêmes' because in them 'on [. . .] retrouvait exagérées, épurées, dotées d'un saisissant relief les attitudes et les passions des gens qu'on appelle normaux.'[2] Beauvoir mentions a number of specific cases which caught their attention, including Violette Nozières and the Papin affair, traces of which are to be found in 'Erostrate', a story in Sartre's collection *Le Mur*;[3] but events in *La Nausée*, which take place during 1932 in Bouville/Le Havre, also bear the unmistakeable stamp of the rubric's influence on the author.

Antoine Roquentin has an existence which is systematically on the margins of conventional life. 'Moi je vis seul, entièrement seul. Je ne parle à personne, jamais; je ne reçois rien, je ne donne rien' (N, 11).[4] In particular, he has drifted beyond the framework of narrative transactions which accompanies social integration: 'Ces gens m'émerveillent: ils racontent, en buvant leur café, des histoires nettes et vraisemblables. [. . .] Quand on vit seul, on ne sait même plus ce que c'est que raconter: le vraisemblable disparaît en même temps que les amis' (N, 12).[5] In the place of the socially-sanctioned norms which are what the *vraisemblable* in effect codifies, Roquentin's day-to-day existence is characterized by unsettling visions that embody the senselessness and contingency of the world. In an effort to grasp what it is that makes his existence suddenly so disquieting, he attempts to formulate the ordinary in terms other than those which betray its arbitrariness by fitting it into conventional patterns of meaning. He recounts in his diary a series of proto-narratives, 'des histoires sans queue ni tête' whose strange ordinariness exemplifies, as he puts it, 'tout l'invraisemblable [. . .] tout ce qui ne pourrait pas être cru dans les cafés'

(N, 12): which is what characterizes his experience of the real. A woman running backwards round a corner as she waves goodbye bumps into a black man; a glass of beer sits on a table; an old man in the Luxembourg Gardens, wearing a boot on one foot and a slipper on the other, stares in fright at the booted foot (N, 12–14). These episodes have no point, except that they happened: they represent crude, unshaped slices of the real.

Sartre thus has Roquentin set down examples of what Georges Perec would later term 'l'infra-ordinaire' or endotics, as a challenge to the doxa.[6] This aspect of Roquentin's writing might be seen, in fact, as a *mise en abyme* for what the author does: Sartre himself challenges the conventions of the novelistic by having elements of Roquentin's story evolve within what is in effect a network of *faits divers*.[7] It is curiously appropriate that Roquentin's ontological disorientation should be triggered in the first instance as a result of his predilection for picking up 'des bouts de journaux [. . .] lourds et somptueux, mais probablement salis de merde', which he spots lying among the detritus on the ground (N, 15). This serves as an apt figure for his attraction to the lurid vulgarity of the *faits divers* – not quite what is known in English as the 'gutter press'; moreover, it inaugurates a series of episodes in which Roquentin's attacks of nausea are framed by allusions to the *fait divers*. Indeed, the effectiveness of Sartre's depiction of Roquentin's malaise is determined in part by the peculiar atmosphere associated with its reminiscences of the rubric, in which the grotesque and the out of the way become the norm. In addition, the very sense of Roquentin's nausea is communicated to the reader by means of meditations that frequently have the *faits divers* as their object.

Roquentin likes to retreat to the café Mably for the feeling of secure normality it affords him: 'Dans les cafés, tout est toujours normal et particulièrement au café Mably, à cause du gérant M. Fasquelle, qui porte sur sa figure un air de canaillerie bien positif et rassurant' (N, 11). However, one morning this normality is threatened by the absence of the *gérant*. The episode coincides with Roquentin's efforts to repress a rising panic in himself at the prospect of acknowledging the problematical nature of History and hence the futility of the biography of Rollebon he is working on: 'Ne pas trop réfléchir sur la valeur de l'Histoire' (N, 85), he notes. It triggers a crisis which crystallizes Roquentin's dawning sense of the contingency of the universe. Moreover, as the overarching authority of the discourse of History wanes we note that Roquentin's perceptions are increasingly couched in the style of sensational newspaper reports which will underpin ensuing developments.

A customer asks to see M. Fasquelle and the waiter replies with some surprise that he has not yet come down from his room. The customer's casual suggestion that he might have died prompts an apprehensive reaction in Roquentin. At the thought of the *gérant* lying dead upstairs, the situation appears to Roquentin as an item in the *fait divers* rubric: 'Trouvé mort dans son lit, un matin de brouillard. – Et en sous-titre: dans le café, des clients consommaient sans se douter . . .' (N, 88). The *fait divers* serves Roquentin as the appropriate vehicle to bring home the nature of the irruption, into the humdrum everyday world, of horror in the shape of the facticity of death. Notwithstanding its banal sensationalism, the rubric communicates an implicit sense of what is veiled by conventional verisimilitude. Roquentin's imagination embroiders patterns of journalistic stereotypes around his initial vision: 'Mais était-il encore dans son lit? N'avait-il pas chaviré, entraînant les draps avec lui et cognant de la tête contre le plancher?' (N, 88). The fantasies associated with the *fait divers* are shown to be founded in a fundamentally authentic perception: there is a repressed real contingency which haunts the stable fictions of the everyday. The intuition hangs in the air of the café: unable to go upstairs to check for himself, Roquentin steps outside to escape the charged atmosphere. As he walks past a *charcuterie* and sees the counter assistant reach into the window for a 'bout de chair morte', he notes, again in *fait divers* style: 'Dans sa chambre, à cinq minutes de là, M. Fasquelle était mort' (N, 90).

Clearly, there is about all this a touch of satire at the expense of the stylistic register of the rubric, with its melodramatic rhetorical effects and highly-coloured juxtapositions. But the irony does not protect Roquentin from the contagion of horror: he looks around for 'un appui solide, une défense contre mes pensées', but in vain, for 'quelque chose d'inquiétant restait à traîner dans la rue' (N, 90). His existence has lurched into the world of the *fait divers*, which Sartre exploits to achieve a specific literary-cum-philosophical aim. A red droplet on the mayonnaise of *œuf à la russe* in the shop window reminds Roquentin of blood: whereupon his overheated imagination assails him with another vision of everyday violence and bloodshed: 'Quelqu'un était tombé, la face en avant et saignait dans le plat' (N, 90).

Roquentin seeks refuge in the library, where he finds he cannot concentrate on his work as his mind keeps returning to the café Mably and the state of the *gérant*. It is not that he really believes the man is dead, but that the possibility of such an event has unsettled his perception of the world: 'Au fond je ne croyais pas trop à sa mort et c'est précisément ce qui m'agaçait: c'était une idée flottante dont je ne pouvais ni me persuader ni me défaire' (N, 91). Speculative horror is enough to contaminate his environment with 'une espèce d'inconsistance des choses' (N, 92). He senses that 'Le monde attendait [. . .] sa crise, sa Nausée' (N, 92). What his nightmarish awareness highlights is that reality and events are contingent, not bound by patterns of human understanding – an insight he shares with the *fait divers* rubric: '*Tout* peut se produire, *tout* peut arriver' (N, 92) he murmurs as he realizes that the laws of physics and the categories of human understanding make no perceptible mark on the facticity of the universe. He has lost his faith in the veneer of normality that the world habitually presents, suddenly seeing it as liable to veer wholesale into a sinister otherness. Like the surface of the sea, its superficial appearance conceals lurking monsters (N, 94). He is quite clear that 'à l'origine de ce malaise il y a l'histoire du café Mably' (N, 93), and he is impelled to rush back there to conjure the sickening spell it has cast over him. But the café is deserted, as is to be expected at two in the afternoon: 'Oui, mais voilà, j'avais *besoin* de voir M. Fasquelle' (N, 93). In any case, by now Roquentin's horror has gone beyond what mere facts can remedy. He is seized with panic: 'Où aller? où aller? *Tout* peut arriver' (N, 94).

The ensuing narrative vindicates this perception while at the same time ironically challenging plot structures which exploit coincidence to drive home their message. As Roquentin wanders the streets in his paranoid and aimless state, fearful of both objects and people he encounters, he passes three times by the public garden, in which he notices on each occasion a man dressed in a cape (N, 90, 93, 95). The third time, however, he observes that a young girl is in the garden with him – and realizes that the man is in fact an exhibitionist, about to subject the child to his attentions. Roquentin takes in the intensity of the brief relationship: the grotesque fascination that links him to the spectacle and the girl to the man, the 'puissance obscure de leurs désirs' which attaches predator and victim to each other, the 'espèce d'attente' that connects the scene to Roquentin's perception of a world in which anything can happen. 'J'aurais voulu empêcher ça,' he says, and after considering coughing, he pushes open the gate to forestall the man's intentions and addresses him with the words: 'Une grande menace pèse sur la ville' (N, 95–6).

The multiple ironies here will repay further scrutiny. The impact of this entire café Mably sequence is largely due to the fact that effectively it starts and ends in *fait divers*. While it builds from the supposed death of M. Fasquelle to the climactic '*Tout* peut arriver', there is clearly an ironic anticlimax inherent in the choice of an incongruous sordid incident as the culmination of the sequence. The declaration Roquentin directs sardonically at the potential 'flasher' makes this point eloquently. If anything can happen, the vulgar commonplace is just as likely as the calamity. But in fact, of course, nothing *does* happen: by sheer coincidence – anything can happen, after all – Roquentin stumbles upon the scene at the crucial moment in order to stop the exhibitionist. The contrived nature of this arrival in the nick of time is hinted at in the triple reference to the man in his cape. Overall, this play with contingency and with the overlap between the apocalyptic and the trivial, while in keeping with the metaphysical aims of the novel, constitutes another link with the *fait divers*.

This is not the end of the story. The motifs explored here will recur subsequently, generating a pattern of echoes centring on the *fait divers* as a device that contributes to the novel's overall coherence.

Already, as Roquentin sought security in the library, the Autodidact, trembling and weak, has greeted him with the words: 'Il m'arrive une histoire abominable' (N, 91). We later realize with hindsight that this remark prefigures the scandal of the Autodidact's denunciation, towards the end of the novel, for interfering with young boys; and as such it connects also with the improper advances of the exhibitionist on the girl in the garden. We shall consider the connections at greater length in due course; for the moment it will suffice to point out that these allusions to illicit sexual behaviour are developed further in a reference to a more brutal *fait divers* that occurs at the next crisis point in Roquentin's story.

As in the previous instance, a new development is ushered in by Roquentin's changing attitude to his biography of Rollebon, which he now decides to abandon altogether. Foregoing the narratives of history he falls a prey once more to those of the *faits divers* as, finding himself a victim of his body's facticity, he buys a newspaper to divert his thoughts from the 'horreur d'exister' (N, 119). Again, the headline forces itself upon him: 'Sensationnel. Le corps de la petite Lucienne a été retrouvé!' (N, 120). The prior knowledge of the case presupposed by the definite article in 'la petite Lucienne'[8] implies a familiarity which, as is intended, draws the reader into a phantasmatic intimacy with the story. Roquentin also notes: 'Odeur d'encre, le papier se froisse entre mes doigts': the tactile and olfactory sensations involved in reading newsprint recall the predilection for paper which led to his first experience of nausea. This combination of *fait divers* phantasms and sensations of facticity associated with newsprint will lead Roquentin to his most acute attack so far.

As has been admirably illustrated by Rhiannon Goldthorpe, the fevered meditations provoked by news of the rape and death of the girl dramatize central features of Sartre's phenomenology.[9] They highlight Roquentin's growing sense of his own facticity, for example as he remarks: 'Son corps existe encore. [. . .] *Elle* n'existe plus' (N, 120). They also give expression to a number of the obsessions that haunt him (and the text) as he uneasily acknowledges his own sexual arousal on reading the story, feeling his consciousness slipping into the grip of his body – and colluding in the 'empâtement', in accordance with Sartre's ontology of desire.[10] Another kind of complicity is alluded to as he imagines the girl's body, 'ses doigts crispés dans la boue' and refers to his own actions: 'Je roule le journal en boule, mes doigts crispés sur le journal; couleur d'encre.' His private fetishes are coming into play and intensifying the phantasms the story triggers. As Roquentin's sense of his separate identity blurs in the swooning of fantasy and desire, the 'doigt de la petite maculé de boue' becomes his own 'doigt qui sortait du ruisseau boueux' (N, 120) after picking up scraps of discarded newspaper; but by extension, as he evokes the finger 'qui gratte dans ma culotte' (N, 120) an indirect but fairly obvious allusion can be discerned to his own penis – 'le doigt se lève' (N, 121) – manifesting his involuntary sexual arousal on reading the details of the crime. He records the phrase, 'l'ignoble individu a pris la fuite' (N, 120), clearly a quotation from the stereotypical moralizing text of the *fait divers*. Again, however, the irony such a style gives rise to is no defence against its implications as Roquentin's self-disgust calls up this phrase repeatedly, attaching it to himself: 'Je fuis, l'ignoble individu a pris la fuite' (N, 120). The language of the news story has insinuated itself into his consciousness: 'Ce journal est-ce encore moi?' Under the pressure of the thoughts, impulses and sensations assailing him, Roquentin's reflections degenerate into barely-rational incoherence which Sartre articulates through a version of the stream-of-consciousness technique. By this means he is able both to record insights into the devious play of sexual desire, as well as phenomenological data, through the recurrent motifs of Roquentin's obsessions.[11] Roquentin's consciousness thus becomes the unwilling instrument of sexual impulses which make him fantasize that he is the rapist: 'Un doux désir sanglant de viol me prend par derrière [. . .] j'ai mal, doux à ma chair meurtrie. [. . .] Je fuis, je suis un ignoble individu à la chair meurtrie' (N, 120–1).[12] Other references that echo his periodic sexual encounters with the *patronne* of the *Rendez-vous des Cheminots* are called up and threaded into this already rich fantasy material,[13] which shows Sartre offering a telling testimony to the insidious evocative power of the *fait divers*.[14]

The text of the novel offers no explicit link between this news, reported on the Monday, and the sexual assault Roquentin has averted in the *jardin public* the previous Friday; but we do not need any diegetic connection to perceive what the two have in common. Rhiannon Goldthorpe comments on the latter incident that 'the atmosphere of tension and potential violence suggests that self-exposure might lead to rape or murder.'[15] Indeed, aberrant sexuality hangs over the text like the 'menace' Roquentin himself refers to.[16] Evocations of its threatening force seem to be used by Sartre to underpin the disquieting nature of the world's contingency which he elsewhere dramatizes in nightmare visions of nature and vegetation invading the town or monstrous hallucinations being enacted in the streets, for instance (N, 186–9).[17]

True to this mingling of transgressive sexuality with disturbing metaphysics, the novel reaches its conclusion, on the day of Roquentin's final departure from Bouville, via an episode in the library in which the Autodidact is caught making improper advances to a pair of young boys. Roquentin's diary entry recording the event begins with the announcement that 'le scandale' has befallen the poor man, though such a fate seems entirely disproportionate to what Roquentin half-jokingly calls his 'humble amour contemplatif pour les jeunes garçons – une forme d'humanisme, plutôt' (N, 189). However, the damage is done: it is evident that henceforth the Autodidact is exiled from society, condemned to the margins like Roquentin himself. He has become a denizen of the *fait divers* – and Roquentin's retrospective account of the incident that follows this prelude contains numerous motifs and allusions to indicate that this is indeed the culmination of the elements we have been examining.

Paying a final visit to take his leave of the library, Roquentin completes certain formalities and then reaches for the newspaper. The first item he reads is a classic *fait divers*: 'Sauvé par son chien'. The text we are given is truncated, but is characteristic of the unprepossessing ordinariness that ushers in the 'strange but true': 'M. Dubosc, propriétaire à Remiredon, rentrait hier soir à bicyclette de la foire de Naugis . . .' (N, 190). The title is sufficient indication of the rest, with its logic and codes so beloved of the rubric: a potential tragedy resolved by a down to earth intervention; the reversal of roles implied by a dog playing the part of a saviour; the vindication nonetheless of the received commonsense wisdom about man's best friend. This fairly light-hearted, innocuous story contrasts with the indecent sexual items that have preceded and will immediately follow. However, Sartre will have Roquentin keep the newspaper in his hands throughout the ensuing episode, sometimes hiding behind it, sometimes punctuating his narrative with quotations from it, repeatedly referring to it. While he reads the humdrum reports in his paper, in effect, a scandalous *fait divers* will be acted out before him. Sartre's systematic framing and counterpointing of the narrative with news copy represents a variant on a technique he has used earlier when Roquentin reads Balzac's *Eugénie Grandet* in the restaurant and *La Nausée* intercuts the literary dialogue of the traditional novel with the considerably less stylised and coherent conversation of the customers at the next table (N, 58–61). Here too, then, we are implicitly invited to compare actual events with what conventional representations – here the press – habitually make of such material.

Moreover, as the unsuspecting Autodidact is maliciously lured by two schoolboys into making the gestures that condemn him in the eyes of the respectable people who witness them, Sartre takes care to apply to the incident key terms that relate it to the other *fait divers* references in the novel. Noticing the first hints of the boys' provocations, Roquentin admits, 'J'attendais, en feignant de lire mon journal [. . .] les autres attendaient aussi' (N, 193). The air of expectancy, echoing the earlier perceptions that '*Tout peut arriver*' in the café Mably sequence, ultimately becomes so acute that the librarian's eventual explosion of outrage will come as a relief: 'l'attente était trop pénible' (N, 195). Another set of connections with previous incidents is established in the declaration: 'Je comprenais bien que quelque chose d'ignoble allait se produire, je voyais bien aussi qu'il était encore temps d'empêcher que cela ne se produisît. Mais je n'arrivais pas à deviner ce qu'il fallait empêcher' (N, 194). *Ignoble* links with the *individu* who raped and murdered Lucienne, while *empêcher* is what Roquentin sought and managed to do in the case of the exhibitionist. In this latter instance, too, he had thought that a cough might forestall the offence (N, 95), just as in the library 'je toussai fortement, pour l'avertir' (N, 195). Similarly, the 'gros doigt jauni par le tabac' which the Autodidact stretches out towards the 'chair inerte' of the child has 'toute la disgrâce d'un sexe masculin' (N, 195): which allusions recall precisely the imagery of Roquentin's visions after reading the *fait divers* about *la petite Lucienne*.

The mingled horror and rapt attention that fascinated both onlooker and participants in the scene Roquentin witnessed in the park is also reiterated here, as the 'grosse dame' notices what is happening in the library and watches transfixed: 'Elle semblait fascinée' (N, 194). In fact the entire scene unfolds in an atmosphere of mesmerized collusion which hints at the hidden impulses that make the *fait divers* enduringly compelling: Roquentin, glancing surreptitiously at the Autodidact, is aware of others watching too, with their 'lourds regards qui pesaient sur lui sans qu'il le sût' (N, 194). The furtive spectacle has the ritual air of a public execution: 'Ce silence me parut tragique: c'était la fin, la mise à mort' (N, 194). The hypnotic qualities of events as they occur are redolent of some primal scene that corresponds to deep-seated compulsions on the part of the watchers: their voyeuristic tendencies are manifest in Roquentin's remark: 'Je sentais clairement que le drame allait éclater: ils *voulaient* tous qu'il éclatât' (N, 194).[18] It can hardly be more clear how much the scandalous incident actually meets the needs of the public who will be outraged by it: as in the exhibitionist episode of the *jardin public*, protagonists and witnesses are 'rivés l'un à l'autre par la puissance obscur de leurs désirs' (N, 95). Though these events in themselves are less unusual than those in the *fait divers* which Sartre cites as the prelude to this sequence, their sexual content, permitting an unacknowledged complicity on the part of onlookers, generates the sort of scandal that marks an effective collusion between the outcast and his judges. The challenges to normal causality and to the man–animal hierarchy in the 'Sauvé par son chien' story, while they highlight the contingency of the universe, do not after all mobilize the same impulses as the *fait divers* of sexual misdemeanour. The scandal of facticity, the fascinated collusion of consciousness with the *en-soi* that occurs in sexual arousal and which we are reminded of shamefully in the spectacle of sexual behaviour in others[19] perhaps explain the distinction Sartre implicitly draws between the two types of item that appear in the rubric. A preoccupation with the phenomenology of sexuality appears to predominate here over other features in *La Nausée*'s exploitation of *fait divers* material.

On this, his last day at Bouville, Roquentin goes on to call at the *Rendez-vous des Cheminots*, where he will take his leave of the *patronne*. By now he is feeling completely estranged from the town, a state that exacerbates his being *de trop* in metaphysical terms, and as his consciousness floats queasily he thinks of the Autodidact with a kind of envy. The latter's mishap has made him a focus of attention: not just the outraged lady and the Corsican librarian, but 'peut-être tout le monde, dans la ville' know of him by now – presumably through the *fait divers* and *la rumeur*.[20] As an object of vilification, the Autodidact's *être pour autrui* at least offers some relief from the sickening contingency of the *pour soi* to which Roquentin is condemned (N, 201–2). With this example of a *fait divers* in mind, once in the bar Roquentin reaches for the *Journal de Bouville* – but then abandons the idea, remembering that he has already read the paper, 'de la première ligne à la dernière', in the Library (N, 203). His recalling this serves to remind the reader also of the first item that caught his eye then: 'Sauvé par son chien' (N, 190). And this modest headline will turn out to be the harbinger of the novel's conclusion just as so many other turning-points in the narrative have been initiated by *faits divers* references. The notion of salvation coming from an unexpected quarter is precisely the theme of these closing pages, and is made explicit as Roquentin listens for one last time to the recording of 'Some of these days' which has brought him relief from previous attacks of nausea. On this occasion it helps him clarify the differences between his formless existence and the mode of being of the melody and the performer. Thinking of the composer and the singer of the song, he notes: 'En voilà deux qui sont sauvés: le Juif et la Négresse. Sauvés.' (N, 209)

The insistence on the key term emphasizes the seriousness with which it is to be taken, despite its evident outlandishness in a novel from which religious themes are notably absent except as a butt of ridicule or satire. But the story of M. Dubosc, returning homewards after an outing to the fair at Naugis, who encountered some mishap from which he had to be saved by his dog, also prefigures the fate of Roquentin, heading back to Paris after this interlude in Bouville where he too has fallen foul of misfortune. The jocular note suggested by the *fait divers* does not preclude a real escape from a real danger: but it also serves unobtrusively to set the tone for Sartre's conclusion in which Roquentin, inspired by the music, determines to write a novel which will redeem his existence. The closing pages of *La Nausée* effectively combine the two senses of *sauvé*; the strategy is a risky one, since it has features which are grandiose, melodramatic, incongruous and contrived. 'Man at the end of his tether rescued from despair by ragtime record'? The retrospective glance at the *fait divers* implicitly endorses the novel's conclusion via a smiling sense of the modest coincidences that nourish the rubric and of which, we might allow,

Roquentin's story is one more example. It comes coloured by that ambivalence the novel as a whole reserves for the *fait divers* elements it draws on.[21]

Notes

1. See above, chapters 6, 7, and 8.
2. Simone de Beauvoir, *La Force de l'Age*, Paris, Gallimard, 1961, p.135.
3. See above, pp.92–3.
4. Jean-Paul Sartre, *La Nausée* (hereafter N), in *Œuvres romanesques*, ed. M. Contat and M. Rybalka, Paris, Pléiade, 1981.
5. Sartre stated that the challenge to 'vraisemblance' as an expression of bourgeois orthodoxy was one of the purposes of the novel: see *Œuvres romanesques*, p. 1730, and Rhiannon Goldthorpe, '*La Nausée*', London, Harper-Collins, Unwin Critical Library, 1991, pp. 83–8.
6. See Georges Perec, *L'infra-ordinaire*, Paris, Seuil, 1989, and David Bellos, *Georges Perec, A Life in Words*, London, Harvill, 1993, pp.521–5.
7. On the self-conscious features of the novel, see Paul Reed and Roger McLure, '*La Nausée* and the problem of literary representation', *Modern Language Review*, no.82, 1987, pp.343–55.
8. That it is typical of *fait divers* style is borne out by the case of 'le petit Gregory' we have seen Duras comment on.
9. Goldthorpe, '*La Nausée*', pp.169–75.
10. Cf. Andy Leak, 'Nausea and desire in Sartre's *La Nausée*', *French Studies*, vol.43 , no.1, January 1989, pp.61–72.
11. See Goldthorpe, '*La Nausée*', pp.174–5, for an analysis of stylistic techniques used here. Keith Gore, in 'Lucienne, Sex and Nausea', *Forum for Modern Language Studies*, vol.26, no.1, 1990, pp.37–48, corrects Leak's interpretation of the sexual impulses in play by pointing out that the evocation of homosexual rape is merely a figure for facticity grasping consciousness.
12. Cf. Goldthorpe, '*La Nausée*', p.170: 'He identifies himself with the "ignoble individu" who raped and murdered the little girl, but he is himself a victim, violated by desire.'
13. N, 121: 'caresser dans l'épanouissement des draps blancs la chair blanche épanouie'.
14. See *Œuvres romanesques*, pp.1776–7, for the even more explicit and insistent sexual content of this section in the manuscript.
15. '*La Nausée*', p.152.
16. See A. Leak, *The Perverted Consciousness: Sexuality and Sartre*, London, Macmillan, 1989; and S. Doubrovsky, 'Le Neuf de Cœur. Fragment

d'une psycholecture de *La Nausée*', *Obliques*, nos. 18–19, 1979, especially at p.71; 'Phallotexte et gynotexte dans *La Nausée*: "feuillet sans date"', in Michael Issacharoff and Jean-Claude Vilquin, eds., *Sartre et la mise en signe*, Paris/Lexington Kentucky, Klinksieck/French Forum, 1982, pp.31–55.

17. In an interesting article, S. Beynon John examines the episodes we are considering and sees in them the prefiguration of an apocalyptic destruction of the conventional urban existence which is the culmination of Roquentin's fantasms. The reading retains its suggestive force despite the fact, acknowledged by Beynon John, that the apocalyptic vision precedes the last of these incidents (see below, pp.210–13). Moreover, in overlooking the *fait divers* allusions that link them and the novel's conclusion, this critic's argument lacks a dimension that permits a more comprehensive reading, embracing more of the narrative elements. See S. Beynon John, 'Sartre's *La Nausée*: the City and Apocalypse', *Romance Studies*, no.22, Autumn 1993, pp.53–65.

18. Generations of readers of the *Livre de Poche* and *Folio* editions have been presented with a defective text which rendered this allusion virtually impenetrable.

19. See Jean-Paul Sartre, *L'Etre et le néant*, Paris, Gallimard, 1943, pp.317–9, and Goldthorpe, '*La Nausée*', pp.152–4.

20. On *la rumeur*, see above, pp.7, 145, 152n20, 190.

21. Cf. *Œuvres romanesques*, pp.1672–3, on Sartre's own ambivalence about the ending of the novel.

14

Textual Hide-and-Seek:
Alain Robbe-Grillet

Alain Robbe-Grillet acknowledges that the development of his writing practice owes much to both the Camus of *L'Etranger* and the Sartre of *La Nausée*. Indeed, in a notable article which established him as a leading spokesman for the *nouveau roman*, 'Nature, humanisme, tragédie', published in 1958,[1] he analyses these two novels as failed attempts to break through conventional representations and to depict the neutral presence of objects – 'l'être-là des choses' – in the reality outside the human mind. Though setting out to measure objectively the distance that separates human consciousness from nature and the universe, argues Robbe-Grillet, both novels ultimately capitulate to the anthropocentric metaphors in language and thereby reestablish the myth of a dubious collusion with the world. If he chose to criticize these two novels, he explains, it was not a gesture of hostility, but an indication that he was greatly indebted to them and identified profoundly with the ambition that inspired them.[2] In many respects, they stand as a joint urtext in relation to his own output.

Robbe-Grillet characterizes his writing project as a struggle with the humanistic clichés and emotional stereotypes of bourgeois ideology –which he as readily sees embodied in journalism as elsewhere in modern culture. A section of his quasi-autobiographical text *Le Miroir qui revient* evokes his encounters with the press on occasions when he was involved in *faits divers* such as an aeroplane accident in 1961 and a bomb alert on the liner *Queen Elizabeth II* some years later. Interviewed after these experiences, Robbe-Grillet found that his accounts of them failed to impress the reporters, who actually wrote up his comments in terms that sensationalized and misrepresented the incidents –and made him something of a figure of fun as a man who contrived to achieve an artificially impassive style in his novels but who apparently gave way to lurid and emotional outpourings when real experience was involved.[3] He concludes that 'la descendance du pire Zola est donc censée, aux yeux du grand public et à en croire ses porte-parole officiels, représenter la façon la plus naturelle de parler, comme d'écrire' (LM, 155). Though by this stage in his career he had decisively distanced himself from the culturally-conditioned reflexes that reproduce unthinking ideological commonplaces in writing, he admits that as an apprentice he too had written 'des passages entiers que n'auraient pas sans doute désavoués ni mon interviewer de l'A.F.P. [Agence France Presse] ni le courriériste de *L'Express*' (LM, 163). For Robbe-Grillet there can be no question of banishing from his writing all traces of the dominant ideology: it is in fact the only material available for the writer to work on, and he therefore embraces it – in order to subvert it. His achievement as a creative artist has been to assert his freedom to manipulate the discourses he inhabits, to play with clichés and stereotypes with the precise aim of preventing us from accepting them as natural or taking them for granted. What he calls 'la banalité du toujours-déjà-dit' (LM, 220) is the substance on which he works, as a sculptor might assemble a work of art from materials that lie to hand. He calls such representations 'le matériau mythologique qui m'environne dans mon existence quotidienne' and presents them collectively as the site within which humans can exercise imaginative freedom, rather than being imprisoned by the unspoken ideological presuppositions and intellectual prejudices they embody: 'ces images ne fonctionneront plus comme des pièges du moment qu'elles seront reprises par un discours vivant, qui reste le seul espace de ma liberté,' he declares.[4]

A prime example of this ideologically-charged substance on which the artist must work is the *fait divers*. Robbe-Grillet singles it out as such: 'Lorsque je lis les faits divers scandaleux ou criminels [. . .] je me trouve assailli par une multitude de signes dont l'ensemble constitue la mythologie du monde où je vis, quelque chose comme l'inconscient collectif de la société, c'est-à-dire à la fois l'image qu'elle veut se donner d'elle-même et le reflet des troubles qui la hantent.'[5] This stands as an eloquent reiteration and reminder of the key issues we are discussing. It also offers a useful introduction to instances of Robbe-Grillet's own dealings with *faits divers*, which are marked by telling displacements and ambivalences.

Robbe-Grillet has offered new readings of *L'Etranger* since his article of 1958. At a conference in 1982 he presented the novel as a portrayal of an aspect of Husserl's phenomenology.[6] In this reading, Meursault exemplifies the intentionality of consciousness: the character's consciousness is a void constantly projected outward into the world of objects, whose plenitude balances this subjective emptiness in a fragile and deceptive equilibrium – until, with the murder of the Arab, Meursault's consciousness implodes and is invaded by the 'trop plein' of the world. As a result of this cataclysm Meursault finds himself trapped in interiority: in prison, where he has only his memories for company – plus the *fait divers* he finds beneath the mattress. In retracing Robbe-Grillet's exposé we need not concern ourselves unduly with its methodological or textual accuracy: phenomenologists could examine the technical foundations of his argument in the light of an article by Sartre which he refers to,[7] while Camus specialists will register some puzzlement at Robbe-Grillet's repeated assertion that Meursault had the *fait divers* in his pocket all the time. As we shall see, Camus's novel is a pretext for a form of creative fantasizing on Robbe-Grillet's part.

The *nouveau romancier* systematically avoids all reference to the specific content of Meursault's 'coupure de presse', though he acknowledges what we have already observed, that its substance recurs in *Le Malentendu* and elsewhere in Camus's work.[8] For Robbe-Grillet the news cutting 'probablement est déjà le signe de la tentation humaniste':[9] although Meursault had appeared to achieve the phenomenological purity of the 'conscience vide', in fact he illustrates the practical impossibility of such a notion. This is brought home to us 'sous la forme dérisoire d'une coupure de journal, l'imprimé légué par la société'; the *fait divers* represents 'l'échec de sa liberté à l'intérieur de sa poche'.[10] In other words, though Meursault first strikes the reader as an innocent, a pagan, resistant to conventional modes of thought or behaviour, ultimately he turns out to be deeply marked by the commonplaces of culture and ideology which are represented by the news cutting he carries (according to Robbe-Grillet) on his person. In sum this reading of the novel repeats the story of failure set out in the 1958 article: but whereas there Robbe-Grillet impugned a technical flaw or a failure of nerve on Camus's part, here − in a manner that would have shocked his disciples in the 1950s − he sympathizes with the character in what seems the inevitable tragedy of a reversion to bourgeois ideology: 'Sans que je sache pourquoi, le fait qu'il lise et relise cette coupure [. . .] m'a toujours énormément touché. Ce qui le reliait, lui, en tant que conscience husserlienne, au monde de Balzac ou de Zola, c'était cette coupure de presse qu'il avait gardée sur lui, et il savait que c'était le signe que sa liberté serait un échec.'[11] There is a certain poignancy about this evocation of *L'Etranger*, made all the more telling by the fact that in passing Robbe-Grillet adopts the first-person pronoun to retrace the experience, as if acknowledging thereby the defeat of his own youthful aspirations to ideological purity.[12]

His empathy for the character, in addition to the textual inaccuracy indicated above, can be corroborated as indications that Robbe-Grillet is incorporating the novel within a framework of fantasms stemming from his own fiction. This is made manifest in the following paragraph:

Cette coupure de presse [. . .] m'a toujours impressioné et j'y fais même allusion dans *Le Voyeur*. Mathias a dans sa poche une coupure de presse qui relate le même crime commis par quelqu'un d'autre auparavant; donc il a déjà sur lui, depuis toujours, la coupure de presse qui désigne l'acte pour lequel il va être emprisonné et condamné.[13]

It is Robbe-Grillet's character Mathias, not Meursault, who carries the *fait divers* in his wallet, as we shall see; but it is Meursault, not Mathias, who is imprisoned and condemned. (Indeed the structure of *Le Voyeur* makes it impossible to assert that Mathias actually committed any crime at all.) Robbe-Grillet is constructing an amalgam of the two texts, his own and that of Camus, on the strength of the *fait divers* that features in both.

The content of the *fait divers* in *L'Etranger* does not of course correspond to that indicated in *Le Voyeur*. Robbe-Grillet's amalgamation of the two characters is legitimate, however, in that they both fall foul of the 'toujours-déjà-dit'. The *fait divers* can be said to function in both cases as the figure of their ultimate subjection to the discourses of society, even if the anecdotal content does not coincide. We have seen that Meursault's press cutting of the son murdered by his mother and sister is applicable to his own case in that it highlights the contingency inherent in human affairs. And yet, in the light of Robbe-Grillet's argument we may wish to reread it as a more specific résumé of his fate: Meursault, the prodigal son who keeps his distance from family/society in Part 1, returns to it in the courtroom in Part 2 but is not recognized by his *familiers*, who kill him in pursuit of their own vision. Mathias, for his part, whether he has committed a crime or not, is caught up within the criminal fantasies of his readership who impose a murderous reading onto the possibly innocuous details of his visit to the island on which the novel is located – just as the judiciary force an incriminating pattern upon Meursault's day-to-day behaviour prior to the crime. In this sense the text that condemns them both already exists prior to, and independently of, their own stories.

Robbe-Grillet's rumination on *L'Etranger* is rewritten into *Le Miroir qui revient*, a section of which reproduces the broad lines of the interpretation we have set out (LM, 166–72). However, here the element of hallucinatory identification with Meursault is much more intense and extensive, the opening phrase announcing *a contrario* an oneiric exploration of the textual amalgam we have indicated:

Et aussitôt je me réveille, ayant implosé, dans l'envers du monde où j'ai vécu jusqu'à présent: moi qui prétendais ne pouvoir exister qu'en me projetant vers le dehors, voici que je suis maintenant, par une cruelle inversion topologique de l'espace, emmuré dans une cellule de prison, quelque chose de fermé, de cubique, de blanc selon toute probabilité, et il n'y a rien à l'intérieur de ces quatre murs qui représenteront désormais mon seul extérieur possible, ni meubles, ni gens, ni sable, ni mer, rien d'autre que moi. [. . .] (LM, 171)[14]

The passage culminates once more in an evocation of the *fait divers*; but under the pressure, presumably, of the increased phantasmatic impetus, previously repressed details come to light. (The implied psychoanalytic model claims only figurative validity, as it is not easy to distinguish the involuntary from the studied in this text, as Robbe-Grillet is the first to point out.) The passage requires to be quoted at length, as numerous details call for comment:

> Pour me reposer, je relis alors, une fois de plus, ma coupure de presse. C'est un fait divers découpé il y a très longtemps dans un journal: un crime sexuel sans doute (mais la bienséance a interdit au rédacteur de raconter les choses clairement) commis sur une petite fille par un nommé Nicolas Stavroguine. La reconstitution descriptive de la chambre, ainsi que le fragment de journal, devenu difficilement lisible à cause de l'usure le long des plis du papier, de qualité médiocre, se trouvent à présent rangés dans mon troisième roman, *Le voyeur*. (LM, 172)

Once more, then, Robbe-Grillet alleges an intertextual connection between *L'Etranger* and *Le Voyeur*. But, as he puts it, the *fait divers* is becoming difficult to read because of the folds in the paper . . . We are in fact moving away from the *fait divers* in Camus's novel as the paedophilic sexual elements that characterize Robbe-Grillet's text become more explicit.

The reference to the central character of Dostoyevsky's novel *The Devils* calls to mind 'Stavrogin's confession', a chapter that was cut from the original published text at the instigation of the censor and was thought lost until it was discovered among the papers of Dostoyevsky's wife in 1921 and was first published separately in 1922. Later in *Le Miroir qui revient*, Robbe-Grillet will make much of the gap left in Dostoyevky's novel as a result (LM, 214–16). It exemplifies his own principle that the *trou* is essential in a text, as the empty space which enables fixed meaning to drain away and permits the full play of the writing.[15] The enigmatic Stavrogin is central to *The Devils* though frequently on the margins of the narrative: his unpredictable behaviour and outrageous gestures provoke intense speculation. In the rediscovered chapter he 'confesses' to Tikhon, giving the latter an autobiographical text he has written – but from which, it seems, he has removed the second of five sheets, so that even now the full truth does not emerge.[16] Contrary to what Robbe-Grillet asserts, the intended place of this chapter in the novel is known, though it is nowadays normally printed as an appendix to the main text. Its status as a revelation therefore remains problematic, the more so as Stavrogin is not averse to lying about himself. As one critic has written, 'It is not clear whether Stavrogin is confessing genuinely, nor even whether there is really anything to confess':[17] which confirms Robbe-Grillet's views on the significance of his confession, first excised, then restored as a truncated, unreliable document – all the while remaining the elusive displaced centre of the novel.[18]

Robbe-Grillet asserts (LM, 216) that in *Le Voyeur* he sought to produce a similar formal effect of textual play structured around the sign of an absence – in effect, the absence of proof concerning the crime supposedly committed during Mathias's visit to the island. Throughout his discussions of Stavrogin, however, he says nothing more than the sketchy comment quoted above on the actual crime which Dostoyevsky's character may or may not have committed. Nevertheless, the nature of Stavrogin's crime is germane to our discussion. His confession suggests that he had sexual relations with a twelve-year-old girl who subsequently committed suicide. In an earlier section of the novel, Shatov has confronted Stavrogin with rumours that in Petersburg he was a member of a group that indulged in sadistic sexual practices, including the seduction and debauchery of children; and Stavrogin himself has made passing reference to abusing and raping a little girl. His reason for confessing to Tikhon is that he is haunted by visions of the girl who killed herself following his sexual assault on her.[19] In all these respects, therefore, we can see that Stavrogin mirrors substantial elements of the obsessive thematics which accompany Mathias in *Le Voyeur*. However, in *Le Miroir qui revient*, Robbe-Grillet, after pointing out the structural similarities between his novel and that of Dostoyevsky, declares: 'Je n'avais pas lu *Les Démons* à l'époque où j'écrivais *Le Voyeur*' (LM, 216).[20] If the display of intertextual associations is ultimately to be repudiated in this way, why should the novelist indulge it? This extensive intertextual play has served to do little more than implicitly highlight the sado-sexual elements which distance *Le Voyeur* and its *fait divers* from *L'Etranger* and Meursault's press cutting, despite the link which Robbe-Grillet is at pains to indicate.

The suggestion that the central concerns of *Le Voyeur* have significant affinities with other literary texts – but crucially *not* with those Robbe-Grillet names in this connection – is indirectly alluded to in an extension of the prison-cell phantasm in which Robbe-Grillet assimilates himself to Meursault:

> Mais par moment je soupçonne aussi, dans ma cellule de prison où j'ai tout le temps pour réfléchir à ces problèmes, que j'ai dû confondre en quelques occasions, par certains aspects similaires de leurs troubles aventures politiques, Henri de Corinthe avec le marquis de Rollebon, auquel il vient d'être fait allusion quelques pages plus haut, à propos de *La Nausée*. [. . .] Tel justement Stavroguine d'un bout à l'autre du roman de Dostoïevsky, Corinthe est presque toujours en voyage, durant cette période fiévreuse et sans pitié. (LM, 172–3)

Robbe-Grillet thus associates his mythical predecessor whose history he is seeking to reconstruct alongside his own, with Rollebon who stands in a not dissimilar relationship *vis-à-vis* Roquentin in *La Nausée*. He uses the term 'amalgame' to refer to this confusion of the two characters – a confusion not unlike what we have seen occurring between Meursault and Mathias – and then brings Stavrogin into play as well. This effects a transition (a *glissement*, to use a term characteristic of Robbe-Grillet's aesthetic) bringing the paedophilic issues we have discussed so far into the orbit of Sartre's novel – a novel which, as we have seen, is precisely constructed around a series of episodes involving sexual assaults on children and young girls, converging in turn upon the *fait divers* of the rape and murder of Lucienne. This would appear to be the unavowed urtext for *Le Voyeur*, a matrix whose significant absence is marked through the complex intertextual labyrinth that has led us to it.

It is hard to know how seriously to take this play of concealment that ultimately reveals what it hides.[21] In one sense it invites detective work, an 'enquête policière' which so much of Robbe-Grillet's writing openly derides;[22] in another sense it mimics the displacements and projections familiar in psychoanalytic theory when a failure of repression brings these other mechanisms into play to protect the ego against admissions it finds painful. But since for Robbe-Grillet the real object of his (and our) research is properly that which is perpetually deferred, these 'pièces à conviction'[23] we have been induced and enabled to track down might be assumed to be worthless simulacra of truth. In both cases there is a clear temptation to view the investigation and its outcome ironically: though in both cases we could be dealing with a 'double-bluff' strategy. In considering Robbe-Grillet's exploitation of this *fait divers* it is tempting to recall his own words on the form as 'à la fois l'image qu'[il] veut se donner [de lui]-même et le reflet des troubles qui [le] hantent'.[24] This game of hide and seek centres on obsessions which may mean more to the author than his ludic practices might lead us to suppose.

Be that as it may, the narrative and the *fait divers* in *Le Voyeur*, once they are brought into conjunction with *La Nausée* and the *fait divers* of 'la petite Lucienne', generate fertile intertextual readings. Early in Robbe-Grillet's novel,[25] before the reader is in a position to infer much from the problematic narrative, Mathias finds himself in front of a cinema poster announcing a forthcoming feature. It is a picture 'aux couleurs violentes' of 'un homme de stature colossale' who is brutally holding 'une jeune personne' clearly about to become the victim of this sadistic 'bourreau' (V, 45). It calls to mind a tattered display of cinema posters on a hoarding in Sartre's Bouville. The latest one has been defaced and torn, but the fragments that remain combine with parts of those revealed beneath: 'une autre unité s'est établie d'elle-même entre la bouche tordue, les gouttes de sang, les lettres blanches, la désinence "âtre": on dirait qu'une passion criminelle et sans repos cherche à s'exprimer par ces signes mystérieux' (N, 32–3). Robbe-Grillet's poster – indeed the whole of *Le Voyeur* – might have been designed with Roquentin's commentary in mind: in both novels the evocation of a cinema poster is followed by series of motifs and episodes illustrating the impulses of a 'passion criminelle'. In *La Nausée*, as we have seen, a number of children undergo varieties of sexual abuse at the hands of adults. In *Le Voyeur* the sado-erotic suggestions implicit in the poster associate with a variety of textual allusions – string, cigarette ends, sweets – to converge on a story of the rape and murder of a young girl which is actually alluded to most directly for the first time in the novel by means of a *fait divers*.[26]

Mathias has wandered into an empty bedroom while looking for the wife of a café proprietor to whom he hopes to sell a watch. The bedroom décor keeps returning to his mind, along with other potentially suggestive images including some of fearful young girls, and later as he sits on rocks overlooking the sea he is prompted to finger his wallet in which is a press cutting taken from the previous day's local paper. Twice he does this, just to check that it is there, but the third time he finally takes out the article and 'rel[i]t le texte attentivement, une fois de plus, d'un bout à l'autre' (V, 74–5). Even before we learn anything more about it, this news item is clearly presented as the object of a set of compulsive, even fetishistic behaviour patterns.

The text of the *fait divers* is not quoted directly, apart from the isolated adjectives 'horrible', 'ignoble' and 'odieux' which, we are told, 'ne servaient à rien, dans ce domaine' (although the second connects with the *fait divers* of Lucienne while also confirming thereby its status as a cliché of the rubric). The narrator appears to convey frustration on Mathias's part in indicating that half of the report is taken up with 'les circonstances oiseuses' of the discovery of the body, and that the final section discusses details of the police investigation, with the result that 'il restait fort peu de lignes pour la description du corps lui-même et rien du tout pour la reconstitution de l'ordre des violences subies par la victime.' (We might note in passing that Mathias's lack of interest in the discovery and the police manhunt offers evidence of his innocence so far as the crime itself is concerned.) Clearly it is these latter details which interest Mathias: he is hoping to gratify fantasies of erotic violence through his reading of the text. However, he is denied the satisfaction he seeks, owing to the hackneyed moralizing or euphemistic nature of the language employed. The trite adjectives are of no use, as we have seen; likewise 'les lamentations vagues sur le sort tragique de la fillette' do nothing for him. 'Quant aux formules voilées employées pour raconter sa mort, elles appartenaient toutes au langage de convention en usage dans la presse pour cette rubrique et ne renvoyaient, au mieux, qu'à des généralités. On sentait très bien que les rédacteurs utilisaient les mêmes termes à chaque occasion similaire, sans chercher à fournir le moindre renseignement réel sur un cas particulier dont on pouvait supposer qu'ils ignoraient tout eux-mêmes' (V, 76). These remarks offer pointed comment on journalistic writing, and sit interestingly alongside Robbe-Grillet's strictures on the banal sensationalizing his own experience was to undergo at the hands of reporters.[27] But at the same time, of course, they constitute a telling reflection on the dubious referential capacity of language in general, and connect with that self-consciousness about writing which is an important theme of this and other *nouveaux romans*.[28] The effect of the expressive shortcomings of language, in the *fait divers* and by implication in all texts, is this: 'Il fallait réinventer la scène d'un bout à l'autre à partir de deux ou trois détails élémentaires, comme l'âge ou la couleur des cheveux' (V, 76). Because he transforms the *fait divers*, in effect, into a *mise en abyme* of the novel as a whole, Robbe-Grillet both invites a greater imaginative engagement on the part of the reader and demystifies the questionable fantasizing involved in fiction as well as in the *fait divers*. The impact on Mathias of reading the sensational news item is immediately obvious in the ensuing pages. His vision of the bedroom recurs, this time peopled by a large man and a compliant, vulnerable young girl whose demeanour and relationship to the aggressive male are drawn from the cinema poster. The phantasmatic energy stimulated then frustrated by the *fait divers* is evidently drawing the scattered motifs together, animating them into an enactment of the sadistic events resulting in the girl's murder (V, 76-80).

Throughout the rest of the novel the text will rework and permute these motifs in patterns of themes and variations corresponding to Mathias's guilty voyeuristic obsession with the material of the *fait divers*. The repetition compulsion we have seen elsewhere associated with such material[29] is highlighted by the new cinema poster which inaugurates part 2 of *Le Voyeur* by announcing the title 'Monsieur X. sur le double circuit' (V, 167).[30] At the same time the description of this poster overlaying its predecessors and entering into a confusing relationship of signification with what it conceals and reveals alludes once more to the text of *La Nausée* – both the tattered poster and the novel as a whole, fragments of which can be perceived in the interstices of *Le Voyeur*. Ironically, for his part 'Mathias n'y reconnut plus rien du tout – incapable, même, d'affirmer qu'il y eût là deux images différentes superposées, ou bien une seule image, ou trois, ou même une plus grande nombre' (V, 167-8). Mathias, Meursault, Stavrogin, Roquentin: how many images are contained here? Mathias becomes entangled in versions of the story that haunts him to the extent of colouring his perception of people and things around him – and perhaps, for the novel neither confirms nor denies anything, of actually committing (or dreaming of committing) a crime himself. We can see that like Roquentin after reading of Lucienne, he too is violated by the desire that drives him to fantasize about committing a rape. He suffers from voyeurism, he is a victim of a sado-erotic fixation.

His involvement with the community entailed by his work as a watch salesman brings Mathias into contact with other manifestations of the *fait divers* via the gossip and rumour among those who knew the victim. Already in the café he has overheard fragments of a conversation between sailors about a certain girl and what 'elle mériterait' (V, 59). Now a sailor tells how local fishermen found the body and gives details about its condition – precisely the details Mathias regretted the absence of in the *fait divers* (V, 174–7). The tone here is speculative, also characteristic of a certain kind of news reporting:[31] expressions such as 'sans doute', 'improbable', 'elle devait avoir perdu l'équilibre', 'peut-être même' accompany discussion of various hypotheses as to how the death occurred. At the same time the wounds on the corpse are mentioned, with a clinical precision that suggests their cause – contact with the rocks, bites from fish or crabs – without reference to sadistic possibilities. The information is exchanged, assessed, assimilated, in the course of the conversation, by the various customers in the café: with only the slightest hint to the contrary, 'tout était clair, évident, banal' (V, 175). The narrative presentation of this sequence, making of it an innocuous if unfortunate event, devoid of suspicious circumstances, may as some critics suggest betray its mendacity by its very naturalness.[32] Certainly, though such engagement in social discourse may prove capable of calming Mathias's propensity to feverish visions, tell-tale signs of his repressed impulses can emerge in his commerce with those around him. Earlier, when paying for his drink in the café, for example, 'Il prit son portefeuille dans la poche intérieure de sa veste et en tira un billet de dix couronnes. Il en profita pour remettre en place une coupure de journal dont le bord dépassait légèrement les autres papiers' (V, 120). As long as he has the *fait divers* on his person he is a prey to the obsessions it articulates. As we have seen Robbe-Grillet suggest, the press cutting designates those patterns of behaviour always already laid down for us by ideology amd culture, the model 'légué par la société':[33] if Mathias is to escape the obsessions that haunt him, he must abolish this fetishistic inheritance.

Mathias manifestly does achieve a certain peace of mind as his stay on the island draws to a close.[34] His attainment of this state is accompanied, significantly, by his burning the press cutting, using the cigarette previously associated with sadistic practices. This process is described at length and in some detail, to suggest the deliberate liquidation of a private fetish: 'Il lit le texte imprimé d'un bout à l'autre, y choisit un mot et, après avoir fait tomber la cendre de sa cigarette, approche la pointe rouge de l'endroit favori' (V, 236). It is also significant that Mathias effects the destruction of the *fait divers* by reducing it to a series of holes: 'De nouveaux trous succèdent à ceux-là, d'abord groupés par paires, puis intercalés tant bien que mal aux emplacements disponibles. Le rectangle de papier-journal est bientôt entièrement ajouré' (V, 236). The operation therefore represents precisely the liberation from unhealthily fixated readings through the introduction of gaps into the text. The holes, as we have seen, are a figure for that which disseminates meaning, defers sense, and permits the free play of writing and reading (LM, 211–16). In this way the ideological 'piège' of the *fait divers* can be 'repri[s] par un discours vivant, qui reste le seul espace de ma liberté'.[35] The inauguration of *l'écriture* as a site for the free play of meaning is affirmed as we learn that a new cinema poster has not arrived, and that in place of the fetishistic images previously displayed, 'Il va [. . .] falloir annoncer le programme de dimanche prochain par une simple inscription à l'encre. Mathias quitte l'homme en train déjà de commencer son ouvrage, traçant d'une main ferme une lettre O de grande taille' (V, 250). This reiterates how the novel reaches its conclusion by tracing holes in what the voyeuristic eye seeks out: 'Il ne subsiste ainsi du fait divers aucune trace repérable à l'oeil nu' (V, 237).

Thus the final pages of the novel both depict and complete a therapeutic function. Robbe-Grillet has subjected sado-erotic phantasms to the liberating play of creative writing with the aim of freeing the imagination from voyeuristic fixations. Perhaps this is why, having defused his sexual obsessions in this way, Robbe-Grillet will apparently have such difficulty in his autobiography in unearthing and reading the real *fait divers* that stands at the centre of *Le Voyeur*.

Notes

1. Later republished in *Pour un nouveau roman*, Paris, Gallimard, collection Idées, pp.55–84.
2. See Alain Robbe-Grillet, 'Monde trop plein, conscience vide', in *Albert Camus: œuvre fermée, œuvre ouverte?* Proceedings of a colloquium at Cérisy-la-Salle, June 1982, Cahiers Albert Camus 5, Paris, Gallimard, 1985, pp.215–27; and *Le Miroir qui revient* (hereafter LM), Paris, Minuit, 1984, pp.163–6.
3. See *Le Miroir qui revient*, pp.153–63. Relevant documents are reproduced in the special number of *Obliques* devoted to Robbe-Grillet (nos.16–17, 1978, pp.154–6).
4. 'Présentation de *Projet pour une révolution à New York*', *Nouvel Observateur*, 26 June 1970.
5. Ibid.

6. Robbe-Grillet, 'Monde trop plein, conscience vide'.
7. 'Une idée fondamentale de la phénoménologie de Husserl: l'intentionnalité', in *Situations* I, Paris, Gallimard, 1947, pp.31–5. Originally published in 1939.
8. See above, pp.143–5.
9. Robbe-Grillet, 'Monde trop plein, conscience vide,' p.225.
10. Ibid., p.226.
11. Ibid., pp.225–6.
12. '*L'Etranger* c'est moi aussi,' he has said earlier (ibid., p.215).
13. Ibid., p.225.
14. Readers of *Dans le labyrinthe* (1959) will recognize here the scenario of interiority from which is drawn the linguistico-phantasmatic material of that novel.
15. Cf. the interview in *Littérature*, no.49, February 1983, pp.16–22, in which Robbe-Grillet says: 'Les structures narratives qui m'intéressent sont justement les structures lacunaires.'
16. Curiously, the Penguin Classics English translation does not allude to this absence within the relevant chapter, and specialist colleagues have been unable to locate evidence of it in the original Russian text. However, the gap is attested to by R. Peace, *Dostoyevsky, an Examination of the Major Novels*, Cambridge, Cambridge University Press, 1971, p.211; by Albert Camus in his adaptation from the French translation by Boris de Schloezer, TRN, 1070; and by Robbe-Grillet himself, LM, pp.215–6. So far as I have been able to ascertain, the gap first appears in de Schloezer's French translation which was published in *La Nouvelle Revue Francaise*, vols.18 and 19, June and July 1922. In vol.19, p.30 of this version, Tikhon points out that the text stops short and the second of five sheets is missing. 'Le second est censuré en attendant . . .' replies Stavrogin. In the absence of corroboration from elsewhere, this may in fact be nothing more than an act of censorship on the part of the translator.
17. Peace, *Dostoyevsky*, p.325 n9; cf. ibid., pp.179–217.
18. See Malcolm Jones, *Dostoyevsky, the Novel of Discord*, London, Paul Elek, 1976, pp.128–9, 140–2.
19. See *The Devils*, translated by David Magarshack, Harmondsworth, Penguin Classics, 1971, pp.260, 243, 696, 702. The motif of sadistic violation of young girls casts a shadow across Dostoyevsky's life and work: see Georges Auclair, *Le 'Mana' quotidien: structures et fonctions de la chronique du fait divers*, Paris, Editions Anthropos, 1970, p.211.
20. Robbe-Grillet makes the same statement in *Obliques*, nos. 16–17, 1978, p.62, where he also sketches for the first time the structural analogy between Dostoyevsky's novel and his own – going one better, he argues, than the critics who had pointed out a sado-sexual thematic

link.

21. Studies of *Le Miroir qui revient* and its companion volume in the *Romanesques* series, *Angélique ou l'enchantement*, have shown how textual play and internal mirroring are central to Robbe-Grillet's aesthetic in them, but do not refer to the 'coupure de press' sequence. See Roger-Michel Allemand, *Duplications et duplicité dans les 'Romanesques' d'Alain Robbe-Grillet*, Paris, Archives des Lettres Modernes, 250, 1991; and Roger-Michel Allemand, Alain Goulet, *Imaginaire, écritures, lectures de Robbe-Grillet*, Lion-sur-Mer, Editions Arcane-Beaunieux, 1991.

22. *Les Gommes* (1953) is based on a mockery of the detective investigation; Robbe-Grillet reiterates his subversive stance on the phenomenon in the 'Entretien' on *Le Roman policier* in *Littérature*, no.49, February 1983.

23. We have noted Robbe-Grillet's fondness for the oneiric, rather than strictly forensic, qualities associated with the presence of 'pièces à conviction' at the scene of a crime, as he indicates in 'Joe Bousquet le rêveur', in *Pour un nouveau roman*, and restates in 'Entretien' in *Littérature*, no.49, February 1983, pp.21–2. See above, p.74.

24. See above.

25. *Le Voyeur*, Paris, Minuit, 1955; hereafter V.

26. For Ludovic Janvier, the *fait divers* is the 'source même de la tentation' which assails Mathias: *Une Parole exigeante: le nouveau roman*, Paris, Minuit, 1964, p.121.

27. See above, pp.216–7.

28. For insightful comments on this and other aspects of the novel, see Alastair B. Duncan, 'Robbe-Grillet's *Le Voyeur*: a reassessment', *Symposium*, Summer 1980, pp.107–24, especially at pp.114–20; B.G. Garnham, *Robbe-Grillet: 'Les Gommes' and 'Le Voyeur'*, London, Grant and Cutler, 1982.

29. See above, the discussion of Duras, pp.193–6.

30. Incidentally this evocation of two circuits around the same course is perhaps deliberately reminiscent of the two acts of Beckett's *En attendant Godot*, on which Robbe-Grillet also wrote an influential article and in which, famously, according to another critic, 'Nothing happens – twice.' These facts might also be adduced to exonerate Mathias of guilt for the commission of any real crime . . . One should not overlook echoes of *Les Gommes*, which features a similar cyclic repetition – and an enigmatic cinema poster.

31. See above, p.54, on the article on Lafcadio's crime in *Les Caves du Vatican*.

32. See R. Holzberg, 'Décryptage du *Voyeur*', *The French Review*, vol.52, no.6, May 1979, pp.848–55, especially at pp.851, 852, 854; Duncan, 'Robbe-Grillet's *Le Voyeur*', pp.116–18.

33. 'Monde trop plein, conscience vide', p.226.
34. Cf. Garnham, *Robbe-Grillet: 'Les Gommes' and 'Le Voyeur'*, pp.59–60; Duncan, 'Robbe-Grillet's *Le Voyeur*', pp.119, 121.
35. Robbe-Grillet, 'Présentation de *Projet pour une révolution à New York*'.

PART VII

Setting the Record Straight

15

Setting the Record Straight:
J.M.G. Le Clézio

With titles such as *Le Déluge* (1966), *La Guerre* (1970), *Les Géants* (1973), the early novels of J.M.G. Le Clézio offer apocalyptic surveys of the modern city, society and civilization.[1] However, an important aspect of the author's writing is given over to the transcription of minute, apparently trivial experiences that culminate in catastrophe at the level of the individual. This feature finds perhaps its most typical expression in his short stories, characterized by a feverish awareness of how precarious are the conditions of normal existence. The preface to *La Fièvre*,[2] a collection published in 1965, communicates this vision quite explicitly: 'Nous vivons dans un monde bien fragile' (F, 7). Humans are constantly vulnerable to prosaic accidents that can shatter their lives. A typical aside in one story has a character look up from the street to see a man at his balcony: 'Il avait les deux bras appuyés sur la balustrade de fer forgé, et la tête inclinée en avant, sans souci pour les tuiles qu'il pouvait recevoir, d'une seconde à l'autre, sur sa nuque ainsi offerte' (F, 42). This is unmistakably the universe of the *fait divers*. However, the stories in *La Fièvre* concentrate on the subjective sources of calamity rather than on external accidents. The author explains in his preface: 'La vie est pleine de folies. Ce ne sont que de petites folies quotidiennes, mais elle sont terribles, si on les regarde bien' (F, 7). Repudiating great emotions, Le Clézio depicts minor niggles which work at first unobtrusively on a person's sensibilities: 'Parfois, ces minuscules flèches noires se réunissent, et la raison des hommes perd l'équilibre' (F, 7). The sheer incessancy of sense perceptions can become overwhelming: 'Nos peaux, nos yeux, nos oreilles, nos nez, nos langues emmagasinent tous les jours des millions de sensations dont pas une n'est oubliée. Voilà le danger' (F, 8). In terms which recall themes familiar to us, the writer indicates how, through imperceptible accumulation, trifling incidents or sensations in private lives 'prennent une ampleur et une gravité exceptionnelles'.[3] Thus the stories in this volume will illustrate a basic pattern, whereby human experience attests to the apocalyptic: 'Tous les jours, nous perdons la tête à cause d'un peu de température, d'une rage de dents, d'un vertige passager. [. . .] Cela ne dure pas longtemps, mais cela suffit. [. . .] Nous sommes de vrais volcans' (F, 8).

The examples Le Clézio quotes here allude to three of the most substantial narratives in the volume. In the title story, the protagonist, hallucinating in the extreme heat, kills his wife in a 'moment de crise, de maladie, d'amour, ou de ce que vous voulez' (F, 58). The hero of 'Le jour où Beaumont fit connaissance avec sa douleur' awakens in the night with toothache. After hours of solitary agony and tormented visions, daybreak finds him crouching on the rooftop, on the verge of suicide. In 'L'homme qui marche', J.-F. Paoli is drinking his coffee the morning after a quarrel with his lover when the sound of dripping water imposes itself upon his perceptions. Its rhythm drives him 'lentement, royalement, vers les domaines de la folie' (F, 109): in a manic effort to harmonize his steps with it, he walks the streets incessantly, oblivious to the passers-by and car horns that follow in his wake.

'Les gens commençaient à me regarder bizarrement' (F, 94), says one character in the grip of his compulsions. Despite their systematically private perspective, these texts provide pointers to the relationship between the eccentricities they depict, and those such as journalists who make it their business to report back from the boundaries that circumscribe normality and sanity. The sufferer is accosted by a former school friend who knows him better now from newspaper articles about his recent success as a playwright, which she has distractedly read and vaguely retained. This second-hand acquaintance via the press accounts prevents her from appreciating the intimate drama of the man sitting before her (F, 96–7). Journalists who record the prodigious for public consumption compound such misunderstandings. In the story entitled 'Martin' we see them conducting an interview with a hydrocephalic boy genius. The dialogue between the reporters and the twelve-year-old is punctuated by the paragraph subheadlines which will encapsulate the sense of the discussion for the casual newspaper reader: the presentation caricatures its subject.

Le Clézio's concern with *faits divers* and journalism in general is more comprehensive than this simple critique would suggest. 'La Fièvre' examines the impact on Roch of reports of violence in the *faits divers*. In his fevered condition, Roch perceives something momentous in 'ces condensés d'aventures bizarres et mystérieuses, les bouts d'épopée que les hommes des quatre coins du monde laissaient traîner là, sur cette feuille de papier, en énigmes' (F, 14). Race riots in the United States are experienced with striking immediacy: 'on arrivait sur les lieux de l'histoire' (F, 14). An effect of geographical authenticity emanates from the page layout: 'Les faits étaient écrits sur la terre comme sur le journal, carrés, insérés au milieu d'autres, résumant avec douleur, avec compassion, les autres exploits et les autres massacres' (F, 14). The violence he reads about explodes into the present as if he is undergoing it himself: 'La peau se bleuissait sous les matraques, les cheveux étaient collés par une sueur mauvaise [. . .] et à l'intérieur du crâne où résonnent les coups, les idées sont mortes' (F, 15). This vision of the world at large inhabits Roch's mind now: 'La violence éclatait partout [. . .] les histoires des crimes sont terribles, car plus rien n'a de raison [. . .] tout s'est fait souffrance et meurtrissure' (F, 15–16). The reporter's copy becomes one with the reader's own language, informing his subjective expression: 'Les paroles du journal se sont décomposées et ont écrit, d'un seul coup, sur une grande feuille blanche, comme à l'intérieur d'un rêve, ceci' (F, 16): there follows a poem invoking a vision of furious crowds beneath banners bearing the word 'COLERE', concluding with the words 'Ils sont morts pour vous' (F, 16–17). News reports can clearly be a source of imaginative solidarity and creative inspiration. However, Le Clézio's story is less about inspiration than hallucination, a malignant distortion of it: Roch's subsequent reading of the *fait divers* co-opts his generous emotions, attaching them despite himself to a more sordid phantasm belied by the innocuous words on the page:

> Cet autre texte, fixé dans le papier du journal, ineffaçable, et pourtant tellement fuyant, ce misérable attentat, nu, sordide, toujours présent dans le monde, et à quoi on participe, petit à petit, sans y croire. [. . .] Oui, cela est sûr, cet événement, ce crime, cette pulsation infime qui monte en soi, qui résonne, qui se répercute, qui fait vraiment mal avant de se dessécher et de périr sous forme de mots. (F, 17)

Again we are given the text of the news report, in which the brutal murder of an elderly shopkeeper is counterpointed by the characteristic attention paid to the fact that while the killer escaped with some 20 francs from the till, 20,000 francs of his victim's savings lay unguarded in a cupboard upstairs.[4] Equally significantly, though, the criminal is reported as having been 'hanté par le désir de tuer la vieille femme' (F, 18), and Roch proves susceptible to the same phantasm: 'Voilà. Ces vieilles femmes sont mortes, comme ça, sans difficulté; leurs vies en un cri rauque et déchiré, ont été étouffées dans un mouvement brusque qui s'est abattu sur elles comme une marée' (F, 18). The shift to the plural suggests that Roch accepts it as a commonplace.[5] More than this, its effect on Roch, starting with what we might almost call tropisms in the manner of Sarraute, is marked: 'Une sorte de frémissement étrange monta dans le corps de Roch.' He is overwhelmed by an 'onde brûlante et froide à la fois', a sort of 'explosion nerveuse, triturant la vie de Roch'; the blood in his veins seems to turn to molten lava as a 'spasme' grips him (F, 18). This disturbing experience is the prelude to the fever that takes hold and drives him out of the house, a prey to that sensation of impending violence beneath the surface of the ordinary which corresponds to an intuition of contingency in the universe: 'un rien [. . .] pouvait [. . .] donner le signal de départ d'un cataclysme infini' (F, 21). Pursued by such visions, Roch will wreak havoc in the town before returning home, where his peaceful domestic interior strikes him also as nothing more than 'une feinte, une comédie fragile qu'un rien pouvait démasquer' (F, 49). When his wife comes in, the violence he has read about affects his perception of her: 'Sous ce front, c'était l'os du crâne, épais et solide, prête à recevoir les coups' (F, 53). The nightmare culminates in evocations of 'Elizabeth, au corps troué' (F, 57) as she becomes the object of a brutality that manifestly emanates from the gruesome news reports.

Another part of the author's purpose is to demonstrate that the 'petites folies quotidiennes' do not always issue in visible crises at all. This he does notably in *La Ronde et autres faits divers*.[6] Here, despite the title, there is no mention of news reports: the author indicates by implication that not all human life does find its way into the columns of the papers. What these stories have in common with *La Fièvre* is that they present a world poised on the brink of calamity. Indeed, the characters in *La Ronde et autres faits divers* are drawn from groups which habitually provide items in the *faits divers* rubric. They include delinquent adolescents, petty thieves, truants and runaway children, escaped prisoners, illegal immigrants, the unemployed and others whose lives are more obviously vulnerable than others to the vagaries of a universe in which the worst can happen.

The risks to which such people are exposed are perhaps best illustrated by the opening two stories. 'La Ronde' sketches three ingredients in a casual calamity: a woman standing at a bus stop with a handbag whose clasp catches the sunlight; an antiquated removal van going about its business in a neighbouring street; and Martine, a teenager who seeks to prove herself in the eyes of her best friend's gang by participating in a handbag-snatch on *vélomoteurs*. Almost from the start Martine herself has the sense that 'cela est réglé d'avance, et qu'elles s'approchent de ce qui va arriver sans pouvoir se détourner' (R, 13). The onlookers are also mysteriously aware that this conjunction of banal, everyday items will eventuate in a disaster, which they seem to will on: 'Leurs yeux impitoyables suivent la cavalcade des deux vélomoteurs le long du trottoir. Qu'est-ce qu'ils attendent, donc? Qu'est-ce qu'ils veulent?' (R, 14). The spectacle is one of those which fulfils a collective need for violence and disaster, at once a realization and conjuration of common fears, as Baudrillard puts it, which we have seen elsewhere.[7] The story ends as Martine, having collided with the removal van, lies bleeding in the road alongside the handbag she has snatched, its gilded clasp reflecting the light in 'des éclats meurtriers' (R, 20).

The reader acts as onlooker in the second story, entitled 'Moloch'. No connection is explicitly made between events in the narrative and the eponymous ancient god to whom first-born children were ritually sacrificed. However, an air of impending horror is generated by the presence of a wolfhound sharing a caravan with Liane, a pregnant woman who lives alone, her contacts with humanity limited to the social worker. Both are hungry, but Liane is prevented from letting the beast out to hunt for its food when she goes into labour; she gives birth while 'Le chien-loup aux yeux jaunes regarde fixement [. . .] chaque nerf de son corps [. . .] tendu à se rompre' (R, 39–40). The awful prospect contained in this situation is sustained over several tense pages: but it is not realized. The faithful dog proves in fact to be Liane's protector against the authorities, 'les médecins, les policiers, les assistantes, les conducteurs d'ambulances' (R, 28) who were hunting for her and who will now come for her baby 'qu'on va venir prendre, qu'on va emporter, qu'on va dévorer' (R, 45). The ironic reversal of expectations implicates the reader as one who has virtually willed the worst as in the previous story. We salve our conscience by taking Liane's side against society and endorsing her determination to stay ahead of 'l'avancée des hommes qui les cherchent' (R, 47).

Le Clézio attends with compassion to lives which are neglected – as opposed to being travestied – by the press. We understand Martine's reckless escapade in terms the papers would hardly bother with. Elsewhere we see that the nine-year-old David, caught stealing money from a till, is really trying to emulate and thereby make contact with his elder brother who has disappeared from home. The thief interviewed in 'Oh voleur, voleur, quelle vie est la tienne?' demonstrates a connection between criminality and unemployment that is overlooked in establishment moralizing, as do the clandestine immigrants in 'Le passeur'. The husband drives his car over a cliff at the spot where his wife crashed to her death: in Le Clézio's hands there unfolds a moving, understated story of intolerable bereavement which it is almost unseemly to compare with the maudlin *fait divers* it so poignantly avoids. Like some of the people they portray, these stories have escaped the clutches of stilted official reports.

The encounter with the language of authority is crucial to an understanding of Le Clézio's first novel, which systematically addresses the whole range of issues associated with the *fait divers*.[8] Its title, *Le Procès-verbal*, refers precisely to an official record of an event (sometimes with judicial consequences). In evoking such documents as a charge-sheet, a statement made to police, the transcript of an interrogation, or the proceedings of formal deliberations or debate, the novel takes as its theme the subjection of the real to institutional or establishment discourses.

Adam Pollo is a man whose memory (and hence his identity) is unclear: he does not know 's'il s'était échappé d'un asile d'aliénés ou s'il était déserteur' (PV, 91), a condition the author highlights in his preface.[9] There is evidence that he has indeed served in the army.[10] He finds it hard to make a connection between visions of the military life and the existence he now leads, based though it is on the belief 'qu'on a besoin de se défendre contre tous ceux [. . .] qui voudraient bien vous assassiner' (PV, 54). The feeling that his life is threatened in this way may not be unrelated to dangers undergone as a soldier, or to the risks run by deserters. Moreover, Adam appears to be haunted by military memories whose status he cannot be certain of: he annoys a French soldier by asking him about postings in Algeria, recollections of which, coming to him he knows not how, may derive from his own time there (PV, 54–5). But try as he may, resuscitating whatever fragments he can grasp, 'Il n'y avait rien, dans la composition même de ces choses horribles, qui lui indiquât de façon certaine s'il sortait de l'asile ou de l'armée' (PV, 57).

Nonetheless, war is obsessively present in his thoughts. He questions his girlfriend insistently on people's opinions about the possibility of a nuclear war (PV, 64), and in response to her shrug of the shoulders responds with a story of battle horrors that might stand as a warning of the dangers entailed by such ignorance or indifference. He catalogues it all: tanks invading the town; soldiers directing jets of napalm into houses; bazookas, dumdum bullets, mortars and grenades; a port being bombed; the recoil of cannons as they are fired. 'Où est-ce que j'ai bien pu voir ça?' (PV, 65) he asks at the outset; but in the next breath he refers to 'la bombe qui tombe sur le port quand j'ai huit ans et que je tremble' (PV, 65).

Michèle points out the inconsistencies in his version of events. 'De quelle guerre tu parles? De l'atomique? Elle n'a pas encore eu lieu. De la guerre de 40? Tu ne l'as même pas faite, tu devais avoir douze ou treize ans à ce moment-là . . .' (PV, 66). Adam is forced to agree about the Second World War: 'J'aurais été bien trop jeune pour m'en souvenir actuellement.' However, having conceded his mistake, he continues in terms which suggest that beyond the private confusion of his recollections, a more significant collective pathology, inscribed in the public discourse of History, is at work: 'Il n'y avait pas eu de guerres depuis, sans quoi elles auraient été mentionnées dans les manuels d'Histoire Contemporaine. Or, Adam le savait pour les avoir lus, relativement récemment, on ne signalait nulle part de guerre depuis celle contre Hitler' (PV, 66–7).

Beyond the general satirical force of this flagrant falsification, the detail calls for further comment. We have previously noted allusions to military service in Algeria, and later the novel reproduces a news headline on Ben Bella's triumphant return to Oran (PV, 255). The former is vehemently repudiated by the French soldier who denies having ever set foot there (PV, 55); no pertinent explanation accompanies the news item either. But clearly both refer to the Algerian war, which began in 1954 and was finally resolved by way of the Evian agreements of 1962, the year in which *Le Procès-verbal* is set. The conflict was not acknowledged as a war by the French government, for whom it was fundamentally a matter of public order in three *départements* which formed an integral part of the the the Republic.[11] This equivocation means that the military chapters of Contemporary History, in its official version signalled by capital letters in Adam's text, are subject to what Foucault calls *l'interdit*.[12] The official discourse represses uncomfortable memories, making it impossible to speak of them. The analogy with the lacunary condition of Adam Pollo's memory is obvious – the Algerian compaign coincides chronologically with what we can infer of his supposed military career. Hence his obsessive awareness of an experience of war and violence he cannot be sure of having undergone. He might well be a former soldier who has been undergoing treatment for battle trauma at a clinic from which he escaped or was discharged before the start of the novel. The dynamic of the narrative derives from components which would fit this hypothesis.

The society he inhabits will have difficulty accommodating what his experience has made of him, since by definition he embodies that which has been censored from the documents constituting its collective consciousness. As a refugee from two institutional frames which embody models of social integration, Adam is a marginal figure, an outsider. On the one hand, his sensibility, intensified by exposure to violence, is in a state of general perceptual hyperaesthesia: his apprehension of reality is heightened to a point bordering on apocalyptic visions redolent of warfare. On the other hand, the narrative depicts society's reflexes when confronted with the raw violence which Adam records and which it has denied itself the means properly to acknowledge.

Adam's painful consciousness of the pervasive violence in the world is summed up in his declaration: 'La guerre, elle est totale et permanente. Moi, Adam, j'y suis encore, finalement. Je ne veux pas en sortir' (PV, 66).[13] Just as Adam likens soldiers in battle to ants (PV, 65), so he will place his vision of communal cataclysm at the centre of the novel's concerns when he scribbles a text in his diary under the heading 'Procès-Verbal d'une catastrophe chez les fourmis' (PV, 219). Adam looks for evidence of this terrifying contingency in both the news of possible wars and 'les nouvelles en dehors de celles qui sont dans les journaux [. . .] des choses [. . .] que tout le monde sait [. . .] les opinions des gens, les bruits qui courent' (PV, 63–4). In so doing he demonstrates that his preoccupations are informed by the spirit of the *fait divers*. With Michèle he discusses the ramifications of day to day brutal occurrences in terms that bear this out: 'On fait de la métaphysique [. . .] devant un chien écrasé dans la rue' (PV, 69). This leads to the question that manifests the sense of impending calamity colouring Adam's existence: 'Tu as l'impression d'attendre quelque chose, hein?

Quelque chose de déplaisant ? [. . .] Moi aussi [. . .] en fin de compte, je n'attends plus rien de déplaisant, mais quelque chose de *dangereux*' (PV, 69). We shall see that like the onlookers in the *faits divers* of 'La Ronde' and 'Moloch', Adam's presentiment of disaster is fraught with ambiguity.

In one sense the violence Adam anticipates is something he aspires to: he is drawn by death which, in extinguishing conscious existence, puts an end to conflict and negativity and restores the body once and for all to the life of the elements: 'Il attendait solitaire au bout de son corps grêle l'accident bizarre qui l'écraserait contre le sol, et l'incrusterait, à nouveau chez les vivants, dans la boue sanglante de ses chairs, de ses os en miettes, de sa bouche ouverte, de ses yeux aveugles' (PV, 92). He is tormented by conscious life and the torrents of 'sensations synesthésiques' it entails: 'Je suis écrasé sous le poids de ma conscience. *J'en meurs*, c'est un fait' (PV, 72). This paradoxical reversal of conceptions of life and death explains the discomfort associated with the precariousness of existence, which consciousness contemplates with an ambivalence it attaches to the prospect of its own extinction. While clinging on to life, Adam recognizes that consciousness represents a flaw in the universe: he expects to be condemned and punished for 'la faute de vivre' (PV, 132).[14]

The aberrations inherent in the everyday mean that the *fait divers* is intrinsic to this novel as to Le Clézio's other writings. Adam's story starts with his failure to appear in the papers following Michèle's reporting to the police that he raped her (PV, 42–5). It culminates in a news report of his being taken into custody for a variety of possible offences committed on the promenade and elsewhere. In between these items, *fait divers* cases accompany the narrative, contributing both to the general tone and to the development of key specific themes. For example, Adam and Michèle, strolling by the sea, sit on a bench 'dont le dossier avait été arraché, trois mois auparavant, par un accident d'automobile: un camion six-tonnes avait fauché un Vélo Solex débouchant sur sa droite, et, perdant le contrôle de sa direction, s'était renversé sur le trottoir – d'où le banc mutilé et 2 morts' (PV, 46). Nothing more is said: the local catastrophe simply forms part of the narrative background, having been absorbed into the everyday landscape.[15] The novel is interspersed with other passing allusions to newspapers and the incidents that have appeared or might appear in them. An old lady unexpectedly dies of sunstroke in the street and in contrast an Italian takes a cigarette from a packet, 'et ce qu'on pouvait attendre arrive: il fume' (PV, 191). The 'Grand Prix Automobile' is likely to produce a fatal accident which will have limited impact – until it appears in printed form: 'On mettra de la sciure par terre, et on attendra le journal du lundi. Ce sera: "Tragique bilan des Courses du Grand Prix" et pas plus mal qu'ailleurs' (PV, 198–9). The dispassionate way in which such items are recorded, the random interleaved with the routinely predictable, challenges the interpretative hierarchies we may apply and recalls the analogy between humans and ants we have noted elsewhere. On the other hand, a true 'catastrophe chez les fourmis' occurs as Adam moves to greet Michèle: 'Il écrasa sans s'en apercevoir deux fourmis rouge et noir, dont l'une portait une dépouille de bousier' (PV, 61). These instances evince varying attempts to make sense of the universe's arbitrariness: the simple record of the predictable alongside the unpredictable; the occurrence, plus a satirical commentary on its aftermath; the reversal of scale, levelling the minuscule up to the human.

Around the mid-point of the novel Adam has a particularly acute insight into the inevitability of death (PV, 146–8). The sequence that deals with it, however, is steeped in allusions to contingency and random events. Adam could have reached his intuition at a number of different times, in a variety of ways: the text lists the alternative forms the revelation might have assumed (PV, 146–7). The circumstances and events around him when it has occurred are themselves a matter of equal indifference: a further page or so catalogues the possibilities. The absolute of death renders the detail irrelevant. Ways in which Adam might meet his death are then presented, in two pages (PV, 148–50) which read like a compendium drawn from the *fait divers* rubric. Some twenty-eight possibilities are envisaged, each as likely – or unlikely – as the other; death as contingency denies plausibility as much as any other human construction: 'Un volcan pouvait surgir sous ses pieds, là, à chaque seconde.' Adam sits down to rest, 'las d'avoir à se défendre sans cesse contre tous ces dangers' – whereupon a passing cyclist announces that the body of a drowned man has just been found washed up on the shore. This scenario, not considered among the previous twenty-eight, ironically confirms that the *fait divers* of death will defy even the most meticulous anticipation.

The serio-comic tribute to contingency introduces a study of the reception and publication of this latter incident, explicitly referred to as a 'fait divers' (PV, 162). It constitutes a *mise en abyme*, since the pages dealing with it rehearse both the themes and broader structure of the entire novel. The corpse is in a state of decomposition – or rather, as Adam notices, 'tout a fondu' (PV, 153). The cadaver is in fact reverting to the elements in which it has been immersed: the man has become 'un homme liquide' or a 'monstre amphibie', a sort of fish or a 'têtard géant' (PV, 152–3). Clothes, face, feet, hands, all are 'imbibés d'eau de mer'. Bones, hair, teeth and mouth are associated respectively with 'gelée', 'goémons', 'graviers', and 'une anémone' (PV, 153). These motifs reiterate the dream of quitting conscious existence through confusion with the other realms of being – animal, vegetable and mineral. Hence the sea in which this man died is referred to, paradoxically, as 'l'élément de sa résurrection' (PV, 154).

Adam, looking on, is likened to the drowned man, himself a 'noyé sous la pluie': 'il avait lui-même, à force d'être resté sous la pluie, l'air d'un noyé' (PV, 152). The other onlookers who have gathered in the rain also 'ressemblaient de plus en plus à des noyés' (PV, 153, 162). The analogies confirm that death by drowning, a 'divertissement de choix' (PV, 151), carries profound existential reverberations: 'Pour montrer aux autres comment il faut faire; pour les mettre en demeure de périr' (PV, 151). The mingled emotions and reactions of the spectators confer a quasi-totemic significance on the victim: 'Tous heureux, en dépit de ce léger pincement des narines et du cœur, où l'impudeur s'arrêterait un instant, le temps de se charger d'un rien de honte, avant de déferler [. . .] vers celui-*ci*, vers l'*objet*' (PV, 151).

The body ritually discloses an ontological truth: 'Il était un drôle d'archange. [. . .] Il était enfin vainqueur, unique et éternel. Sa main impérieuse, gantée de bleu, nous montrait la mer d'où il était né' (PV, 154). This death intimates the 'passage étrange' (PV, 154) from conscious existence to that state of being which Adam's 'extase matérialiste' (PV, 204) borders on and also points to. As such it represents a temptation and an imperative: 'Nous devrions [. . .] laisser aller nos corps au milieu du flot [. . .] pénétrés par le dard de l'osmose [. . .], nous serions immobiles et doux'. Hence people retrieved from the sea are conducted simultaneously 'vers la morgue et le paradis' (PV, 155).[16] The next chapter begins with the assertion that there is nothing to add to this fundamental truth: 'Quand on a compris pourquoi il y a des gens qui se noient [. . .] le reste ne compte pas' (PV, 156). Only those who are blind to this essential 'drame permanent' attend to 'les détails qui semblent justifier l'événement, lui donner une réalité, mais qui n'en sont que la mise en scène' (PV, 156). When such people 'composent [. . .] se lamentent [. . .] élucubrent et écrivent des poèmes' (PV, 156), they 'font petit à petit partie de ceux qui ont noyé le type' (PV, 158): in articulating trivia which obscure essential truths they condemn their fellow humans to a life without revelation, that leads to despair and suicide.

The aftermath of the *fait divers* – the very condition of its manifestation as a published *fait divers* – is therefore dismissed as a diversionary transformation. Nonetheless, Le Clézio goes on to show how the incident is assimilated for (and by) the public at large. The urge to truth is indeed not the principal driving force behind this process. Rather, in the ensuing 'choral scene', social interaction is staged through the jostling of discourses striving for authority and status. Recollections of an analogous incident are ratified by the rejoinder 'Oui, je me rappelle avoir lu ça dans les journaux' (PV, 162), which is where all this activity is tending. At this point the narrator formally lists names and occupations as if in preparation for a news report – or *procès-verbal*. One character is imagined at some future point referring back to what he saw, speaking 'une ultime fois de ce fait divers' with the words 'J'ai vu un homme qui était noyé. [. . .] On en a parlé dans le journal, d'ailleurs, le lendemain' (PV, 162–3). Whereupon the novel reproduces the story in facsimile from a *fait divers* rubric. The exchanges exemplify the mechanisms whereby a community comes to an official version of events to which it can subsequently refer as a check on assertions made about them – in an essentially circular pattern which actually excludes the elemental truths involved. The *fait divers* is the stuff of social cohesion and social integration: 'Le dernier souvenir de cet homme mort [. . .] les rendait solidaires sans amour,' we learn of the group as it begins to disband and its members return to 'ce long voyage solitaire à travers l'abîme' (PV, 162).[17]

The publication of the *fait divers* in the newspaper marks the official reassertion of the social consensus in reaction to that which most challenges it. The victim's profession and social standing – 'honorablement connu dans les milieux commerçants' – are restated and thereby validated (PV, 163). 'La thèse de l'accident devant être repoussée,' we are told, 'l'enquête a conclu au suicide,' and the evidence points to 'une crise de neurasthénie', all of which places a reassuringly impassive clinical veneer over potentially disturbing questions. Regret and condolences conclude the ritual of the rubric.

However, the reaction of the man's widow and daughter provides a telling postscript: 'On n'en parlera jamais plus, ni à table, ni le soir, au salon, avec les parents et amis. [. . .] Entre elles et lui, ce sera bien fini. [. . .] Il n'avait jamais existé' (PV, 164). Shamed – or relieved – at the nature of his passing, they suppress his actual existence from their lives and mythologize him in contradictory versions. In this respect his ontological status is rendered comparable to that of the war and military experience from which Adam Pollo's story derives. The gap in the women's life-stories is papered over with narratives from the two domains that the novel as a whole brings into play, History and *la factidiversialité*: 'Son mari était mort à la guerre, en héros, en montant à l'assaut d'une forteresse japonaise. Le père d'Andrée avait été tué dans un accident d'auto, ou d'avion, quand elle n'avait que trois ans' (PV, 164). This sequence concludes with the statement: 'Voilà à peu près ce qui a dû se passer, hors d'Adam, entre quelques hommes, le jour où ce type a été retiré noyé' (PV, 165). Adam has been an outside observer of this process – so far. The novel will reach its overall conclusion by showing how he becomes a victim of it himself.

Before we learn the details of Adam's arrest, we are given an intimation of his story coming into contact with, and being taken in hand by, an authoritative, official-seeming discourse: 'Voici comment Adam raconta la suite, plus tard [. . .] dans un cahier d'écolier jaune. [. . .] On retrouva le tout, à moitié calciné' (PV, 206). Adam's testimony is thereby turned into a *pièce à conviction*, an element in the *procès-verbal* which the narrative here acknowledges itself to be.

The arrest, presented as one of several reports in three facsimile pages from a newspaper, is headlined: 'Un maniaque arrêté à Carros' and features at the bottom of a front page whose lead story is Ben Bella's return to Oran to join the GPRA (*Gouvernement Provisoire de la République Algérienne*). Alongside are two stories of drowning, and a third concerning the recovery from the sea of the bodies of two German tourists. In addition to reports of forest fires disrupting train journeys and a seamen's strike suspending crossings to Corsica and Africa, we can read of the verdict and sentences at the conclusion of 'l'affaire Locussol', evidently a murder case, and of the discovery in a ravine of the body of a Toulon man whose death is as yet shrouded in mystery.

The *fait divers* is not read in isolation, contrary to what normally happens in novels with their focus on one story or group of associated stories. We have seen Roch read the page layout as a geographical simulacrum, but it also constructs the fragmentation and heterogeneity of reality. Its distribution of narratives influences the attention we bring even to the subject we are chiefly concerned with. 'Maniaque arrêté à Carros,' though not the front page lead, is continued above 'Enigme en Corse (suite de la page 1)' on page 7. However, since this latter story runs on to a third page – reproduced by Le Clézio to satisfy our curiosity – we inevitably digress to it, temporarily leaving Adam Pollo behind. At the same time, the novel subjects this divergent miscellany to the associative pull of its own thematic structure. We have noted that the Ben Bella headline subsumes the *fait divers* within a specific historical context and interacts with the novel's implicit allusions to the Algerian war. The stories of drownings echo the earlier *fait divers*, and Adam's predicament is thereby associated with the techniques and themes we have seen conveyed through this item. Moreover, the broad themes of disruption, calamity, and death that inform the novel are also made manifest in the particular instances that here contribute their colouring to the environment in which we absorb the news report about Adam.

Many implications of Adam's appearance in a *fait divers* have been prefigured through the story of the drowned man.[18] What is new here is the contrast produced by the shift in focalization from private to public. The peremptory characterization of Adam as 'un maniaque [. . .] visiblement privé de ses facultés mentales' disrupts the empathy that the narrative up to now has carefully nurtured. From the case of the drowned man we recall that certain elemental or ontological truths fall by the wayside in the progression to a chronicle of circumstantial detail in the rubric: the issue is made graphically clear at this point.

However, this *fait divers* is not merely a restatement in different terms of what we know already: it is only here that we discover Adam has indulged in 'des exhibitions qualifiables d'attentat à la pudeur' and has unconvincingly confessed, it appears, to being a pyromaniac (PV, 256). The narrative of his pursuit and arrest, followed by details of the psychiatric hospital and personnel in whose care he is placed, are similarly left to the columns of the newspaper. Thus the narrative of the *fait divers* is absorbed but not superseded by that of the novel.

It also emerges here that Adam's case falls between the medical and judicial authorities:

> Si le docteur Pauvert [. . .] diagnostique des troubles mentaux, le jeune homme sera interné à la clinique psychiatrique sans répondre des accusations. Au cas contraire, il sera poursuivi sur deux chefs d'accusation: violation de domicile avec vagabondage et attentat à la pudeur. (PV, 256)

This marks a potential clash of official discourses in the attempt to make sense of the affair, evoking in relations between professions what we have seen happen among individual members of a group in connection with the drowned man.[19] The novel renews its narrative dynamic by engaging with the issues at this institutional level.

The final section of the novel depicts Adam Pollo in the psychiatric hospital, where he is interviewed by a group of students and the head doctor (PV, 271–2). Though not like the reporters he saw on his arrival, and though they will not 'faire un canard' about him, they are 'un peu des journalistes', the nurse explains. This prelude, undeniably somewhat contrived, connects the earlier journalistic practices to medical modes of investigation and forms of knowledge, suggesting that the latter do not necessarily supersede the former. The examination itself, conducted by students under the supervision of the expert, neatly formalizes that assimilation of evidence and production of discursive knowledge of which the *fait divers* furnishes a rudimentary, picturesque example. The students precisely mirror the group of onlookers encircling the corpse of the drowned man earlier.[20] However, the process of investigation and diagnosis here incorporates a principle of authority present only in an unstable embryonic form earlier.

The effect of this authority is made clear as the sympathetic approach of a female student begins to elicit from Adam a response which is recognizably authentic and pertinent. The head doctor intervenes to indicate that his trainees are proving insufficiently inquisitorial and judgemental: 'Vous laissez passer des indices' (PV, 281). He corrects their case notes, proposing technical terminology where they are recording Adam's subjective experience. Typifying institutional discourse, he shows they must fit observation to prior knowledge if they are to produce the required 'début de diagnostic' (PV, 281). Furthermore, as the female student, empathizing with her subject, is driven to question whether or not Adam is really mad, the doctor again perceives a need to set the record straight: there is an essential line to be drawn between sanity and madness, and it is only beyond this line that distinctions can be dispensed with (PV, 286). He then invites the young woman to continue her interrogation with a view to verifying his conclusions rather than pursuing her own (PV, 287). The seduction of power, knowledge and authority is thus counterposed to the attraction of intersubjective projection.

Adam goes to some lengths to explain himself, but 'ses paroles avaient résonné bizarrement dans l'infirmerie'; the institutional context, standing as a metaphor for the received discourse, 'faisait s'éteindre le sens des mots' (PV, 291). If he is to get his point across, he must achieve communication with his fellow humans. He has previously managed a form of this by telling stories to the crowd on the beach: the closest he comes to it here is by telling stories to his questioners – of his former friend Tweedsmuir, for example (PV, 289–92). He recognizes that the discourses they practise make no provision for 'le genre anecdotique'(PV, 302–3), and he too is sick of literature; but as long as they remain in the realm of 'la psychopathologie [. . .] il n'y a plus rien à comprendre' (PV, 307). He therefore proposes to the young woman simply to swap stories: 'Vous me raconterez une histoire . . . Et pour les autres, pour tous les autres, je continuerai mon histoire à moi. Vous savez, cette histoire compliquée, qui explique tout' (PV, 307–8). The others want to bring to an end 'cette histoire de l'autre monde' (PV, 308), but she recognizes the prospect of something else in his offer: 'Elle attendait quelque chose. Quelque chose, non point de nouveau, d'étrange, mais de fatalement social' (PV, 309). In the presence of the story-telling impulse, the expectation we have seen associated in Le Clézio's writing with contingency and impending catastrophe is transformed into a force for communication and social cohesion. Adam seems to be on the verge of discovering the secret of social interaction through narrative. However, the story he has to tell, like others that have preoccupied him in the course of the novel, opens fissures in the fabric of intelligibility: this time he breaks off, actually struck dumb by the implications for language, logic and fact of the humdrum anecdote from which, he has said, the rest all stemmed.

Adam suffers a psychological crisis. This is evoked in terms of a series of metamorphoses: in particular, 'On aurait dit qu'il émergeait sans cesse d'une eau trouble et jaune [. . .] Adam se transformait en mer' (PV, 311). With this reminiscence of the earlier *fait divers* of the drowned man, Adam is seen mentally at least to succumb to the primal embrace of the elements; by the same token the doctor and his apprentices who tried to formulate his case in terms which actually exclude its essentials can be grouped with the onlookers described earlier: 'ils font petit à petit partie de ceux qui ont noyé le type' (PV, 158: see above, pp.00–00).

The diagnosis of 'aphasie', written down as Adam subsides into silence (PV, 312), marks another point at which his experience is inscribed within the circuit of public writing and reading. The 'crayon à bille' and the 'cahier' used to record the diagnosis are noticeably reminiscent of Adam's own writing implements (cf. 206): this mode of discourse is not entirely alien to him. He has previously indicated that for him speech is merely a preliminary to real communication: 'L'important, c'est de toujours parler de façon à être écrit' (PV, 48). His school-friend Tweedsmuir, whose story he has recounted as a form of self-projection, embodies an ideal that conforms to this principle: 'S'il avait réussi à aller jusqu'au bout, on aurait fini par parler de lui dans les journaux' (PV, 292). As we learn that Adam, having gone beyond even this achievement, 'entrait dans la légende' (PV, 312) we may surmise that his story has achieved the form of required reading he aspired to.

If the official record has gaps, distortions and omissions, as we have seen to be the case, then it can only be remedied by rewriting it for more authentic readings. This is what the narrative of Adam appears to do, both in its substance and in its form. From the outset it takes a standard model and reshapes it: 'Il y avait une petite fois [. . .]'. The *fait divers*, as we have attempted to show, is an important feature of such a 'passage étrange' (PV, 154) from life to new modes of existence.

Notes

1. The detail of Le Clézio's work has yet to receive the sensitive critical scrutiny it calls for. Two introductory volumes remain at the level of generalities: Jennifer Waelti-Walters, *J.M.G. Le Clézio*, Boston, Twayne, 1977; and idem, *Icare ou l'évasion impossible*, Sherbrooke, Editions Naaman, 1981. Germaine Brée, *Le Monde fabuleux de J.M.G. Le Clézio*, Amsterdam, Rodopi, 1990, provides a more penetrating survey.
2. J.M.G. Le Clézio, *La Fièvre* (hereafter F), Paris, Gallimard, 1965.
3. Pierre Lhoste, *Conversations avec J.M.G. Le Clézio*, Paris, Mercure de France, 1971, p.62, on *La Fièvre*.
4. One is tempted to assume that this is an authentic press report, if only because the distortion of the place name Hem-Hardinval to Ham-Hardival seems a genuine or at least characteristic typographical error. The case is a classic example of a type discussed by Jean Paulhan: see above, p.40.
5. It is of course all the more a feature of our culture in that it virtually replicates the story in Dostoyevsky's *Crime and Punishment*. It is worth

noting that Dostoyevsky's novel also begins with words which seem to prefigure 'La Fièvre' as do Raskolnikov's horrific dreams, fever and fantasies: 'One evening, during an exceptional heatwave at the beginning of July, a young man went out into the street.'

6. J.M.G. Le Clézio, *La Ronde et autres faits divers* (hereafter R), Paris, Gallimard, 1982.

7. Jean Baudrillard, *La Société de Consommation*, Paris, Gallimard-Folio, pp.30, 34: it corresponds to a desire on the part of 'gens sans histoire, et heureux de l'être', to 'déculpabiliser la passivité . . . il faut que cette quiétude de la sphère privée apparaisse comme valeur *arrachée*, constamment menacée, environnée par un destin de catastrophe.' Georges Auclair presents a complementary interpretation of the way in which the readers or spectators of *faits divers* actually will on the destruction and misfortune of others: *Le 'Mana' quotidien: structures et fonction de la chronique des faits divers*, Paris, Editions Anthropos, 1970, pp.186–7, 197–8. Compare with the onlookers at the downfall of the Autodidact in *La Nausée*.

8. *Le Procès-verbal* established his reputation by winning the Prix Renaudot in 1963. Quotations refer to the Gallimard-Folio edition, hereafter PV.

9. Le Clézio calls him 'un homme qui ne savait trop s'il sortait de l'armée ou de l'asile psychiatrique' (PV, 12).

10. He indicates to a girlfriend that as a deserter he is 'à la merci de la moindre petite dénonciation' (PV, 44). When questioned directly on the subject, he says he has done his military service (PV, 284), and a letter from his mother appears to suggest that he has been recovering from 'les récentes fatigues' it entailed (PV, 235); elsewhere, in conversation with American sailors doing their military service, he declares 'Moi, je l'ai fini' (PV, 51), though the evidence of his own ruminations offers the possibility that he may have re-enlisted first, the more so as the blank period in his life extends back some ten years (PV, 53, 54).

11. See for example P. Avril and G. Vincent, *La IVe République*, Paris, MA Editions, 1988, pp.14–17; André Nouschi and Maurice Augulhon, *La France de 1940 à nos jours*, Paris, Nathan, 1984, pp.149–58; Jean-Pierre Rioux, *La France de la Quatrième République*, vol.2, *L'Expansion et l'impuissance*, Paris, Seuil, collection Histoire, 1983, pp.66–7. The *Manifeste des 121*, a document signed in 1960 by intellectuals in protest against the use of military force in Algeria, develops the public equivocations about it in its opening paragraph. Note too the trauma associated with the war that affects Laurence in *Les Belles Images*: see above, p.176.

12. *Leçon inaugurale au Collège de France*, quoted in Avril and Vincent, *La*

IV *République*, p.15.

13. Cf. Le Clézio's statement that what he is seeking to convey is the fact that 'On vit dans une société en guerre permanente. Guerre de la masse contre l'individu, guerre des objets contre l'être humain, guerre des êtres humains entre eux. C'est ce sentiment d'agression permanente qu'il y a autour de moi.' He adds also a reference to 'une guerre à l'intérieur de soi-même': Lhoste, *Conversations avec J.M.G. Le Clézio*, pp.30; 54–5. Cf. also the novel J.M.G Le Clézio, *La Guerre*, Paris, Gallimard, 1970, especially at pp.7–8.

14. Underpinning Adam's story is an ontological theory reminiscent of Sartre's phenomenological analysis of consciousness as the source of *le néant* amidst the plenitude of *l'être*. For Adam, the sense of the precarious nature of things stems from the fact that consciousness introduces 'une part négative' into the Parmenidean unity and indivisibility of being. (PV, 70; see the later references to Parmenides, 71, 300). One aspect of Adam's response to this perception will be developed in his attempts to attain oneness with the elements – for example as he lies among the rocks and 's'éteignait insensiblement [. . .] dans le gel minéral' (PV, 77–8) or when we watch him 'se laisser étouffer, envahir, violenter, [. . .] par un monde seul et unique' (PV, 91–2). The narrator will later refer to his experience of the 'extase matérialiste' (PV, 204), in terms that point to the title *L'Extase matérielle* Le Clézio gives to his own book of 1967 on the subject: and under clinical interrogation Adam will once more evoke an 'état d'extase', associating it again with the philosophy of Parmenides (PV, 300). This conception of existence is also evident in the stories of *La Fièvre*.

15. It will of course recur elsewhere, the girl on the Vélosolex being alluded to in *Le Déluge* (pp.20–1) and the incident forming the subject of the first 'fait divers' in *La Ronde*.

16. See above, note 14.

17. See Auclair on the role of the *fait divers* in ensuring social cohesion in the face of what threatens it, *Le 'Mana' quotidien*, p.197.

18. The fact that the latest news item redeems what it can for social propriety in referring to Adam's family as 'honorablement connue dans la ville' (PV, 256) – the same phrase as used in the case of the drowned man (PV, 163) – confirms the link, earlier prefigured in the *fait divers* headline 'Las de la vie' which echoed Adam's 'las de vivre' (PV, 150).

19. Michel Foucault has shown how such instances exemplify the incipient conflict between newly-emerging disciplines in the course of the nineteenth century over the delinquent, 'l'individu dans lequel l'infracteur de la loi et l'objet d'une technique savante se superposent – à peu près' (*Surveiller et Punir*, Paris, Gallimard, 1975, pp.259–60). See also *Moi, Pierre Rivière . . .*, Paris, Gallimard, 1973; and Ruth

Harris, *Murders and Madness: Medicine, Law and Society in the 'fin de siècle'*, Oxford, Clarendon Press, 1989. We have seen effects of related tensions with respect to the Papin sisters: see above, pp.92–4.

20. Adam implies a connection as he perceives that his questioners are 'avides d'entourer tout le monde et lui-même dans la puissance de la connaissance' (PV, 282). Cf. PV, 158: 'Encerclant la tache d'eau de mer, où flottent des débris.'

16

Conclusion

In *The Girl at the 'Lion d'Or'*, a novel by the English writer Sebastian Faulks, the male protagonist is a lawyer in 1930s France who, like Camus's Clamence, has encountered more than his fair share of *faits divers*.[1] In the face of scandal, crime and catastrophe, his faculties are overwhelmed. As with the 'sublime but frightening feeling' inspired in him by a piece of music, he can find no way to explain the 'base but equally frightening feeling' involved in the powerful impulses that drive an individual to sexual or other transgressions. His typically French faith in the power of the intellect to comprehend such matters has given way to an admission of defeat:

> I can see no way in which they can be brought within my experience and reason, and I have to admit this. And so, instead of taking on every challenge and finding a way to assimilate it, you have to shy away, and say, 'This is too disturbing. This is dangerous'. [. . .] It's the only reasonable way to react – to admit that your life will be, in some senses, incomplete.[2]

This reasoned response to unreason indicates why the *fait divers* continues to fascinate, even when it defies understanding. The incompleteness of lives informed by an awareness of not having been ravished by the unspeakable constitutes the ground of a residual affinity with such extremes. The pursuit of 'ravissement' on the part of Duras and her characters is perhaps the most graphic instance of this phenomenon; but it is equally evidenced in the collusion we have seen evoked between onlookers and the horror or scandal they compulsively partake of even while censuring or recoiling from it. The skewed relation with the real that this can produce is formulated by Baudrillard as comprising neither involvement nor practical interest, but curiosity. The vicarious experience furnished by the *fait divers* constitutes neither knowledge nor ignorance, but what Baudrillard calls 'méconnaissance'.[3]

The *fait divers* implicates writing as such in the vicious circle. Words dictated by the incomplete sensibility Faulk's character adumbrates are in danger of ringing hollow, or of veering into colourful evasions or substitutions. Thierry Lévy writes as a barrister to impugn the language of the entire judicial system and its journalistic appurtenances, which he considers profoundly compromised in their attitude to the 'belle affaire': 'Le juge est là pour approuver le crime,' he argues, and characterizes the writing of *faits divers* as a 'laisser-aller général'.[4] For Lévy, writing about the *fait divers* constantly risks betraying the purpose of writing: 'l'écriture est le contraire de la sensation' and at its best 'fait passer la sensation à la compréhension': 'Le langage [. . .] est un refuge contre la menace d'être détruit par des sentiments qu'on n'aura même pas eu la force d'éprouver jusqu'au bout.'[5] Though Lévy's terminology still blurs matters somewhat in conflating *langage* and *écriture*, it would seem, nonetheless, that writing is, after all, a potential protection against the unavoidable incompleteness of a life that accepts the need to rein back emotions and impulses that are dangerous or disturbing.

The language of reason accepts its limited horizons; the language of sensation gestures unreliably at phenomena beyond this limit. Both are inadequate and both compromise themselves when evoking individually the extremes of the *fait divers*. The *écriture* of the creative writers we have been considering might be said to enact the dialogue between these two languages, pointing to possibilities of synthesis. The implicit effects of this dialogue are perhaps illustrated most clearly when a novel concludes with a *fait divers* to which it has itself provided the context and background. At the end of Conrad's *The Secret Agent* (1907), the characters contemplate the death they have been a party to through the enigma evoked in lines intoned from a news report: 'An impenetrable mystery seems destined to hang for ever over this act of madness or despair.' *Un Crime* (1935), by Georges Bernanos, concludes as the criminal, bent on suicide, places her head on the railway line upon a newspaper headlined 'Accident, crime, ou suicide' over a report of the death of her companion 'qu'elle ne devait jamais lire'. Etcherelli's *Elise ou la vraie vie* (1967) likewise juxtaposes the climax of its narrative with a news report, couched in typically formulaic terms, of the death of the heroine's brother in a road accident. We have seen *Histoire d'un fait divers* stop just short of this, and *Les Faux-Monnayeurs* eschew it in a similarly ostentatious manner; *Le Procès-verbal* varies and highlights the device by focusing first on a *fait divers* with its aftermath, and then on a *fait divers* to which we have been given the antecedents. The novels we have been reading separate out the sensational from their narrative, locate it in a *fait divers*, and then articulate an important part of their own significance – often, in fact, via a rhetoric of silent juxtaposition – through such encounters between imperfect news text and literary narrative context.

Literary art retrieves the *fait divers* from ephemerality, and such novels as we have considered replace its subjection to history by incorporation into their narrative. The *fait divers* thus achieves a different kind of reading, referred to by both Genet and Le Clézio as *la légende*, as its text interacts with the thematic and formal structures of the writing that has assimilated it. The incipient sensationalism and prurience of the *fait divers* are transmuted in the environment of the literary text with its rigour and control; the fiction, for its part, is able to produce an effect of conjunction with reality. While adding another voice to its polyphonic texture, the novel signals its own incompleteness in acknowledging the need to accommodate the news report.

Notes

1. Sebastian Faulks, *The Girl at the 'Lion d'Or'*, London, Vintage, 1990 (first published: Hutchinson, 1989). This fine novel, situated in 1936, is strikingly faithful to the period atmosphere we have surveyed in part III of the present book: it draws its inspiration from a rising sense of the forces of history impinging on a climate of scandal and *faits divers*. The climax of an adulterous love affair which drives the narrative is mirrored in a news report of the suicide of Roger Salengro, then Minister of the Interior, which occurred on 17 November 1936 following 'l'affaire Salengro', sustained anti-Semitic attacks on his personal life and military record. Several other English novels provide specific instances of the impact across the Channel of the *fait divers*: see John Fowles, *The French Lieutenant's Woman* (1969) and Julian Barnes, *Before She Met Me* (1982) and *A History of the World in 10½ Chapters* (1989).
2. Faulks, *The Girl at the 'Lion d'Or'*, pp.183–4.
3. Jean Baudrillard, *La Société de consommation*, Paris, Gallimard-Folio, pp.32–3.
4. Thierry Lévy, *Le Crime en toute humanité*, Paris, Grasset, collection Figures, 1984. See pp.69–94, 95–116.
5. Ibid., pp.130, 133. The chapter entitled, 'Ecriture, trahison' (pp.117–46) is a useful exposé of some of the issues at stake.

Select Bibliography

Primary Sources

Where the reference edition is a paperback, the date of first publication is given in parentheses.

Aragon, Louis, *Anicet ou le panorama, roman*, Paris, Gallimard, 1921
——, *Le Libertinage*, Paris, Gallimard, 1924
——, *Le Paysan de Paris*, Paris, Livre de Poche (1926)
——, *Traité du Style*, Paris, Gallimard, 1928
——, *Les Cloches de Bâle*, Paris, Gallimard-Folio (1934)
——, *Les Beaux Quartiers*, Paris, Gallimard-Folio (1936)
Beauvoir, Simone de, *Le Sang des Autres*, Paris, Gallimard-Folio (1945)
——, *La Force de l'Age*, Paris, Gallimard, 1960
——, *Les Belles Images*, Paris, Gallimard-Folio (1966)
——, *Tout Compte fait*, Paris, Gallimard, 1972
——, *Les Belles Images*, ed. B. Stefanson, London, Heinemann Educational, 1980
Breton, André, *Manifestes du Surréalisme*, Paris, Gallimard, collection Idées (1924, 1930)
——, *Les Pas perdus*, Paris, Gallimard, 1924
——, *Nadja*, Paris, Gallimard-Folio (1928)
——, *Point du Jour*, Paris, Gallimard-Folio Essais (1934/1970)
——, *L'Amour fou*, Paris, Gallimard-Folio (1937)
——, *Poèmes*, Paris, Gallimard, 1948
——, et al., *Violette Nozières, Poèmes, dessins, correspondence, documents, Preface de José Pierre*, Paris, Editions Terrain Vague, 1991
Camus, Albert, *Carnets I*, Paris, Gallimard, 1962
——, *Théâtre, récits, nouvelles*, Paris, Pléiade, 1962
——, *Carnets II, Janvier 1942–Mars 1951*, Paris, Gallimard, 1964
——, *Essais*, Paris, Pléiade, 1965
——, *La Mort Heureuse*, introduction and notes by Jean Sarocchi, Paris, Gallimard, Cahiers Albert Camus 1, 1971
——, *Fragments d'un combat*, edited, with an introduction and notes by Jacqueline Lévi-Valensi and André Abbou, Paris, Gallimard, Cahiers Albert Camus 3, 1978, vol. 2

——, *Albert Camus, éditorialiste à 'L'Express'*, Introduction, commentaries and notes by Paul-F. Smets, Paris, Gallimard, Cahiers Albert Camus 6, 1987

——, *Carnets III, Mars 1951–Décembre 1959*, Paris, Gallimard, 1989

Camus, Albert, and Grenier, Jean, *Correspondance 1932–1960*, Paris, Gallimard, 1981

Desnos, Robert, *Domaine public*, Paris, NRF/Le point du jour, 1953

Duras, Marguerite, *Les Petits Chevaux de Tarquinia*, Paris, Gallimard-Folio (1953)

——, *Moderato cantabile*, Paris, Minuit, collection Double, 1958

——, *Les Viaducs de la Seine-et-Oise*, Paris, Gallimard, 1959

——, *Le Ravissement de Lol V. Stein*, Gallimard-Folio (1964)

——, *L'Amante anglaise*, Paris, Gallimard, 1967

——, *Moderato cantabile*, ed. Thomas Bishop, Englewood Cliffs, Prentice Hall, 1968

——, *Les Parleuses*, Paris, Minuit, 1974

——, *Outside*, Paris, POL, 1984

——, *Le Théâtre de l'Amante anglaise*, Paris, Gallimard, collection L'Imaginaire, 1991

——, *Le Monde extérieur*, ed. Christiane Blot-Labarrère, Paris, POL, 1993

Eluard, Paul, *Œuvres complètes*, Paris, Pléiade, 1968

Fénéon, Félix, *Nouvelles en trois lignes*, edited, with an introduction by Patrick and Roman Wald Lasowski, Paris, Editions Macula, 1990

Gautier, Jean-Jacques, *Histoire d'un fait divers*, Paris, Julliard, 1946

Genet, Jean, *Journal du Voleur*, Paris, Gallimard, 1949

——, *Œuvres complètes de Jean Genet*, vol.2, Paris, Gallimard, 1951

——, *Œuvres complètes*, vol.3, Paris, Gallimard, 1953

——, *Œuvres complètes*, vol.4, Paris, Gallimard, 1968

——, *Œuvres complètes*, vol.5, Paris, Gallimard, 1979

Gide, André, *Journal des Faux-Monnayeurs*, Paris, Gallimard, 1927

——, *Journal 1889–1939*, Paris, Pléiade, 1951

——, *Romans, récits et soties, œuvres lyriques*, Paris, Pléiade, 1958

——, *Ne Jugez Pas*, Paris, Gallimard, 1969

Grenier, Roger, 'Utilité du fait divers', *Les Temps Modernes*, no.17, 1947

——, *Le Rôle d'Accusé. Le Mythe du fait divers*, Paris, Gallimard, 1948

——, *Les Monstres*, Paris, Gallimard, 1953

——, 'Le pays des poètes. Le fait divers: de l'acte à la parole', *Nouvelle Revue de Psychanalyse*, vol.31, 1985, pp.19–27

——, *Soleil et Ombre*, Paris, Gallimard, Collection Folio (1987)

Jarry, Alfred, *Œuvres complètes*, vol.2, edited by Henri Bordillon with the collaboration of Patrick Besnier and Bernard Le Doze, Paris, Pléiade, 1987

Le Clézio, J.M.G., *Le Procès-verbal*, Paris, Gallimard-Folio (1963)

——, *La Fièvre*, Paris, Gallimard, 1965

——, *L'Extase matérielle*, Paris, Gallimard, Idées (1967)

——, *La Guerre*, Paris, Gallimard, 1970

——, *La Ronde et autres faits divers*, Paris, Gallimard, 1982

Mallarmé, Stéphane, *Œuvres complètes*, edited with notes by Henri Mondor and G. Jean-Aubry, Paris, Pléiade, 1945

Mauriac, François, *Thérèse Desqueyroux*, Paris, Livre de Poche (1927)

——, *Thérèse Desqueyroux*, ed. Cecil Jenkins, London, University of London Press, Textes Français Classiques et Modernes, 1964

——, *Œuvres romanesques et théâtrales complètes*, ed. Jacques Petit, vol.2, Paris, Pléiade, 1979

Montherlant, Henri de, *Mors et Vita. Service Inutile*, Paris, Gallimard, 1954

Philippe, Charles-Louis, *Marie Donadieu*, Paris, Bibliothèque Charpentier, Fasquelle Editeurs, 1951

——, *Œuvres complètes*, vol.5, Moulins, Editions Ipomée, 1986

Proust, Marcel, *Contre Sainte-Beuve*, preceded by *Pastiches et mélanges* and followed by *Essais et articles*, edited by Pierre Clarac with the collaboration of Yves Sandre, Paris, Pléiade, 1971

——, *Les Pastiches de Proust*, critical edition with commentary by Jean Milly, Paris, Librairie Armand Colin, 1970

Queneau, Raymond, *Zazie dans le Métro*, Paris, Gallimard-Folio (1959)

Robbe-Grillet, Alain, *Le Voyeur*, Paris, Minuit, 1955

——, *Pour un nouveau roman*, Paris, Gallimard, collection Idées (1963)

——, 'Présentation de *Projet pour une révolution à New York*', *Nouvel Observateur*, 26 June 1970

——, 'Entretien' in *Littérature* no.49, 'Le Roman policier', February 1983, pp.16–22

——, *Le Miroir qui revient*, Paris, Minuit, 1984

——, 'Monde trop plein, conscience vide', in *Albert Camus: œuvre fermée, œuvre ouverte?* proceedings of a colloquium at Cérisy-la-Salle, June 1982, Cahiers Albert Camus 5, Paris, Gallimard, 1985

Sarraute, Nathalie, *Portrait d'un inconnu*, Paris, Union Générale d'Editions, collection 10/18 (1948)

——, *L'Ere du Soupçon*, Paris, Gallimard, collection Idées (1956)

Sartre, Jean-Paul, 'Une idée fondamentale de la phénoménologie de Husserl: l'intentionnalité', in *Situations I*, Paris, Gallimard, 1947 (1939), pp.31–5

——, *L'Age de Raison*, Paris, Gallimard-Folio (1945)

——, *Huis Clos suivi de Les Mouches*, Paris, Livre de Poche (1947)

——, *Saint Genet, comédien et martyr*, Paris, Gallimard, 1952

——, *Situations VIII*, Paris, Gallimard, 1972

——, *Œuvres romanesques*, ed. M. Contat and M. Rybalka, Paris, Pléiade, 1981

Tournier, Michel, *Le Roi des Aulnes*, Paris, Gallimard-Folio (1970)

——, *Le Vent Paraclet*, Paris, Gallimard-Folio (1977)

Vitrac, Roger, *Victor ou les Enfants au Pouvoir*, Paris, Gallimard, Le Manteau d'Harlequin, 1946

Secondary Sources

Allemand, A., *L'œuvre romanesque de Nathalie Sarraute*, Neuchâtel, Editions de la Baconnière, 1980

Allemand, R.-M., *Duplications et duplicité dans les 'Romanesques' d'Alain Robbe-Grillet*, Paris, Archives des Lettres Modernes, 250, 1991

——, and Goulet, A., *Imaginaire, écritures, lectures de Robbe-Grillet*, Lion-sur-Mer, Editions Arcane-Beaunieux, 1991

Amar, D., and Yana, P., '"Sublime, forcément sublime": à propos d'un article paru dans *Libération*', *Revue des Sciences Humaines*, no.202, April–June 1986, pp.153–76

Apter, E., 'Allegories of reading/allegories of justice: the Gidean fait divers', *Romanic Review*, vol.80, no.4, 1989, pp.560–70

Ascher, C., *Simone de Beauvoir, a life of freedom*, Brighton, Harvester Press, 1981

Assouline, P., *Gaston Gallimard*, Paris, Balland/Seuil, Collection Points, 1985

Auclair, G., *Le 'Mana' quotidien: structures et fonctions de la chronique des faits divers*, Paris, Editions Anthropos, 1970

Avril, P., and Vincent, G., *La IVᵉ République*, Paris, MA Editions, 1988

Barthes, R., *Mythologies*, Paris, Seuil, collection Points, 1957

——, 'Structure du fait divers', in *Essais critiques*, Paris, Seuil, 1964, pp.188–97

——, 'L'effet de réel,' in Barthes, Bersani *et al.*, *Littérature et Réalité*, Paris, Seuil, collection Points, 1982

——, *Le Bruissement de la Langue*, Paris, Seuil, 1984

Baudrillard, J., *La Société de consommation*, Paris, Gallimard, Folio-Essais (1970)

Beaumont, K., *Alfred Jarry. A Critical and Biographical Study*, Leicester, Leicester University Press, 1984

Bell, D.F., '*La Chandelle verte* and the *fait divers*', *L'Esprit Créateur*, vol.24, 1984, pp.48–56

Bell, S., *Nathalie Sarraute: 'Portrait d'un Inconnu' and 'Vous les entendez?'*, London, Grant and Cutler, 1988

Bellanger, C., Godechot, J., Guiral, P., Terrou, F., *Histoire générale de la presse française*, vol.3, *De 1871 à 1940*, Paris, Presses Universitaires de France, 1972

Bellos, D., *Georges Perec, A Life in Words*, London, Harvill, 1993

Béraud, H., Bourcier, E., Salmon, A., *L'Affaire Landru*, Paris, Albin Michel, 1924

Beynon John, S., 'Sartre's *La Nausée*: the City and Apocalypse', *Romance Studies*, no.22, Autumn 1993, pp.53–65

Borgomano, M., *Marguerite Duras, une lecture des fantasmes*, Paris, Cistre, 1987

Borne, D., and Dubief, H., *Nouvelle Histoire de la France Contemporaine*, vol.13, *La Crise des années 30*, Paris, Seuil, 1989

Boros, M.-D., *Un Séquestré, l'homme sartrien*, Paris, Nizet, 1968

Brée, G., *Le Monde fabuleux de J.M.G. Le Clézio*, Amsterdam, Rodopi, 1990

Britton, C., 'Fiction, fact and madness: intertextual relations among Gide's female characters', in M. Worton and J. Still, eds., *Intertextuality: theories and practices*, Manchester, Manchester University Press, 1990, pp.159–75

Brooks, P., *Reading for the Plot*, Oxford, Clarendon Press, 1984

Cardinal, R., 'The air of eventuality', *Aura*, no.1, January 1993, pp.72–81

Catteau, J., *La Création littéraire chez Dostoïevski*, Paris, Institut d'Etudes slaves, 1978

Chénieux-Gendron, J., *Le Surréalisme et le Roman*, Paris, L'Age d'homme, 1983

Chevalier, L., *Classes laborieuses et classes dangereuses à Paris pendant la première moitié de XIXᵉ siècle*, Paris, Plon, 1958

Clausse, R., *Le journal et l'actualité*, Paris, Marabout Université, 1967

Colette, *Œuvres complètes de Colette*, vol.13, Paris, Le Fleuron, chez Flammarion, 1950

——, *Œuvres complètes*, vol.14, Le Fleuron, chez Flammarion, 1950

——, *Œuvres*, vol.3, general editor Claude Pichois, Paris, Gallimard, Bibliothèque de la Pléiade, 1991

Collier, P., 'Surrealist city narrative: Breton and Aragon', in E. Timms, D. Kelley, eds., *Unreal city: Urban experience in modern European Literature and Art*, New York, St Martin's Press, 1985, pp.214–29

Colombani, R., *L'Affaire Weidmann*, Paris, Albin Michel, 1989

Courrière, Y., *Joseph Kessel, ou sur la piste du lion*, Paris, Plon/Presses-Pocket, 1986

Coward, D., *Duras: 'Moderato cantabile'*, London, Grant and Cutler, 1981

Crastre, V., *André Breton: Trilogie surréaliste*, Paris, SEDES, 1971

Davis, C., 'Genet's *Journal du Voleur* and the ethics of reading', *French Studies*, vol.68, no.1, January 1994, pp.50–62

Dichy, A., and Fouché, P., *Jean Genet: Essai de chronologie 1910-1944*, Paris, Bibliothèque de littérature française contemporaine de l'Université Paris 7, 1988

Dostoyevsky, F., *The Devils*, translated by David Magarshack, Harmondsworth, Penguin Classics, 1971

Doubrovsky, S., 'Le Neuf de Cœur. Fragment d'une psycholecture de *La Nausée*', *Obliques*, nos.18–19, 1979

——, 'Phallotexte et gynotexte dans *La Nausée*: "feuillet sans date"', in Michael Issacharoff and Jean-Claude Vilquin, eds., *Sartre et la mise en signe*, Paris/Lexington Kentucky, Klincksieck/French Forum, 1982, pp.31–55

Drieu la Rochelle, P., 'Le cas Violette Nozières', *Marianne*, 6 September 1933, p.10

Duncan, A.B., 'Robbe-Grillet's *Le Voyeur*: a reassessment', *Symposium*, Summer 1980, pp.107–24

Evans, M., *Simone de Beauvoir: a feminist mandarin*, London and New York, Tavistock, 1985

Fallaize, E., *The Novels of Simone de Beauvoir*, London and New York, Routledge, 1988

Faulks, S., *The Girl at the 'Lion d'Or'*, London, Vintage, 1989

Flower, J.E., *Intention and achievement. An essay on the novels of François Mauriac*, Oxford, Clarendon Press, 1969

——, *Literature and the Left in France*, London and Basingstoke, Macmillan, 1983

Foucault, M., *Moi, Pierre Rivière . . .*, Paris, Gallimard, 1973

——, *Surveiller et Punir*, Paris, Gallimard, 1975

Frese Witt, M.A., *Existential Prisons. Captivity in Mid-Twentieth-Century French Literature*, Durham, Duke University Press, 1985

Garfitt, J.S.T., *Mauriac: 'Thérèse Desqueyroux'*, London, Grant and Cutler, 1991

Garnham, B.G., *Robbe-Grillet: 'Les Gommes' and 'Le Voyeur'*, London, Grant and Cutler, 1982

Gavillet, A., *La Littérature au Défi. Aragon Surréaliste*, Neuchatel, Editions de la Baconnière, 1957

Gindine, Y., *Aragon prosateur surréaliste*, Geneva, Droz, 1966

Goldmann, L., 'Le Théâtre de Genet et les études sociologiques', *Cahiers Renaud-Barrault*, no.57, November 1966, pp.90–125

Goldthorpe, R., *'La Nausée'*, London, Harper-Collins, Unwin Critical Library, 1991

Gore, K., 'Lucienne, Sex and Nausea', *Forum for Modern Language Studies*, vol.26, no.1, 1990, pp.37–48

Gritti, J., *Elle court, elle court, la rumeur*, Ottowa, Editions Stanké, 1978

Harris, R., *Murders and Madness: Medicine, Law and Society in the 'fin de siècle'*, Oxford, Clarendon Press, 1989

Hill, L., *Marguerite Duras, apocalyptic desires*, London, Routledge, 1993

Holzberg, R., 'Décryptage du *Voyeur*', *The French Review*, vol.52, no.6, May 1979, pp.848–55

Jackson, E.R., 'André Gide et les faits-divers: un rapport préliminaire', *Bulletin des Amis d'André Gide*, vol.20, no.93, January 1992, pp.83–91

Janvier, L., *Une parole exigeante: le nouveau roman*, Paris, Minuit, 1964

Jones, M., *Dostoyevsky, the novel of discord*, London, Paul Elek, 1976

Jost, F., general editor, *Obliques*, nos.16–17, special 'Robbe-Grillet' number, 1978

Jouhandeau, M., *Trois crimes rituels*, Paris, Gallimard, 1961

Kapferer, J.-N., *Rumeurs*, Paris, Seuil, 1987

Keefe, T., *Beauvoir: 'Les Belles Images', 'La Femme Rompue'*, Glasgow, University of Glasgow French and German Publications, Introductory Guides to French Literature 12, 1991

Kessel, J., *Nuits de Montmartre*, Paris, Christian Bourgois collection 10/18, 1990

Kidd, W., 'Oedipal and pre-Oedipal elements in *Thérèse Desqueyroux*', in J.E. Flower, B. Swift, eds., *François Mauriac, Visions and Reappraisals*, Oxford, Berg, 1989

Kundera, M., *The Unbearable Lightness of Being*, London, Faber and Faber, 1985

Lacan, J., 'Motifs du crime paranoïaque: le crime des sœurs Papin', in *De la psychose paranoïaque dans ses rapports avec la personnalité*, Paris, Seuil, 1975, pp.389–98

Lalou, R., *Histoire de la Littérature française contemporaine*, Paris, Presses universitaires de France, 1953

Leak, A., 'Nausea and desire in Sartre's *La Nausée*', *French Studies*, vol.43, no.1, January 1989, pp.61–72

——, *The Perverted Consciousness: Sexuality and Sartre*, London, Macmillan, 1989

Lecerf, M., *Les Faits Divers*, Paris, Larousse, collection Idéologies et Sociétés, 1981

Le Guillant, L., 'L'Affaire des sœurs Papin', *Les Temps Modernes*, no.210, November

1963, pp.868–913

Lejeune, P., 'Les projets autobiographiques de Georges Perec', in *Parcours Perec*, edited by Mireille Ribière, Lyon, Presses Universitaires de Lyon, 1990

Lévi-Valensi, J., *Aragon romancier*, Paris, SEDES, 1989

Lévy, T., *Le Crime en toute humanité*, Paris, Grasset, collection Figures, 1984

Lhoste, P., *Conversations avec J.M.G. Le Clézio*, Paris, Mercure de France, 1971

Lipovetsky, G., *L'Empire de l'éphémère*, Gallimard, Folio-Essais, 1987

Lottmann, H., *Albert Camus*, Paris, Seuil, 1978

McLure, R., 'Duras *contra* Bergson: time in *Moderato cantabile*', *Forum for Modern Language Studies*, vol.25, no.1, January 1989, pp.62–76

Maeder, T., *The Unspeakable Crimes of Dr. Petiot*, London, Penguin Books, 1990

Maitron, J., *Le Mouvement anarchiste en France*, vol.1, *Des origines à 1914*, Paris, François Maspéro, 1975

Malgorn, A., *Jean Genet qui êtes-vous?*, Lyon, La Manufacture, 1988

Martin, C., *La Maturité d'André Gide*, Paris, Klincksieck, 1977

Maucuer, M., *Thérèse Desqueyroux*, Paris, Hatier, collection Profil d'une œuvre, 1970

Merleau-Ponty, M., 'Sur les faits divers', *Signes*, Paris, Gallimard, 1960, pp.388–91

Monestier, A., *et al.*, *Le Fait Divers*, catalogue of an exhibition organized at the Musée national des arts et traditions populaires, Paris, Editions de la Réunion des musées nationaux, 1982

Morin, E., *et al.*, *La Rumeur d'Orléans*, edition supplemented by *La Rumeur d'Amiens*, Paris, Seuil, collection Points, 1969

Mouret, F., 'Gide à la découverte de Browning et de Hogg, ou la technique romanesque de la multiplicité des points de vue', in *Cahiers André Gide*, no.3, Paris, Gallimard, 1972, pp.223–39

Nadeau, M., *Histoire du Surréalisme*, Paris, Seuil, collection Points, 1964

Nizan, P., *Pour une nouvelle culture*, Paris, Grasset, 1970

Nouschi, A., Augulhon, M., *La France de 1940 à nos jours*, Paris, Nathan, 1984

O'Callaghan, R., 'A construction of desire: *Le Voyeur* and *Moderato cantabile*', *New Zealand Journal of French Studies*, vol.5, no.1, May 1984, pp.25–48

Paganini, M., 'L'inscription juridique dans *Les Bonnes* de Jean Genet', *Romanic Review*, vol.80, no.3, 1989, pp.462–82

Palle, A., 'Petiot "faux résistant"', *Les Temps Modernes*, no.10, July 1946, pp.157–62

Paulhan, J., *Les Causes célèbres*, Paris, Gallimard, 1950

——, *Entretien sur des faits divers*, in *Œuvres complètes*, vol.2, Paris, Cercle du Livre Précieux, 1966

Peace, R., *Dostoyevsky, an examination of the major novels*, Cambridge, Cambridge University Press, 1971

Perec, G., *Je me souviens. Les Choses communes*, I, Paris, Hachette, 1978

——, *L'infra-ordinaire*, Paris, Seuil, 1989

Pierre, J., 'Violette Nozières et les surréalistes', preface to *Violette Nozières. Poèmes, dessins, correspondence, documents*, St. Niklaas, Belgium, Terrain Vague, 1991

Poulaille, H., *Nouvel âge littéraire*, Bassac, Plein Chant, 1986

Quincey, T. de, *On Murder as a Fine Art*, London, Philip Allan, 1925 .

Raimond, M., *La Crise du Roman, des lendemains du naturalisme aux années vingt*, Paris, Corti, 1966

Reed, P., and McLure, R., 'La Nausée and the problem of literary representation', *Modern Language Review*, no.82, 1987, pp.343–55

Ricouart, J., *Ecriture féminine et violence: Une étude de Marguerite Duras*, Birmingham, Alabama, Summa, 1991

Rifkin, A., *Street Noises, Parisian Pleasure, 1900–1940*, Manchester and New York, Manchester University Press, 1993

Rioux, J.-P., *La France de la Quatrième République*, vol.2, *L'Expansion et l'impuissance*, Paris, Seuil, collection Histoire, 1983

——, 'Camus et la Seconde Guerre Mondiale', in *Camus et la politique*, ed. Jeanyves Guérin, Paris, Editions L'Harmattan, 1986, pp.97–106

Roe, D., *Charles-Louis Philippe, la vie et l'œuvre*, Charles-Louis Philippe, *Œuvres complètes*, vol.1, Moulins, Editions Ipomée, 1986

Romi, *Histoire des faits divers*, Paris, Editions du Pont-Royal, 1962

Savona, J., *Jean Genet*, Basingstoke, Macmillan, 1983

——, 'Théâtre et univers carcéral: Jean Genet et Michel Foucault', *French Forum*, vol.10, no.2, 1985, pp.201–13

Schwob, M., *Mœurs des Diurnales, Traité de journalisme*, n.p., Editions des Cendres, 1985 [first published under the pseudonym of Loyson-Bridet, Paris, Mercure de France, 1903]

Séguin, J.-P., *Nouvelles à sensation: Canards du XIXᵉ siècle*, Paris, Armand Colin, 1959

Sheringham, M., 'Knowledge and repetition in Le Ravissement de Lol V. Stein', *Romance Studies*, no.2, Summer 1983, pp.124–40

——, 'Narration and experience in Genet's *Journal du Voleur*', in *Studies in French Fiction: a Festschrift for Vivenne Milne*, ed. Robert Gibson, London, Grant and Cutler, 1988, pp.289–306

Smets, P.-F., 'Camus chroniqueur judiciaire à *Alger Républicain* en 1939', in *Albert Camus, dans le premier silence et au-delà*, Brussels, J. Goemaere, 1985, pp.142–88

Stewart, H.E., 'Louis Ménesclou, assassin and source of the "Lilac Murder" in Genet's *Haute Surveillance*', *Romance Notes*, vol.26, no.3, Spring 1986, pp.204–8

——, 'Jean Genet's favorite murderers', *The French Review*, vol.60, no.5, 1987, pp.635–43

Stewart, H.E., and McGregor, R.R., *Jean Genet: a biography of deceit 1910–1951*, New York, Peter Lang, 1989

Stubbs, J., 'From De Quincey to Surrealism: an art that kills', *Digraphe*, special number: 'Thomas de Quincey', June 1994

Thibaudet, A., *Histoire de la Littérature française de 1789 à nos jours*, Paris, Stock,

1936

Thody, P., *Jean Genet, a study of his novels and plays*, London, Hamish Hamilton, 1968

Tison-Braun, M., *Marguerite Duras*, Amsterdam, Rodopi, 1985

Vircondelet, A., *Duras*, Paris, Editions François Bourin, 1991

Waelti-Walters, J., *J.M.G. Le Clézio*, Boston, Twayne, 1977

——, *Icare ou l'évasion impossible*, Sherbrooke, Editions Naaman, 1981

Walker, D., *André Gide*, London and Basingstoke, Macmillan, 1990

—— 'Le criminel chez Camus', in *Albert Camus, les extrêmes et l'équilibre*, proceedings of the Keele colloquium, edited with an introduction by David H. Walker, Amsterdam, Rodopi, collection 'Faux Titre', 1994, pp.17–32

White, E., *Genet*, London, Chatto and Windus, 1993

Wilson, E., 'Tournier, the body and the reader', *French Studies*, vol.47, no.1, January 1993, pp.43–56

Wolgensinger, J., *L'Histoire à la une*, Paris, Gallimard, collection Découvertes, 1989

Wright, G., *Between the Guillotine and Liberty. Two Centuries of the Crime Problem in France*, New York and Oxford, Oxford University Press, 1983

Index

Index

Index

Index